W9-DHF-666

In Service and Servitude

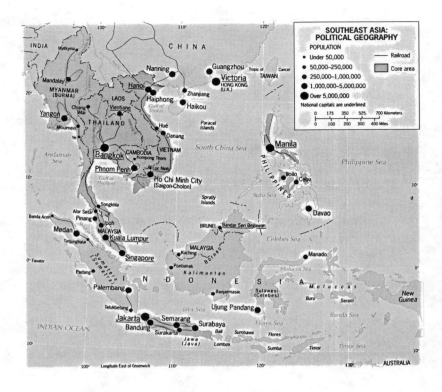

Southeast Asia, Political Geography.

From Harm De Blij and Peter Muller, *Geography: Realms, Regions, and Concepts.* New York: John Wiley and Sons. Copyright © 1997 John Wiley and Sons. Reprinted by permission of John Wiley and Sons, Inc.

In Service and Servitude

Foreign Female Domestic Workers and the Malaysian "Modernity" Project

Christine B. N. Chin

Columbia University Press

New York

Columbia University Press
Publishers Since 1893
New York   Chichester, West Sussex
Copyright © 1998 Columbia University Press
All rights reserved

Library of Congress Cataloging-in-Publication Data
Chin, Christine B. N.
    In service and servitude : foreign female domestic workers and the Malaysian
"modernity" project / Christine B.N. Chin.
        p.   cm.
    Includes bibliographical references and indexes.
    ISBN 0–231–10986–5 (cloth). — ISBN 0–231–10987–3 (paper)
        1. Women domestics—Malaysia.   2. Alien labor, Philippine—Malaysia.
3. Alien labor, Indonesian—Malaysia.   4. Women, Filipina—Employment—
Malaysia.   5. Women, Indonesian—Employment—Malaysia.   6. Master and
servant—Malaysia.   I. Title.
    HD6072.2.M4C48   1998
    331.4'8164046'09595—dc21   97–43048
                                                                CIP

Casebound editions of Columbia University Press books are printed on permanent
and durable acid-free paper.
Printed in the United States of America
c 10 9 8 7 6 5 4 3 2 1
p 10 9 8 7 6 5 4 3 2 1

For my grandparents, my mother, and nanny.

Contents

List of Tables

Preface

This narrow path has been trod many a time already, it's only that this time the journey is one to mark the way.
　　—Pramoedya Ananta Toer, *This Earth of Mankind*, 1975

My interest in the relationship between domestic service and development can be said to have been "years in the making." I was brought up in an upper-class Malaysian Chinese extended family that was the very model of the classic Chinese "three generations under one roof" wherein family members were served twenty-four hours a day by nannies, housemaids, and cooks. In time, nannies grew old, while housemaids and cooks were difficult to employ because of the expanded employment and education opportunities for working-class women that were brought about by development. Consequently, by the late 1970s and early 1980s, my extended and nuclear families, along with the families of the expanding Malaysian middle classes, began employing female domestic workers from the Philippines and Indonesia.

Until only a few years ago, however, that interest in the relationship between domestic service and development existed only in the remotest periphery of my intellectual consciousness. The patriarchal-class environment in which I was socialized as a young child ensured that the issue of housekeeping unmistakably was the responsibility of my mother, my aunts, and my paternal grandmother. Whether or not servants performed household tasks in a timely manner, or indeed if there even were enough servants to perform the tasks at all, remained the sole responsibility of the older women in my extended family, while the men went to work in their respective offices and the grandchildren were free to pursue the less mundane tasks of everyday life.

The relationship between domestic service and development was not a *problematique* since I pursued, in higher institutions of learning in the West, an intellectual path characterized by inquiry into matters of national, regional, and global concern that, in turn, were steeped in contestations over political, economic, and/or explicitly cultural resources. Along that path I also encountered important topics such as women and war, economy, politics, development, and literature. Rarely, if ever, was the relationship between domestic service and development deemed important enough for discourse or even cursory inquiry.

To be sure, in the context of scholarship on Malaysia and Southeast Asia, studies of the effects of development structures and processes on women have centered mostly around the nature of women's participation in rural and urban (especially manufacturing industries) economies. The inference is that domestic service performed by women was and continues to be perceived as too removed from the spotlight of development in its political and economic dimensions. Some of the key reasons for this, I believe, are the physically segregated nature of domestic service that obscures its contribution to development along the political, economic, and social dimensions; and the association of paid reproductive labor with upper-class or aristocratic pursuit of physical comfort.

My gradual awakening to the importance of the relationship between contemporary domestic service and development in Malaysia occurred in the summer of 1993, when I returned to Kuala Lumpur to visit with relatives. Early one morning, as I was having breakfast in the kitchen of a relative's house, I heard the sound of muffled crying that emanated from the neighbor's backyard. I walked out of the kitchen and into the backyard in search of the source. As I leaned over the metal fence (the majority of the modern houses are two-story link or row houses separated by fences in the front and back of adjoining structures), a horrifying image confronted me.

I saw a young woman crouched in a corner below the neighbor's kitchen window. Around one of her legs was a long chain (normally used to restrict the movement of house pets that are let loose in backyards) attached to the kitchen's sliding metal door. I asked her who she was since I did not recognize her as a member of the neighbor's family. She cried as she said that she was the family's Filipina servant. Her female employer, who was going out to shop for groceries in a nearby farmers' market, had chained her to the back of the house to ensure that she would not eat the family's food in her absence.

Feeling disgusted, I went back into my relative's house and asked Margaret (pseudonym), the Filipina servant, all of what she knew about the frequency with which her compatriot was abused in that specific manner. Margaret looked away and kept quiet as I spoke to her. I then asked the other members of the household if they were aware of the way in which the female neighbor abused her servant, and if so, had they ever challenged the woman's behavior. The very prompt reply instructed me to mind my own business: it was not the concern of the household because the neighbor was "crazy." Consequently, I decided to wait for her to return from the market. Suffice it to say that my conversation with her left two feuding families in its wake. Hindsight warrants that I acknowledge having sowed the seeds for this study on that day, even though I had no idea that my encounter with the abused servant would shape the future direction of my intellectual thought and career.

A few days later, Margaret who had spoken merely a few words to me since I arrived, began to engage me in conversation about life in the United States. She considered me as her employer's strange, long-lost relative who was not only "brave" (to use her word) enough to challenge a crazy neighbor, but who also voluntarily fetched her own clothes and drinks, and washed her own dinner plates—arguably, habits that may have been the result of the manner in which living away from my extended and immediate families, and equally important, living without the benefit of another woman's domestic labor for so many years, could not but encourage a "self-serving" lifestyle.

Acknowledging that I was as curious about her life as she was mine, I asked if she would allow me to accompany her to the Sunday church service (the overwhelming majority of Filipina domestic workers are Christians). It was there that I entered a different world—the "public" world of foreign female domestic workers. It was there that the seeds of this study began to sprout.

During the 1993 visit in Kuala Lumpur, I spoke with a variety of Malaysians. Among them were activists who counseled foreign female domestic workers—in particular, women who had run away from abusive employers. I learned that Filipina and Indonesian servants complained of insufficient food and rest, physical assault, and in certain cases, even rape. Not only was I ashamed to "discover" that educated ("civilized") Malaysians were capable of mistreating and abusing foreign domestic workers, I was surprised also by the responses of many with whom I conversed on the topic: they did not consider employers' denial of sufficient food and rest days for foreign domestic workers as incidences of mistreatment. Indeed, I felt even more bothered when I thought back to my boarding school days in England in which I had to constantly remind my peers at school (especially those who consistently marveled at my ability to use a toothbrush to clean my teeth, and/or the way in which my verbal enunciations reflected a command of the "Queen's English") that Malaysians were neither uncivilized ("No, we do not live on top of coconut trees"), nor were we entirely illiterate.

After all, Malaysian society had excavated itself from the tutelage of British colonial masters in 1957, and the people had survived the May 13, 1969 ethnic riots—the one time there had been a mass outbreak of physical violence between Malays and Chinese which had threatened to undermine the perceived political and economic progress that was made after independence. In the attempt to quell physical fighting between Malays and Chinese, the Malay-dominated state immediately instituted emergency rule.

In 1971, when Malaysian society emerged from emergency rule, the state implemented the New Economic Policy (NEP) 1971–1990, essentially an affirmative action export-oriented development program for Malays, the politically and numerically dominant ethnic group in the country. The NEP was charged with correcting socioeconomic imbalances in interethnic relations that had originated in the period of colonial rule—i.e., real and perceived Chinese control of the economy at the expense of Malays, the heirs of the country.

In spite of or perhaps because of the NEP, sustained economic growth since the mid and late 1980s has been achieved in Malaysia. Today, the country and the peoples are well on their way to coveting the much-prized "developed" status that is synonymous with the advanced industrialized world. The NEP's successor, the National Development Policy (NDP) 1991–2000 that further encourages export-oriented development, embodies state elites' efforts to create a developed society and country by the year 2020.

Upon my return to the United States at the end of the summer of 1993, I reviewed reports published by transnational nonstate organizations concerned with foreign female domestic workers' welfare all over the world. I quickly realized that the phenomenon of employer-abuse of foreign servants is not restricted to Malaysia. Many employers throughout Asia, the Middle East, and the West are implicated similarly in abusing foreign servants. Employer-related abuse may be and is facilitated, if not reinforced, by the absence of national labor legislation that protect Filipina and Indonesian domestic workers in Malaysia and many other labor-receiving states, while labor-sending states such as the Philippines and Indonesia continue to encourage female out-migration.

Various reports of rising transnational incidents of abuse implied that there was a yet-to-be explored relationship between the state-led transnationalization of migrant female domestic labor and the global expansion of neoliberalism that celebrates open markets and free trade—including the trade in and market for foreign female domestic workers. This knowledge offered to me the possibility of conducting a comparative study of transnational migrant female labor, especially given the increasing global valorization of neoliberalism.

Instead of pursuing this research path, I chose to return to Malaysia in 1994, formally to begin field research of the relationship between contemporary domestic service and development. While it can be said that I did so largely because of key intellectual reasons that are presented in the introductory chapter of this study, I am compelled also to acknowledge that my identity as a Malaysian cannot be divorced or suspended from my identity as a scholar. The global move to deregulate, privatize, and/or liberalize national economies, places multidimensional pressures on postcolonial societies and states such as that of Malaysia. What is called (economic) "globalization," and its oft-lauded promise to improve everyday life, can and does harbor the potential to undermine the individual and collective sense of self that is at the core of humanity. As such, the denigration of Filipina and Indonesian women as domestic workers, in Malaysia and elsewhere, should not be accepted as part of the global, regional, national, and personal journeys toward economic prosperity.

Acknowledgments

This study would not have been possible without the cooperation of the many Malaysian employers, and Filipina and Indonesian domestic workers who overcame their reservations to speak to me about the various aspects of domestic service. Many of the employers did not see how the subject of foreign servants could be of intellectual interest, and some even wondered out loud that perhaps I was unable to find something better to do in life. Despite our difference in outlook, some of us will enjoy but none of us can fully escape the interlocking effects of the movement of transnational capital across the globe. As employers live the daily exigencies of pursing careers, having families, and building other social networks, I hope they will pause to contemplate the contradictory ways in which the processes of global, regional, and national economic restructuring shape their consciousness and lives.

Some of the most challenging and enjoyable periods of field research were my interactions with Indonesian and Filipina domestic workers. Their hopes, dreams, pain, and fear left me feeling empowered and helpless at the same time. Several of the more outspoken women asked if I intended to publish my study because they wanted the world to know about some of the conditions under which they worked and lived. In many ways, they made me grapple with the question of the relationship between *theoria* and *praxis*. Capturing their voices in print in a scholarly prose is one step, albeit small, toward revisiting the barriers between objectivity-subjectivity and aloofness-commitment.

Here in the United States, I acknowledge a number of individuals who had had a direct and indirect hand in shaping the form and content of this study. Diane Singerman's patience and faith in me gave me the courage to push the limits of my intellect. The framework of modernity via consumption would have had a more difficult path to articulation had it not been for her never-ending questions that, nearly, were impossible to answer. Nevertheless, the puzzle was put together bit by bit as I struggled to answer them.

Cynthia Enloe, who long has paved the way for those of us interested in researching women and international/global politics and political economy, was tremendously instrumental in polishing the finished puzzle. She was as encouraging as she was critical in her incisive comments on the "forest and the trees," so to speak. Her ability to critique without tearing down the author's sense of self-worth indeed is a rarity that should be validated over and over again. Thank you Cynthia for your warmth, your brilliance, and your humanity.

To James H. Mittelman, please know that the past few years have been invaluable to the development of my intellectual voice. Jim spent a considerable amount of time and effort engaging me in dialogue on the theoretical aspects of this and other scholarly efforts. He was ever so kind and forthcoming in his advice—and, to be sure criticisms—of different chapters. I am deeply appreciative of his consistent support and his ability always to bring out the best scholarly work in me.

It is said that with "age comes wisdom." In this sense, I pay homage to Hamid Mowlana, who tried to instill in me the values and strength to be a productive and independent researcher. My thanks also to a good friend and colleague, Mustapha Kamal Pasha. He is a kindred spirit who understands and can articulate the kinds of theoretical and ethico-moral struggles experienced by those of us from postcolonial societies who live and work in the West today. His brilliant mind and generosity are what give me the strength to face my fear of falling into the pit of mediocrity.

I owe the first half of the book's title to Renée Marlin-Bennett who, during a telephone conversation one day, would not let me hang up until we had produced an acceptable title. Given her present research on intellectual property rights, it behooves me to tell her that she may not collect any royalties on this one.

Other scholars, near and far, commented on a version of chapter 4 in particular, and in general, the theoretical framework of the entire book at the York-MUNS (Multilateralism and the United Nations System) Symposium, York University, Toronto, Canada, May 4–6, 1994. With much respect, I acknowledge Robert W. Cox, Stephen Gill, Craig Murphy, Kees Van der Pijl, Fantu Cheru, Mustapha Kamal Pasha, Rianne Mahon, Hélène Pellerin, Ezz-Edine Chouckri, Brian Ford, John-Paul Halucha, Martin Hewson, Nilgün Önder, Magnus Ryner, and Timothy Sinclair.

Formal and informal conversations with other critically oriented intellectuals would influence the form and content of every chapter in this book. I humbly acknowledge the help of J. Ann Tickner, Simona Sharoni, Marsha J. Darling, and Sylvia C. Tiwon, whose dedication to critical feminist pedagogy and scholarship continues to give me consistent intellectual and emotional sustenance.

The completion of my manuscript was made possible with the institutional support of the School of International Service (SIS) at American University. The Dean of SIS, Louis W. Goodman, and the staff, especially Rana el-Khatib and Steven Carlson, ensured that the postdoctoral fellow had just about everything she needed to do so. From the theoretical to the lascivious, William P. Brady, Fanta Aw, Gary R. Weaver, and Beth I. Wachs, in their own ways, helped me keep a healthy sense of humor as I walked and at times hobbled along the path of the scholar-educator.

Various individuals in Malaysia and the United States were indispensable to different stages of producing the manuscript. Mrs. Khoo Siew Mun graciously gave me access to the resources of and her staff at the Clearing House on Women in Development, Women's Affairs Division of the Ministry of National Unity and Social Development, Kuala Lumpur, Malaysia. She made it possible for me to work with the library staff at Universiti Malaya. Special thanks to Sharifuddin Mohamad Sharif, executive at the New Straits Times Press Resource Center, who spent two and one-half weeks with me shifting through piles of old newspapers and microfiche in a refrigerated room.

Fieldwork would have been much more difficult had it not been for the following activists who warmly welcomed me back to Kuala Lumpur: Caridad Tharan, International Council on Management of Population Programmes; Nedra Weerakoon, Asian and Pacific Development Centre's Gender Project; Irene and Agile Fernandez, Tenaganita; and Ivy Josiah, Women's Aid Organization. At Universiti Malaya, Loh Lee Lee and Shanmugam Paramasivam graciously shared with me respective information on domestic workers and Indonesian migrant labor. Patrick Pillai, senior fellow at the Institute for Security and International Studies, Kuala Lumpur, also devoted a considerable amount of time discussing with me the various dimensions of international migration theory, and the political economy of development in Malaysia.

I do not know how to express fully right here my indebtedness to and love for several life-long friends. They are Yolanda, Meng Fui, Esther, and

Ellen Chan, who (despite their not-so-secretly held hopes that I would do better in the corporate as opposed to the academic world) stood by me and helped fight some of my battles and doubts in the course of producing the manuscript. As I write these words, I think that Meng Fui finally understands my drive to be a scholar-educator. I hope to be able to reciprocate at some point, even though I still believe that he would make a better professor than a wealthy businessman from an Asian NIC.

Nzinga Robinson opened her Washington D.C. home to me, my pets, and my books as a safe (read: distraction-less) haven from which to write the initial incarnations of the manuscript. She and her daughter, Ngozi Temitope Robinson, welcomed me in their lives fully aware that the processes of writing could and frequently did turn me into a monster. Words fail to capture adequately the hilarious and heartbreaking moments as a privileged Malaysian Chinese woman negotiated her voice, space, and identity in the home of a middle-class African-American family in Washington D.C. Nzinga courageously and patiently put up with constant comments such as "I have no life" and "I think I've lost my mind" until my utterances drove members of the household near-crazy. At times, her responses were met with much incredulity that could only fuel the spirit to conquer a fear-based disease called procrastination: "Do you know that the 'Mo-tea-sir' tribe is long dead? Please sweep the staircase . . . you may as well act like a maid if you're going to write about one." As an adult and as a guest in the house, I consciously surrendered my civil-political rights, even though I was not always able to acknowledge then that I would gain, in return, an even deeper understanding of the limitations and privileges of my identity. It should be said that my temporary surrender of civil-political rights during that period in no way affirmed the viability of the authoritarian path to democracy.

As an author, I could not have asked for a better working relationship with the editorial staff at Columbia University Press. Kate Wittenberg, editor-in-chief, took the manuscript and "ran with it." She was both encouraging and understanding, but also firm in the ways that she dealt with the logistics of taking the manuscript to press. Thanks also to Alex Coolman and Leslie Bialler. Leslie, who provided uninhibited and hilarious comments on the manuscript, kept me engaged in the project during the most isolationist period of reviewing the final changes. I, alone, am responsible for any and all errors.

Above all else, the Chin family and especially my father K.V. Chin, gallantly fielded criticisms of how I had given up avenues to increase my material wealth (or is it many times the ability to meet basic human needs?) only to settle for a study of "maids." Yet, individually and collectively my father and my siblings Sandra, B.Y., Beek See, and Beek Yin, help me remain committed to my vocation in a way that balances the intellectual with the spiritual and the material. My father worked hard to ensure that regardless of my career path, I would neither lose sight of the value of my choices nor my person in relation to my spiritual upbringing and teachers. This book tells him that I may be a bit closer to finding that particular kind of peace in my heart.

Christine B. N. Chin
September 1997

Abbreviations

ABIM	Angkatan Belia Islam Malaysia
APDC	Asian and Pacific Development Centre
ASN	Amanah Saham Nasional
BCIC	Bumiputera Commercial and Industrial Community
CCA-URM	Christian Conference of Asia—Rural Urban Mission
DAP	Democratic Action Party
DOM	Privately-owned domestic employment agency
FELCRA	Federal Land Consolidation and Rehabilitation Authority
FELDA	Federal Land Development Authority
FIDA	Federal Industrial Development Authority
FPE	Financial Public Enterprise
FTZ	Free Trade Zone
EO	Executive Order
EOI	Export-Oriented Industrialization
GDP	Gross Domestic Product
GNP	Gross National Product
HICOM	Heavy Industries Corporation of Malaysia
ICA	Industrial Coordination Act
IMF	International Monetary Fund
IMP	Industrial Master Plan
ISI	Import Substitution Industrialization
MARA	Majlis Amanah Rakyat Malaysia
MCA	Malayan/Malaysian Chinese Association
MCP	Malayan Communist Party
MIC	Malayan/Malaysian Indian Congress
MPHB	Multi-Purpose Holdings Berhad
MRL	Malay Reservation Land Enactment

MTUC	Malayan/Malaysian Trades Union Congress
NDP	National Development Policy 1991–2000
NEP	New Economic Policy 1971–1990
NFPE	Non-Financial Public Enterprise
NGO	Nongovernmental Organization
NIC	Newly Industrializing Country
NIDL	New International Division of Labour
NPP	National Population Policy
OEDC	Organization for Economic Co-operation and Development
OPEC	Organization of Petroleum Exporting Countries
OWI	Overseas Workers Investment Fund
PAS	Partai Al-Islam SeMalaysia
POEA	Philippine Overseas Employment Agency
PNB	Permodalan Nasional Berhad
RISDA	Rubber Industries Small Holders Development Authority
RLA	Rice Lands Act
RM	Ringgit Malaysia
SEDC	State Economic Development Corporation
SPLP	Sijil Perjalanan Laksana Paspot
TNC	Transnational Corporation
UDA	Urban Development Authority
UMNO	United Malays National Organization
UMNO Baru	"New" United Malays National Organization
Wanita UMNO	UMNO Women
Wawasan 2020	Vision 2020

"Scenes of Malaysian Life" Series.

Originally published in *New Straits Times*, March 12, 1988. Used by permission of the cartoonist, Lat.

In Service and Servitude

CHAPTER I

Introduction

By the year 2020, Malaysia can be a united nation, with a confident Malaysian society, infused by strong moral and ethical values, living in a society that is democratic, liberal and tolerant, caring, economically just and equitable, progressive and prosperous, and in full possession of an economy that is competitive, dynamic, robust, and resilient.
—Dr. Mahathir Mohamad, Prime Minister of Malaysia, 1991

We are part of Vision 2020. Without us, our employers would not be able to work so much. We also contribute to the Malaysian family.
—"Anita," a Filipina domestic worker in Kuala Lumpur, 1994

The rapidly industrializing Southeast Asian country of Malaysia plays host to a growing number of Filipina and Indonesian female domestic workers: from a few hundred in the 1970s to approximately 70,000 by 1994.[1] Together with the exponential increase in foreign female domestic workers are two other phenomena that can be discerned readily from a cursory examination of major Malaysian newspapers such as *New Straits Times*, and *The Star*. Since the mid 1980s, when state authorities officially began to regulate the in-migration of foreign servants, newspaper articles have portrayed Filipina and Indonesian servants either as house thieves and prostitutes or as victims of horrific forms of sexual and physical assault by their employers.

While newspaper reports graphically detail how some Filipina and Indonesian domestic workers are abused violently by their employers (e.g., servants who are raped, kicked, and/or punched by employers), little is mentioned of the women's complaints that they are made to sleep on kitchen floors, along corridors, or in storage rooms with no ventilation; that they have to work 18–20 hour days; that they are denied rest days; and that they do not get enough to eat.

With the growing population of transnational migrant domestic labor in the country, police and immigration officials make it a point to ensure law and order by searching for and deporting foreign domestic workers who offer sex-for-sale on their rest days and/or who steal their employers' belongings. Meanwhile, domestic service remains unlegislated. Employers are rarely, if ever, prosecuted for their abusive actions.

Significantly, there appears to be relatively little public and private concern and outrage with regards to the dehumanizing conditions in which some Filipina and Indonesian domestic servants live and work. During the course of my 1993 visit with family and friends in Kuala Lumpur, I was surprised by the lack of media attention to the welfare of foreign female domestic workers as a group, and also the apathy of fellow Malaysians who employed servants from the neighboring countries of the Philippines and Indonesia. The cause of improving transnational migrant workers' welfare is left to a small group of activists who are committed to penetrate the wall of silence that surrounds the complaints of Filipina and Indonesian domestic workers in the country (e.g., lobbying the state for transnational migrant workers' rights).[2]

The contemporary institution of domestic service in Malaysia that, in the last two decades, gradually has been characterized by the in-migration and labor of Filipina and Indonesian domestic workers, together with reports of the dehumanizing manner in which some women are treated, elicit compelling theoretico-normative issues. The majority of foreign female domestic workers began arriving on Malaysian soil during the period of the New Economic Policy (NEP) 1971–1990. The NEP was implemented in the aftermath of the 1969 general elections that disintegrated into arguably the one and only mass outbreak of violence between Malays and non-Malays in the country's modern history. The NEP had an official two-pronged objective: to eradicate poverty and to redress real and perceived interethnic inequalities held over from British colonial rule that left the majority of Malays— the politically and numerically dominant ethnic group in Malaysia—primarily associated with a rural subsistence lifestyle while the more modern urban areas and occupations were perceived to be dominated by non-Malays, namely the Chinese. Subsequently, the NEP encouraged Malay urban in-migration while it instituted a quota system for Malays in most areas of social life, e.g., education, employment, and banking/finance.

The in-migration of Filipina and Indonesian domestic workers that began during the NEP's era of state-led socioeconomic restructuring continues today. The present National Development Policy (NDP) 1991–2000 is a continuation of the NEP, albeit with an even greater emphasis on export-oriented development in which open markets and free trade are considered the major avenues to sustaining economic growth.

According to the current Prime Minister of Malaysia, Dr. Mahathir Mohamad, the ultimate objective of export-oriented development is to realize " *Wawasan 2020*"/Vision 2020, or what I call the Malaysian state's "modernity project." The modernity project involves constructing a developed multiethnic Malaysian society with the "caring family" as its social base:

> [W]e should aim for is a Malaysia that is a fully developed country by year 2020.
> . . . By the year 2020, Malaysia can be a united nation, with a confident Malaysian society, infused by strong and ethical values, living in a society that is democratic, liberal and tolerant, caring. . . . [T]he challenge of establishing a fully caring society and a caring culture, a social system in which society will come before self, in which the welfare of the people will revolve not around the state or the individual but around a strong and resilient family system. . . . [T]he challenge of establishing a prosperous society with an economy that is fully competitive, dynamic, robust and resilient.[3]

TABLE I.I

Malaysia

Basic Indicators

Year	Population ('000)	Urban Population % of Total	Current per Capita (US$)	Labor Force Total Female ('000)	%	GDP Average Annual Growth % 1970–80	1980–92*
1973	11,675	36.0	600	4,131.3	32.3		
1980	13,763	42.0	1800	5,337.4	34.6	7.9	
1990	17,671	49.8	2400	7,071.1	35.1		
1993	19,047	52.1	3140	7,652.7	35.4		6.2

Source: World Bank, 1995.

* The 1980-92 average includes the 1985-87 recessionary period. In the 1990s the average annual growth is approximately 8 percent.

In the context of the modernity project, "Anita" a Filipina domestic worker stated in a 1994 newspaper interview that foreign female domestic workers were important to the Malaysian family, hence Vision 2020. Introduced as one of the epigraphs in this chapter, her remark that Filipina servants facilitate the realization of the modern Malaysian family, was made in relation to Filipina and Indonesian domestic workers' complaints of mistreatment and abuse at the hands of Malaysian employers.[4]

This study, which analyzes the relationship between transnational migrant female domestic labor and the political economy of development in Malaysia, is informed by two central questions. Why is unlegislated live-in domestic service, an essentially premodern social institution and peopled mostly by female domestic workers from the Philippines and Indonesia, increasingly prevalent in the context of constructing a modern developed Malaysian society by way of export-oriented development? If the in-migration of foreign female domestic workers is important to nurturing the modern caring Malaysian family—at the very least by way of substituting for the domestic labor of working Malaysian mothers—then why is there an overall absence of public and private concern regarding the less-than-human conditions in which some Filipina and Indonesian domestic workers exchange labor for wages?

A "problem-solving" approach to these questions would provide immediate answers. It can be said that foreign female domestic workers' presence in Malaysia is a consequence of transnational wage differentials that encourage migration-for-employment; that Malaysian demands for Filipina and Indonesian servants result from enhanced personal purchasing powers during a period of declining supply in local servants; and that employer insensitivities can and do lead to the abuse of foreign domestic workers. Taken to its logical conclusion, the attendant solutions are not without merit. Economic growth should be strengthened in labor-sending countries to equalize wage differentials; Malaysians should be trained to better supervise foreign servants, encouraged to use childcare centers and/or to hire part-time or day servants; and domestic service should be legislated to protect servants from abuse.

Defining one of the problems and solutions in terms of transnational wage differentials, however, sidesteps the need to explain how and why states have become actively involved in facilitating labor migration, not to mention that efforts to equalize wage differentials mostly will have the effect of alleviating the symptoms and not the larger structural constraints of global and regional economies from which emerges the phenomenon of transnational migration-for-employment. Similarly, the solutions of legislating domestic service and training employers neither explains how and why employers may and do abuse foreign domestic workers nor the real or perceived need for servants, especially from the Philippines and Indonesia.

The major limitations of a problem-solving approach are conceptual parameters that privilege ahistoricity, and that divide social life into discrete, mutually exclusive dimensions and levels which have little bearing on one another. It is assumed that a problem in any dimension and level of social life can be isolated and dealt with singularly, immediately and effectively. As Robert W. Cox argues in his discussion of the differences between problem-solving and critical theories:

> There is problem-solving theory which takes the present as given and reasons about how to deal with particular problems within the existing order of things. Then there is . . . critical theory . . . [which] stands back . . . to ask how that order came about, how it may be changing, and how the changes may be influenced or challenged. *Where problem-solving focuses synchronically upon the immediate and reasons in terms of fixed relationships, critical theory works in a more historical and diachronic dimension. Its aim is the understanding of structural change* [emphasis mine].[5]

I adopt, in this study, a critical interdisciplinary approach to examine the relationship between domestic service and a development path that is constituted by and that constitutes responses of the state elite and private citizens to forces of change on, as well as interactions among the transnational, national, and household levels. The conceptual framework, which locates the performance and consumption of paid reproductive labor in the midst of various dimensions of development within and beyond Malaysia, allows me to explain how and why contemporary domestic service has become an integral component in efforts by the Malaysian state elite to garner consent from key social forces for the construction of a developed socially stable multiethnic polity.

The "Good Life": Integrating the Politics of Governance with the Politics of Social Reproduction

To propose that the politics of governance are related to the politics of social reproduction (i.e., who does what aspect of reproductive labor, under what conditions, and in what kind of family form), is to insist that the Malaysian state actively shapes the demands for, and the consequent in-migratory and employment structures and processes of, female domestic workers from the neighboring Southeast Asian countries of the Philippines and Indonesia.[6] The question is how, why, and with what consequences?

Existing scholarship of changing state-society relations in rapidly industrializing Asian countries continues to ignore the relevance of paid reproductive labor to the unfolding of late-twentieth-century modernity. For the last two decades, sustained economic growth in Asia has strengthened scholarly interest in how Asian states bring about and manage rapid industrialization. Borrowing from critical scholarship on the political economy of Latin America, the model of the developmental state is used by some scholars of Asian political economy to explain the state's involvement in the economy and society: "The conceptualization of a 'developmental state' focuses on the political will, the ideological coherence, the bureaucratic instruments, and the repressive capacity to formulate and implement effective economic policies to promote high speed capitalist growth."[7]

The developmental state is conceptualized as "an amalgam of social, political, ideological and economic elements organised in a particular manner."[8] It is not a neutral entity but an expression of power embedded in complex overlapping social networks. Institutionalized state power is embodied in the bureaucratic, coercive, and judicial arms that constitute the state apparatus.

The coercive-repressive dimension of the developmental state is considered an important independent variable in the restructuring of the economy. In rapidly industrializing Asian countries, the state's coercive-repressive power is seen to be increasingly class-based, and in some cases, racialized-ethnicized. Yet, the centrality of scholarly focus on legislation that coerces big business to behave in distinct ways to capture transnational capital and markets, and that represses dissent from various oppositional groups in society, cannot adequately account for continued economic success and social order.[9]

Coercive-repressive legislation is designed to do just that: coerce and repress. It is not intended to fundamentally alter peoples' values, beliefs, attitudes, perceptions, and behavior. Intellectual inquiry of state-society relations in rapidly industrializing Asia has not examined the more surreptitious ways in which the state elite implement policies to construct consent among new social forces that are engendered by industrialization and that have the potential to challenge state legitimacy.

Emphasis placed on the class and/or racial-ethnic dimension of the developmental state has obscured an equally important and related modality of identity and power, i.e., gender. Analyses of the gendering of the developmental state—in which the state apparatus is controlled mainly by elite men from various racial-ethnic backgrounds who conceptualize and implement policies and legislation—can contribute to a deeper understanding of strategies of coercion and consent that are used to maintain social order.

The phenomenon of state-supported transnationalization of migrant female domestic labor since the 1970s deserves closer attention than is given by critical political economists of Asian state-society relations.[10] The ways in which labor migration are incorporated in development policies can point researchers in the direction of identifying the more surreptitious strategies of consent—implicating the state elite and apparatus in the changing form and content of domestic service—that help normalize different forms of social relations and organization in society to support export-oriented growth, hence reinforce state legitimacy. Such strategies can and do involve official, albeit covert, manipulation of the various dimensions of identity formation, maintenance, or transformation that affect the nature and path of development.

On the other hand, and until recently, scholarship of domestic service, or the performance and consumption of paid household labor in most regions of the world, has been informed by conceptual frameworks or templates that focus mostly on employer-domestic worker relations. Absent from many but not all of these studies are conceptualizations of state involvement in the changing form and content of domestic service.[11] A key consequence of this is the lost opportunity to explicate the evolving gender-class-racial/ethnic dimensions of the state.

I am not suggesting that inquiries of employer-domestic worker relations in the West and elsewhere that have yielded knowledge of gender, class, and racial-ethnic negotiations of power in the household are no longer appropriate or relevant to conceptualizing and researching contemporary domestic service. On the contrary, given that foreign female domestic workers increasingly are found throughout Asia, the Middle East, Western Europe, and North America, it is to be expected that analyses of employer-domestic worker relations will enhance our understanding of the construction and exercise of power that is circumscribed by specific intersections of nationality, gender, class, race/ethnicity, and religion in the private or domestic domain. My point is that many of the existing templates (including those that examine the changing form and content of domestic service as a particular indicator of gendered capitalist development paths in the so-called Third World which leave open little more than jobs as servants for local and foreign migrant women) have not fully explored or conceptualized the state's involvement in shaping contemporary domestic service.[12] This serves to reinforce the persistent and unstated assumption within academic circles and in everyday life that domestic service is a mostly personal-private issue best left to feminists who analyze negotiations of power in the household.[13] Implicit in this assumption is the notion that while transformations in domestic service are a consequence of economic development, they remain unrelated to the conceivably more important topic of the politics of governance.

The failure of literature on the political economy of rapid industrialization, and on domestic service to theoretically and normatively account for multicausal linkages among the regional, national, and household levels leaves us with an implicit picture of the state as a protector and perpetrator of capitalist-patriarchal and/or racial-ethnic ideologies. We still do not fully know why, how, and with what consequences policies that directly and indirectly encourage demands for paid reproductive labor shape the lives of female employer-supervisors and foreign servants in particular, and in general, the development path along which society is encouraged to evolve.

State-supported transnationalization of migrant female domestic labor today more clearly implicates the labor-sending and labor-receiving state elite and apparatus in the changing form and content of domestic service. Why do states encourage the out- and in-migration of female servants rather than male servants? Is it merely an issue of labor demand and supply? Or does the transnational migration of female servants also facilitate labor-sending and labor-receiving states' explicit and/or implicit economic and noneconomic objectives?[14]

Analyses of the transition from local to foreign domestic workers can reveal even more than the knowledge that paid reproductive labor is characterized by specific intersections of nationality, gender, class, and race-ethnicity. Especially given contemporary high levels of economic interpenetration, the boundaries separating phenomena within and beyond specific geopolitical borders are blurred. As one consequence, it is increasingly difficult to sustain the argument that the practices of "private" and "public patriarchy" are mutually exclusive.[15] Our understanding of social life at the household or national levels then must take into consideration forces that interpenetrate them. Feminist scholars of International Relations such as Cynthia Enloe and J. Ann Tickner continue to stress this point with regards to the complex and intimate relationship between gender, and household, national, and international politics.[16]

Contemporary domestic service can be and is related to the issue of governance, i.e., how and why labor migration policies become part of efforts among the labor-sending state elite to maintain legitimacy while they restructure the economy to facilitate open markets and free trade, including the trade in female domestic workers. At the labor-receiving end, official regulation of the in-migration and employment of foreign female domestic workers indicates that contemporary domestic service is intricately tied to the negotiation of legitimacy between the state elite and key social forces, particularly the employing social class(es).

There exists a relatively small but growing body of literature on the state's relation to foreign female domestic workers in the advanced industrialized world. The United States and Canada, for example, in order to encourage the legal in-migration of foreign female domestic workers (especially from the Caribbean and Central America) at least as a partial solution to middle-class pressure for the provision of childcare services, have constructed immigration rules that bind foreign domestic workers to their employers for a specified time period.[17] As Sedef Arat-Koc argues in the context of foreign female domestic workers' relation to the Canadian state:

> The state plays an active role in structuring and controlling not only the volume but also the conditions of these workers. There is a striking contrast between the *laissez faire* approach that the liberal state has taken, which favours private solutions to problems in the domestic sphere, and its rigid intervention in the provision, organization and control of 'help' for that sphere. Given the specific combination of state policies in areas of child care provision, labor legislation and immigration, domestic service is not simply a private but *a politically constructed solution to the crisis of the domestic sphere.*[18]

In North America, the politico-economic motives of the state elite are seen to contribute to the ongoing gendered, racialized-ethnicized, and class-based nature in the performance and consumption of live-in paid housework.[19]

The study of contemporary domestic service that is characterized by transnational migrant domestic labor offers a monumental opportunity to conceptually bridge the household, national, regional, and global levels on the basis of the construction and pursuit of what can be called the "good life." In the present context of the global expansion of neoliberalism, the state elite have the task of negotiating effectively between demands that emanate both from within and from beyond geopolitical borders.[20] Particularly given neoliberalism's promise that open markets and free trade are the most viable and natural routes to what Jeremy Bentham, in the eighteenth century, called the pursuit of the real and perceived "greatest happiness of the greatest number [of peoples]," contemporary legislation and policies have to be designed to encourage the emergence of a shared vision and ways to achieve this vision with key social forces.[21] The shared vision, to be sure, partly is constituted for countries that are in the processes of liberalizing, deregulating, and/or privatizing national economies.

In most countries, since the state apparatus is grounded in particular intersections of class-based, gendered and racialized-ethnicized power, then so will be the definition and pursuit of the good life in today's world. Yet, neoliberalism's blueprint for development obscures this foundational proposition by ignoring different conceptualizations of development and by conflating the complexity and multidimensionality of development structures and processes with economic success. Success is measured by a series of indicators such as percentage of sustained annual economic growth, per capita income, level of savings and investment, and debt-GNP ratio to debt-export ratios.[22]

The pursuit of the "good life," real or perceived, continues at all levels to revolve around an emphasis on more efficient ways to generate, accumulate, and utilize material wealth. According to this schema, whatever facilitates the pursuit of the good life on all levels is promoted as, and coterminous with, whatever is morally acceptable.

The *raison d'être* of the contemporary state has become the ability to provide the context for, and to convince citizens to pursue and to realize, neoliberalism's version of the good life. Utility becomes the principal legitimating moral criterion on which are justified methods employed in the pursuit of the good life: i.e., an action or a policy is valid if it brings about responses that are favorable to the actor.[23] In spite of how structural adjustment and stabilization policies marginalize peoples from certain classes, racial-ethnic groups, and gender, state elites in the developing world (at the insistence and with the help of the World Bank, the IMF, and the OECD) continue to restructure their economies to facilitate the unobstructed movement of transnational capital.[24] It is assumed that all peoples want to and will achieve neoliberalism's promise and version of the good life.

To be sure, not all peoples agree to this definition of the good life. The gendered, racialized-ethnicized, and class-based dimensions of the exercise of state power in the service of neoliberal utilitarianism (or, in Gramscian terms, the "hegemonic historic bloc") continues to be challenged by different groups of peoples in different ways ("counterhegemonic historic bloc"), e.g., feminists, environmentalists, human rights activists, and Islamicists operating on the local, national, and transnational levels.[25]

If state legitimacy is to be maintained, then key social forces somehow must be encouraged to share a similar vision of the good life and ways to pursue it. Strategies of coercion-repression can be used to silence dissent. Nonetheless, it is the strategies of garnering consent that facilitate the construction and/or maintenance of a shared vision between those who govern and those who are governed.

To paraphrase Antonio Gramsci, the state is both repressor and educator. Especially in periods of rapid social change, strategies of coercion-repression silence dissent while strategies of consent proceed less coercively, if not unobtrusively, to encourage peoples to adopt different perceptions, values, and/or forms of social relations and organizations.[26] Significantly, the processes of educating a new form of citizenry might be made free of class-based, nationalistic, gendered and/or racialized-ethnicized ideologies; but they are not.

Implicit in my study is a detailed exposition of the gendering of state power and apparatus in relation to contemporary domestic service. The analysis is made even more compelling because the construction and pursuit of the good life in Malaysia must take into account two interrelated factors: the regional context of Southeast Asian interstate competition in capturing transnational capital and markets, and the modern Malaysian history of interethnic material and symbolic contestations that have shaped nearly every, if not all, aspects of social life.

Finding the State in the Family: Consumption of Paid Reproductive Labor and the Construction of Middle-Class Hood

> If every State tends to create and maintain a certain type of civilization and of citizen (and hence of collective life and of individual relations), and to eliminate certain customs and attitudes and to disseminate others, then the Law will be its instrument for this purpose (together with the school system, and other institutions and activities) . . . In reality, the State must be conceived of as an "educator," in as much as it tends precisely to create a new type and level of civilization.
> —Antonio Gramsci, *Selections from the Prison Notebook*, 1971

Historically, the emergence of the middle classes, along with their politics, have affected the adoption of different development paths and forms of state.[27] This point is not any less important today, especially since the growth of the middle classes in Asia has been linked intimately to changing forms of state. In countries such as South Korea, Taiwan, and Thailand, the middle classes are seen to have spearheaded successfully demands for political democratization, while there is no indication that the middle classes in other Asian countries such as Malaysia and Singapore are about to follow suit.

Conceptually, the middle classes continue to present a challenge for Neo-Marxist and Neo-Weberian class theorists since members of the middle classes range from school teachers and low-level bureaucrats to lawyers, computer scientists, and owners of small businesses (see chapter 6).[28] To reflect the heterogeneity of those located at various points between the capitalist and the proletarian or between the upper and lower classes, I consistently use the phrase in its plural form, the "middle classes."

That the middle classes are a consequence of, and an important factor in, shaping the political economy of rapid industrialization is not the immediate issue here. Rather, the issue is how and why the state elite devise strategies of consent to police middle-class identities and politics. The potential of the expanding middle classes to strengthen the path of export-oriented development in Malaysia is indirectly acknowledged in official discourse: "Recognizing that a larger population constitutes an important human resource to create *a larger consumer base with an increasing purchasing power* [emphasis mine] to generate and support industrial growth through productive exploitation of natural resources, Malaysia could, therefore, plan for a larger population which could ultimately reach 70 million."[29] Indeed, contemporary capitalist development necessitates the restructuring of social relations and organizations, especially peoples' relation to production *and* consumption processes.[30]

Especially in Malaysia, the middle classes increasingly place an emphasis on what Pierre Bourdieu called the "pursuit of distinction," in which the consumption of goods and services are seen as a key way to construct identities and lifestyles that distinguish them from the lower or working classes.[31] Analysis of contemporary domestic service and development in Malaysia or other labor-receiving countries ought to be located in the context of the state elite's relation to the employing social classes or the middle classes in general, and changing middle-class consumption patterns in particular. Malaysian demands for transnational migrant domestic labor signal that such changes are occurring visibly at the level of the family or the household.

It also should be noted that throughout this study, I frequently and deliberately use the noun "family" as opposed to "household" even though

I am aware that the more critically oriented feminist scholarship objects to the use of the former noun in relation to discourse on social relations in the domestic domain since it reinforces patriarchal-capitalist ideology that legitimates the husband as the main wage-earner and the wife as the home-maker. The uncritical use of the noun "family" can and does mystify the nature of unpaid reproductive labor that is performed by the wife. I, most certainly, do not take issue with this position. Rather, the noun "family" is used to emphasize specifically the Malaysian state's ideological position toward constructing a modern Malaysian middle-class family in which men, in theory, remain the main wage-earners while women assume the responsibility for performing housework or supervising servants. When the noun "household" is used in this study, it refers to the level of analysis at which a servant works for and resides with the employing family.[32]

According to the schema of the public-private dichotomy, the reach of the state apparatus does not and cannot extend to the innermost sanctum of society, i.e., the family. Unlike this picture drawn by classical philosophers of the family as an entity located in the private emotive realm secluded from activities in public space, the institution of the family has and continues to be an intricate component in the processes of state formation, maintenance, and/or disintegration.[33]

> At the most fundamental level, the state is involved in the definition of what constitutes a family, marriage, and parenthood. What counts as genuine and legal marriage, the claims of "natural" as against step parents, definitions of dependents, family, and household are all called upon the framing of legislation. . . . Thus, the basic coinage of family relations, the understanding of the central terms of marriage, family . . . are built into the relationships between state and the family. In an important sense, the state is a key agency in telling and reminding us what the family is.[34]

If the state is to maintain the cohesion of its historic bloc that binds social forces, then it relates to families from different classes in different ways. Jacques Donzelot and Christopher Lasch have argued in different contexts that state elites in the West directly and indirectly promote the development of particular models of science, education, law, and medicine that construct new forms of citizenry to achieve social order within different historical contexts. For instance, in France during the *ancien régime*, the state governed through the family by investing the patriarch of the household with respect, status, and protection. In return, the patriarch provided labor, revenue, and "faithfulness to public order."[35] Today in the United States, welfare agencies that regulate Medicaid or Food Stamp programs are designed, in theory, to help the working poor. In practice, agencies' rules of eligibility constitute and reinforce particular types of family structures for the poor.[36]

Demands for paid reproductive labor can be influenced by way of legislating (or not legislating) areas of social life that, in turn, affect peoples' real and perceived need for domestic servants. The analysis in this study ascertains that by enframing the larger possible fields of actions and responses in which peoples live and interact, the Malaysian state elite are able to coopt domestic service as a key educative institution to encourage and legitimize the middle classes' adoption of the nuclear family form. It is "educative" in the Gramscian sense, in that legislation and policies on various aspects of social life, including the in-migration and employment of foreign female domestic workers, covertly or surreptitiously socialize peoples into different ways of perceiving and organizing social relations.[37]

The implementation of the NEP during the 1970s, i.e., in the midst of what some would call the emerging New International Division of Labour, opened the window of opportunity for greater state involvement in shaping the middle-class family. The supply of Malaysian servants declined as newly built factories owned by transnational corporations demanded female factory workers. By refusing to legislate domestic service, state authorities hastened the decline as young Malaysian Malay, Chinese, and Indian women elected to work in factories that paid higher wages and that offered more structured work environments with clearly defined rest periods and rest days.

Encouraged by the transnationalization of migrant female domestic labor, Malaysian employers began to hire servants from the Philippines and Indonesia. Immigration, child care, employment, reproduction, and personal income tax legislation and policies affect everyday life in a way that continues to fuel Malaysian demands for foreign female domestic workers.

By the mid 1980s, Filipina and Indonesian domestic workers were key to the state elite's defense of the NEP as migrant women became boundary markers for and of the expanding Malaysian middle classes. Official regulation of the in-migration of foreign female domestic workers led to the construction of rules that govern Malaysian employment Filipina and Indonesian servants. Of importance is that the in-migration of servants from other labor-sending countries is discouraged partly because of the politics of population distribution in multiethnic Malaysia.

A key strategy of garnering consent was embodied in employment rules which objectified the social and material boundaries of the Malay and non-

Malay middle classes. By delineating entry into the community of the expanding Malaysian middle classes, the rules indirectly addressed criticisms from certain groups within society that the NEP had not benefitted the majority of Malays in particular, and Malaysians in general.

The employment rules also insisted on Malay and non-Malay middle-class adoption of the nuclear family form. On the normative level, the middle-class nuclear family "(re)drafts morality" by emphasizing women's reproductive roles as wives and mothers who also supervise foreign female domestic workers.[38] On the political economic level, the middle-class nuclear family strengthens the growth of capitalist markets as members of the nuclear family are expected to be more dependent on the capitalist market than on the extended community or family for the provision of goods and services. Middle-class consumption of foreign female domestic workers' labor (provided by the transnational capitalist labor market in domestic servants) is part of the Malaysian state elite's promotion of enhanced middle-class consumption of goods and services as symbolic of personal and national progress.

The pursuit of "modernity via consumption," of which the performance and consumption of paid reproductive labor is a part, facilitates the development of a particular kind of "middle class-hood" in Malaysia that is not premised exclusively on ethnic, cultural, and religious differences. Malaysian Malay, Chinese, and Indian middle-class employers of Filipina and Indonesian domestic workers increasingly construct a similarly distinctive lifestyle of consuming goods and services. To a great extent, contemporary state apparatus and power are gendered without regard to ethnicity in the efforts to police the Malaysian middle classes.

Direct and indirect state support for Malaysian employment of Filipina and Indonesian female domestic workers continues to have negative consequences on the lives of migrant women. Growing demands for foreign domestic workers have given rise to and sustain a transnational "trade in maids," in which migrant women are "exported and imported," and bought and sold, like consumer goods. The dehumanization of foreign female domestic workers is constituted and reinforced by the interplay between the maid trade; the unlegislated status of domestic service; and the manner in which state authorities—in an effort to control the public activities of tens of thousands of migrant women—contribute to negative public and private discourse, perception, and treatment of foreign female domestic workers. Reports of Filipina and Indonesian domestic workers' deplorable working conditions (e.g., emotional, physical, economic, and sexual subordination) are not matched by public outcry to legislate domestic service or to punish abusive employers.

The principle of utility that inheres in the global expansion of neo-liberalism influences, and is reinforced in, the development path of Malaysia. Filipina and Indonesian female domestic workers' presence in the country, and especially their responses to inhumane and inhuman working conditions, highlight the extent to which utilitarianism has penetrated the many dimensions of social life to become a key principal legitimating moral criterion that guides social actions and interactions. Benefits accrued to the state and the middle classes from foreign female domestic workers' presence in Malaysia is perceived to far outweigh the negative aspects of employer-foreign servant relations, if not to naturalize public acceptance of reported and unreported incidences of employer abuse. In a multiethnic context, the official policy of restricting foreign female domestic workers' movement in public space is justified to ensure social order. Domestic employment agencies and employers are complicit, for example, in denying Filipina and Indonesian domestic workers rest days to prevent them from being exposed to criminal elements beyond the home. Employers who provide foreign domestic workers with board and lodging in addition to wages expect and insist that servants earn their keep by working longer hours, and sleeping and eating less.

Malaysian employers and society-at-large remain generally silent on the servitude of foreign female domestic workers. The interests of the state elite and the Malaysian middle classes have converged in a way that perpetuates the silence, since the plights of many foreign female domestic workers are deemed inconsequential to the modernity project of *Wawasan 2020*. The mistreatment and abuse of Filipina and Indonesian domestic workers are rationalized as valid and moral because the women are not considered and treated as human beings, but as objects to be controlled for order, sold for profit, and consumed for status.

Transnational migrant female domestic labor has become an integral component in the state elite's strategy of garnering consent for export-oriented development. Today, the service and servitude of foreign female domestic workers result from, and contribute to, the modernity project of nurturing the continued growth of the Malaysian middle classes, and legitimizing the form of the middle-class nuclear family—irrespective of ethnicity—as the foundation of and for a modern multiethnic polity.

The Creation or Recovery of Knowledge in an Era of Neoliberalism

" 'How you must envy my delighted existence!' it [a frog in a broken-down well] said to the giant turtle of the Eastern Sea. 'If I want to go out, I jump along the railing around the well, then I come back and rest where the brick lining is missing from the wall. . . . Turning around, I see crayfish and tadpoles, but none of them is a match for me. Furthermore, I have sole possession of all the water in this hole and straddle all the joy in this broken-down well. This is the ultimate! Why don't you drop in some time, sir, and see for yourself?' " But before the turtle of the Eastern Sea could get his left foot in, his right knee had already gotten stuck. After extricating himself, he withdrew a little and told the frog about the sea, saying, 'A distance of a thousand tricents is insufficient to span its breadth; a height of a thousand fathoms is insufficient to plumb its depth. During Yu's time, there were floods nine years out of ten, but the water in it did not appreciably increase; during Tang's time, there were droughts seven years out of eight, but the extent of the shores did not appreciably decrease . . . [T]his is the great joy of the Eastern Sea. 'Upon hearing this, the frog in the broken-down well was so utterly startled that it lost itself in bewilderment.' "
—Master Chuang, *Chuang Tzu*, circa 350 B.C.

To reiterate, this study is informed and driven by the interest in the critical analysis of the identification, formation, and maintenance of social institutions and structures that are shaped by and that shape human beliefs, values, attitudes, perceptions, and interactions. Of increasing interest today is the seemingly natural global expansion of capitalist free markets. The phenomenon of economic liberalization, privatization, and deregulation throughout the world may well lead peoples to perceive capitalist expansion as if it were part of the natural order of social life in the sense that human beings are inherently inclined toward the accumulation of wealth. Therefore, many practitioners and supporters of neoliberalism have come to believe that state intervention in economies can only obstruct this law of nature.

However, the capitalist orientation of social life is not natural as if it were the result of human nature per se. It is natural only so long as we understand that particular patterned behavior and interactions in the Euro-American world gave rise to institutions and structures that, over time, were naturalized and objectivated throughout the rest of the world. The objectivation and expansion of distinct beliefs, values, attitudes, perceptions, and interactions between the material and nonmaterial world appear to make natural the capitalist orientation of social life.[39] Critical analysis is designed to "deconstruct" this objective world to reveal the bases, and on many occasions, the unequal distributions and exercises of power that inhere in social relations, institutions, and structures.[40]

The process of critical analysis insists on a diachronic approach to the study of any "sphere of human activity." Equally important, critical analysis involves the examination, and if appropriate, the consequent need to redress prevailing (dominant) ways in which scholars problematize issues: "Critical theory is directed to the social and political complex as a whole rather than the separate parts . . . [and] leads toward the construction of a larger picture of the whole of which the initially contemplated part is just one component, and seeks to understand the processes of change in which both parts and whole are involved."[41]

From this perspective, analysis of domestic service that focuses exclusively on employer-domestic worker relations in the household is conceptualized within the larger national and regional contexts in which the relationship occurs. To do so is not to undermine the importance and centrality of employer-domestic worker relations per se, but to be able to identify and understand a myriad of forces interacting across regional, national, and household levels that shape the relationship. In chapter 2, I offer a discussion of the historico-empirical foundation for the argument that the Malaysian state elite rely on strategies of coercion and consent to restructure the economy and society. Analyses of the respective waves of low-wage migrant labor during the colonial and postcolonial periods are integrated in the discussion to explicate the relation between migrant labor and strategies of consent.

Having established the larger context for the contemporary in-migration of foreign workers per se, the discussion is narrowed considerably in chapter 3, which examines the historical relation between the state and the institution of domestic service. I ask and answer the question as to how and why personnel changes in domestic service were distinguished first with the displacement of foreign male servants by foreign female servants during the 1930s, and eventually, the substitution of foreign female domestic workers for the labor of their Malaysian counterparts in the late twentieth century. This is followed by an analysis of the reasons underlying state regulation of the in-migration and placement of Filipina and Indonesian domestic workers in Malaysian households. The key argument in this chapter is that specific employment rules facilitated the objectivation of the social and material boundaries of the middle classes in response to public criticisms that development had not benefitted the majority of Malaysians.

Chapter 4 begins with the global context out of which occurs the contemporary state-supported transnationalization of migrant labor. The key actors involved in the Malaysian-Philippine-Indonesian "maid trade" are identified, and their actions and policies are discussed in relation to foreign female domestic workers' migratory and employment chain. This chapter demonstrates that the transnational labor market in foreign female domestic workers did not arise "naturally." Rather, it is actively constructed and maintained by state and nonstate actors. In the maid trade, many Filipina and Indonesian domestic workers are viewed and treated as children at best, and as commodities at worst in the exchange of servants for cash on the transnational domestic labor market.

The focus in chapter 5 expands on the theme of the dehumanization of foreign female domestic workers by providing an analysis of employer-servant relations on the household level. In this chapter, employer-servant relations are conceptualized from the perspective of the "public" and "hidden" transcripts of domestic service, i.e., the public/observable deference of foreign female domestic workers in their relationship with employers ("public" transcript) is juxtaposed with what foreign servants say and do when they are away from their workplace ("hidden" transcript).[42] Various methods of supervision and surveillance are found to be constitutive of the processes of the construction of middle-class identity in the household, and subsequent acts of employer-related mistreatment and abuse. Filipina and Indonesian domestic workers, however, are not entirely passive or powerless in their responses to abusive employers. Their strategies of negotiating and renegotiating control over the use of time and space are identified and analyzed.

Chapter 6 provides a more in-depth discussion on Malaysian demands for transnational migrant domestic labor, and the manner in which the employing social classes and the public-at-large have been able to ignore the mistreatment and abuse of Filipina and Indonesian domestic workers. The interplay between the socioeconomic requirements and consequences of export-oriented development in Malaysia, and prevailing Asian patriarchal attitudes toward middle-class Malaysian women, make inevitable middle-class families' demands that domestic workers facilitate the construction and pursuit of the good life. I revisit the Immigration Department's rules governing the employment of domestic workers within the context of policies and legislation designed to (re)construct middle-class women's roles and status within the nuclear family form, and to legitimize the notion of "modernity via consumption."

Chapter 7 concludes with a summary of the major arguments in this study and offers a critique of utility as a guiding moral principle in the conduct of the everyday life of the Malaysian middle classes.

Forays Into the Field: The Field Research Process

Words are for catching ideas; once you've caught the idea, you can forget about the words. Where can I find a person who knows how to forget about words so that I can have a few words with him [her]?
—Master Chuang, *Chuang Tzu*, circa 350 B.C.

The methodological approach taken is that of a nonpositivist manner of recovering and generating knowledge pertaining to the relationship between contemporary domestic service and the political economy of development in Malaysia. This is not to say that methods such as attitudinal surveys will not aid in the task of identifying factors that lead to Malaysian demands for and eventual employment of Filipina and Indonesian domestic workers. Nonetheless, surveys can constrain our ability to understand the complexity of various forces at work in shaping the performance and consumption of paid reproductive labor since, "[S]urveys are also limited instruments. One limitation is the fact that they oversimplify complex issues by reducing them to the responses to a limited number of questions."[43]

Feminist inquiry that remains within the boundaries of positivism insists that a feminist reinterpretation of the scientific method rectifies many androcentric biases. It is argued that the context of discovery is as equally important as the context of justification, i.e., making clear the researcher's identity will lead to a more objective study. While I support the move to acknowledge the researcher's identity (gender, nationality, ideological position, and so forth), we still would labor under the illusion in which the complexities of social life can be distilled into a series of hypotheses and categories to be tested, and the ensuing results effectively lauded as "truth."

There also was a practical consideration that mitigated the use of survey instruments. In 1993, while I was visiting family and friends in Kuala Lumpur, I became acutely aware not only of the presence of foreign female domestic workers in Malaysia, but also of the refusal by many employers to even speak about domestic service, let alone answer a list of prepared questions (see preface). Students at Universiti Malaya who had conducted or were in the process of conducting surveys of Filipina and Indonesian domestic workers, and activists from nongovernmental organizations that offered counseling services to abused foreign domestic workers, complained of the difficulty in gaining access to this population as a whole and in convincing migrant women to answer surveys.

I elected instead to conduct multimethod ethnographic research—archival analysis, observation, and interviews—that would help construct a picture of domestic service in which are embedded various dimensions of the lives of employers and domestic workers. It can be said that interviews conducted within the framework of ethnographic research are unscientific in the sense that there is no way to evaluate the validity and replicability of the data. I concede that this argument, indeed, is valid *if* the assumption is that the many different and complex ways in which social actors, in their everyday lives, perceive and interact with their environment are accessible to formal social scientific inquiry. This study follows the guidelines established for ethnographic validity: i.e., to make explicit the relation between theory and ethnographic methods, or "theoretical candor"; to map the "ethnographer's path"; and to offer extensive "fieldnote quotations" as evidence.[44]

A key intent in this study was to capture, as much as possible, the structural impact of development on the lives of employers and foreign female domestic workers in their own words. My refusal to structure the question-answer sessions, choosing instead to allow employers and domestic workers the right to speak about any issue they so pleased, produced a wealth of information on the ways in which they understood and expressed their understanding of social relations and structures that affected their lives.

Analysis of the interviews fall under the aegis of the "study of narrativity." Narrativity should not be conflated with the method of presenting historical knowledge or a mode of "representation." Rather, it should be considered a part of social epistemology and ontology: the employers and servants' narratives, in and of themselves, were informative of how and why the respondents respectively constituted their identities, or conversely and in distinct ways challenged identities constructed on their behalf.

Put simply, we come to construct our identities by locating ourselves in narratives in which we process our understanding of ourselves and the world around us: "Ontological narratives make identity and the self something that one *becomes*. Thus narrative embeds identities in time and spatial relationships."[45] Take, for example, the voice that I develop in this chapter, and ultimately throughout the entire study. It is through what, how, and why I say what I do—in this case, in written form—to my reader, that I come to understand, construct, and project my identity as a scholar. Out in the field, the process is somewhat similar in the sense that employers and domestic workers construct their identities as they narrate to me or others that which they consider important. I share the construction and presentation of parts of this study with the voices of the peoples whose everyday lives help to shape decisionmaking at the national level, and who are affected by transnational forces generally beyond their control.

In January 1994, I traveled back to Malaysia for approximately six months to conduct ethnographic research on the causes and consequences of Malaysian employment of Filipina and Indonesian domestic workers. The initial stages of fieldwork involved archival research and interviews of policymakers and activists. It is important to emphasize here that there is little secondary literature on domestic service in colonial and postcolonial Malaysia. Yet, the challenge of analyzing the relationship between state-led expansion of export-oriented development and the institution of contemporary domestic service that is currently dominated by the labor of foreign female domestic workers necessitates examining the past.

The processes of reconstructing a picture of domestic service from colonialism to the point in which transnational migrant domestic labor literally has displaced Malaysian female domestic workers involved archival research and analysis of newspaper articles, colonial literature, and scholarship on Malaysian women and development. Unstructured interviews of former Malaysian female domestic workers whom I encountered while in the field contributed to the discussion of how and why Filipina and Indonesian domestic workers have come to work for Malaysian families (see chapter 3).

Interviews of policymakers, representatives from the Philippine and Indonesian embassies, and Malaysian activists were conducted to ascertain the state's policy on the in-migration of foreign female domestic workers. Malaysian state officials and representatives of the labor-sending states consented to interviews only under the expressed agreement of anonymity. If and when there are citations to such interviews, only the date and/or place of interviews are identified.

I was informed by activists and several state officials in 1994, that the Home Affairs Ministry (arguably, the most powerful ministry and one that is controlled directly by the Prime Minister) had imposed a "gag order" prohibiting official interviews on low wage labor in-migration. According to a state official, given the unending low wage labor demands of key industries, "The state opens one eye and closes the other [to the issue of low wage labor in-migration]." Chapters 2, 3, and 4 offer more detailed analyses of why labor in-migration has become a politically sensitive issue in the country.

Analysis of the causes and consequences of Filipina and Indonesian domestic workers' in-migration to Malaysia also required investigating Malaysian citizens' demands for household help, privately owned companies that specialize in supplying foreign domestic labor, and the domestic workers' perspectives of the in-migration and employment processes. The knowledge generated in the process of field research, and consequently organized, analyzed, and presented—especially in chapters 4, 5, and 6—derive from a combination of observation and unstructured interviews of Malaysian employers, Filipina and Indonesian domestic workers, and private domestic employment agencies (DOMs).

During the period of field research, I lived in various neighborhoods in Kuala Lumpur with the intent of observing some of the working conditions and relations between employers and foreign female domestic workers, and possibly the opportunity to interview the employers and their domestic servants. While some employers agreed to speak with me, only in rare cases was I given permission to speak with domestic workers before or after interviews with employers. Even so, employers were always within a comfortable listening distance. In lieu of employers' consent in these neighborhoods, I interviewed Filipina and Indonesian domestic workers at churches, shopping malls, supermarkets, "*pasar malam*,"[46] bus/taxi stands, and on rare occasions, domestic employment agency houses.[47]

Filipina servants were more accessible than their Indonesian counterparts. A major reason is that the Philippine Overseas Employment Agency (POEA) negotiated a standardized contract governing salary and working conditions. Among the requirements are four rest days or days off every month. During the period of research, domestic workers were allowed only two rest days a month, at best. On their rest days, most of the women attend Sunday church services, after which they would either go shopping, back to their employers' houses, or even to "afternoon" discotheques.

The Indonesian state has yet to negotiate for and insist on a standardized contract for their female nationals. Employers are advised by DOMs to pay Indonesian servants approximately RM10–15 (at an approximate exchange rate of RM2.6 to US$1 in 1994) in lieu of one rest day per month to keep the women from leaving their workplace. Public perception and discourse that associate legal and illegal foreign female domestic workers with crimes of theft and prostitution play a major part in employers' refusal to allow Indonesian servants (who do not have standardized work contracts) to leave their houses unaccompanied, or even to converse with friends at the house-gates.

Some Indonesian domestic workers, to be sure, did not wish to be interviewed for fear that I was an undercover immigration official conceivably interested in their legal or illegal status. Potential Indonesian respondents then, were recommended by a variety of peoples: Indonesian and Malay informants in the informal economy (e.g., hawkers in the Chow Kit area); Filipina servants who identified Indonesian servants in their neighborhoods; Indonesian migrant workers waiting to have papers processed at their embassy; and Indonesian female restaurant workers.

The "ethnographer's path," as it evolved was never that of a direct path from points A to Z.[48] Rather, the road that I found myself traveling on was at times rough, bumpy, and bent at a ninety degree angle; and at other times it was smooth and straight.[49] It is not possible to offer a precise sense of the duration of unstructured interviews because there were no clearcut markers that distinguished when an interview proper began or ended—short of my taking physical leave of the respondent. Interviews were conducted while Filipina and Indonesian domestic workers worked (e.g., hanging clothes in the front of the house, buying groceries at the wet market), shopped, ate their meals, or even while they supervised children in neighborhood playgrounds. There were quite a number of times when the interviews could be and were interrupted by friends of foreign domestic workers who either wanted to join the conversation, or who wanted the respondents to leave with them to go elsewhere. For the most part, Filipina and Indonesian domestic workers' control over their use of "free" time was severely constrained by their employers. Some women were given one day off a month while others had two rest days or even none at all. Even so, a typical rest day could range from a few hours to a maximum of twelve hours. My intention was to gather information with the least amount of intrusion or interruption in the women's activities.

In almost every interview, foreign female domestic workers were the first to assume the role of the interviewer. They wanted to know what I did in America, my experience living there, and if I knew anyone (e.g., a "nice" employer) in Kuala Lumpur or America who wanted to hire a domestic worker, and so forth. Once they were comfortable with the fact that I neither worked for the state nor for DOMs, they would ask me what I wanted to know. I then inquired about their lives, e.g., why they chose to work as servants, their views of Malaysian employers, what they considered problems at work, and how they dealt with the problems. These were the general questions I had in mind for the workers. Whether or not the questions were asked in a specific order, or even were needed to be asked, depended on the context of each interview. Approximately eighty-nine interviews of Filipina female domestic workers and forty-seven interviews of Indonesian female domestic workers were conducted over the course of the field research period.

Interviews with employers occurred in their houses, country clubs, restaurants, offices, and on several occasions, brokerage firms—i.e., wherever the respondents could fit interviews into their schedules. I began with my social and professional networks, and over time, the snowball approach produced sixty-eight respondents. Most, upon learning that I studied overseas, "claimed" me as belonging to the middle class. Consequently, narratives were interspersed with "You know-lah . . . ," "I tell you . . . ," "[N]o need to say any more, am I right?" and so forth. I read these prefixes and suffixes to the employers' narratives as their attempt to establish some degree of commonality with me—i.e., as a Malaysian, and as one who was perceived to belong to the same social stratum—that ultimately gave them the license or the justification for sharing their candid views of Filipina and Indonesian domestic workers (see especially chapters 5 and 6). Indeed, I would ask a respondent to clarify his/her statements if they were not clear to me. Many times, a respondent either would organize a "get together" with other friends in her house or invite me to a social function as a way to facilitate my research or to "make life easier for you, so that you don't need to call them one by one."[50]

Although I did not make any efforts to single out male or female employers, the majority of the respondents were female. Husbands of female employers, even when present during the interviews, deferred to their wives in discussing "maids," and would interject to emphasize or add what they thought were important points in narrating the processes involved in hiring and evaluating the performance of foreign domestic workers.

The names of all employers and foreign servants in this study are pseudonyms because of the respondents' requests for anonymity. Filipina and Indonesian domestic workers were fearful of negative repercussions from employers, DOMs, and the Immigration Department, while employers did not wish to divulge their identities and their narratives on foreign female domestic workers. The interviews were not tape recorded. Notes were taken either with permission during the interview, or immediately afterward.

There were several occasions when an informant or a respondent would call me the day after a social function for a "debriefing" session, i.e., to convey to me his/her interpretation of fellow conversants' behavior and/or statements about issues discussed the previous night. In these sessions, I would remember what Simon Ottenberg calls "head notes" or information previously unrecorded in field notes, but that could and would surface when triggered by an event or a conversation.[51] These head notes were included in the field notes.

Several key issues arise from the method of unstructured interviews. Bonnie Dill, in her study of African-American domestic servants, discussed Aaron Cicourel's identification of the five issues that emerge from conducting interviews in general: "[T]rust; status discrepancies; varying perceptions and interpretations of questions; tension between sensitive areas which may cause a subject to withdraw; and the fact that much that is meaningful to both parties remains unstated."[52] I dealt with the first four challenges by considering the interviews as interactions in which the interviewer and the respondent worked out issues of trust and honesty. As Clifford Geertz argued, "It is dialogue that does it, however delicate and liable to misfire, not inquisition, however orderly and straight from the shoulder."[53]

In the duration of my field work, employers' and foreign female domestic workers' narratives on their respective experiences with regards to domestic service were interspersed with long discussions on matters that seemed, at the outset, barely relevant to the central topic. I nevertheless sat patiently and listened to advice on the latest *haute couture*, how to choose a good husband, and so forth.

Cicourel's last challenge, I believe, is central to those who choose to conduct research in their home country, since most of the "social cues" that they consider part of everyday life easily would and could be problematized or made "alien" by researchers from other countries. Consequently throughout the course of my field research, it required a conscious effort on my part as the researcher to engage in what I call a "self-induced ethnomethodological stance"; to be constantly aware that all of what I normally took for granted in everyday Malaysian life might and did generate relevant/pertinent information for this study.[54]

DOMs would represent one of the most challenging aspects of fieldwork. I obtained a list of legal DOMs furnished by the Immigration Department, and having been forewarned by NGOs of their uncooperative nature, I nevertheless called a few to request interviews. The requests were denied almost instantaneously. Upon learning that a friend and a close relative were in the process of selecting DOMs to facilitate the process of hiring foreign female domestic workers, we sat down and devised a list of questions for the DOMs such as the fees charged for processing an employer's application form, and the difference in the cost involved in hiring a Filipina as opposed to an Indonesian domestic worker. In the role as a prospective employer, I "interviewed" via the telephone and/or in person, representatives from twenty DOMs (see especially chapter 4).

Ethnographic research supports my epistemic position which, among other issues previously discussed, "repudiates the idea of a social reality out there independent of the observer."[55] My identity as a Malaysian woman cannot and is not bracketed or suspended from my identity as a researcher in the course of organizing, analyzing, and presenting the body of material derived from field research.

It is appropriate here to anticipate and address the argument that this study is not "objective" in the sense that the researcher was not value-neutral in conceptualizing and researching the relation between domestic service and development. Indeed, from the perspective of critical theory (whether it is critical theory informed by the sensibilities of the Habermasian, Coxian, feminist, and/or postmodern positions), a key goal of engaging in intellectual inquiry and discourse is to search for the possibilities of change from an existing social order in which discrimination and oppression are based on nationality, race-ethnicity, gender, class, and/or religion.[56]

The ultimate objective in this study is to help ascertain potentialities for the transformation of, or emancipation from, the constraints of seemingly natural social relations, institutions, and structures.[57] The question becomes emancipation for whom and for what?

To be sure, the plight of Filipina and Indonesian domestic workers in Malaysia can be temporarily solved, at the very least, by the implementation of standardized work contracts, grievance mechanisms, legislation that defines and enforces the rights of domestic workers, and so forth. These various mechanisms, however, do not address present capitalist-patriarchal structures and processes that are constituted by and that constitute a warped conception of the good life as it is currently packaged and promoted throughout the world. The good life today is characteristically consumption-oriented, most visibly at the expense of the working poor and the physical environment. From the perspective of labor-sending states, structural adjustment and stabilization policies that promise the potential for state elites to provide their peoples with the context to pursue and to enjoy the good life increasingly necessitate the "export" of female nationals as foreign domestic workers. At the labor-receiving end, state-encouraged middle-class Malaysian pursuit of the good life via enhanced material consumption also involves consuming the labor or services of Filipina and Indonesian domestic workers. Most importantly, the processes of consuming migrant domestic labor occur in a context in which foreign female domestic workers are denied labor protection while employer-related abuse, for the most part, remains unpunished.

In the race to realize the good life via more efficient means to accumulate wealth that allow for greater acts of consumption, it is assumed that the most basic values of human decency and respect can and will remain intact. The real danger of failure by officials to address the causes of Malaysian demands for and abuse of Filipina and Indonesian domestic workers, together with middle-class employers' refusal to confront a development path that greatly shapes their lifestyles, is that it may well lead to the emergence of a future generation of middle-class citizens who may be socialized in the art of consumption in a way that disregards or dismisses the negative consequences on those who serve them. The emancipation of foreign female domestic workers from oppressive and dehumanizing working conditions, then, is dependent on the emancipation of middle-class employers and the state elite from the idea that modernity should and can be reduced to, and made synonymous with, enhanced consumption.

At the level of scholarly discourse, emancipation takes on the equally urgent and fundamental restructuring of the ways in which we conceive and execute research problems. The study of social change in this era of the global expansion of neoliberalism may be likened to making decisions to renovate or to raze an old building. As "architects" and "construction" workers then, should we demolish the house and use new tools and material to rebuild? Do we have the means to do so? Or should we renovate the house, recycle the tools and material, and use them in innovative ways to build a different house?

As far as the intellectual project of generating knowledge is concerned, emancipation is related to understanding, acknowledging, and acting to undo received disciplinary and epistemological boundaries that segregate the pursuit of knowledge. I neither argue that any intellectual division of labor is unfruitful, nor the idea that we should critique received traditions for the sake of engaging in critique. Rather, I question how and why we have come to defend constructed boundaries such as the separation of political science from anthropology, and/or literature that have obstructed the pursuit of knowledge. Some of the consequences of this kind of intellectual segregation are the production of unidimensional pictures of social change, and the silencing or marginalization of voices within the academy that struggle to paint a more "human," thus more complex and less definitive picture of social change.

In the past, the belief that the human mind was passive (it did not interfere with the experience of sensory data) and ahistoric (static through space and time) led us on a grand search for laws—universal laws of social change that were believed to be immutable. In doing so, the intellectual project became one of conceptualizing and acting upon such laws as "truth," whereas "truth" as we have had to confront it is the inherent placing and valuing of hidden worldviews, values, perceptions, beliefs, and attitudes within conceptual frameworks as "natural" and "objective," thus free from distortion or critique. The epistemic and methodological positions of "objective truth" have been problematic for what and how they obscure value choices. The demise of the tenets of mind as passive and ahistoric, truth as objective and immutable, imply that as social change is grounded in history; so too are the ways in which we conceptualize or problematize issues. As scholars, precisely because we are members of society, we participate in generating, validating, opposing, constructing, deconstructing, and reconstructing social phenomena. The pursuit of knowledge cannot and does not exempt us from influencing and obviously being influenced by the changing environment.

The heated verbal and written ideological debates over the control of intellectual territory leaves the task of studying and explaining social change even more difficult as "disciples" or scholars-to-be are caught in the crossfire. It also masks the initial and overriding motive of engaging in the intellectual project. If the stated and unstated intentions are to understand social change and to search for possibilities of reconstructing an alternative social order premised on different grounds, then self-reflexivity is a necessity and not a luxury.

> The best feminist analysis, insists that the inquirer her\himself be placed in the same critical plane as the overt subject matter, thereby recovering the entire research process for scrutiny in the results of the research. That is, the class, race, culture, and gender assumptions, beliefs and behaviours of the researcher her\himself must be placed within the frame of the picture that she\he attempts to paint . . . Introducing this 'subjective' element in the analysis in fact increases the objectivity of the research and decreases the 'subjectivism' which hides this kind of evi-

dence from the public. . . . This requirement [to be up front with one's assumptions] is no idle attempt to 'do good' by the standards of imagined critics in classes, races, cultures (or of a gender) other than that of the researcher. Instead we need to avoid the objectivist stance that attempts to make the researcher's cultural beliefs and practices invisible while simultaneously skewering the objects, beliefs and practices to the display board.[58]

To this end, I have explicitly integrated my nationality, class, and ethnic backgrounds to acknowledge that my schemata for viewing and understanding the world must necessarily be the product of the interactions between two received traditions. They are the class-ethnic-gender socialization processes I experienced as a member of Malaysian society; and the legacy of academic and intellectual training in higher institutions of learning in Europe and North America. The synthesis, and at times, contradictions between these two traditions have driven the formulation and articulation of this study.

In the following chapters, I examine the forces at work on the transnational, national, and household levels in which the Malaysian state elite and the middle classes gradually come to share a similar vision of the good life that involves the in-migration and employment of foreign female domestic workers.

Notes on the Epigraphs

(In order of appearance): Mahathir Mohamad, "Malaysia: The Way Forward," in *Malaysia's Vision 2020: Understanding the Concept, Implications and Challenges* (Petaling Jaya: Pelanduk Publications, 1991), p. 404; Interview of "Anita" in *The Star* April 10, 1994; Antonio Gramsci, *Selections from the Prison Notebooks*, ed. and trans. Quintin Hoare and Geoffrey Nowell Smith (New York: International Publishers, 1971), p. 246; *Wandering on the Way: Early Taoist Tales and Parables of Chuang Tzu*, trans. by Victor H. Mair (New York: Bantam Books, 1994), pp. 161–162, and p. 277.

CHAPTER 2

Arranging and Rearranging the Interior Frontiers
of Society

An enlightened ruler in regulating the livelihood of his people will make sure that in the first place they are well enough off to look after their parents and able to support wife and child, that in good years they get as much as they can, eat at every meal. . . . [O]nly when this has been assumed does he 'gallop onto goodness,' and the people will have no difficulty following him.
—Mencius, *Mencius,* circa 390–380 B.C.

The ruler's subjects, on the other hand, are incapable of taking long views. What they hate is toil and danger, what they want is immediate ease and peace, and they are too stupid to see that ultimate safety can only be served by immediate discomfort and danger. If the ruler pesters them with laws and regulations and threatens them with terrifying penalties, this is the objective of 'saving mankind from disorder and averting calamities that hang over the whole world.' . . . No greater service to the people could be imagined; but there are some so stupid as not to realize this and insist upon regarding the ruler's measures as tyranny.
—Han Fei Tzu, *Han Fei Tzu,* circa 350 B.C.

The presence of low-wage migrant labor on Malaysian soil today is not unprecedented, since Malaysia is a country born, in part, of immigrant peoples. During the colonial period, low-wage migrant labor from China and India helped build a natural resource-based export economy. The presence of a growing population of Chinese and Indian migrant workers (many of whom eventually settled in the country) led the British to implement legislation that defined and protected specific Malay rights. A key consequence was the association of different peoples with different economic function and geographic space. In the late twentieth century, low-wage migrant labor from the Philippines and Indonesia would facilitate efforts by post-colonial elites to rearrange Malaysian society without undermining social stability in the multiethnic country and/or the economy's competitiveness in the regional and global arenas.

This chapter analyzes the relationship between the colonial and post-colonial in-migrating waves of low-wage labor, and state strategies of coercion-repression and consent used to arrange and rearrange the interior frontiers of society.[1] The discussion sets the larger context of this study's argument that the contemporary in-migration of Filipina and Indonesian domestic workers is integral to the postcolonial state elite's defense of the New Economic Policy (NEP) 1971–1990, and to the normalization of the modern middle-class nuclear family.

Opening of the Immigration Gates: Colonial Arrangement of the Interior Frontiers of Malayan Society [2]

In precolonial Malay society on the peninsula, rulers established their principalities along river estuaries to facilitate the collection of revenue:

> They were rivermouth societies, for the most part, centered on port towns lying where the river debouched onto the sea, placed so as to control what came down and to participate in what passed by. The political power, the "state" or *negeri*, at the mouth of the river, sought to establish sufficient authority over the peoples upriver and, in the interior, to ensure a flow of produce that could be taxed or sold. . . . [S]tate boundaries tended to be vague and relatively unimportant, for what mattered was control of waterborne traffic, not land.[3]

Malay peasant use of land was governed by usufructuary laws: a peasant owned land so long as he actively cultivated it.[4] A portion of the land's produce was given to the ruler in return for physical protection and royal recognition of the peasant's identity as a Malay or an individual who lived and served under a particular Malay ruler.[5]

Malay society was organized hierarchically by political bonds linking Malay rulers (*raja* or sultan) at the top of the political structure to their peasant subjects (*rakyat*) at the bottom.[6] Malay rulers' adoption of Islam (hence the *raja* became the sultan) circa the fifteenth century, and consequent diffusion of the religion throughout Malay society, failed to significantly alter the vertical bonds, or Malay folk religion.[7] Instead, existing hierarchical social arrangements became the major vehicle for transmitting Islam.[8]

Malay women's status and roles in the precolonial economy and society differed according to class. Aristocratic women were confined mostly to the socialization of children, although some were known to have been active traders. Peasant women, however, had reproductive and productive roles in their capacities as wives, mothers, daughters, and farmers. It is argued that with the exception of female debt-bondage (see chapter 3), Malay men and women had a complementary rather than a superior-subordinate relationship.[9]

As early as the sixteenth century, European commercial interests were present on the peninsula. The entrépot of Melaka, which overlooked the Straits of Melaka on the west coast of the peninsula, was of immense strategic and commercial importance to the India-China trade route. Portuguese, Dutch, and British mercantilists successively conquered Melaka in 1511, 1641, and 1795. Of the three European mercantilist maritime powers, the British gradually penetrated, expanded, and consolidated colonial control over the peninsula. Colonial policies eventually would be embodied by the Kiplingesque notion of the "white man's burden" in which the British assumed moral responsibility for civilizing their native nonwhite brethren, while developing a natural resource-based export economy.[10]

Initial consent for British presence on the peninsula was solicited in the following way. Colonialists signed treaties with Malay rulers of the "Straits Settlements" of Penang, Singapore, and Melaka for the right to trade and establish military bases to oversee their India-China trade route. In return for British military and commercial presence, rulers were given physical protection from enemies within and beyond their principalities.

During the early years of colonial presence, a small population of Chinese men worked as sugar smallholders and tin miners. By the mid nineteenth century, Chinese tin mine workers eventually displaced their Malay counterparts as male-dominated Chinese secret societies' organization and control over labor proved more efficient in generating revenue. Different rulers made alliances with different secret societies organized along clan lines.

Constant fighting between secret societies encouraged colonial military intervention to prevent the disruption of European trade.[11] From 1874 to 1930, the British extended their presence on the peninsula by signing treaties with the rest of the Malay rulers. The treaties expanded colonial administrative and bureaucratic rule throughout most of the peninsula.

The colonial system of rule, or the "resident system" as it was called, placed a resident advisor with each sultan in return for colonial guarantee of the symbolic continuity of Malay governance, the sultans' position as protector of Islam, and the recognition of Malays as the indigenous peoples.[12] Decision-making power within the Malay political structure shifted to British hands as the resident advisor replaced the *bendahara* (chief minister to the ruler), and appointed colonial district officers who took over the responsibilities of Malay chiefs.[13]

To facilitate capital accumulation, the British implemented the Torren Land Laws (patterned after the South Australian Torren Land Laws of the 1850s) that institutionalized the concept of private property complete with permanent and transferable rights to land. Colonial land legislation was implemented ostensibly to "protect" Malay society by clearly delineating land ownership in the midst of increasing foreign presence. In practice, the private property concept justified the alienation of large portions of unused or uncultivated land for commercial purposes: "Above all for British officials, this turning of the greater part of the peninsula into 'State land' offered an unparalleled opportunity to make land available in the future, at the most nominal rents, to settlers and to British and Chinese capitalists for their use."[14]

From the mid to late nineteenth century, American and British industrial and commercial demands hastened the growth of tin and rubber industries or the "twin pillars" of colonial Malaya's export economy. Yet, weak colonial control over the supply of labor threatened to undermine the emerging economy. European capitalists, who were unable to attract Malay labor because of the availability of land for cultivation, responded by "importing" predominantly male migrant workers from China and India.

Colonial administrators had a reason for initially neither prohibiting the in-migration of Chinese and Indian labor, nor actively recruiting Malay peasants to work in the tin and rubber industries. Taxes on migrant consumption activities such as gambling, smoking opium, and visiting brothels provided the colonial state treasury with additional revenue.[15]

Development in colonial Malaya was synonymous with the establishment and growth of an export economy geared toward supplying international demands for tin and rubber, as well as the import of manufactured British consumer goods. Infrastructural (especially public works) projects were designed to facilitate communication between the hinterland and coastal cities and ports, rather than to improve the living standards of the peoples. Instead of financing projects with taxes on the export of tin and rubber, and the import of manufactured goods, the British relied mostly on revenue from state monopolies on the sale of alcohol and tobacco, and taxes on migrant brothels, opium, and gaming dens.

Together with the demands for and consequent in-migration of Chinese and Indian male labor was the colonial construction of ascribed racial-gender traits and concomitant socioeconomic segregation of the Malay, Chinese, and Indian peoples. Below, I discuss how a racial-gender division of labor, or the association between occupational segregation and racial-gender traits began to emerge in response to the nexus of moral and economic justification for and of colonialism. In my analysis of British rule in Malaya, I have deliberately used the words "race" and racial groups as opposed to ethnicity and ethnic groups, specifically to highlight colonial perception and treatment of Malays, Chinese, and Indian peoples. Colonial construction of the categories of "Malay," "Chinese," and "Klings" presumed that physiognomic differences and subsequent lifestyles among the peoples could be traced to different biological foundations, hence the social construction of "races" of peoples—and concomitant hierarchical ordering—as opposed to a race of human beings. (Depending on the context in postcolonial Malaysia, government publications and official speeches categorize the peoples either according to racial or ethnic groups.)

Colonialists initially were unable to exercise extensive control over the in-migration and employment of Chinese male labor. The early stages of the mining industry were controlled by Chinese secret societies with well-developed financial and labor organizational networks.[16] Labor brokers or work leaders traveled back to their villages to recruit mostly male kin or village folk who, almost always, could not pay their own passage to Malaya. Many labor recruits migrated as indentured workers whose debts were deducted from future earnings.[17] By keeping labor costs to a minimum, the indentured labor system facilitated Chinese as well as European capital accumulation in Malaya.

Several pieces of legislation were introduced in the late 1800s that curbed wealthy Chinese miners' ability to compete with their European counterparts in the production and distribution of tin ore. The Chinese Immigration Ordinance 1877 regulated labor in-migration; the Societies Ordinance 1889 outlawed Chinese secret societies; and the amended Labour Contract Ordinance 1914 banned indentured Chinese labor.[18]

Prior to the Societies Ordinance 1889, Chinese secret societies' control and influence over mining labor prompted the colonialists to protect another emerging commercial interest, i.e., rubber plantations.[19] Below is an excerpt from a letter written by a colonial officer to plantation owners:

> To secure your independence, work with Javanese or Tamils, and if you have sufficient experience, also with Malays and Chinese, you can thus always play one against the other. . . . [I]n case of a strike, you will never be left without labor,

and the coolies of one nationality will think twice before they make their terms,
if they know that you are in a position that you can do without them.[20]

This "divide and rule strategy" was used to police the migrant workforce.
Of interest is that South Asian workers were not the first choice of alternative migrant labor to that of the Chinese.

In the mid to late nineteenth century, Malay peoples were known to migrate freely between the peninsula and the archipelago. What the British did was to formalize Malay migration mechanisms by establishing labor brokers in Malaya and the Dutch East Indies to facilitate in-migration from the neighboring island of Java.

Demands for Javanese labor quickly fell as the workers proved difficult to control because of illness, opium addiction, and recalcitrance.[21] Migrant labor from South Asia would be considered more suitable for estate work since the British believed that colonialism in India already had "conditioned" Indians for plantation and construction work: "The Indian labourer had none of the self-reliance nor the capacity of the Chinese but he was the most amenable to the comparatively lowly paid and rather regimented life of estates and government projects. He was well behaved, docile and had neither the education nor the enterprise to rise, as the Chinese did, above the level of manual labour."[22]

The British controlled Indian labor at the sending (India) and receiving (Malaya) ends. In 1907, the Tamil Immigration Fund, which was administered by the Indian Immigration Committee, required all employers to finance Indian labor in-migration as a major way to eliminate indentured labor: (a) the *kangany* system in which *kanganies* or male head workers from plantations were sent back to India to recruit kin or village folk; and (b) the system of nonrecruits or "walk-ins" to the Malayan Immigration Commission in India.[23] The Fund financed both systems as a major way to eliminate indentured labor.

Migrant women from India and China were not a significant presence in colonial Malaya until the early decades of the twentieth century. The predominance of male migrants in the late nineteenth century was due to social customs in countries of origin that discouraged female out-migration (so as to induce the eventual return of the men).[24] In 1871, there were 307 Indian and 200 Chinese women respectively per thousand men from each ethnic group. By 1911, for every one thousand Indian and Chinese men respectively there were only 308 Indian and 249 Chinese women.[25]

The predominantly single male migrant population in Malaya was seen as a potential threat to social stability and order. Entire Indian families were encouraged to migrate in order to ensure the stability of the Indian migrant community, and to provide a continuous supply of low-wage labor. The Indian Immigration Committee offered incentives for female in-migration: employers were taxed at lower rates per female laborer; recruiters were given higher allowances for the migration of entire families; and nonrecruits were given cash bonuses if children migrated with them. Since Indian men were paid a single wage as opposed to family wage in colonial Malaya, women and children then were compelled to work.[26]

Even though scholars are divided over the extent of Indian women's participation in the colonial economy, it is generally accepted that Indian women worked as rubber tappers and weeders in plantations/estates, and as laborers for state infrastructural projects. Little is known of the age or marital status of Indian women workers except for various historical references to separate estate housing for married women, migrant worker fights over women, and forced sex between Indian women and (European) plantation owners and (Indian) managers.[27] Historical records tell of incidences in which women were kidnapped from India to work as prostitutes on plantations/estates. The 1941 strike by Indian laborers in Selangor is revealing of the extent of sexual abuse on estates: among the striking workers' demands was an end to the molestation of their womenfolk.[28]

Colonial policy constructed dual roles for Indian women in Malaya—they were considered as both productive and reproductive workers. Women worked alongside men in the plantations; reproduced the future low-wage workforce; ensured stable home environments for Indian men; and provided European plantation owners and Indian managers with sexual services.

The colonial practice of capitalist-patriarchal ideology also shaped Chinese migrant women's participation in the economy. During the late 1800s, female out-migration was actively discouraged by Ch'ing dynasty officials at ports of departure. Women who migrated did so primarily as wives of male workers, or they were kidnapped to work as prostitutes and *mui-tsai* (girl-slaves between the ages of six and thirteen). Chinese secret societies controlled the in-migration and employment of the latter two categories of migrant women.[29]

The institutionalization of Chinese prostitution in Malaya reflected colonial dependence on Chinese women's reproductive/sexual roles to stabilize the Chinese male migrant population. Between 1900–1927, legalized brothels were major revenue contributors to the state treasury. Prostitution was banned finally in 1930 in response to public outcry in Britain.

The *mui-tsai* system, in which families sold or pawned girl children to wealthier households in order to settle debts, was not legislated until the Domestic Servants Ordinance 1925. Wealthy Chinese families provided board and lodging, and "moral guidance" in return for the household services of young girl-slaves. Once the girls reached the age of eighteen or when debts were settled, they were either free to leave, or were taken as mistresses or daughters-in-law.

With the help of the Chinese Protector (colonial officer in charge of Chinese affairs) in 1885, wealthy Chinese businessmen established the *Po Leung Kuk*, which was charged with imparting economic skills to runaway *mui-tsai*. In practice, the institution, which originated from Chinese philanthropic activity, quickly became a supplier of properly trained young wives-to-be rather than one providing the skills for independent living.[30]

It has been argued that the *mui-tsai* system persisted because of British failure to control the in-migration of Chinese girl-slaves.[31] The question is that if prostitution could be legalized, then why not the *mui-tsai* system? Until the Domestic Servants Ordinance 1925, legislative silence on young girl-slaves could not have been largely due to the failure to control the immigration gates. First, there was not a perceived need to regulate *mui-tsai* in-migration because the latter, unlike prostitutes, did not contribute to state revenue. Second, young girls were crucial to the stability of the Chinese male migrant population. Given the low numbers of Chinese women in Malaya between the late 1800s and early 1900s, the partnership between colonialists and wealthy Chinese businessmen (embodied in the institution of the *Po Leung Kuk*) ensured the socialization of runaway *mui-tsai* as eligible and desirable wives for single Chinese men.

The majority of Chinese female migrants arrived in Malaya between 1933 and 1938. Worldwide economic depression prompted the British to pass the Aliens Ordinances 1930 and 1933, which instituted a quota system severely restricting the in-migration of male workers, but that did not exclude women. Since the passage for one male quota ticket was made considerably higher, a labor broker would take a male migrant only if four women bought tickets to travel with him. Within five years, approximately 190,000 Chinese women had arrived in Malaya, and they worked as domestic servants, construction laborers, *dulang* washers (the process is a method of salvaging residue tin ore), and rubber tappers.[32] In these occupations, women were paid less than men. Particularly in the mining industry, women were restricted to *dulang* washing, and they were prohibited from working underground or tending machines. Such rules ostensibly protected women from physical danger. However, protection had the effect of denigrating or devaluing women's work: they were hired as piece rate workers with salaries substantially lower than men, and they were not provided with board and lodging. Mine owners assumed that women lived with their husbands or fathers, and that women's wages were supplementary income or what is now commonly known as "pin money."

Even before the mass arrival of Chinese women, colonial concern for the growing number of Chinese and Indian migrant workers led to the Malay Reservation Land Enactment (MRL) 1913 that set aside land to be used, sold, and mortgaged only among Malays. Table 2.1 shows that in 1911, Malays constituted more than one-half of the population in colonial Malaya. By 1931, Malay share of the population had dropped below 50 percent.

The colonial policy of protecting traditional Malay lifestyle by segregating land for exclusive Malay use did not prevent Malays from threatening the processes of European capital accumulation. Wealthy Malay landowners, and Chinese businessmen who were given proxies by them, purchased reservation land for commercial agricultural production. Equally significant was that Malay peasant smallholders began cultivating rubber on reservation land for sale to Chinese and European traders: "By 1921, there were no less than 415,799 acres of peasant rubber 'smallholdings' in the Federated Malay States, comprising *33.4 percent* [italics mine] of the total planted rubber acreage."[33]

TABLE 2.1
Percentage Distribution of Population by Ethnicity

Year	Malays	Chinese	Indians	Others
1911	58.6	29.6	10.2	1.6
1921	54.0	29.4	15.1	1.5
1931	49.2	33.9	15.1	1.8
1947	49.5	38.4	10.8	1.3
1957	49.8	37.2	11.1	1.9
1970	53.1	35.5	10.6	0.8

Source: adapted from Saw, *Peninsular Malaysia*, p. 65.

Colonial fear of economic competition from Malays led to the Rice Lands Act (RLA) 1917 that prohibited the cultivation of any cash-crop other than rice on reservation land. A colonial officer provided the official rationale for the RLA:

> Our trusteeship for the Malay people demands that we administer the country on lines constant with their welfare and happiness, not only for today but for the future ages. That end will be attained by building up a sturdy and thrifty peasantry living on the lands they own and living by the food they grow than by causing them to forsake the life of their fathers for the glamour of new ways which put money into their pockets today but leave them empty tomorrow, and to abandon their rice-fields for new crops which they cannot themselves utilize and the market for which depends on outside world conditions beyond their orbit.[34]

In practice, the RLA was a double-edged sword colonialists wielded to eliminate an emerging competitive Malay capitalist class, and also the rising cost of importing food for migrant workers: "[RLA] stipulated that all Malay land which had originally in name been alienated for padi [rice] production had to be cultivated in padi. The legal penalties were confiscation of the crop and money fines."[35] Rice had become the largest import item in British Malaya from the late 1800s to the 1920s.[36] Insatiable low-wage labor demands of the colonial export economy, and the consequent rising cost required to maintain the migrant labor force, had begun to undermine European capitalists' rates of return on their investments. Colonialists anticipated that rice produced on reservation land would curb the unacceptably high food bill.

The MRL and RLA that constituted the colonial set-aside land program to ensure the socioeconomic survival of Malay peoples prevented the emergence of a Malay capitalist class. Subsequently, the set-aside land program was expected to increase, or at the very least maintain, capitalist profit margins by producing enough rice to feed the migrant population.[37]

Colonial trusteeship of Malay peoples was reinforced further by an education policy that naturalized the socioeconomic segregation of Malays, Chinese, and Indians. English medium schools were established for male children of the Malay elite; vernacular schools for the rest of Malay peasantry; and Chinese and Tamil vernacular schools for the children of migrant workers. The education policy helped lay the foundation for the emergence of the Malay middle classes who were dependent on the state. English-medium schools supplied white-collar Malay male labor for the lower echelons of the bureaucracy (the Malayan Administrative Service), while the British retained control of the more powerful upper echelons (the Malayan

Civil Service).[38] Malay vernacular schools, on the other hand, were not structured to impart any vocational skills that could improve peasants' socioeconomic welfare. Rather, textbooks used were translations of palace literature (e.g., those of the *hikayat* genre), and Malay oral stories. The intent was to construct a more "cultured" Malay yeomanry.[39]

> By encouragement and teaching, the Malays are not incapable of being led on to industrious pursuits . . . [T]here exists no reason why the Malay should not become in all points a good citizen; and though he may not possess the native intelligence of the Chinese as a trader and artisan, nor the shrewd cleverness of the Kling [Indian] in his business and monetary transactions, he will be found no whit behind them in agricultural pursuits . . .[40]

The later establishment of separate schools for boys and girls legitimized gendered roles and identities for Malay peasants: girls were instructed in housework and boys learned to be literate farmers and fishermen.

By the early twentieth century, colonial construction of different identities for different peoples was well underway. "Benevolent" colonialism and its labor, land, and education policies arranged the physical, social, and mental interior frontiers of Malayan society according to the association of racial-gender traits with economic function and geographic space. At the community level, Malay and non-Malay identities were constructed in opposition to one another: migrant workers (particularly the Chinese who had more economic clout as a group than the Indians) almost always were perceived and treated as more intelligent, more hardworking, but more conniving than Malays, the lazy but peaceful heirs of the country.[41]

The dyadic or oppositional construction of racial identities conflated colonial efforts to prohibit Malays from actively participating in capitalist accumulation, led by the Europeans, with that of protecting Malays from political and social emasculation by the Chinese and Indian migrant populations. Colonial protection basically took the form of physical and socioeconomic segregation: Malays were to be seen predominantly as farmers on reservation land, the Chinese mostly as entrepreneurs in rural and urban settlements, and the Indians primarily as plantation and public works laborers.[42] Malay women's roles were left largely intact, whereas Chinese and Indian women were encouraged to participate in the colonial economy.

The divide and rule strategy of racial-occupation-gender segregation not only mitigated the formation of horizontal interethnic class bonds (instead, segregation was seen to provide the social order needed for capital accumulation), but also, and more importantly, it deflected Malay attention from

European to Chinese economic activities. This strategy sowed the seeds of interethnic contestations that would arise at key points in twentieth-century Malaysian history.

Toward the end of colonial rule, European trading or agency houses owned at least two-thirds of the economy, as they controlled approximately 65 percent of the export-import trade, while Chinese share of the economy amounted to 16 percent.[43] Even though the mining industry initially was controlled by alliances between Malay royalty and the Chinese, the introduction of European technology coupled with European control of international finance and trade networks displaced Chinese mining methods and the small local clan-based financial and distribution networks. Yet, Malays eventually would associate the Chinese with control of the economy because "it was probably the ubiquitous presence of Chinese traders and shopkeepers in nearly every village that was to make the Chinese economic role seem more threatening and exploitative to the Malays than the European rule, although the Europeans were far more dominant economically."[44]

Road to Independence and Closing of the Immigration Gates

Segregationist policies pursued by the British did not prevent Malays from confronting the need to reconstruct their identities vis-à-vis non-Malays on the peninsula. The early decades of the twentieth century witnessed the emergence of nationalist discourse that grappled with the meaning of Malayness in a growing sea of non-Malays.[45]

Malay demands for independence from Britain were bolstered by the Japanese who occupied Malaya during World War II. Malay support for the Japanese would be juxtaposed with what appeared to be Chinese nationalist and communist support of initial British resistance to the Japanese invasion.[46] British military retreat from Malaya identifiably left the Malayan Communist Party, which was predominantly Chinese, engaged in a lonely and protracted anti-Japanese insurgency that could only exacerbate Malay-Chinese relations.

The British, upon their return to Malaya after the war, proposed a Malayan Union in which all eleven "states" on the peninsula were to be unified under a central government administered by the British. Included with the proposed plan was the granting of citizenship to all who were born or who had lived in Malaya for at least ten years.[47] The proposal elicited overwhelmingly negative responses from the Malay community because of the belief that the British and the Chinese would dominate the country's political and economic systems. Malay rejection of the Malayan Union proposal, together with the Malayan Communist Party's growing influence over labor unions, finally convinced the British that Malayan independence was the only viable route to sustaining capitalist development.[48]

Malayan public discourse soon focused on who would govern, under what conditions, and in what form.[49] Chinese and Indian migrant workers who eventually settled in Malaya insisted on citizenship as a symbol of their legitimacy in the birth of a new country. The question of acknowledging non-Malay presence, contributions, and demands without negatively affecting Malay claims to political power, was resolved in what is known as the "Bargain of '57": Chinese and Indians were granted citizenship in return for Malay dominance of the political process and state structures.[50]

The Bargain of '57 was the result of "consociational" alliances between elite men from the three major ethnic political parties that were nurtured and supported by the British: United Malays National Organization (UMNO), Malayan Chinese Association (MCA), and Malayan Indian Congress (MIC). Collectively, they formed the Alliance party that was dominated by UMNO, and that led the country to independence. Leadership transferred from the British to conservative Western-educated, pro-British male elite in the three political parties: e.g., Tunku Abdul Rahman (UMNO), Tan Siew Sin (MCA), and V.T. Sambanthan (MIC).

Women in Malaya had no clearly defined voice or role in the independence movement. Within UMNO, Malay women formed *Kaum Ibu* to organize women's participation. Nonetheless, *Kaum Ibu* only played a supportive role to UMNO. The organization became *Wanita* UMNO in the early 1970s when younger generations of Malay women assumed leadership and pressed for changes within UMNO's governing structure. Neither MCA nor MIC had a women's section until the 1970s.[51]

On August 31, 1957, the postcolonial state of Malaya or the Federation of Malaya, was born and armed with a Federal Constitution that defined executive, judicial, and legislative responsibilities. The president of UMNO, Tunku Abdul Rahman, became the country's Prime Minister or head of the executive branch. The bicameral legislature consisted of an elected and appointed Senate (*Dewan Negara*) and an elected House of Representatives (*Dewan Rakyat*). Governance in the newly independent country took the form of a federal government that oversaw the eleven "states" of Johor, Melaka, Negeri Sembilan, Selangor, Perak, Pulau Pinang, Pahang, Kedah, Perlis, Kelantan, and Trengganu.

The official definition of Malay identity was inherited from colonialism: "The modern Malaysian constitution's definition of a Malay is derived from a 1913 colonial enactment in which a Malay was 'a person belonging to any Malay race who habitually speaks the Malay language . . . and professes the Muslim religion.' "[52] Enshrined in Articles 152, 153 and 181 of the 1957 Federal Constitution were Malay Special Rights/Privileges or the collective term for Malay reservation land; Malay quotas in education, business, and civil service; the continuation of Malay royalty's symbolic role as protectors of Islam and leaders of the peoples and country; Islam as the national religion; and Malay as the national language. Nonetheless, the political ascendancy of Malays occurred without a restructuring of Malay, Chinese, and Indian peoples' participation in the economy, or a prior deconstruction of social identities based on physiognomy and sex that placed certain peoples in certain occupational positions.

In 1957, the immigration gates were closed officially to the mass immigration of low-wage foreign labor so as not to disrupt the delicate ethnic balance. Malays constituted approximately one-half of the total population of 6,278,758 in Malaya. The Malay, Chinese, and Indian share of the population respectively were 49.8 percent, 37.2 percent, and 11.1 percent (see table 2.1).[53]

A series of events between 1963 and 1965 would leave Malays the undisputed numerically dominant ethnic group in Malaya. Communist threat to capital accumulation (the Malayan Communist Party that was driven underground by the British in the 1950s gradually had infiltrated labor unions in Singapore and Malaya) led to the 1963 inclusion of Singapore into the Federation of Malaya. Since Singapore's 75 percent Chinese population would upset the already slim Malay majority, Sabah and Sarawak (the British protectorates on Borneo island) also were included in the Federation to balance the ethnic distribution of the Malayan population.[54]

The Federation of Malaya became the Federation of Malaysia in 1963. The total Malaysian population jumped from approximately eight million to eleven million. Singapore left the Federation two years later because of irreconcilable differences between Chinese and Malay political elites over Malay political dominance of the country. By 1970 the population distribution was 53.1 percent Malay, 36.5 percent Chinese, and 11.4 percent Indian and others (see table 2.1).

Postcolonial Rearrangement of the Interior Frontiers of Malaysian Society

In the mid 1980s, the immigration gates were reopened officially to the mass in-migration of low-wage foreign labor. At issue is not whether industry demands for labor led to the reopening of the immigration gates, but rather the manner in which the postcolonial in-migrating wave of low-wage foreign servants, and construction and agriplantation workers, resulted from the state elite's efforts to balance demands that emanated from within and from beyond the geopolitical borders.

Specifically, the in-migration of Filipina and Indonesian servants is related to the demands for household labor from the Malaysian middle classes. As Joel S. Kahn argued, the growth of the Malaysian middle classes should be understood within the three interlocking factors of an enlarged state with parastatal limbs; the effects of changes in transnational economic structures and processes; and the practice of "money politics" in Malaysia.[55]

In the rest of this chapter, I first examine the strategies of coercion-repression and consent that were used to legitimize different development paths pursued by the postcolonial state elite. The three factors that encouraged the growth of the middle classes, together with the gendering of state apparatus and power, will be discussed in this context. The last section offers an analysis of the political economic conditions in Malaysia from which emerged the demands for, and state regulation of low-wage foreign migrant labor.

The Era of The New Economic Policy 1971–1990

> The Plan aims at the creation of a viable and dynamic commercial and industrial community of Malays and other indigenous people, and the emergence of a new breed of Malaysians, living and working in unity to serve the nation with unswerving loyalty.
> —Tun Abdul Razak, second Prime Minister of Malaysia, 1971

For at least a decade after independence, the postcolonial state basically retained the ethos of its predecessor. With the exception of introducing the policy of import substitution industrialization (ISI) to reduce the economy's dependence on imported manufactured goods, the state apparatus ensured a conducive context for non-Malay capital accumulation. Economic wealth remained primarily in the hands of European trading houses, and a small but growing number of Chinese conglomerates.[56]

Inherent ISI contradictions and the global spatial reorganization of production (New International Division of Labour or NIDL) prompted a shift in the industrialization policy from ISI to a mixture of ISI and EOI (export-oriented industrialization).[57] Industries in the advanced industrialized countries that wanted to relocate certain steps in the production process to countries with low-wage labor markets were invited to invest in Malaysia.[58]

The addition of EOI to existing ISI policies came too late. Different social forces' perceptions that the postcolonial state elite had been mortgaging the material and symbolic aspects of their future found expression in what the British had so painstakingly nurtured during colonialism, i.e., the identification of ethnicity with economic function and geographic space. In spite of and because of the contradictory positions of protecting Malay rights; ensuring interethnic social order and stability; and facilitating capital accumulation at the very same time, the Western-educated pro-British leadership was unable to define and/or to meet the demands of new social forces that were engendered by development.[59]

The Malay state elite's (for example, Prime Minister Tunku Abdul Rahman) *laissez-faire* relationships especially with non-Malay capitalists were blamed for rising economic gaps not only between the Malays and Chinese, but also within the Malay community.[60] In 1965, the First Bumiputera (Malay) Economic Congress, which mainly consisted of the small but growing population of the Malay middle classes (such as professionals, academicians, civil servants, and small businessmen) chastised the state for its failure to protect Malay rights, since most Malays neither owned nor controlled Malaysian companies.[61] A key colonial legacy left unaddressed was that most Malays lacked the capital, and the technological and organizational skills, to develop a viable Malay entrepreneurial or business class. Hence, the "Ali-Baba" relationship emerged wherein Malays ("Ali") sold their business quotas, i.e., licenses and permits to non-Malays (read: Chinese or "Babas") who, after decades of colonial tutelage, were more experienced in managing companies. Chinese businessmen financially compensated their Malay "sleeping partners" for the privilege of using the latter's names in business contracts and so forth. Four years later, the Second Bumiputera Economic Congress assailed the state for the way in which a handful of Malays had come to monopolize major corporations' boards of directors. The low numbers of successful Malay businessmen reinforced the Malay middle classes' sense of continued market closure to Malays as the country developed.

While the Chinese business elite took advantage of their relationship with Malay politicians and bureaucrats, middle-class Chinese voiced their dissatisfaction with Malay quotas in education and employment. Chinese fears rose when the Malay state elite discussed reducing subsidies to schools that used Chinese as the medium of instruction.[62] Preferential Malay access in education and employment fueled the fear of eventual market closure to the Chinese community.

The postcolonial state's growing legitimation crises would be compounded by its capital-intensive industrialization policy that relied heavily on the expertise of expatriates. Unemployment rose from 2 percent in 1957 to 8 percent in 1968. The legitimation crisis climaxed in the aftermath of the May 1969 elections or what Malaysians would come to call the "May 13" riots, an event that led to severe restrictions on the future expression of civil-political rights.

In the election, the ruling multiethnic Alliance Party had lost the coveted two-thirds majority needed for amending the Constitution without prior consultation with opposition parties. The Democratic Action Party (DAP), which was predominantly Chinese, celebrated its electoral gains with a victory parade in Kuala Lumpur. Verbal altercations erupted between Chinese celebrants and Malay bystanders. UMNO Youth retaliated by staging a demonstration that ultimately disintegrated into bloodshed.[63]

An Expansive State with Parastatal Limbs

Physical violence between Malays and Chinese made evident postcolonial state elites' unavoidable task of redressing a key legacy of British colonialism. Just as the British constructed a racial division of labor that facilitated predominantly European capital accumulation, the postcolonial state elite were compelled to rearrange the interior frontiers of Malaysian society. The question was how and on what grounds?

The 1969 riots immediately led to an approximate two-year repression of civil-political rights: the suspension of Parliament and the Constitution severely restricted the right to free speech and association in society. Under siege from real and perceived criticisms of his close ties to the British and Chinese elites, Tunku Abdul Rahman stepped down as Prime Minister (1957–1970) and he was replaced by Tun Abdul Razak (1970–1976). Among the changes implemented when Parliament reconvened in 1971 were the replacement of the old guards within UMNO by young Malay leaders (e.g.,

Dr. Mahathir Mohamad) who were more nationalistic and vocal in their pro-Malay stance. The Alliance Party was restructured into Barisan Nasional (National Front), which coopted several opposition parties. UMNO remained the dominant partner in Barisan Nasional. Constitutional amendments were passed to prohibit public discussion, including parliamentary debates on Malay Special Rights/Privileges. It was assumed that interethnic contestations could be eliminated in part by suppressing public discourse on the "sensitive issue" of Malay Special Rights/Privileges.[64]

Paradoxically, the blueprint for restructuring society that was introduced in the same year could only heighten and reinforce the production of difference in almost every aspect of Malaysian social life. The blueprint was the NEP, a twenty-year development plan with a two-pronged objective of eradicating poverty regardless of ethnicity, and restructuring society in a way that eliminated the identification of ethnicity with economic function and geographic space:

> The plan incorporates a two-pronged New Economic Policy for development. The first prong is to reduce and eventually eradicate poverty, by raising income levels and increasing employment opportunities for all Malaysians, irrespective of race. The second program aims at accelerating the process of restructuring Malaysian society to correct economic imbalance, so as to reduce and eventually eliminate the identification of race with economic function.[65]

The first decade of the NEP oversaw the transformation of a small state apparatus inherited from the British, to an expansive state with parastatal limbs. The state's constitutionally defined role as trustee for Malays would be placed firmly in the foreground. The NEP marked the beginning of an era of "development by [overt] trusteeship,"[66] which legitimized the transition from unregulated capitalism to "planned" capitalism.[67]

Implicit in the NEP were strategies of garnering consent from the Malay community, and conversely coercing non-Malays to adhere to state-led capitalist development that was conceptualized with a specific slant toward uplifting the socioeconomic welfare and status of Malays vis-à-vis the Chinese and Indian communities. Existing state financial and nonfinancial enterprises were enlisted and new ones were established to realize the two-pronged objective. Examples of Financial Public Enterprises (FPEs) are Bank Bumiputera and Bank Rakyat. Among the Non-Financial Public Enterprises are the Federal Land Development Authority (FELDA), Federal Land Consolidation Authority (FELCRA), and Urban Development Authority (UDA).

FPEs and NFPEs were expected to create a Bumiputera Industrial and Commercial Community (BCIC) or a community of Malay bourgeoisie and middle classes.[68] A key intent was the transfer of corporate wealth from non-Malays to Malays: in 1970, Malays owned only 2.4 percent of total corporate wealth. The NEP target was 30 percent Malay corporate ownership by 1990.[69]

The growth of the Malay middle classes was tied to the expansion of the state apparatus. Education, employment, credit, and urban in-migration policies and legislation had the task of disassociating the notion of Malayness with rural subsistence and lifestyle.[70] Malay quotas in tertiary and vocational education, and fellowships for local and overseas study, would increase the number of Malay students, while public universities such as Universiti Malaya admitted three Malays for every non-Malay student.[71] In the area of employment, between 80 to 90 percent of civil service jobs on all levels were reserved for Malays, and a quota of 30 percent Malay employees was implemented in the private sector:

> Toward this end, the government has not only openly displayed hiring prefer-
> ences in the public sector, but has also pressured private enterprises to add Malays
> to their payroll. This is especially obvious in the civil service, where an estimated
> 90 percent of employees are Malays, heads of departments are almost always
> Malays and nearly all employers in the powerful Public Services Department,
> responsible for hiring and promoting civil servants are Malays.[72]

By way of coercive policies toward non-Malays, the NEP began to "indi-genize" (to increase the number of Malays in) urban areas and employment sectors that previously were "sinicized" (or made Chinese) during colonial rule. Of the three ethnic groups, Malays experienced the highest rate of urbanization: from 2.2 percent in 1970 to 5.2 percent in 1980. In large towns of 75,000 or more inhabitants the Malay share increased from 21.9 percent in 1970 to 38.2 percent in 1980, compared to the Chinese share of 61.4 percent in 1970 and 49.4 percent in 1980.[73]

Policies that brought about "state capitalism" in the 1970s were not at all premised on capital accumulation per se.[74] Rather, the NEP's "redistribute first, growth later" philosophy was implemented to increase Malay participation in, and ownership of the economy—albeit with the Malay or UMNO-controlled state as trustee. The initial overriding objective was not the pursuit of export-oriented industrialization.

The expansive state with parastatal limbs was informed and character-ized by more than a specific class-ethnic nexus. State apparatus and power increasingly were gendered as well: the implementation of the NEP was based on the assumption that the needs and conditions of women in general, and Malay women in particular, were similar to and could be subsumed under the respective aegis of society and community. Emphasis was on the relationship between ethnicity and class, in spite of the officially acknowledged need to restructure Malaysian society and economy.

Women made little overall progress in the public arena. In politics, for example, although the ratio of male to female members of parliament gradually decreased (see table 2.2), the number of Malay women in cabinet positions remained few and far between. Chinese and Indian women have yet to be appointed to cabinet positions. During Tunku Abdul Rahman's tenure as Prime Minister there was only one Malay female minister. The number increased to two female ministers during Tun Abdul Razak's tenure. His successor, Tun Hussein Onn (1976–1981) appointed three women to his cabinet. By 1996 there were two female ministers and two female deputy ministers in Prime Minister Dr. Mahathir Mohamad's cabinet.

TABLE 2.2
Ratio of Male to Female Members of Parliament

Year	Ratio of Male: Female
1959	33.7:1
1969	71:1
1974	30:1
1978	21:1
1982	18.3:1

Source: adapted from Jamilah Ariffin, *Women and Development*, p. 111.

TABLE 2.3
Percentage of Male and Female Staff in Government Service

Sex	1957	1960	1967	1980	1987
Male	86.3	82.9	79.0	73.0	69.4
Female	13.7	17.1	21.0	27.0	30.6

Source: adapted from Jamilah Ariffin, *Women and Development*, pp. 117-8.

The NEP period legitimized what Jamilah Ariffin called the "feminization of government jobs."[75] Although many more women were employed in government service by 1987 (see table 2.3), the majority of women were in the positions of Grade C and D low level support staff (see table 2.4). Specific intersections of gender-class-ethnic ideologies then became the basis of and shaped the expansive state apparatus in Malaysia.

Changes in Transnational Economic Structures and Processes

The relocation of production plants from advanced industrialized to developing countries facilitated the NEP's two-pronged objective. Foreign firms were exempt from taxes if they employed a certain number of workers, and if they located their industries in special areas targeted by the state.[76] Free Trade Zones (FTZs), established under the Free Trade Zone Act 1971, began

TABLE 2.4
Distribution of Women According to Salary Groups in Government Jobs

Salary Group	1968 No.	%	1987 No.	%	Growth Rate (%)
Group A (university degree)	244	1.1	19,032	8.9	22.9
Group B (diploma & higher school cert.)	748	3.2	15,066	7.0	15.8
Group C (Malaysian cert. of education)	15,804	68.5	104,153	35.6	9.9
Group D (no Malaysian cert. of education)	23,064	27.2	76,563	35.6	13.2
TOTAL	23,064	100.0	214,814	100.0	

Source: adapted from Jamilah Ariffin, *Women and Development*, p. 121.

the process of integrating the Malaysian economy into the NIDL, and at the very same time increasing Malaysian employment opportunities. While the state was the largest public employer of Malays, FTZs were major private sector employers of rural-urban migrants (see chapter 6 for further discussion on Malaysian women and the NEP).[77]

From 1971 to 1975, the Malaysian economy grew at an average annual rate of 7.3 percent, while the last half of the decade witnessed an average growth rate of 8.6 percent per annum.[78] The discovery of offshore oil and global increases in the price of commodities during the 1970s provided the necessary revenue for state expenditure in the NEP's first decade. State-led development, however, remained predominantly the export of primary commodities. Tin, rubber, oil, and timber exports consistently out-performed nonresource-based exports.[79] By 1980, the export of manufactured products merely constituted 18.8 percent of total exports (see table 2.7).

Dr. Mahathir Mohamad's ascent to the Prime Ministership in 1981 marked a shift from an emphasis in light to heavy industrialization in preparation for Malaysia's entry into "NIC-dom." The "Look East" (1981) and "Malaysia, Inc." (1983) slogans called on Malaysians to emulate the East Asian (especially Japanese and South Korean) work ethic and to support state-led industrialization programs.

The shift to heavy industrialization occurred in a context in which the economy did not have access to transnational markets, a skilled labor force, a developed domestic market, or the technology and capital.[80] In a period of global economic downturn, the emphasis on heavy industrialization contributed to the 1985–87 economic recession in Malaysia.

The interplay between global, regional, and national economic restructuring processes during the first half of the 1980s left an indelible mark on the direction of development in Malaysia. On the global level, the decline in commodity prices and the debt crises signalled and legitimized the expansion of neoliberalism. The World Bank and IMF responses to the crises were to attach conditionalities to future loans: structural adjustment and stabilization policies dictated public sector expenditure. Consequently, economic liberalization, privatization, and/or deregulation were pursued throughout the developing world. It was within this global context that the Malaysian state elite found it necessary to modify the fiscal and overall development policies:

> [T]he state was increasingly beset by debt and revenue difficulties exacerbated by declines in taxes obtained from the oil sector . . . Public sector debt jumped from M$11,349 million in 1981 to M$30,199 million in 1985, from 21% to 41% of GNP.

. . . When the recession of 1985/86 arrived the government could no longer simply borrow its way out of trouble. In 1986, it was forced to cut development
expenditure to M$13.6 billion, substantially down from M$18.7 billion in 1982.[81]

The changing Asian regional division of labor would only hasten the
need to redefine the state's role in development in general, and the speci-
ficities of export-oriented industrialization. Singapore, in an attempt to
insert itself in the hierarchy of higher value added goods and services
between Japan and the rest of Southeast Asia, pursued its "second industrial
revolution" policy.[82] Following Hong Kong's lead, Singaporean firms began
specializing in small-batch, high-cost semiconductors, while Malaysian
firms were left with the large-batch low-cost assembly work.[83]

Malaysia's ability to attract and retain transnational electronic industries
increasingly was jeopardized by emerging low-wage competition from Southeast Asian countries such as Indonesia and the Philippines.[84] Yet, it was not
easy to shift to value-added goods and services, in part, because policymakers
had failed to encourage human-resource development in the country.

The Industrial Master Plan (IMP) 1986–1995 that was released in 1986
highlighted the causes of Malaysia's economic malaise. Among them were the
NEP goal of 30 percent Malay ownership in the economy, and the lack of
human-resource development. Solutions included relaxing the 30 percent
equity rule; liberalizing foreign investment; reducing tariffs in protected
industries; strengthening export promotion; and integrating FTZs with the
rest of the economy. In sum, the IMP laid the groundwork for the state's
apparent retreat from the economy: key enterprises were to be sold to private-
sector interests. Nonetheless, economic privatization centered mostly on the
transfer of state assets to key individuals, and investment conglomerates
owned by the three dominant mainstream ethnic political parties of UMNO,
MCA, and MIC.[85]

The policy of industrial deepening in the 1980s encouraged the rapid
growth of the Malaysian Malay and non-Malay middle classes. It is estimated that the Malaysian middle classes constituted at least 37.2 percent
of the workforce by 1986.[86] Particularly in the electronics industry,
demands for skilled workers and professionals such as lawyers, computer
scientists, engineers, and middle-level managers increased. Together with
this came a growth of related service-industry personnel such as lawyers,
bankers, and architects.[87]

Private-sector employment did not evince any serious attempts at wage
equalization between men and women. For example, the 1992 Ministry of

Human Resources' report of employment occupations and average monthly wage rates for men and women in the manufacturing industries paint a bleak picture, as seen in table 2.5. Women were not even represented in upper-level management positions and their monthly wages were higher than men's wages in mostly low-level positions traditionally occupied by what can be called the "nurturing" sex.

While the Malaysian Malay, Chinese, and Indian middle classes have expanded, wage rates for women in government service and the corporate world continue to lag behind those of men.[88] Although the NEP increased Malay control and ownership of the economy, the practice of what Sylvia Walby in a different context called "public patriarchy" continues to define women's activities in public space.[89] The notion that women who work beyond the home are considered and treated as appendages to men is reinforced by and reinforces the practice of "private patriarchy" within the household. The interplay between public and private patriarchy will strongly influence state policies and legislation on women in the workplace, and real and perceived middle-class demands for transnational migrant domestic labor.

Money Politics

During the NEP period, the boundaries between the state and UMNO blurred. As the Malay-controlled state apparatus encroached in the economy, so too did the reach of UMNO. Gomez's research of the "money pol-

TABLE 2.5

Average Monthly Salaries for Men and Women in Manufacturing Industries
by Select Occupations
1992

Occupation	Men	Women
General Manager	$4674.50	—
Managing Director	$5497.77	—
Executive Director	$2547.74	—
Accountant	$3342.35	$2861.37
Sales/Marketing Manager	$3247.22	$2372.21
Confidential Secretary	$1155.41	$1346.64
Stenographer	—	$818.57

Source: Ministry of Human Resources, 1992.

itics" phenomenon in Malaysia ascertained that UMNO's entry into the corporate world had begun in earnest during the early 1970s when Tengku Razaleigh Hamzah (then treasurer of UMNO) formed Fleet Holdings Sdn. Bhd. to acquire *The Straits Times Press*. That which began as an effort to Malaysian-ize the country's leading English-language newspaper, led to the close linkage among the corporate, political, and bureaucratic worlds. During the 1970s and 1980s, UMNO, MCA, and MIC respectively would build and control complex webs of interlocking corporations. Of the three, UMNO's dominance of Barisan Nasional and the state apparatus meant that the Malay politico-bureaucratic elite and their supporters overwhelmingly controlled FPEs and NFPEs.[90]

By the second decade of the NEP, the Malay middle classes had become the major base of UMNO, as the Malaysian middle classes in general were becoming key social forces of the state. The number of Malays among all registered professionals (architects, accountants, engineers, dentists, doctors, veterinary surgeons, lawyers, and surveyors) increased from 47 percent in 1970 to 58.8 percent by 1990. The NEP's apparent success in restructuring Malay employment was evident in higher Malay employment rates in the primary, secondary, and tertiary sectors. Similarly, Malay ownership of wealth increased from 2.4 percent in 1970 to 20.3 percent in 1990 (see table 2.6).

The Malaysian economy's annual growth rate averaged 8.8 percent in the last half of the NEP's second decade. The incidence of poverty declined from 49.3 percent in 1970 to 15 percent in 1990 or 1 percent better than the 16 percent target set by the state.[91] Exports of manufactured products improved vastly. In 1970, manufactured products only contributed 6.5 percent of the total value of exports. By 1990, manufactured products constituted over 50 percent of the total value of exports (see Table 2.7).

However, heightened public discourse on corruption and theft in parastatals coupled with the internal crisis within UMNO during the second half of the 1980s, would bring about state strategies of coercion-repression and consent that were used respectively to silence opposition to the NEP, and to manage the politics of the expanding Malay and non-Malay middle classes (see below).

Polanyian Double Movement: The Rise and Response of New Social Forces

In spite of statistics indicating the NEP's success in restructuring society, the affirmative action development policy was extended beyond 1990, in the form of the National Development Policy (NDP) 1991–2000.[92] The NDP places greater emphasis on export-oriented development with an increased role for the private sector; on upgrading human resource and agricultural development; and on the growth of the BCIC. The Malaysian economy, like its Southeast Asian neighbors, continues to move away from a reliance on primary commodity exports to that of exports in manufactured products (see table 2.8).

The NDP's overall objective is to ensure Malaysia's coveted membership in the group of developed countries by 2020, hence the slogan "Vision

TABLE 2.6

NEP Restructuring Targets and Achievements

	Target (%)		Achieved (%)
	1970	1990	1990
EMPLOYMENT RESTRUCTURING			
Bumiputera/Malay			
Primary Sector[a]	67.6	61.4	71.2
Secondary Sector[b]	30.8	51.9	48.0
Tertiary Sector[c]	37.9	48.4	51.0
Non-Bumiputera/Non-Malay			
Primary Sector	32.4	38.6	28.8
Secondary Sector	69.2	48.1	52.0
Tertiary Sector	62.1	51.6	49.0
OWNERSHIP RESTRUCTURING			
Bumiputera[d]	2.4	30.0	20.3
Other Malaysian	32.3	40.0	46.2
Foreigners	63.3	30.0	25.1
Nominee Companies[e]	2.0	—	8.4

Source: Government of Malaysia, 1991.

a. agriculture

b. mining, manufacture, construction, utilities and transport

c. wholesale and retail trade, finance, government and other services

d. includes trust agencies and other related institutions

e. blind trust companies

2020." The construction of the modern caring Malaysian family is expected to be the social foundation of a developed Malaysian society. As Prime Minister Dr. Mahathir Mohamad put it, the goal is to establish "a fully caring society and a caring culture, a social system in which society will come before self, in which the welfare of the people will not revolve around the state or the individual but around a strong and resilient family system."[93]

TABLE 2.7
Export Structure By Select Categories

	1970	1975	1980	1985	1990
Total Value of Exports (millions)	1686.6	3846.6	12,944.7	15,637.9	29,418.7
Agriculture & Other Raw Materials (%)	50	34.1	30.9	18.3	11.3
Manufactured Goods (%)	6.5	17.3	18.8	27.2	54.2

Source: UNCTAD, 1993.

TABLE 2.8
Merchandise Exports of Select Southeast Asian Economies

	% Share of Merchandise Exports									
Country	Fuels, Minerals, Metals		Other Primary Commodities		Machinery & other Equipment		Other Manufactures		Textile Fibers Clothing Fibers	
	1970	1993	1970	1993	1970	1993	1970	1993	1970	1993
Malaysia	30	14	63	21	2	41	6	24	1	16
Philippines	23	7	70	17	0	19	8	58	2	9
Indonesia	44	32	54	15	0	5	1	48	1	16
Thailand	15	2	77	26	0	28	8	45	8	15
Singapore	25	14	45	6	11	55	20	25	6	4

Source: World Bank, 1995.

The expansion of the Malaysian middle classes is considered a key component of successful export-oriented development. In 1991, the Prime Minister insisted that, "A developed Malaysia must have a *wide and vigorous middle class* [emphasis mine] and must provide full opportunities for those in the bottom third to climb their way out of relative poverty."[94] Chapter 6 presents a detailed analysis of the official vision for the Malaysian middle classes, and the role that Filipina and Indonesian domestic workers are expected to play in this vision.

While economic statistics may reflect the successful rearrangement of the interior frontiers of Malaysian society, they do not speak to the different ways in which opposition to the NEP emerged during the 1970s and 1980s. The period of the NEP gave rise to a Polanyian double movement in which certain groups within society mobilized and demanded protective measures against the real and perceived negative socioeconomic consequences of Malaysia's integration into the global capitalist economy.[95] Such opposition was met, most visibly, by the repressive powers of the state apparatus.

Aside from what may be considered the "usual and expected" contestations between Malays and Chinese over issues such as education and language, the most potent challengers emerged from within the Malay community.[96] Fiscal policies that privileged the industrial sector had had an adverse effect on rural Malays.

The Malay peasantry increasingly were exposed to global fluctuations in commodity prices without state support that could buffer the peoples against downward trends. Peasant protesters would be joined by mostly Malay university students who rallied against a capitalist development path that neglected the poor and the rural. On several occasions, peasants and students clashed with the authorities, e.g., the 1974 Baling incident over declining rubber prices, and the 1980 Kedah strike over state elimination of cash subsidies. The University and University Colleges (Amendment) Act 1975 was implemented to prohibit on and off-campus demonstrations by students and staff. To quell middle class support for peasants and students, civil servants were coopted by wage raises.[97]

Many of the Malay students who participated in peasant strikes also were members of Angkatan Belia Islam Malaysia (ABIM) or the Malaysian Islamic Youth Movement, which was led by local and foreign-educated Malay students.[98] During the 1970s, ABIM openly criticized the Malay state elite's promotion of a Western capitalist development path that was perceived to encourage the socioeconomic and cultural decline of the Malay community.

The NEP was accused of promoting un-Islamic attitudes and values since it was premised fundamentally on ethnic, religious, and class discrimination.

ABIM called for the establishment of an Islamic state complete with Islamic judicial and economic systems. Other *dakwah* (literally, to proselytize) groups such as Darul Arqam and Tabligh, soon joined the Malayo-Muslim critique of the state.[99] The *dakwah* groups were far from united in their critique and response to the direction of Malaysian development. Tabligh, for example, focused on proselytizing activities, whereas Darul Arqam advocated a retreat from capitalist modes of production and western lifestyles.[100] Collectively, however, they projected an anti-Western and anti-capitalist assault on the NEP, hence state legitimacy:

> Suggestions raised by some elements of the dakwah brigade that serious Muslims should be prepared to substitute spiritual for material values and that excoriate all forms of materialism, in general, particularly when derived from the west, thus clearly strike at the very heart of the government's economic philosophy, and undermine its strategies for creating a united Malay front, and vote, as the basis of its own power.[101]

Partai Al-Islam SeMalaysia (PAS), the only registered Islamic (opposition) political party, added to the chorus of Islamicists by framing UMNO's promotion of capitalist over Islamic values in terms of "*kafir-mengafir*" (literally, to be infidel-ized).[102] Public discourse gradually focused on the issue of whether the state and its pro-state Malay supporters were true Muslims or infidels. Islamicists painted a picture of the way the Malay state elite had successively mortgaged Muslim lifestyles and values for a Westernized culture and society. A recurrent theme was the perceived increasingly "loose" morality and sexuality of female factory workers in FTZs (see chapter 6).

Preferential treatment for rural supporters of UMNO contributed to the perception that the UMNO-controlled state apparatus was intent on undermining Islamicists. There were cases in which rural peoples were "punished" for refusing to support UMNO during key elections: development aid to certain areas either was delayed or at times simply ignored.[103]

The widening economic gap between elite and poor Malays was important in fueling the argument that state-led capitalist development had become the bane of Malay social existence. Senior and retired politico-bureaucrats who managed the resources of NFPEs and FPEs had used their positions to accumulate wealth and to dispense patronage to supporters of UMNO.[104] Rural and urban Malays who did not enjoy access to state resources and patronage were marginalized from the processes of redistributing old wealth and generating new wealth.[105] Some Malays felt increasingly disinherited, especially since official rhetoric of improving the socioeconomic lot of all Malays meant, in practice, reinforcing the processes of wealth accumulation by those who already were in positions of power and by those who had access to bureaucrats and politicians.[106] During the NEP's first decade, intraethnic income inequality had surpassed that of interethnic income inequality.[107]

The Third Bumiputera Economic Congress demanded that state enterprises relinquish their control of acquired corporate assets to privately owned Malay businesses.[108] State authorities responded by establishing the Amanah Saham Nasional (ASN), or National Unit Trust Scheme in 1981 to purchase Permodalan Nasional Berhad's assets and to transfer them to the private sector. To keep corporate assets in Malay hands, ASN shares could be bought and sold only through ASN. By 1987, 2 million Malays had purchased ASN shares. However, 75 percent of the shares were owned by 1.3 percent of the Malays. Put simply, wealthy Malays continued to accumulate wealth at an uninterrupted pace.[109] Conventional wisdom among Malay small-business owners was that the average Malay ("Ali") was no longer a "sleeping partner" of a Chinese ("Baba") businessman. Rather, he had become the "sleeping partner" of Malay-controlled state enterprises such as Majlis Amanah Rakyat Malaysia (MARA) that were responsible for promoting Malay entrepreneurship. General sentiment was reflected in a popular phrase during that period: "First it was the Ali-Baba relationship, now it's the Ali-MARA relationship, soon it'll be all MARA and no Ali."[110]

The NEP was seen to have nurtured a "statist capitalist class," a "bureaucratic capitalist class," or "a business/capitalist class," that exhibited rent-seeking behavior.[111] High-level Malay bureaucrats, politicians, and members of the Malay royalty, together with a handful of Malay and non-Malay capitalists, gradually came to control Malaysia's economic resources.[112]

Newspaper reports (especially by the foreign press) of corruption and mismanagement in NFPEs and FPEs reinforced public perception that the NEP had benefitted only a small number of elite Malays, and simultaneously had legitimized irresponsible behavior among state bureaucrat-managers.[113] Chinese capitalists and political leaders also were not immune to criticisms from the Chinese and Malay communities. The 1980s failure of MCA-supported Deposit Taking Cooperatives had fragmented the Chinese community.[114]

Given the context of modern Malaysian politics, Islamic criticism arguably was the only politically legitimate avenue by which Malays could challenge the UMNO-controlled state and its policies that engendered wide economic gaps between elite and poor Malays.[115] In the context of export-oriented development, the Malay middle classes' pursuit of distinctive lifestyles had pitted Malays against one another. Heightened Islamic discourse in public space helped fragment the Malay middle classes according to different categories of social identity such as "Malayness in Muslim dress" or "Malayness in modern dress."[116] Some scholars have maintained that the *dakwah* movement enjoyed a degree of urban middle-class Malay support partly because Islam provided the spiritual foundation for coping with rapid physical and social dislocation brought about by the NEP.[117] The NEP's objective of creating a BCIC via the series of interrelated policies discussed earlier meant that urban Muslim and/or modern middle-class Malay lifestyles were remarkably different from that of the fisherman and farmer.

The state's coercive-repressive apparatus was unabashedly employed in response to public discourse on corruption in FPEs and NFPEs, and to the Islamicist challenge. A slew of repressive legislation (and later amendments to some of them) was used to silence oppositional discourse and public dissemination of information critical of state policies: the Internal Security Act 1960, the Official Secrets Act 1972, the Printing Presses and Publications Act 1984, and the Societies Act 1966 are but a few of the repressive legislative weapons.

In the early 1980s, ABIM's charismatic leader Anwar Ibrahim was coopted by an offer to become the Minister of Culture (today, he is Deputy Prime Minister). The state elite also overtly pursued an Islamization program to emphasize that their policies could be and were more "Muslim" than the Islamicists. Officially sanctioned *dakwah* groups, and various Islamic institutions such as the Islamic International University, the Islamic Foundation and Social Welfare, and the Islamic Insurance Scheme, reflected the Islamic orientation of the state.[118]

As the Islamicist threat abated, opposing opinions arose from within UMNO. Prior to 1970, 62.3 percent of UMNO's constituency were rural Malays. By 1985, that proportion had dropped to 41.3 percent as the Malay middle classes, e.g., professionals, bureaucrats, academicians, and the small-business owners gradually came to dominate UMNO's rank and file.[119] The expanding Malay middle classes had become major social forces of UMNO and the state.

The second half of the 1980s would characterize overt state encroachment in the realm of civil-political rights. Unresolved political differences between the Prime Minister and the Deputy Prime Minister led to the latter's resignation. Prime Minister Dr. Mahathir Mohamad's selection of Ghafar Baba to replace Musa Hitam in 1986 continued the in-fighting within UMNO.[120] The crisis intensified in 1987 when a breakaway faction of UMNO politicians assumed the lead in criticizing the way in which the NEP had been used by certain high-level bureaucrats and politicians for self-aggrandizement purposes. At the UMNO General Assembly meeting, Musa Hitam and Tengku Razaleigh Hamzah (then UMNO's most senior Vice-President) challenged the incumbents for the presidency and deputy presidency of UMNO. The election winners would take control of the Prime Minister and Deputy Prime Ministership, assuming that the UMNO-led National Front coalition retained its majority.

The challengers, dubbed "Team B" by the media, accused "Team A," the incumbents, of perpetuating inequality within the Malay community by disbursing NEP funds to garner favor, influence, and patronage.[121] The fight for control over UMNO, and thus the country, fragmented members of the General Assembly. When the votes were tabulated, Team A had won by a slight margin, and the dispute disintegrated into a lawsuit filed by Team B.[122]

In that very same year, the Chinese community mobilized over the issue of the UMNO-controlled state's promotion of non-Mandarin speaking Chinese headmasters in Chinese vernacular schools. When the major Chinese mainstream and opposition political parties organized a protest rally, UMNO's Youth division responded with a proposed rally of its own to oppose Chinese cultural self-determination. It seemed as if the May 13, 1969 riots were on the verge of resurrection. The state resorted to "Operation Lallang." Malay and non-Malay mainstream and opposition political party members, academicians, professionals, labor union members, artists, activists, and Islamicists were arrested under the Internal Security Act that empowered the authorities to retain anyone for two years without trial or justification.[124]

In this period, the powers of the judiciary and the Malay royalty—the two legitimate avenues to which dissidents could appeal—were severely circumscribed. The Lord President of the Supreme Court was dismissed, and

Malay royalty's legal immunity gradually would be eroded by a series of politico-legal maneuvers.[125]

The frequent exercise of repressive legislation was seen by the state elite as necessary to ensure social order in the midst of restructuring the economy and society in Malaysia. Scholars of Malaysian development would identify the 1980s with a distinctly authoritarian mode of governance.[126] Nonetheless, the NEP era also embodied a key strategy of garnering consent that involved the in-migration of low-wage labor from the Philippines and Indonesia.

"Guest" Workers

In spite of the NEP, rapid economic growth allowed Chinese and Indians to continue participating in the labor force. From 1970 to 1980, Malay, Chinese, and Indian participation rates respectively increased from 48.4 to 50.6 percent, 47.7 to 50.8 percent, and 48.5 to 53.5 percent.[127] Within the Malay community, the rate of labor force participation in the agricultural sector dropped from 73 percent in 1970 to 46.8 percent in 1980, as Malay participation rates in the service and industrial sectors respectively increased from 5.6 to 26 percent and from 2.7 to 11.8 percent.[128] Malaysian Malay, Chinese, and Indian women continued to be associated primarily with jobs such as nursing, teaching, and clerical work, that highlighted their reproductive role.[129]

A key consequence of the NEP in general, and the establishment of TNC-owned factories to FTZs in particular, was the decline in the low-wage labor supply. In the late 1970s, Malaysians already were employing female domestic servants, and female and male construction and plantation workers from Indonesia and the Philippines.

> [The NEP's] simultaneous emphasis both on urbanization/industrialization and rural development created an acute labor shortage in the agricultural sector when the rural Malay population moved into urban areas in response to the government's urbanization policy. The short-fall in labor in the rural sector was overcome by the solicitation of Indonesians by contractors and sub-contractors such as FELDA (Federal Land Development Authority) RISDA (Rubber Industry Small Holders Development Authority), and FELCRA (Federal Land Consolidation and Rehabilitation Authority). Such labor, it appears, was brought in surreptitiously, either through illegal syndicates or informal social networks.[130]

Table 2.9 shows that the unemployment rate averaged approximately 6 percent in the second half of the 1980s. Malaysian employment of illegal foreign or "guest" workers was related, in part, to the NEP's urbanization and employment policies that had heightened expectations of rural Malays for better-paying white-collar employment in urban areas. The predominant Malay perception was that white-collar urban employment, as more "modern," carried with it a higher social status.

Between 1978 and 1985, the declining supply of low-wage labor had threatened to undermine the viability of export industries based on natural resources, hence the economy's competitiveness overseas. The rubber industry reported severe labor shortages that resulted in the loss of more than 50,000 tonnes of rubber at a cost of RM123 million.[131] The oil palm industry faced similar problems. Even during the mid-1980s economic recession with an average unemployment rate of approximately 8 percent (see table 2.9), these two industries failed to attract local labor.

It was reported that Malaysians, especially the youth, increasingly refused to work in plantations because of low wages and bad working conditions. Wage differentials between the industrial and agricultural sectors were identified as the major cause of declining local labor supply.[132] Agriplantation employers consistently refused to raise wages to attract local labor since raising wages on one level would necessarily entail raising wages on all levels, which then would decrease profits.

TABLE 2.9
Participation & Unemployment Rates

Year	Total Labor Force ('000)	Employed ('000)	Unemployed (%)
1976	4662	4376	6.1
1979	4955	4700	5.2
1980	5122	4835	5.6
1983	5727	5429	5.2
1986	6222	5707	8.3
1989	6850	6390	6.7
1990	7042	6686	5.1
1991	7241	6926	4.3
1992	7441	7148	3.9
1993	7646	7371	3.6

Source: Asian Development Bank, 1994.

*Total number of people economically active as a percentage of the total number in the working age population (15-64 years)

In 1979, major newspapers reported approximately 100,000 illegal Indonesian and Filipino migrant plantation workers respectively in Johor and Sabah. Mainstream and opposition political party members, together with labor unions, responded to the reports by demanding that the Immigration Department put an end to the illegal in-migration of foreign workers. Critics argued that illegal migrant workers were threats to national security (e.g., Indonesian "communist" infiltration and covert Philippine-Christian proselytizing activities).[133] In spite of protests, the federal government refused to regulate or ban illegal migrants, asserting instead that migrant workers "were necessary to fill the manpower needs of the state [in reference to the issue of illegal migrants in Sabah]."[134]

I argue that the initial refusal to regulate or to ban illegal migrant labor was due to two key reasons. It was not politically feasible to undermine the NEP's pro-Malay urbanization policy by openly encouraging rural Malays to be agricultural workers in private and state-owned agriplantations, or to work in the low-status occupation of urban domestic servant. The irony, in the case of the agricultural sector, is that agriplantations managed by NFPEs such as FELDA, were designed to increase rural Malay employment opportunities. There also was no economic justification, especially within the multiethnic context, to officially open the country's immigration doors: "Malaysian officials note that the country has a 6 per cent unemployment rate [in 1980]; hence there are locals available to do estate work, but they are too 'choosy.' "[135]

According to Richard Dorall, implicit in non-Malay public criticism of state authorities' refusal to ban especially illegal Indonesian migrant workers (many of whom were the ethnic, religious and cultural cousins of Malays), was the belief that the Malay-controlled state apparatus had wanted to increase covertly the Malay population at the political, economic, and social expense of the non-Malay communities: "From the very beginning, non-Malay objections to the large-scale and uncontrolled presence of Indonesian migrant workers were based less on economic reasons . . . but more on their fears that the Indonesians, being Muslims and culturally almost identical to the Malays, would in fact stay as immigrants and numerically increase the Malay population number."[136] Yet, if state authorities officially banned the in-migration of illegal Indonesian workers, then the low-wage labor woes of the agriplantation industry (of which NFPEs were major participants), would be left unaddressed.

Newspaper reports of the growing presence of illegal Indonesian migrant workers highlighted a potential clash between state authorities, non-Malays, and even Malays who objected to their presence: by 1983, there were approximately 300,000 to 600,000 illegal Indonesian migrants in Malaysia. The political leadership acted by signing the 1984 Medan Pact with Indonesia to control illegal migration. Specific procedures were delineated for the legal in-migration of Indonesian workers.[137] Three years later, the pact was rescinded because it could not effectively control the in-migration of illegal Indonesian workers: migrants considered the legal route too time-consuming, complicated, and costly.[138]

As the Malaysian economy began to recover from the 1985–87 economic recession, employers from all ethnic groups openly complained of the increasing difficulty in hiring Malaysian workers for domestic service, plantation, and construction work. The Ministry of Labour (which was later renamed the Ministry of Human Resources) was pressured to officially acknowledge the economy's demands for low-wage foreign migrant labor:

> In Malaysia, as in the case with most countries, unemployment and labor short-ages exist. These shortages are concentrated in the plantation and some agricul-tural sectors in low paying and low status jobs. Given the general rise in the stan-dard of living and improved job opportunities in Malaysia, the youth of today are not prepared to undertake these jobs and prefer to migrate to urban areas in search of better jobs. Some would even "wait" for better employment opportu-nities. Towards the end of this period, the government began to initiate the process of legalizing the use of migrant labor to alleviate these shortages.[139]

The confluence of several factors prompted the formal reopening of the immigration gates: the NEP's objective of restructuring society; the state and private sector-owned industries' common goal of maintaining the competi-tive edge in Malaysian commodity exports; and the IMP recommendation of improving Malaysian human-resource development in response to changing regional economic structures and processes. At the very same time, the transnationalization of migrant labor provided an easy solution for public and private sector employers. Labor out-migration from neighboring countries supplied the Malaysian economy with an unending stream of legal low-wage plantation, construction, and domestic workers (see chapter 4).

At the outset, there appears to be nothing surreptitious about the Immi-gration Department's willingness to reopen the gates and regulate the in-migration of "guest" workers.[140] Similar to the in-migration of Chinese and Indian workers in the late nineteenth and early twentieth centuries, the in-migration of Filipino and Indonesian workers in the late twentieth century is encouraged to sustain capitalist accumulation. However, the timing and content of postcolonial state regulation of foreign female domestic workers is crucial to understanding the relationship between contemporary domestic service and the strategy of consent.

During the second half of the 1980s, the negative socioeconomic consequences engendered by the NEP had put into question the continued viability of the development path. In this context, the mutually reinforcing processes of Malaysian demands for domestic servants and the transnationalization of migrant female domestic labor would help maintain state legitimacy. A closer analysis of specific rules governing the in-migration and employment of foreign female domestic workers reveals the state elite's strategy of garnering consent from key social forces, namely the expanding Malaysian Malay and non-Malay middle classes. In the next chapter I discuss how and why official regulation of the in-migration and employment of Filipina and Indonesian domestic workers addressed indirectly criticisms that the NEP had not benefitted Malays, and subsequently allowed the state elite to police the form and content of the Malaysian middle classes.

Notes on the Epigraphs

(In order of appearance): Arthur Waley, ed., *Three Ways of Thought in Ancient China* (Garden City: Doubleday, 1939), pp. 111, 161; Tun Abdul Razak, "Foreword" to *Second Malaysia Plan 1971–1975*, Government of Malaysia (Kuala Lumpur: Government Printing Press, 1971), p. vi.

CHAPTER 3

"Boys, *Amahs*, and Girls":
Domestic Workers of the Past and Present

Classification itself is the object of a discourse . . . [T]here is always a stake in where things are: tell me how you classify and I'll tell you who you are.
—Roland Barthes, *The Semiotic Challenge*, 1988

It can be argued that Malaysian demands for Filipina and Indonesian servants are a consequence of successful economic growth in the country. By this reasoning, the continued in-migration of foreign female domestic workers is a testament to a development path that offers Malaysian servants alternative employment opportunities, as many more middle-class and upper-middle-class Malaysians feel the need, and possess the purchasing powers, to hire live-in domestic workers.

My argument, however, is that personnel changes in domestic service are more complex and revealing of the state's "relations of ruling" than the above explanation suggests.[1] By refusing to intercede overtly in meeting demands for household help, the colonial and postcolonial state authorities in Malaysia exhibit relative similarities respectively in structuring and restructuring the larger fields of possible actions and responses in a society that constitutes particular peoples as domestic servants.

Hylam Boys and Klings

One of the earliest available historical references to paid domestic service tells us that Chinese and Indian migrant men worked as servants in European households during the mid to late 1800s.[2] Malay women, as well as Chinese and Indian migrant women, performed unpaid reproductive labor in their capacities as wives, mothers, and daughters. Malay and Chinese debt-bondswomen, in particular, also are known to have performed unpaid reproductive labor in households other than their own.

We have seen in the previous chapter how and why paternalistic colonial policies were conceived to "protect" the rural Malay lifestyle. Colonial protection included leaving relatively intact the Malay institution of debt-bondage wherein men and women who could not repay money borrowed from rulers or chiefs were then taken to live with and work for their creditors.[3]

In debt-bondage, a creditor held the right to determine when and how the debt was to be repaid. Young debt-bondswomen were known to be taken to satisfy the sexual and household needs of Malay rulers and their male followers. Rulers offered the sexual services of debt-bondswomen as a way to elicit the loyalty of male conscripts without homes and families.[4] A debt-bondswoman was quoted as having said, "Our chief works are cooking, working, carrying water, splitting firewood, pounding rice, and at nights, we are to prostitute ourselves, giving half of this earning to the raja and half to supply ourselves with clothing and provision for the sultan, the house and other slaves."[5] Many times, a debt-bondswoman could gain her freedom if she gave birth to her creditor-master's child, and/or if her creditor-master selected her as his concubine.

From the way that the British constructed specific roles for Malay, Chinese, and Indian women's participation, it is clear that the colonial state was gendered in its relation to women. Regardless of different ethnic backgrounds, women were constituted and treated primarily as domestic-sexual persons. If and when women assumed "productive" roles in economy, they did so under different conditions than men.

The presence of Chinese and Indian male servants during the mid to late nineteenth century raises an interesting question. If the performance of unpaid reproductive labor was associated intimately with women's ascribed roles in the household, then why were men as opposed to women allowed to work as domestic servants?

The high ratio of male to female migrants produced a surplus male workforce that could and did meet European demands for household help without negatively affecting labor supply in key industries. At the end of the nineteenth century, Chinese or "Hylam boys" (Chinese men from the Hailam clan), and "Klings" (a pejorative term used in reference to South Indians) performed paid domestic labor in European households. A colonial writer of that period observed that "Chinese women do not go out to service, they are too proud to be menials."[6] This romantic illusion of women's alleged refusal to be domestic servants glossed over the fact that because of their low numbers, Chinese women were of necessity reserved for more profitable occupations such as prostitution, which helped to maintain a stable male migrant workforce and subsequently to assure a constant inflow of revenue to the state treasury.[7]

Colonial notions of Western cultural and moral superiority delimited the choice of male servants according to race. The absence of references to Malay male servants in European households was due largely to racial and paternalistic attitudes toward Malay men. Within the context of colonial land, education, and labor legislation and policies designed to protect Malay peoples, it would have been morally indefensible to hire the future heirs of the country to work in the low-status job of the domestic servant.[8]

Given a choice between Chinese or Indian male servants, Europeans were partial to the former—a preference that reflected and reinforced racial stereotypes: while Indians were perceived as docile workers, they also were considered less intelligent and less hygienic in their ways, as the following passage demonstrates:

> Chinese are excellent servants. They are sober, industrious, methodical and attentive to their duties. They are limited to Macaos and Hylams . . . ["Natives of Madras or 'Klings' "] invariably drink and are filthy in the extreme. The writer found a Kling cook once beating up a custard pudding with the stump of an old broom. Chinese servants will tell you that Kling cooks do all their work in the kitchen such as ornamenting or whitening cakes with their dirty fingers. A story is told of a Kling cook boiling the plum pudding in the corner of his waist cloth, who hearing his master call, rushed out of the kitchen forgetting the pudding which came flying out of the pot dangling about his heels.[9]

Colonial construction of Chinese men as "boys" defused the threat of the presence of adult males from a different race who worked in close proximity to European women.[10] While Chinese male servants lived in separate quarters on the premises and performed all kinds of housework, there was no indication that they provided childcare services.[11] It was general practice among European employers to hire Chinese men based on *surat* or letters of recommendation from previous employers. Chinese secret societies conducted a lucrative business of forging letters to place male workers, some of whom knew little of housework. By the 1930s, Europeans were complaining bitterly about the frequent use of falsified letters, and Chinese male servants' demands for higher wages and holidays. Employers expressed their outrage in a series of letters to the editor of the *Straits Times.*

I have been a victim on many occasions and have spent many a hard earned dollar on rogues who obviously have never had anything to do with running a house or cooking.

If things stay on much longer as they are doing at present, why before we know where we are, we shall have our servants asking for annual holidays. They might go further. They might ask for an evening off a month. Horrors! Dogs must be licensed. Why not servants? And make them pay for their own license. If they ask for such high wages as $30.00 a month, muzzle 'em.[12]

Employers also rejected Chinese servant demands for "coffee money."

As a class, they should certainly be kept in their place and the government should be called upon to take every strong measure to stamp out the "coffee money" evil. A little dose of the cat or rotan should teach these people that we Europeans are intolerant of such evil practices. No European would descend so low as to ask for coffee money, and it is not expected that we should allow our servants to do so.[13]

Coffee money, in the context of postcolonial Malaysia, is equivalent to "under the table money" given to state bureaucrats for rapid official approval of projects and/or business licenses. Fatimah Halim argues that in the colonial context, coffee money, or the Malay version of *duit kopi*, similarly meant "under-counter payments."[14] It is unclear as to why Chinese male servants would ask their employers for such payments. Perhaps, coffee money embodied the servants' demands for a food allowance in addition to their regular wages since it is not known if they were told to buy their own food, or if meals were provided by employers. Eventually, some Chinese female servants who worked for European employers were told to buy and cook their own food (see section on *amahs* in this chapter).

By the early 1930s, the demands made by Chinese male servants led to a call among the European employers for an official registry of domestic servants, presumably to filter out particular kinds of servants who were considered unfit for service. In 1933, the state publicly announced that it was not prepared to establish an official registry because of the lack of funds.[15] At the same time, Chinese women began arriving on the west coast of Malaya, and in Singapore, to work as *amahs* or domestic servants.

The Cantonese word *amah* is a variant of the romanized version for "mother": "ah ma" is synonymous with "ma ma." Strictly speaking, the word *amah* as opposed to "ah ma" is used in reference to a surrogate mother or a wet nurse.[16] In the 1930s, *amahs* were single celibate Chinese female migrants who performed paid reproductive labor ranging from childcare to washing clothes and cooking.

Amahs

The majority of migrant workers during the 1930s were Cantonese women from the Kwangtung region in Southern China. They belonged to a well-established anti-marriage movement: "Nearly all the girls there had a habit of swearing sisterhood to each other, taking vows of celibacy, and looking upon their prospective husbands as enemies. If, as a result of family pressure, they did marry, they would refuse to consummate the marriage, return home on the third day of the wedding and refuse to return to their husbands."[17]

In order to remain independent from men, young and older unmarried celibate women worked as silk farmers and spinners in Kwangtung's silk industry. They would pool their resources to build *Ku Por Uk* or Old Maids' Houses/Grandaunt's Houses away from their familial homes.[18] Female residents of *Ku Por Uk* accepted collective responsibility for household tasks and finances. Patriarchal Chinese society sanctioned Cantonese women's actions so long as the latter undertook a ritual called *sor hei* (to comb one's hair into a bun at the back of the head) in a temple. The ceremony symbolized religious legitimation of women's newfound rights and status.

The introduction of European technology in the Chinese silk industry during the 1930s, coupled with a series of natural disasters and political strife in Southern China, encouraged women's out-migration. However, migration was not entirely due to economic factors per se. Even though most of the women had lost their jobs as silk farmers and spinners, their decisions to migrate were precipitated also by the desire to remain socially independent from men. In a 1994 interview with a newspaper reporter, a retired *amah* explained that:

> There is no point in getting married. After all, people like us would not be marrying rich men. If we did get married, we would still have to work so hard, have to have babies and all. There is no point slaving for your husband, is there? You might as well do the same work and get paid for it. If you are on your own, whatever money you earn is yours. No one can tell you what to do.[19]

Out-migration was a key avenue by which the women could retain their independence during a period of turbulent socioeconomic and political change. They migrated with the help of male labor brokers called *sui hak* ("water guest"). Upon arrival in Malaya, the women were placed in halfway

houses until they found employment or they lived in rooms rented by their
fellow village/kinfolk.

In the course of fieldwork, I interviewed three retired *amahs* of the 1930s
(well into their eighties at the time of the interviews). The women's names
were Ah Foon Cheh, Ah Lan Cheh, and Ah Ling Cheh.[20] Their first names,
Foon, Lan, and Ling, are substitutes for "ma" in the word "ah ma." The suffix "cheh" means older sister or spinster. Ah Foon Cheh then is Foon, the
spinster or older sister.

Prior to their departure from China, Ah Foon Cheh and Ah Lan Cheh
worked in the silk industry and Ah Ling Cheh worked on her father's farm
land. They came to Malaya as free women, not indentured workers, since
the first two women paid for their passage with their savings while Ah Ling
Cheh had borrowed money from her relatives. The three *amahs* and their
seven *chi mui* ("sisters") rented a room in a shop house in Chinatown and
eventually saved enough money to buy a small flat on the outskirts of Kuala
Lumpur. The flat or *fong chai* (small room) was a place where the women
went on their rest days or at retirement. Many times, the flat was used as a
temporary shelter for unemployed women.

In Malaya, the women reconstituted their informal network of "sisters."
The network protected them from Chinese secret societies that controlled
prostitutes and *mui tsai* ("girl slave"), and at the same time formed the basis
for self-help in a foreign country. Employment was secured via informal
amah networks or with the help of shopkeepers who doubled as informal
domestic employment agents. Even though the three women worked for
Chinese families, it is known that *amahs* also worked in European households.[21] Ah Foon Cheh, Ah Lan Cheh, and Ah Ling Cheh stated that neither they nor their friends had ever entertained the possibility of working
for Malays because of religious differences. The relative absence of Chinese
female servants in Malay households during that period was the result of
low numbers of middle and upper-middle class Malay families, and to be
sure, Muslim prohibition on the consumption of pork. Presently, there is
only one reported case of a Chinese *amah* who worked as a cook in an elite
Malay household, and she neither cooked nor consumed pork throughout
her employment tenure.[22]

Between the 1930s and 1950s, Chinese women began to displace Chinese
male servants as large numbers of women found work for half the monthly
wages of the men. Chinese female servants accepted anywhere between
(Malayan dollars) $5 to $15 per month, while Chinese male servants

demanded at least $30 per month. Women who worked for European employers were paid slightly more than those who worked for non-Europeans, namely Chinese employers.[23]

In wealthy Chinese households, female servants performed a variety of tasks such as cooking, cleaning, ironing, and childcare. At the top of the servant hierarchy were cooks and "baby" *amahs*. Ah Foon Cheh and Ah Ling Cheh respectively worked as a baby nurse and a cook in wealthy Chinese households. Decades later, Ah Ling Cheh was asked to take care of her employers' grandchildren. Ah Lan Cheh, on the other hand, worked as an "all-purpose servant" who cooked, cleaned, and took care of her employers' children until she left to work as a cook in a wealthier Chinese household.

Servants did not have predetermined rest days, and had to ask in advance if they needed time off from work. Employers usually allowed servants one-half of a rest day for religious observances, such as the first and fifteenth day of the month according to the lunar calendar.

Chinese *amahs* were not known to leave their jobs because of disputes over wages or rest days. Ah Ling Cheh explained that most of her sisters negotiated terms of employment with potential employers either at the latter's houses or the *fong chai*. She and her "sisters" privileged mutual respect and trust, over monthly wages.[24]

In the 1960s, Ah Ling Cheh temporarily left her job because of her employer's demeanor toward her:

> Once I had an argument with the mistress. She accused me of breaking the antique vase. I told her that I didn't do it but she accused me all the same. So, I packed my clothes and went back to the *fong chai*. It broke my heart to leave the children. They clung to my trousers and pleaded with me not to leave. Tears flowed down my face as I walked out of the main gate. I told my sisters about her and they helped me look for another employer. After a few days, she [the employer] came to the *fong chai* and apologized to me.

She and her two sisters acknowledged that they were well aware of their "lowly" position or status as servants. In spite of this, they expected employers to treat them with respect: e.g., to address *amahs* politely and to trust the women's judgment in performing various household tasks.

Amah networks established rules and boundaries of employer-employee relations that mitigated physical and sexual abuse. Employers who verbally mistreated their domestic workers were quickly maligned throughout the networks, which could and did jeopardize employers' future ability to hire *amahs*. In my interviews with the three *amahs*, I made the mistake of asking them about love and sex. All three women blushed and then verbally chastised me, a younger Malaysian Chinese woman, for even thinking that a Chinese male employer in that era would demand or dare to approach an *amah* for sexual favors.

I do not assert that physical or sexual harassment never occurred in any *amah*'s tenure as a domestic worker. Rather, *amah* networks acted as safety nets since they provided social, financial, and emotional support for their members. In short, the networks were well-developed self-help institutions of and for this particular generation of Chinese servants in colonial Malaya.

Chinese *amahs* of the 1930s generally enjoyed a reputation of lengthy and dedicated service to their non-European, specifically Chinese employers. Similarities in the ethnic background of employer and employee helped blur class differences. That is, Chinese *amahs* performed physical labor and what has been called "emotional" labor.[25] The emotionally intimate environment in which *amahs* cared for their employers' babies or young children at times, could and did obscure their subordinate class position. The grandchildren of Ah Ling Cheh's employer occasionally visited their retired *amah* bearing gifts of money and foodstuffs. Throughout my interview with Ah Ling Cheh, she referred to her employer's grandchildren as if the latter were her own.[26]

To complicate employer-employee relations even more, not only was an *amah* a surrogate mother to her employers' children, but also depending on the context, she became a surrogate mother to her female employer. Below, Ah Foon Cheh describes a key aspect of her relationship to the employer:

> She used to sit down with me during the early morning or afternoon, after the children had gone to school, and tell me how he [male employer] had a mistress and he kept her in an apartment that he bought for her across town. She said I was lucky because I did not have to experience her heartache. I told her that is precisely why I "*sor hei*" so that I didn't have to feel used [by men]. But I also told her that she was lucky because she had wonderful children of her own.

Nevertheless, emotional labor performed by *amahs* in many instances did not fully conceal the superior-subordinate relationship. Differences between employer and employee's use of time and space in the household markedly constructed and reinforced class differences. *Amahs* who were not baby nurses performed a variety of household tasks such as sweeping floors and cleaning bathrooms: tasks considered too lowly and laborious for female employers who "specialized" in arranging flowers for the dining room table or selecting appropriate curtains to match the living room. Chinese servants rarely ate their meals together with employing families. Instead, meals were consumed in the kitchen, away from the more public areas in the house.

Ah Foon Cheh expressed *amah* class consciousness from a Buddhist perspective: she insisted that the quality of her present life was a reflection of what she had or had not done in past lives. She said, "We were servants; it was our *mang sui* [life's destiny] to serve others. Perhaps we will be more fortunate in our next lives." The class-religious nexus determined Chinese *amahs'* sense of what was possible. A significant consequence was that the *amahs* of the 1930s took great pride in performing loyal and dedicated service to their employers. It can be argued, especially from the perspective of orthodox Marxism, that religion is a superstructural phenomenon constructed for elite manipulation of the masses, or that *amah* class consciousness reflected a sense of fatalistic resignation to class subordination. Even as religious beliefs mitigated the unconditional expression of class consciousness among *amahs*, they also functioned as a restraining force in employer-employee relations. The following is an example of the invocation of a religious belief to renegotiate employer-employee relations. Ah Ling Cheh narrated an incident in which the employer of one of her "sisters " chastised the *amah* for "dragging her feet" in preparing the children's lunch. The servant, who had kept quiet as her employer ranted and raved, finally said calmly: "Are you in a hurry to get your new birth certificate?" The female employer, having interpreted the *amah's* question from a religious standpoint, fell silent and then apologized to the latter. The *amah's* bold retort had invoked the karmatic danger of her employer's impolite speech: reference to a new birth certificate for her employer implied that there would have been no guarantee that her soul would not reincarnate as a poor lowly human being at best, and an animal at worst if she continued to malign her servant.

Amah strategies for coping with European employers were different: they were told directly and indirectly to act like servants. In European households, they did not enjoy the special status, and many times deference, accorded by Chinese employers. *Amahs* were called by their first names without the "cheh" suffix, and they were required to wear black trousers and white tops/blouses as uniforms. Since then, the black-and-white uniform has characterized the 1930s generation of single and celibate *amahs*.[27] Chinese servants were required to use different sets of cooking utensils for themselves and for their European employers. Kenneth Gaw quotes an *amah* as having said that, "I didn't like the idea of working for

Europeans. You'd have to bring your own pots and pans along to do your
own cooking. Also rice, oil, etc. It's like a major move."[28]

European attitudes and behavior that reinforced class-racial differences
meant that their reputations were more susceptible to *amah* gossip than
were the reputations of the non-European employers:

> Amahs working for expatriates tended to gossip more than those employed by
> local Chinese families. Of course, the amahs who were better treated would not
> gossip as much as those less well treated. Many who worked for the Chinese saw
> themselves as part of the families they served and thus, out of loyalty, would not
> gossip about them. This did not apply to the expatriates who were not consid-
> ered as "family," although some amahs working for expatriate employers were
> exceptionally loyal.[29]

Ah Lan Cheh insisted that although most Europeans paid well, they also
expected servants to know their social positions, hence defer to employers at
all times: "They [Europeans] did not like it when their servants answered
them back instead of keeping quiet. Sometimes it cannot be helped because
they [Europeans] are so arrogant. They think they are so 'grand' but they don't
know everything."

By the 1950s, the community of *amahs* was no longer exclusively restricted
to single celibate Chinese migrant female servants. The specific sociocultural
and economic circumstances of migrant women from Kwangtung meant
that they were a finite group who could not reproduce the next generations
of servants.

Amah-hood soon became synonymous with paid female reproductive
labor in general as Malay, and Malayan-born Chinese and Indian women
entered the ranks of domestic servants. Expanding the boundaries of the
amah category meant that the nouns of maid, servant, girl, *amah*, and *mui
tsai* were used interchangeably in reference to female domestic workers.

In 1958, it was reported that five hundred members of the Domestic
Employee's Union had asked state authorities to establish specific hours of
work per day, annual and monthly holidays, workers' insurance, and base
salary. It is not known if the *amahs* of the 1930s belonged to the union.
There was no record of any official response to the demands.[30]

Toward the end of colonial rule, public discourse on independence and
governance did not specifically include women or their participation in,
and contribution to, activities in the public and private domains. Malay,
Chinese, and Indian women's interests were assumed to reflect that of their
respective ethnic communities.[31]

From The Home to The Factory Floor

There exists today a dearth of intellectual inquiry on the relationship between domestic service and development in postcolonial Malaysia.[32] On the one hand, it can be argued that the physical and social segregation of domestic service from public space and attention pose problems of access for researchers. On the other hand, the present black hole in our knowledge of postcolonial domestic service reflects the conventional wisdom that domestic service is not "real" or "productive work":[33]

> Economically, domestic labour is invisible because it is not part of capitalist pro-
> duction which uses wages labour to produce commodities for the market. When
> performed by the housewife, domestic labour is unpaid, it produces use value
> without producing profit. In comparison to that of the housewife, the labour of
> the domestic servant is somewhat more visible because it is paid for. . . . However,
> intertwined as it is with intimate, personal relations, domestic labour is consid-
> ered a private matter, a 'labour of love.' As such, it is ideologically invisible as a
> form of real work, a status that is hard to change even when it is paid for.[34]

What is known is that in 1963, 3,000 out of 10,000 "War Department *Amahs*" went on strike for better working conditions. The women were servants of British military families stationed in Malaysia (again, it is not known if the original *amahs* participated in the strike). The Malayan Trades Union Congress (MTUC) even formed a committee to help organize the servants. Later in the year, the strike was called off because of Indonesia's military action against the creation of the Federation of Malaysia (see chapter 2).[35]

The 1970 Census Report in Malaysia neither provides statistics on the total number of female servants nor distinguishes between women who performed live-in, part-time, or day work. Nonetheless, it is estimated that more than 60 percent of all female rural out-migrants (Malay, Chinese, and Indian) worked as urban domestic servants, which was the second highest employment sector for women (the agricultural sector was the first).[36]

The predominance of female rural out-migrants in urban domestic service prior to 1970 is related to the rate in which the processes of urbanization outpaced industrialization in Malaysia. Urban centers neither had the infrastructural support nor the employment opportunities to absorb large numbers of rural-urban migrants. Female migrants who found employment in urban areas were concentrated mostly in informal jobs such as domestic service that drew on the tradition of women's perceived comparative advantage in performing household labor.[37]

Since Malays were predominantly rural prior to the NEP, one may infer that many Malay female urban in-migrants might have and did work as domestic servants (especially prior to employment in FTZs). Azizah Kassim's research on Malay squatter women and the informal economy indicates that some urban in-migrants worked as servants, although "working as domestic help especially a live-in domestic is considered very demeaning, thus it is only when no other means of employment in the informal sector is available that this type of job is taken. Even then, the domestic help and washerwomen worked on their own terms."[38] She argues that Malay women's reluctance to be live-in servants is related to the "stigma attached to the job; working for a household as a washerwoman or a cook is described as being *hamba orang* (literally, someone else's slave), who, in the traditional Malay society of social stratification occupies the lowest stratum."[39] As previously discussed, debt-bondage was practiced in precolonial and colonial Malaya. The association of live-in domestic service with the condition of enslavement remains today.

During the course of field research, I encountered a Malay day-worker who, in the 1970s, had migrated from a small village in Perak to Kuala Lumpur. Rosita bicycled to work in a middle-class Kuala Lumpur neighborhood five days a week. For more than ten years, she washed and ironed clothes, and swept and/or mopped floors for three families (from different ethnic and religious backgrounds). She chose day-work primarily because she had to care for her own children and that day-work gave her more freedom than live-in domestic service. None of her friends who performed paid housework lived in their employers' houses, choosing instead to commute to work.

Rosita's experience directly contradicts M. Jocelyn Armstrong's study of Malaysian domestic workers in which she argues that Malay female urban in-migrants preferred to perform live-in domestic service because this particular category of work offered "protection from the perceived risks of big city living" and, at the same time, "freedom from female subordination within their own families" (conceivably back in the villages).[40] Indeed, the relative absence of scholarly interest in contemporary domestic service continues to be an effective barrier to a fuller and more complex understanding of different Malaysian women's relations to development processes.

From the late 1960s, the trend in women's employment began to shift from a concentration on "traditional" services, such as paid housework, to that of manufacturing work as a result of newly established FTZs.[41] Among new jobs created were sewing clothes and assembling electronic chips in factories. The gradual feminization of the manufacturing industry is evident in the increase in the number of female workers relative to male workers from 1970 to 1990 (see Table 3.1).

As the number of female factory workers increased, the supply of live-in servants began to decline. Newspaper headlines reflected the exodus of Malaysian servants from the home to the factory floor: "Fewer girls want to be maids," "Amahs are fast becoming a vanishing breed," "More girls seeking jobs in factories," "Seremban in a fix over servant crisis," "It's not just fashionable for girls in Malacca."[42]

Malaysian women's growing reluctance to work in the low-status and low-wage occupation of unlegislated live-in domestic service was captured by newspaper surveys.[43] For example, a former servant explained that: "[Factory work] is more interesting and has brighter prospects . . . and normally a domestic help is not properly treated by a fussy employer. Even if I was offered more pay, I would not become one."[44]

In an unpublished study of Malaysian servants, the major problem identified was the lack of legislative protection: servants labored under conditions of long work hours, low pay, and no rest days.[45] Alternative employment opportunities for women meant that those who had been working or could have worked as domestic servants either left their jobs or used the threat of alternative employment opportunities to make demands that could and did significantly alter employer-employee relations within the household. Women who remained in domestic service were specific in their demands to employers: higher wages, more rest days, and clearly delimited number of work hours per day.[46]

TABLE 3.1

Male and Female Employment in Manufacturing

Year	Males	Females
1970[a]	235,377	111,017
1980	453,599	389,875
1985	479,400	371,000
1990	697,300	635,500

Source: International Labour Organization, 1994.

[a] data for Peninsula Malaysia only. See Fatima Daud, "Women's Economic Role in Malaysia," 1992.

Malaysian employers and potential employers, similar to their European predecessors only a few decades ago in colonial Malaya, openly complained in the newsprint media about domestic servants. Employers' sense of desperation and anger grew as the decline in supply of servants appeared to encourage domestic workers' threats to quit their jobs if demands for more rest-days, reduced working hours, and/or luxurious amenities in the workplace were not met by their employers.[47]

During a few weeks stay in a lower middle class Setapak neighborhood, I interviewed two Chinese female shopkeepers who had worked as servants in the 1970s. Ah Kwan (who is now in her early forties) left her job to marry a Chinese man who sold fresh fruits at one of the farmers' markets in Kuala Lumpur. The couple purchased a two-story building in Setapak: the first floor was used for their laundry business while the second floor housed their living quarters.

Ah Kwan had worked for two Chinese families before quitting her last job because her employer had refused to give her two rest days per month while prohibiting her from watching television. She left after her friends told her that she could easily find paid domestic work since it was a "seller's market." In the end, she opted to marry so that she could have children.

The other former domestic worker, Ah Mun, left her job in the late 1970s after having words with her female employer, who had attempted to deduct a portion of her wages after she had accidentally left a brown iron mark on a shirt. Even as she recalled the incident, she spat on the ground and cursed her former employers. She insisted that she was not even worried about the prospect of getting another job because "to live as a destitute human being was better than to be treated like a dog." It did not take her long to find work: she was hired by a rattan furniture maker to handweave chairs and sofas.

In 1973, a newspaper article reported that the supply of domestic servants had declined so drastically that for several weeks, no women had registered to work with a major domestic employment agency.[48] Informal domestic employment agents also were affected by women's declining interest in domestic service.

During the course of fieldwork in 1994, I met a Chinese taxi driver who used to be an informal employment agent: employers gave him a finder's fee for recommending domestic servants from Chinese New Villages.[49] As he and I discussed my research while we were caught in a massive traffic jam in Kuala Lumpur, he told me that by the early 1980s, he was left with no choice other than to apply for a taxi driver's badge because he could no longer persuade young Chinese women to be servants:

> A couple asked me to get them a *mui tsai*. They offered nearly RM500 [in the early 1980s, wages for domestic servants were between RM200 to RM300] a month. And, do you know what the girl asked me? "Are there any rest days?" I said to her, "It is a live-in job, so probably once a month." The girl laughed and said, "I want one and one half days off every week, just like office workers." Naturally, I said that this couldn't be the case, since she would be hired to serve the family. So I told her, "When they need you to do the work, you must do it." Also, I told her that they were willing to pay her an even higher salary, only if she was good. Still, she refused to work as a *mui-tsai*. So, you can't blame employers for hiring foreigners today because we are not willing to do the work.

The phrase for servant in Cantonese is *kung yan*, literally "work people." The taxi driver's uncritical word choice of *mui tsai* reflects the continued belief that Chinese female servants were considered not so much as workers than as girl-slaves. It is hardly surprising that Chinese women, when offered other opportunities, refused to work as domestic servants. Employers' difficulty in hiring docile, low-wage servants was painfully clear when no women enrolled in the YWCA's free courses designed to train young girls as domestic workers.[50]

By the early 1980s, the Deputy Minister of Information, a woman, proposed promoting domestic service as a profession—to elevate the status of the job, legally and financially, in order to attract servants. Not only did the state fail to respond to the proposal, but also employers openly criticized the plan on the grounds that it would further incite employer-employee contestations over wages and working conditions:

> Why do you have to raise these things in the papers? Even if the proposal does not come through, when my servant reads about how much other servants are being paid, she'll start demanding for more money.

> If I come home at 11 pm, and she has to open the door, does she claim OT [overtime pay]?[51]

The absence of a more structured work environment delineated and protected by labor legislation was *the* key issue in employer-employee contestations. State authorities failed to respond until 1987 when the Minister of Labour, a man, in reference to Filipina and Indonesian female servants' complaints, presented the official rationale for not regulating domestic service: "We will have problems defining, for instance, their hours of work and the value of their accommodation given by their employers, if they were to be included in the Employment Act."[52] Definitional problems became the "reason" for legislative silence on domestic service. Implicit in the minister's rationale was the belief that since the household is synonymous with the private-domestic domain, it then ought to be free from state interference; and that female reproductive labor does not qualify as "work."

A glaring contradiction in the official resistance to legislating domestic service surfaced in 1994, when the Minister of Human Resources asked Filipina and Indonesian female domestic workers to stop airing their complaints in the newspapers. Requesting instead that they report all cases of employer abuse to his ministry,[53] he promised that his ministry "would take action if maids had evidence to substantiate their claims."[54] The burden of proof is placed conveniently on domestic workers, and it is a responsibility that cannot possibly be met or enforced by law since there was and is no enforceable labor legislation delineating work hours or tasks in domestic service.

The specific gender-class-ethnic nexus inherited and perpetuated by the postcolonial state apparatus largely delineated official responses to employer-domestic worker complaints. Clause I of the First Schedule in the Employment Act 1955 covers "any person, irrespective of his occupation who has entered into a contract of service with an employer so long as such person's wages do not exceed $750.00 a month." According to this definition, a female domestic worker could be classified as an employee.

The Employment Act 1955 (Revised 1981) would define officially a domestic servant as

> [A] person [male or female] employed in connection with the work of a private dwelling house and not in connection with any trade, business or profession carried on by the employer in such dwelling house and includes a cook, house servant, butler, child's nurse, valet, footman, gardener, washerman or washerwomen, groom and driver or cleaner of any vehicle licensed for private use.[55]

Yet, servants are conspicuously absent from the Employment Act's categories of female workers who are given such rights as definite work hours per day, and maternity benefits and leave. Domestic workers are not even classified as workers in other key labor legislation that deal with worker benefits and rights: the Employee Provident Fund Ordinance 1951, the Employee Social Security Ordinance 1969, and the Workmen's Compensation Act 1952.[56]

The official position toward domestic service reveals more than the pervasiveness of public patriarchy or the practice of patriarchal ideology in public institutions, legislation and policies. In the aftermath of the 1969 ethnic riots between Malays and Chinese, it would have been politically untenable for the predominantly Malay/UMNO-controlled state apparatus to be seen as actively encouraging Malay women to work in the low-status and low-wage occupation of domestic service.[57] This would have contradicted what is arguably *the* main objective of the NEP—i.e., the promise to enforce the upward socioeconomic mobility of Malays in relation to the non-Malay (read: Chinese) community.

Employers who were disgusted by the seemingly arrogant attitudes of Malaysian servants, and who were frustrated by the increasing difficulty in employing docile household help, began to illegally hire female servants from Indonesia and the Philippines.

Enter The Foreign Maid: Foreign Female Domestic Workers and the Malaysian State

During the 1970s, revenues from commodity exports allowed the two successive Prime Ministers, Tun Abdul Razak and Tun Hussein Onn, and their respective cabinets to increase public-sector expenditure for education and employment. Malaysia's emerging dual labor market structure evolved as a result of a development path that heightened expectations and expanded employment opportunities for Malays specifically, and for Malaysians in general.[58]

The presence of illegal migrants—foreign female domestic workers, and male and female plantation and construction workers—were detected in Malaysia as early as the 1970s. In the late 1970s and early 1980s, inherent in non-Malay complaints about illegal migrant workers was the belief that the Malay-controlled state apparatus allowed the presence of the illegal Indonesian migrants—many of whom are similar to Malays in ethnic, cultural, and religious affiliations—so as to increase the Malay population. Meanwhile, low-wage labor demands of agriplantations continued to rise as a result of the NEP's pro-Malay urbanization policy within the context of export-oriented development. The official response was to maintain the status quo: Malaysian employment of illegal migrant workers was neither banned or regulated.

Public "rediscovery" of illegal migrant workers during the 1985–87 economic recession led to renewed outcries from various groups in society. The MTUC, which had supported "War Department *amahs*" in the early 1960s, reasoned that Malaysian employers preferred foreign servants because the latter were willing to work for lower wages, and that they "carried out their jobs diligently and rarely left the confines of the house for fear of detection by Authorities."[59] In spite of and because of this observation, the MTUC did not act on behalf of or against Filipina and Indonesian domestic workers.[60]

Employers defended their right to hire low-wage migrant workers from abroad as a major way to keep down costs and to solve labor shortage problems. At the very same time, politicians from the three major ethnic groups and various labor unions insisted that the state officially regulate foreign labor in-migration. This fragmentation of interests within society was mirrored in the manner in which the Labour and Home Affairs ministries dealt with the issue of foreign migrant workers.

The Labour Ministry, which coincidentally was led by a Chinese man, moved to protect Malaysian workers and conceivably to ensure interethnic balance, since most of the illegal workers in Peninsular Malaysia were Indonesians. The more powerful Home Affairs Ministry, however, was controlled by Malays (Dr. Mahathir Mohamad held the positions of Home Affairs Minister and Prime Minister), who allegedly were interested in increasing the Malay population (by counting illegal Indonesian workers as Malays, or by issuing illegal Indonesian workers with identity cards given to naturalized citizens) vis-à-vis the non-Malay populations.[61]

The Minister of Labour banned all migrant laborers from entering the country in September 1986: "The Labour Ministry has taken steps to stop totally the employment of foreigners to work as domestic servants and estate workers. It has advised the Immigration Department not to allow such workers to enter the country, Labour Minister Datuk Lee Kim Sai said."[62] Only a few months later, the Malay Deputy Home Affairs Minister Datuk Megat Junid lifted the ban on Filipina and Indonesian domestic workers, "after considering public complaints on the shortage of domestic help."[63] The Labour Ministry explained to the public that while the Home Affairs Ministry had the power to override the ban on foreign female domestic workers, the Labour Ministry would continue to help unemployed Malaysian domestic servants find work.

During the ban on foreign domestic workers, Malay women entered the public debate on foreign versus local servants when *Wanita* UMNO (UMNO Women) publicly requested state authorities to consider training 30,000 unemployed women who had registered as domestic workers with the Labour Ministry.[64] The official response again was to remain characteristically silent on the issue.

To be sure, it was not politically feasible for the Malay/UMNO-controlled state to openly encourage Malay women to work as domestic servants, particularly during a period in which the state was confronted by criticisms within the Malay community that the NEP had only benefitted mostly wealthy Malays who already enjoyed unobstructed access to state bureaucrats and resources. The state elite could not but refrain from directly responding to *Wanita* UMNO's proposal of training unemployed Malaysian women.

Instead in 1986–87, the Immigration Department (housed within the Home Affairs Ministry), established guidelines for privately owned domestic employment agencies (DOMs) to recruit female domestic workers from Indonesia and the Philippines.[65] DOMs and employers in this study said that in the late 1980s, rules of eligibility were implemented for those who wished to employ foreign servants. Specifically, employers' petitions for permission to hire Filipina and Indonesian domestic workers had to include employers' marriage certificates, their children's birth certificates, and copies of the *Borang J* personal income tax return as evidence that employers earned sufficient income to pay foreign domestic workers' monthly salaries.

The family (marriage and birth certificates) and income rules, as I call them, were not made public in the newspapers until 1989, and then mostly in the form of question-answer columns.[66] In these columns, employers who were not sure of the Immigration Department's rules would write to the newspaper editor who, in turn, requested clarification from the Immigration Department. The questions and answers were printed in the same newspaper column.

In 1989, a representative of the Immigration Department answered a potential employer's query. The applicant, who had three children, previously had been denied permission to employ a foreign domestic worker because she failed to furnish an official marriage certificate (she had not gone through a civil marriage ceremony). This particular case was printed in the *New Straits Times* with the headline "No Maid Until Couple Gets Married." The Immigration Department's explanation was that although the woman had submitted her children's birth certificates, she had failed to include her marriage certificate.[67] The marriage and birth certificate rules would be key to normalizing and nurturing a particular form of the modern caring Malaysian family. Chapter 6 presents a detailed analysis of the relationship between this immigration rule and the official effort to redraw the boundaries of public and private morality during the NEP period.

Employers interviewed in this study mentioned that in the late 1980s, the income rule required employers to earn RM50,000 per annum if they wanted to hire Filipina servants. There was no preset income requirement for those who wanted to hire Indonesian women. At that time, a Filipina servant's monthly salary was approximately RM350–400, while an Indonesian servant's salary was anywhere between RM0–180 (depending on whether or not she was an indentured domestic worker). In 1994, the annual income qualification levels were as follows: a combined household income of RM48,000 was required to employ a Filipina servant with a monthly salary of RM500; and a combined household income of RM24,000 was required to qualify for an Indonesian servant with a monthly salary of RM300–330.

Whether the focus is on the late 1980s or 1994, there exists a substantial difference in annual income qualification levels for Malaysians to employ domestic workers from different nationalities. The income rule ensures that employers of Filipina and Indonesian servants respectively are able to pay their employees.

Taken on its own terms, the income rule is not controversial. However, when analyzed together with other employment rules implemented by the Immigration Department, it sheds light on the nature of state regulation of the employment of foreign domestic workers.

From the late 1980s to 1991, the income and family rules were publicized in major newspapers: employers must be married with children and they also must furnish the *Borang J* forms that specified annual incomes. In October 1991, when the state announced its policy of deporting all illegal Indonesian domestic workers by the end of the year, representatives from the Home Affairs Ministry and the Immigration Department insisted that there was a third rule which had been in effect since official regulation of foreign domestic workers began in 1986–87.

That third rule was the "religion" rule, which stated that only Muslims were allowed to employ Indonesian-Muslim servants.[68] In other words, the Home Affairs Ministry insisted that Malays had to employ Indonesian servants whereas non-Malay/non-Muslim employers could hire only Filipina (Christian) servants. As will be discussed shortly, although this particular rule was not publicized until October 1991, the Malaysian public was well aware of its existence.

Analysis of the three employment rules within the larger politics of socioeconomic restructuring in Malaysia reveals the implied objectives in official regulation of the in-migration and employment of Filipina and Indonesian domestic workers. The income rule established the basis for inclusion and exclusion into the Malaysian middle classes. Within the middle classes, the religion rule was used to demarcate intraclass ethnoreligious boundaries since only Malay-Muslim employers were allowed to hire Indonesian servants who, in turn, had to be Muslims. Since there was a lower income requirement level to hire Indonesian servants, then it could be inferred that Malay employment of domestic workers was subsidized by the state. The family rule that required marriage and children's birth certificates was expected to construct and legitimize the middle classes' adoption of the nuclear family form.

During a period in which the NEP was criticized on different fronts by different groups of peoples, the income and religion rules facilitated state elites' ability to "objectify" middle-class boundaries as proof that the choice of development path had benefitted more than a group of politico-bureaucrats and their supporters. Not so coincidentally, the employment rules were established in 1986–87, the same period of political in-fighting within UMNO—the ruling Malay political party—as members debated the future direction of the NEP. "Team A" (Prime Minister Dr. Mahathir Mohamad and supporters) argued that the NEP had benefitted the majority of Malays. "Team B" (Musa Hitam and supporters) insisted that the NEP had nurtured a group of corrupt businessmen and politicians, thus further marginalizing the majority of Malays.

Foreign female domestic workers would become boundary-markers for and of the expanding Malaysian middle classes. Simply put, the presence of foreign servants was to be read as evidence that development had benefitted Malaysians. Within the middle classes, Malay employment of Indonesian servants was subsidized by the state via the income and religion rules.

There were unintended or unanticipated consequences that arose from the income and religion rules. Non-Malays, whose income was insufficient to allow them to employ Filipinas, simultaneously failed to qualify for employing Indonesian servants if they were not Muslims. Those who were denied state permission turned to the illegal route of employing Indonesian servants.

In October 1991, it was officially announced that state authorities would deport all illegal Indonesian servants on the premise that their numbers had reached unacceptable levels (to this day, the exact number of illegal Indonesian servants has not been made public—see the following chapter for more detail). Deputy Home Affairs Minister Datuk Megat Junid insisted at a press conference that, "All employers of illegal Indonesian maids have up to Dec 31 to surrender them to the Immigration Department to avoid prosecution."[69] A few days later, "Datuk Megat Junid said the *Government did not allow Indonesian maids to work in non-Muslim households but it could consider special cases* [emphasis mine]."[70]

Immigration and police officials embarked on a house-to-house search for illegal Indonesian servants.[71] Of significance is that while the Immigration Department refused to process any work permits for illegal Indonesian servants (choosing instead to deport the women), the Department continued to process the work permit applications of illegal Indonesian male and female workers in the plantation and construction sectors.[72]

The illegal status of many Indonesian servants was *not* the only reason for the deportation policy. Non-Malay/non-Muslim middle class employers had blurred the neat boundaries constructed by the religion rule of "only Muslim (Indonesian) servants with Muslim (predominantly Malay) employers."

Since most illegal Indonesian servants migrated with the help of labor brokers called *taikong*, who literally sold the women to employers in order to recoup costs, then even working-class employers could afford to hire illegal Indonesian servants: it was not necessary to pay indentured workers any wages for a considerable length of time. Hawker stalls at farmers' markets and *pasar malam* or neighborhood night markets became illegal domestic employment agencies.[73] Working-class employers had blurred the boundaries constructed by the employment rules for inclusion into, and exclusion from, the middle classes.

The official response was to apply coercion to reconstruct intraclass and interclass ethnoreligious boundaries that had been traversed: all illegal Indonesian servants were to be found and deported immediately. There also was a financial rationale to the deportation policy: extra-legal DOMs had been accumulating profit at the expense of legally registered DOMs, thus future state revenue.

Despite the expectations of the state authorities, the responses of Malaysians did not fall along specific ethnoreligious lines. Employers from all ethnic groups complained vehemently of the planned deportation of Indonesian servants. Malays and non-Malays publicly questioned the religion rule.[74] Even renowned Islamic scholars voiced their objections to the rule and deportation policy.[75]

A key DOM response to sustained employer demands for Filipina and Indonesian domestic workers in the wake of the deportation threat was to request state permission to recruit women from other labor-sending countries such as Sri Lanka.[76] A Chinese member of parliament introduced the motion to recruit domestic servants from East Asia.[77] If granted, the mass in-migration of servants from South and East Asia possibly could tip the population distribution in favor of the Malaysian Indian and Chinese communities.

A few months after the official announcement that illegal Indonesian servants would be deported, the religion rule was rescinded. The Immigration Department issued a statement that allowed employers to hire either Filipina or Indonesian servants. Non-Muslim employers had to ensure that Muslim servants' religious practices would not be subordinated to or reviled by work environments.[78] Muslim employers were allowed to hire Filipina servants (most of whom were Christians), so long as there were no children in the household.[79] The Immigration Department still required children's birth certificates as one of the prerequisites to employ a Filipina or an Indonesian domestic worker.

Representatives from the twenty DOMs with whom I spoke insisted that with the exception of the religion rule, the Immigration Department's requirements had remained unchanged in 1994. A potential employer would have to furnish the Department with marriage and children's birth certificates, and the *Borang J* income tax return. Several DOM representatives, however, offered to help me draft a letter petitioning the Department for permission to employ a servant even if I was neither married nor had children. Yet, I was told that unless I knew someone "powerful," my chances of securing state approval were slim. Other DOM representatives suggested that I financially compensate a friend for using her name and address (provided that she was married and had children, and neither planned to, nor already had employed a foreign domestic worker) in my application to the Department.

State regulation of the in-migration and employment of Filipina and Indonesian domestic workers was key to the defense of the NEP during the mid to late 1980s. This is not to argue that the in-migration of domestic workers was the state elite's solution to accusations of corruption, rentierism, and patronage. Rather, official regulation of the in-migration and placement of Filipina and Indonesian domestic workers objectified the social and material boundaries of the Malay and non-Malay middle classes.

The in-migration of Indonesian and Filipina servants facilitates state elites' efforts to garner consent from emerging key social forces, i.e., the middle classes, for the continued expansion of the path of export-oriented development. Within the institution of contemporary domestic service, employment rules were applied to manipulate specific intersections of class-gender-ethnicity-religion-nationality, in order to address the political challenges to the NEP, and to meet the household needs of the expanding Malaysian middle classes in a way that continued to free working-class Malaysian women to participate mostly in manufacturing industries rather than domestic service.

The historical development of the state's relation to the institution of domestic service is characterized by markedly similar and dissimilar patterns. Twice in the twentieth century, colonial and postcolonial state authorities in Malaysia opened the immigration gates temporarily to solve employer-domestic worker contestations over working conditions and wages. Whereas the British refused to intervene further in the employment of *amahs*, the postcolonial state proceeded to construct rules governing the in-migration and employment of foreign servants to achieve specific objectives.

In the 1930s, Southern Chinese women's desire to remain financially and socially independent from men in the midst of political and socioeconomic turmoil led to the in-migration of *amahs*. The *amah* migratory chain was shaped largely by Chinese women's informal networks of "sisters." Upon arrival in Malaya, *amah* networks could and did exert control over conditions in which their members performed paid reproductive labor. In time, *amahs* gained the reputation of hardworking loyal servants.

Today, the case of Filipina and Indonesian domestic workers is distinctly different from the *amahs*. The following chapter examines the global and regional contexts from which the transnationalization of migrant female domestic labor emerges, and analyzes the women's migratory and employment mechanisms.

Note on the Epigraph

Roland Barthes, *The Semiotic Challenge*, trans. by Richard Howard (London: Hill and Wang, 1988), p. 47.

CHAPTER 4

The Malaysian-Philippine-Indonesian Maid Trade

The preserve of the few, capitalism is unthinkable without society's active complicity.
—Fernand Braudel, *Afterthoughts on Material Civilization and Capitalism*, 1977

In an era of economic liberalization, deregulation, and privatization, the promotion of more efficient ways for the unobstructed transnational movement of capital dominates mainstream public policy and intellectual discourse.[1] So pervasive is the ideology of neoliberalism that the explanatory framework for capital flow from capital-rich to capital-poor countries is also used for labor movement from labor-abundant capital-poor countries to labor-scarce capital-rich countries:

> Countries with a large endowment of labor relative to capital have a low equilibrium market wage, while countries with a limited endowment of labor relative to capital are characterized by a high market wage. . . . The resulting differential in wages causes workers from the low-wage country to move to the high-wage country. . . . The simple and compelling explanation of international migration offered by neoclassical macroeconomics has strongly shaped public thinking and has provided the intellectual basis for much immigration policy.[2]

While the "osmosis" metaphor embodies the macro-level neoliberal explanation in which labor movements are likened to natural push-pull processes of equalizing transnational wage differentials, the micro-level explanation focuses on purposive action. An individual's decision to migrate is based on rational calculations of the costs and benefits involved in migration. Put simply, it is assumed that migrants are rational actors who have unobstructed access to information regarding the migratory process, the availability of jobs, and comparative wages in relation to the cost of living overseas.[3] Consequently, the purposive actions of many, or at least two rational individuals, leads to an equilibrium price, *ceteris paribus*.

The macro-level explanatory framework that is based on a notion of automaticity conveniently overlooks the purposive actions of states. Why is there the need in the Philippines and Indonesia to promote overseas employment, especially as domestic workers for their female nationals? Who are the key actors involved in domestic workers' migratory chain from the Philippines and Indonesia to Malaysia? How do they shape the women's migratory and employment mechanisms, and with what consequences?

I begin this chapter by locating contemporary transnational labor migration within the context of global and regional economic changes. I demonstrate that the theory and practice of labor migration according to the neoliberal push-pull model obscure the constraints of global and regional economic structures and processes, which encourage the incorporation of the "export-import" of labor in export-oriented development paths. Following this is the identification and discussion of key actors—labor-sending and receiving state authorities, domestic employment agencies (DOMs), and employers—who are integral to the domestic workers' migratory chain.

The key argument in this chapter is that the migratory and employment mechanisms of Filipina and Indonesian domestic workers constitute women as objects to be exported-imported, bought-sold, and controlled in the most demeaning ways. A dominant social code of conduct has emerged to govern the actions and perceptions of key actors in the maid trade. The code is premised on the Benthamite principle of utility that allows state and nonstate actors, in the pursuit of their real and perceived greater good, to rationalize the dehumanization of foreign female domestic workers.

Today, the adoption of export-oriented development paths facilitates an acceptance of an almost natural progression in which the trade in goods eventually has come to be complemented by the trade in capital that is constituted as a commodity and, presently, a trade where low-wage migrant workers also are constituted as commodities. The contemporary free trade in goods has found its counterpart in the trade in low-wage foreign female domestic workers.

Overview of Asian Labor Migration in a Global Era of Export-Oriented Development

The 'international is personal' implies that governments depend upon certain kinds of allegedly private relationships in order to conduct their foreign affairs. Governments need more than secrecy and intelligence agencies. . . . [T]hey also

depend on ideas about masculinized dignity and feminized sacrifice to sustain that
sense of autonomous nationhood.

—Cynthia Enloe, *Bananas, Beaches and Bases*, 1989

The migration of peoples is not a new phenomenon in Asian history. What
is new is the degree of overt state support for the transnationalization of
migrant or "guest" workers. Since the 1970s, a key response of Asian states
such as the Philippines, Sri Lanka, Pakistan, Bangladesh, and India to the
processes of global and regional economic restructuring is to institutionalize the out-migration of their able-bodied or productive nationals. The following ascertains that this particular labor policy response is symptomatic
of structural problems inherent in the path of export-oriented development
that had been prepackaged in the 1940s, and that is now repackaged and
sold to states throughout the world.

The global promotion of export-oriented economic growth was institutionalized at the 1944 Bretton Woods Conference that signalled the rise of
Pax Americana.[4] The "Bretton Twins" or the U.S.-led transnational organizations of the International Monetary Fund (IMF) and the World Bank
emerged from the Conference to oversee finance and production.

Noncommunist postcolonial or developing states were born into a system in which states' and peoples' search for the good life in the postcolonial
era was thought to be best pursued via export-oriented growth.[5] Promotion
of this particular path of development could only exacerbate balance of payments deficits, since a majority of developing states emerged from colonialism with export economies, based on natural resources, that had little if
any semblance of manufacturing activity.

In the 1950s, most noncommunist states in the developing world in
general, and Asian states in particular, adopted Import Substitution Industrialization (ISI) policies to help reduce balance of payments deficits.[6] By
the 1960s, when inherent ISI contradictions (such as the saturation of
domestic markets, and rising unemployment due to capital-intensive
industries) could no longer be ignored, a majority of the developing states
began to adopt a mixture of ISI and export-oriented industrialization
(EOI) policies.[7]

To be sure, the "dedomiciling" of capital in the West facilitated the
implementation of EOI policies throughout the developing world.[8]
Transnational Corporations (TNCs), constrained by rising labor costs in
major Keynesian states in the West, and at the very same time bolstered by
innovations in technology, began parceling out steps in the production

process to developing countries in Asia and Latin America that offered low-wage labor within depoliticized investment environments.[9]

Meanwhile, U.S. hegemony began to unravel partly because of fiscal and monetary policies that reinforced capital flight from the country. Gold reserves were close to depletion after the U.S. first financed European and East Asian postwar reconstruction, and then engaged in the protracted war against communist Southeast Asia. Rising labor costs also undercut the ability to compete effectively against exports from German and Japanese economies that were reconstructed with U.S. aid. As a result, interest rates were lowered in the late 1960s to prevent a domestic recession. Lower interest rates, paradoxically, had the effect of stimulating greater U.S. transnational corporate capital flight. In 1971, the U.S. dollar was divorced from gold in response to continuing capital flight and balance of payments deficits.

The absence of a fixed exchange rate meant greater uncertainty in trade and debt payments for the developing world. Export-oriented development since the 1960s primarily has focused on the export of commodities from developing countries endowed with natural resources. Not only were commodity prices slower to rise, but they also were more vulnerable to price fluctuations than those of manufactured goods. Most states in the developing world increasingly depended on foreign aid to facilitate long-term planning, and to sustain economic growth.[10]

The Organization of Petroleum Exporting Countries' (OPEC) decision to raise oil prices in 1973 affected oil-importing states in the developing world in significant ways. Increases in import prices led to greater declining terms of trade and increases in balance of payments deficits. However, liberal petrodollar loans by transnational banks eager to invest financial windfalls from OPEC actions temporarily delayed economic crises throughout most of the developing world.[11]

It is within this changing global economic environment that oil-importing Asian states such as the Philippines, India, Pakistan, and Sri Lanka, began "exporting" all categories of migrant workers from doctors and engineers to construction workers. Labor out-migration was encouraged for two interrelated reasons: to meet the increasing labor demands that emanated from the Middle East without altering existing structures of governance; and to stem real and potential social disruptions (thus, declining state legitimacy) brought about by rising costs of economic development.[12] For example, Philippine President Ferdinand Marcos insisted that, "The export of manpower will be allowed only as a temporary measure to ease underemployment and will be increasingly restrained as productive domestic employment opportunities are created."[13] Approximately two decades later, the World Bank would acknowledge the potential of labor out-migration in mitigating political and economic pressures of unemployment.[14]

The policy of "exporting" labor was considered a temporary and relatively costless solution to increasing foreign exchange earnings and to reducing unemployment. Another perceived advantage of labor out-migration was that migrants, conceivably, would gain new skills and work experience overseas that could be transferred back to their countries of origin.[15] In the early 1980s, the oil-exporting state of Indonesia joined the group of Asian labor-sending states because of declining commodity and oil revenues.[16]

The question remains as to why the state elite in Malaysia, an oil-exporting Asian country, did not officially implement and pursue a labor export policy similar to that of Indonesia during the early 1980s. It is commonly known that Malaysians in the state of Johor commute across the causeway to work on the neighboring island of Singapore. During the Malaysian recession of 1985–87, skilled and semi-skilled construction workers traveled to East Asia to work for substantially higher wages in the booming construction industry. Nonetheless, the Malay/UMNO-controlled state neither openly supported nor prohibited the out-migration of workers to East Asia. Patrick Pillai offers two reasons for the absence of a labor export policy. He argues that, in relative terms, Malaysia did not experience "serious economic or unemployment problems," and that most of the construction workers were Malaysian Chinese.[17] The latter reason implies that within the context of the NEP, in which an affirmative action development program for Malays was actively pursued, the state elite refrained from promoting the out-migration of Malaysian Chinese (as if to be rid of, or at the very least to reduce, the Malaysian Chinese population). In any event, sustained rapid economic growth in Malaysia since the late 1980s has meant that the economy's demands for foreign migrant labor, specifically low-wage workers, appear inexhaustible.

The largest labor market from the late 1970s to mid 1980s for Asian migrant workers was the Middle East—in particular, Saudi Arabia, Kuwait, United Arab Emirates, and Oman.[18] Bolstered by exponential increases in oil revenues, Middle East states undertook large infrastructural projects that required all categories of migrant workers—from engineers, doctors and nurses, to construction workers. In 1975, there were 360,000 South and

South-East Asian migrant workers in the Middle East. By 1983, the official
number of migrants had risen to 3.6 million.[19]

Asian labor-sending states' temporary reprieve from economic crises
ended when OPEC raised oil prices fourfold in 1979, while interest rates
were raised again in the U.S. From the late 1970s to the early 1980s, capital
began to return to the U.S., but it had the simultaneous effect of slowing
down U.S. and global economic growth. Prices and the global demand for
commodities declined. The ability of several Latin American and Asian
states to finance their ever-increasing foreign debt reached crisis levels.

In 1982, the Mexican state's announcement that it could no longer service
the massive foreign debt initiated a series of public acknowledgments by
other large debtor-states of their degree of foreign indebtedness. Brazil,
Argentina, Venezuela, and the Philippines made similar announcements
later in that year. By 1984, a consortium of private transnational banks, the
U.S., the World Bank, and the IMF announced the "Mexico Deal," which
restructured the country's debt package.[20]

The Mexico Deal would hasten the expansion of neoliberalism. Since
then, states in the developing world, to varying degrees, have been and are
subjected to austerity or structural adjustment and stabilization programs.
Among the conditions necessary to qualify for further aid/loans were and are
reductions in state spending, a greater role for the private sector (especially in
industrialization), currency devaluation, and the removal of trade barriers.[21]

The 1980s debt crisis and consequent structural adjustment and stabilization policies made labor out-migration even more indispensable to Asian
sending states. Labor out-migration and migrant remittances might and did
help to cushion against potential political and economic crises hastened by
unpopular structural adjustment programs that insisted on economic
restructuring as the precondition for future aid/loans. This is not to say that
labor out-migration policies were the only or the most important solution
to sustaining state legitimacy. Rather, it is to argue that institutionalized
labor out-migration has become a unique state response to inherent structural problems in the global economic system.

The "quick fix" solution found in labor out-migration policies had the
opposite effect to what labor-sending states such as the Philippines had
anticipated: the policies delayed, rather than hastened industrialization. A
Philippine senator was quoted as having said that:

> Today, the temporary labor export industry has become permanently temporary.
> Moreover it has grown . . . from being a stop-gap measure to being a vital life-

line for the nation . . . [T]he labor export industry is really the biggest economic story for the country . . . *[T]he success of the labor export industry is the best proof that our industrial policies have been a miserable failure* [italics mine]. [22]

In 1976, the Philippines "exported" 47,835 male and female migrant workers to countries all over the world (especially in Asia, the Middle East, and Europe). By 1989, the number of migrant workers had increased tenfold to 458,626.[23]

What had begun as a temporary solution soon became permanent for many South and Southeast Asian labor-sending countries as labor out-migration was incorporated in development policies. Ministries of Labour or Manpower were given the tasks of promoting and regulating migrant workers overseas:

> One of the first steps towards this structural approach was to repeal a number of Labour Ordinances or Labour Codes regulating migration and to establish specific administrative mechanisms within the Ministries of Labour or Manpower, as lead agencies for overseas employment. The Philippine Overseas employment Administration (POEA), the Sri Lanka Bureau of Foreign Employment (SLBFE), the Bureau of Manpower Employment and Training in Bangladesh, and the Centre for Overseas Employment in Indonesia (AKAN) for instance were created to promote and develop overseas employment.[24]

According to the POEA:

> Considered as the crux of the overseas program, *the expansion and maintenance of current international labor markets remain the dominant consideration in future plans and policies of the government* [italics mine]. Backed by in-depth market research activities and joint private and government marketing missions, the systematic development of overseas markets has been intensified and pursued vigorously.[25]

The statement confirms the Philippine state's role in maintaining labor out-migration. Succinctly put, the contemporary transnationalization of labor is not a natural phenomenon. Rather, as Karl Polanyi argued vis-à-vis the emergence of capitalist markets in goods and finance, labor markets also have to be constructed and maintained.[26] As discussed later in this chapter, the real and perceived need to maintain labor markets overseas as a major way to cope with economic, social, and political pressures of implementing export-oriented development paths can and does outweigh several labor-sending states' ability or even political will to address effectively their female nationals' welfare overseas.

It is estimated that migrant remittances via official channels to Asian countries of origin amounted to 3 percent per annum of the GNP during the

1980s, or a total of US$10 billion per year. Table 4.1 shows that in 1983, remittances to Pakistan and Bangladesh respectively were US$2.9 billion (equivalent to 97 percent of merchandise exports) and US$642.4 million (the second largest foreign exchange item after the country's jute export earnings).[27]

Of significance is that some of the official remittance figures are contradicted by estimates of nongovernmental organizations (NGOs). In the case of the Philippines, one of the seven largest debtor-countries during the 1980s, there are large discrepancies between official and unofficial estimates of migrant remittances. Whereas the official total of remittances between 1986–89 was US$1.112 billion (see table 4.1), the *Christian Conference of Asia-Rural Urban Mission* (CCA-URM) estimated that approximately US$3.8 billion was remitted in that period.[28] In 1992, the unofficial estimate of remittances, according to *Asian Migrant Forum*, was US$4.3 billion: more than the country's US$3 billion foreign debt, the US$2 billion trade deficit, or the US$1 billion fresh foreign investments.[29]

Annual remittances to Indonesia pale in comparison to the Philippines and other Asian labor-sending countries. George Cremer posits that the

TABLE 4.1

Workers' Remittances to Select Asian Labor-Receiving Countries
(US$ millions)

Year	Bangladesh	India	Indonesia	Pakistan	Philippines	Sri Lanka
1980	285.5	2743.6	—	2038.0	201.7	136.1
1981	366.8	2274.6	—	2056.5	251.0	203.4
1982	340.0	2599.9	—	2580.0	288.5	264.3
1983	642.4	2650.0	10.0	2926.0	179.0	274.5
1984	500.5	2279.0	53.0	2569.0	59.0	276.5
1985	502.1	2456.0	61.0	2525.0	111.0	265.5
1986	576.3	2223.0	71.0	2435.0	163.0	294.2
1987	747.8	2637.0	86.0	2170.0	221.0	312.8
1988	763.6	2295.0	99.0	1863.0	368.0	320.0
1989	758.0	2567.0	167.0	2008.0	360.0	330.7
1990	778.9	—	166.0	1997.0	262.0	362.5
1991	769.4	—	130.0	1542.0	329.0	401.3
1992	911.8	—	184.0	—	315.0	461.7

Source: Asian Development Bank, 1994.

relatively small value of Indonesian remittances is due to the lateness with which Indonesia entered the labor export market, and that most Indonesian workers were and are in low-wage occupations.[30]

Researchers of transnational labor migration agree that official remittance figures generally are inaccurate because of undercounting[31] and misclassification of remittances by labor-sending states and transnational organizations such as the IMF.[32] In theory, migrant remittances benefit labor-sending states by increasing foreign exchange earnings, national savings and investment, and migrant families' income. The remittance figures in table 4.1 are significant, at the very least, in the reduction of several labor-sending states' balance of payments deficits.[33]

In the early 1980s, remittances were considered so important to the foreign exchange earnings of Asian labor-sending states that a variety of policies were implemented to maximize the flow of remittances through formal banking channels: e.g., establishing overseas bank subsidiaries that offered special exchange rates and eliminating bank commission fees for migrant remittances. In the Philippine case, President Marcos issued the 1983 Executive Order (EO) No. 857, known as the Forced Remittance Law, that required all migrants to remit between 50 and 70 percent of their earnings through formal Philippine banking channels. State coercion took the form of threatening to confiscate migrants' passports and denying future exit permits from the country. Two years later, the EO was repealed as a result of rising protests from migrant workers overseas. In 1983, the unofficial estimate of remittances was US$944.45 million.[34]

The continuation of labor out-migration policies was questionable during the mid-1980s when Middle East states undertook steps to restructure their economies in response to declining oil revenues, the completion of infrastructural projects, and the growing political and social costs associated with maintaining a system of labor apartheid and rigid control of both citizens and foreign workers. Emphasis was placed on human resource development or higher level skills training for Middle East nationals in order to decrease dependence on foreign labor.

From the perspective of Asian labor-sending states, it was fortuitous that Middle East demands for low-wage migrant labor continued to increase even though demands for higher-wage migrant labor decreased. For instance in 1975, Kuwaitis employed 11,921 female domestic workers from Asia. By 1989, there were approximately 100,000 to 120,000 foreign female domestic workers in a population of less than two million Kuwaitis.[35]

In spite of the Gulf War, the migration of Filipino workers to the Middle
East continued relatively unabated. The Overseas Workers Investment Fund
(OWI) was established in 1991 to facilitate migrant remittances. Filipino
workers were encouraged to send remittances to OWI via commercial banking channels. Recipients in the home country could withdraw funds in the
form of certificates issued by the Central Bank to be cashed at commercial
banks, or kept for more than a year to earn a high interest rate between
18–20 percent.[36]

Significantly, as the demand for low-wage labor increased, so too did the
in-migration of foreign female domestic workers. The transition from high
to low wage, or "skilled" to "unskilled" labor also meant the transition from
predominantly male to predominantly female workers. The inextricable
association between female servants and low-wage "unskilled" labor results
from the patriarchal belief that housework performed by women is unskilled
work at best, or invisible work, at worst. Nonetheless, it is assumed that
women are more skilled than men in performing "unskilled" work.

The labor-sending states of Bangladesh and Pakistan banned the out-
migration of female servants in 1983, in response to escalating public
demands for the protection of women from abusive employers overseas.
The labor gap was quickly filled, in part, by Indonesian women. At that
time, the Indonesian state had just entered the labor export market and
subsequently encountered difficulties in placing its nationals within an
increasingly competitive low-wage migrant labor environment. In lieu of
the South Asian policy shifts, the Indonesian state began rigorously to promote Indonesian women as servants.

In that year, women constituted 63 percent of all Indonesian migrant
workers in the Middle East. Four years later, 81 percent of all Indonesian
migrant workers were women, and it was estimated that more than 80 percent of the women were domestic servants (see table 4.2).[37]

The data for Indonesian female workers outside of the Middle East
do not accurately reflect the number of illegal Indonesian female workers
in Malaysia. In the early 1980s, it was estimated that between approximately 100,000 and 300,000 Indonesian women and men worked illegally in Malaysia.[38]

The low-wage foreign migrant labor demands of the Middle East were
matched increasingly by Asia as Japan led a pack of Asian industrializing
countries in the race to capture transnational capital and markets. The "fly-
ing wild geese" phenomenon encouraged Hong Kong, and later Singapore

TABLE 4.2
Indonesian Migrant Workers

Region	1983		1984		1985		1986		1987	
	Women %	All Workers N	Women %	All Workers N	Women %	All Workers N	Women %	All Workers N	Women %	All Workers N
Middle East	63	17,899	65	28,702	81	48,289	84	42,107	87	48,837
Outside of Middle East[a]	7	28,960	19	37,857	11	56,687	4	46,194	17	59,362

Source: adapted from Cremer, "Deployment of Indonesian Migrants," p. 75.
a. Including Singapore, Malaysia, Netherlands, and others.

and Malaysia, to upgrade their economies and workforce to higher value-added and skill-intensive work. Rapid economic growth has created labor markets in these Asian countries in which "guest" workers are segregated in what the Japanese call "3D" jobs (dirty, dangerous, and difficult) in construction, agriculture, entertainment, and domestic service.[39]

Specifically, the growth of the middle classes in Malaysia, Singapore, and Hong Kong, continues to stimulate the mass out-migration of domestic workers, especially from the Philippines, Indonesia, Thailand, and Sri Lanka. In the late 1980s, approximately 76 percent of all Asia-bound Indonesian women, and 60 percent of all Asia-bound Filipinas, migrated as servants.[40] By 1993, approximately 1.4 million women from Bangladesh, Brunei, Indonesia, People's Republic of China, the Philippines, Sri Lanka, and Thailand, worked as servants throughout Asia and the Middle East.[41]

Within the last few years, NGOs concerned with foreign female domestic workers' welfare report rising transnational incidence of physical, emotional, and sexual abuse by employers. Abuse occurs within a context of noninterference by most labor-sending and labor-receiving states.[42] To be sure, the absence of national labor legislation and bilateral and multilateral agreements on foreign female domestic workers' rights allow many forms of employer-related abuse to continue unchallenged.[43]

Aside from the phenomenon of abusive employers, the migratory and employment mechanisms also contribute to the dehumanization of foreign female domestic workers. The rest of this chapter examines the mutually reinforcing processes of the dehumanization and commoditization of Filipina and Indonesian domestic servants that inhere in the policies and actions of state and nonstate actors involved in the Malaysian-Philippine-Indonesian maid trade.

Actors and Migratory Mechanisms in the
Malaysian-Philippine-Indonesian Maid Trade

As previously stated, the in-migration of several hundred female servants began in the late 1970s and has increased exponentially since the mid-1980s. Table 4.3 delineates the number of work permits issued to Filipina and Indonesian servants by the Immigration Department in Malaysia.

The Philippine and Indonesian labor attachés who were interviewed for this study respectively argued that in early 1994 there were approximately 30,000 Filipina and 40,000 Indonesian women working legally as domestic servants in Malaysia. The incredible increase in foreign domestic workers from 1991, or even from the mid 1980s, to 1994 is a controversial issue that can be resolved if and when the Immigration Department releases data by nationality and year. The Department, which is controlled by the Home Affairs Ministry, continues to be extremely secretive of the data, especially given the modern history of interethnic relations.[44]

Below, I discuss the five major sets of actors—representatives from the labor-sending and labor-receiving states, DOMs, employers, and foreign female domestic workers—to ascertain how Filipina and Indonesian servants are treated, and why there is a relative absence of moral outrage.

Labor-Sending State Representatives

Since the site of fieldwork was in Kuala Lumpur, I was not able to interview policymakers in the Philippines or Indonesia. I did, however, interview labor attachés at the Philippine and Indonesian Embassies in Kuala Lumpur.[45] The attachés, both of whom were men, said that it was their responsibility to report the demands for, and the working conditions of, migrant women back to their home countries. They also argued that their respective countries' sluggish economies coupled with the relatively higher wages offered in Malaysia, were responsible for the in-migration of their female nationals.

The labor-sending state representatives consistently used the noun "deployment," with its militaristic connotations, in reference to the out-migration of their female nationals. Increasingly, the term is favored by many scholars and policymakers in discussions of labor out-migration policies.[46]

The noun "deployment" conjures images of female migrants sent abroad by the Philippine and Indonesian states for the purposes of combating economic crises.[47] Competition between the Philippine and Indonesian representatives to promote their female nationals as domestic servants in Malaysia

TABLE 4.3
Domestic Servant Work Permits Issued by the Immigration Department

Nationality	1985	1986	1987	1988	1989	1990	1991
Indonesians	192	394	86	437	524	498	585
Filipinas	3,743	60	2,902	534	1,158	5,340	6,460

Source: adapted from Pillai, *People on the Move*, p. 51.

was evident in the interviews. Below are examples of the male interviewees' perceptions of their womenfolk:

> Our women give less problems than maids from other countries . . . you won't get any problems if you hire our maids, unlike the problems with [–] maids.

> [–] women maintain the edge in the domestic service market because they are educated, they work harder and they are better trained, which is why employers prefer them.

When I asked if male nationals could travel abroad to work as domestic servants, the answers were emphatically in the negative. Instead of identifying the particular *gender* and the occupational sector(s) for which the Malaysian state *only* would issue work permits, the labor-sending state representatives explained in a characteristically gendered manner that "men are not dexterous enough," "men are not docile," and "men do not know how to do housework properly."

The promotion of female nationals as servants betrays at least one official rationale for encouraging overseas employment. Upon returning to their home countries, migrants are expected to serve as agents of change or modernization by "diffusing" new skills training that they have learnt while working abroad. If state promotion of the out-migration of female domestic labor is based on women's "natural" ability to perform housework, then what else can women learn in terms of improving their skills? To argue that women voluntarily migrate as servants is to obscure the fact that domestic service is one of a handful of low-wage labor intensive occupations legally open for them in Malaysia.[48]

Explanations and policies based on the push-pull/equilibrium perspective are inherently flawed since they are premised on the belief that free market forces will bring about equilibrium in population distribution and wages. The theory and practice of transnational labor migration according to an "osmotic"-like movement masks the role of states and DOMs in the transnationalization of migrant female domestic workers. Within the context of labor-sending states' reliance on migrant remittances, and the emphasis in the private sector on the accumulation of profits, states and DOMs filter information in a manner that privileges the positive aspects of overseas work. I am not arguing that labor-sending states do not try to address female nationals' complaints of abuse. Rather, the responses of the Philippine and Indonesian state representatives were shaped or constrained, for the most part, by the perceived advantages accrued from labor out-migration and, to be sure, the fact that domestic workers' relations with Malaysian employers are beyond the jurisdictional boundaries of the Philippine and Indonesian legal systems. Given the choice between marketing female domestic workers or protecting their welfare, labor-sending states almost always privilege the former.[49]

Labor-sending state representatives in Malaysia have the responsibility to investigate female nationals' complaints of abuse. The Philippine representative tries to arbitrate relations between Malaysian DOMs and Filipina servants. Even though he is not empowered by Malaysian law to discipline abusive employers, still he insisted that he could blacklist DOMs in Kuala Lumpur and Manila by refusing to authenticate Filipinas' travel documents. Yet, he failed to give me an approximate number of DOMs that had been blacklisted thus far. Many Filipinas with whom I spoke on this subject insisted that they did not report abusive employers and DOMs to the embassy, as they had no expectations that the embassy would help them.

The Indonesian representative informed me that he personally traveled to employers' houses to investigate complaints. In the several cases that he cited, he insisted that although Malaysian employers were abusive, Indonesian servants also were lazy. The impression I received from the interview was that the servants' attitudes and/or behavior incited abuse.

Discussions on ways to circumvent abuse ultimately took the form of downplaying incidences of abuse: "Only a few cases," "Of course, there are bad employers, but it is rare," "They can always come here [to the embassy] or report to us if they are not well treated by their employers." Indeed in theory, foreign domestic workers can leave their employers' houses to take a taxi or bus ride to their respective embassies with the intent of reporting abusive employers. In practice, servants who are not given any rest days and who are prohibited from using the telephone, receiving visitors, or leaving employers' houses, are physically unable to report incidences of abuse.

There are no official statistics on employer-related abuses. NGOs involved in counseling foreign female domestic workers argue that there are anywhere between five and ten unreported cases of abuse for every documented case.[50] In 1993, the Malaysian Immigration Department released statistics on employers who were prosecuted under Section 56 (1) (d) of the Immigration Act 1959/1963. A total of 174 employers were prosecuted in 1985. By 1992, the number had risen to 978. Employers were prosecuted for various offenses such as "stealing" other employers' servants, hiring illegal migrant servants, and neglecting to renew foreign domestic workers' work permits.[51] There are no available statistics on the specific number of employer-related abuse cases, the nature and frequency of abuse, and/or cases that were prosecuted for abuse.

The POEA established basic requirements such as servants' base salary and number of rest days per month. Work contracts must be signed prior to women's departure from the Philippines.[52] Since the Malaysian state is not legally bound to recognize contracts that are signed overseas, Filipina servants generally are given lower salaries and fewer rest days. Indonesia has yet to negotiate a standardized contract similar to the POEA contract (see following section on DOMs). As of 1994, Indonesia had not negotiated a standardized contract similar to the POEA contract. Overall, the labor-sending state representatives argued that incidences of employer-related abuse were statistically insignificant in comparison to 30,000 Filipina and 40,000 Indonesian domestic workers in Malaysia.

Labor-Receiving State Representatives

Just as the Philippines and Indonesia stand to benefit in economic and noneconomic terms from the out-migration of their female nationals, Malaysia also benefits in a variety of ways. According to a Malaysian male official who insisted on anonymity as the precondition to speaking with me in 1994, the labor in-migration policy allowed *only* Filipina and Indonesian women (not Sri Lankans or women from other nationalities) to enter and work as domestic servants because of "economic cooperation" between Malaysia and the Philippines and Indonesia. Particularly in the last few years, there have been high-level official talks on establishing "growth triangles" such as the Singapore-Johor-Riau growth triangle in which Singapore supplies the infrastructure and skilled labor, while Johor (Malaysia) and Riau (Indonesia) respectively offer low-wage labor, in addition to land.[53]

The history of interethnic relations in Malaysia is the other important but unacknowledged reason for the in-migration of servants from the Philippines and Indonesia. It is quite probable that the mass in-migration of Sri Lankan, Indian, Thai, or Chinese servants is discouraged especially since it could tilt the population distribution in favor of Malaysian Indians and Chinese.

The in-migration of male servants is strictly prohibited on the grounds that "it would create social problems."[54] When I mentioned that there appeared to be more Indonesian than Filipina servants working legally and illegally in Malaysia, I was told by the same state official that: "We let more Indonesians in because Indonesians are more skilled at doing domestic service. So, it depends on comparative advantage. . . ."[55] If we are to believe the

Malaysian representative's statement, then a person's ability to perform paid housework depends not only on gender but nationality as well. The irony is that the presumably higher-skilled Indonesian servants are paid RM300–330 per month, while Filipina servants earn RM500 per month.

The Malaysian state allows, if not encourages, the in-migration of Filipina and Indonesian domestic workers for political and economic reasons. Foreign servants serve as boundary-markers of and for the expanding Malay and non-Malay middle classes in a development era in which the NEP, hence the Malay/UMNO-controlled state, had been criticized for failing to improve the socioeconomic welfare of Malays in particular, and Malaysians in general.

From an economic perspective, the in-migration of domestic workers ensures "low reproductive costs" since the state does not need to pay costs incurred in migrant labor subsistence prior to migration. Subsequently, foreign servants underwrite working-class Malaysian women's participation in the formal economy. Filipina and Indonesian servants' presence delays political pressure on the state elite to provide public child care centers or to encourage Malaysian employers' patronage of privately owned child care centers (see chapter 6).

State-designated short-term contracts (a two-year contract with an extension of an additional and final year) deny foreign domestic workers the right to change employers without prior official approval, keep wages low, and facilitate the repatriation of migrant workers during economic downturns.[56] To offset administrative costs, annual immigration levies are imposed for all categories of foreign workers. In 1994, every foreign female domestic worker or her employer was required to pay a levy of RM360 per annum.[57]

Even with these various control mechanisms in place, Filipina and Indonesian domestic workers' activities in public space are monitored closely. Intent on reducing the population of illegal male and female migrant workers, police and immigration officials conduct raids on known illegal migrant hideouts.[58] The raids, considered as preventive measures in anticipation of future economic downturns, are intended to reduce the number of illegal migrants who could become a social, economic, and political burden. Illegal male and female migrants who are captured are sent to one of eight immigration depots to await deportation, or potential Malaysian employers.[59]

Illegal migrants have been identified as perpetrators of the majority of crimes such as murder, theft, and rape that are committed by foreigners in the country.[60] Newspapers report that both legal and illegal domestic workers, in particular, have participated in "house theft rings" and prostitution.[61] During the period of my field research from January to June 1994, state authorities raided farmers' markets, discotheques, shopping malls, churches, and mosques in search of servants who had failed to register with the Immigration Department; who moonlighted as prostitutes; and/or who operated illegal hawker stalls.[62]

State surveillance of Filipina and Indonesian domestic workers' public behavior extends to the control over women's bodies. Foreign servants are required to undergo three medical examinations: once before arrival in the country, once during the first six months of employment, and once before the end of the two-year contract prior to the renewal of a third and final year of paid housework. The medical examinations are designed to prevent pregnancy and the spread of sexually transmitted diseases.[63] According to the Immigration Department, a foreign servant would be subject to deportation within twenty-four hours of the disclosure of pregnancy because it is "not only morally unacceptable but also against immigration laws."[64]

Male migrants, especially construction workers, who enjoy even greater mobility than domestic workers since they work in public space, and who engage in sexual relations with Malaysian women and/or foreign servants, are not subject to immediate deportation if and when their sex partners become pregnant. Most assuredly, the health policy for foreign female domestic workers, which protects Malaysians and migrant women against diseases, also frees Malaysian and foreign men from taking legal and moral responsibility for their acts of consensual sex with, or their sexual offenses against Filipina and Indonesian domestic workers.

Malaysian newspapers play an important role in sustaining the public's association of Filipina and Indonesian domestic workers with prostitution. Newspaper articles that report the sex-for-sale acts of some are generalized by the public to include all foreign female domestic workers.[65] For example, one Sunday, a friend of my family who was driving past a church in Kuala Lumpur saw a Malaysian friend and me conversing with a Filipina servant. He drove onto the church's driveway, opened his car door, and asked us to get into his car immediately.[66] When we did so, he admonished us for "hanging around low class prostitutes." According to him, certain churches and shopping malls in Kuala Lumpur were known as "get-together" sites for men in search of "foreign" sex. I asked him where and how he had gotten this kind of information. He replied, "the newspapers."

On a different Sunday evening, while I was having dinner with several Filipina servants in a shopping mall restaurant that was filled to capacity, the restaurant manager walked up to our table and said to the women, "Are you finished yet? Don't you see that there are people waiting in line for a table? Hurry up!" Louisa, a Filipina servant replied, "What! I don't have any money, ah?" My attention immediately shifted up from my field notebook to the manager who had not seen me earlier. He quickly and apologetically said to me, "Oh miss, I didn't know you were still eating with your friends. Please, take your time." Later, as I walked past the cashier counter, he muttered to a waitress, "I don't know what that young lady was doing with those prostitutes."

Official efforts to reduce the number of illegal and legal foreign female domestic workers who engage in criminal activities, coupled with sensationalized newsprint reports linking the women and "sex-for sale" acts, simultaneously sexualize and dehumanize migrant women's presence in Malaysian society. The net effect of consistent public discourse associating foreign female domestic servants with the lack of hygiene and morality, constructs and represents the women as workers who are undeserving of public sympathy, and as "social pariahs" who should be captured and placed in "depots" segregated from public space and activities. In spite of these negative representations, the Malaysian middle classes continue to demand the paid reproductive labor of Filipina and Indonesian women.

Middle Class Employers

The analysis in chapter 2 ascertained that the growth of the Malaysian middle classes since the 1970s was tied to the shift from a small to an expansive state, with greater demands for administrative and bureaucratic labor, as the expansion of the electronics and other related service industries was fueled by changes in the transnational economic structures and processes. While the NEP may have focused mostly on nurturing the Malay middle classes per se, the overall export-oriented development path has increased the number of Malay and non-Malay middle strata workers such as corporate managers, computer scientists, accountants, and other credentialed professionals.

Middle-class Malaysian demands for servants occur within the larger context of a national development path in which working- and middle-class women are given more opportunities to participate in public space. However, the practice of public patriarchy in Malaysia is evidenced from the fact that women, on the whole, continue to earn less than their male counterparts, and that women tend to predominate in occupations that emphasize and reaffirm notions of their perceived nurturing capabilities.

The practice of private patriarchy, similarly, reinforces the belief that women who work beyond the home are responsible still for housework and childcare. In the era of the transnationalization of migrant female domestic labor, many middle-class women merely have transferred this responsibility to foreign female domestic workers, and in the process middle class women become household supervisor-managers of Filipina and Indonesian servants. The gendered middle-class intersubjectivity that affirms women's domestic role is given legitimacy by key state policies and legislation. Chapter 6 demonstrates that in addition to pending legislation in 1994 to establish creches in working-class neighborhoods, specific pieces of state policy and legislation encourage middle-class working mothers to employ foreign female domestic workers as a solution to the issue of childcare.

Of importance is that as far as the majority of the sixty-eight employers interviewed in this study were concerned, foreign female domestic workers were more than substitute homemakers. Filipina and Indonesian servants were crucial to middle-class pursuit of distinctive lifestyles: the employment of foreign female domestic workers fell into one of three major categories considered indispensable for the construction of middle-class identity and entry into the "imagined community" of the Malaysian middle classes. Foreign female domestic workers simultaneously are substitute homemakers *and* symbols of Malaysian families' achievement of middle class-hood (see chapters 5 and 6).

Nearly 90 percent of the middle-class employers perceived hiring Filipina and Indonesian servants as similar to possessing or owning material items. The dehumanization of foreign female domestic workers is reflected in statements made by some middle-class employers:

> I pay her a salary every month. She lives in my house, so if I tell her to do something, she should do it.

> So long as she sleeps in my house, and I pay the bills, I own her.

> She prays ten times a day, nothing else gets done. This is my hard-earned money, you know. I told her that unless she finishes her work, she cannot go to sleep.

Unlegislated live-in domestic service perpetuates the perception that employers should have near absolute control over their employees. And indeed, some of them do. The absence of labor legislation clearly delimiting the conditions under which domestic workers perform paid housework reinforces employers' beliefs that they have the moral right to extract more labor from servants—especially since live-in domestic service requires employers to provide board and lodging in addition to monthly wages.

In order to recoup costs incurred in providing Filipina and Indonesian domestic workers with board and lodging, some employers even resort to conducting household food inventories and accordingly charge the servants for what they consume. Over the course of lunch in a Japanese restaurant, three middle-class friends, who employed foreign servants, engaged in a friendly banter about the perceived excesses of their servants, and how they had succeeded in curbing the servants' tendency to eat food in their refrigerators.

> *Suet Ling:* Why must we pay her a higher salary, she uses the electricity, eats our food, she sleeps in our house? It is not fair.
>
> *May Lan:* Hah, you think yours is bad—ah? Mine is worse. She eats our food all the time. The other day, I came home and half the *ayam goreng* [fried chicken] was missing. So, I scolded her.
>
> *Sandy:* Hey, I count the number of eggs in the refrigerator every night. If she wants to eat, she can pay for her own food.

The structures and processes of state-led export-oriented development that, conceivably, have freed many middle-class women from the burden of working both within and beyond the home, simultaneously have imprisoned some women's consciousness vis-à-vis members of the same sex who hail from a different class and nationality. At least 70 percent of 136 Filipina and Indonesian female domestic workers interviewed in this study complained of long work hours, lack of adequate food and proper sleeping accommodations, and no rest days. Employer mistreatment and abuse of foreign domestic workers is facilitated and reinforced not only by the absence of labor legislation, but also by the attitude and advice of DOM representatives.

Private Domestic Employment Agencies

DOMs are indispensable actors in the migratory chain. In neoliberal terms, DOMs are the free market institutions that, based on the free flow of information, accordingly meet employers' demands by supplying Filipina and Indonesian domestic workers.

DOMs can either be extra-legal or legal companies. Prior to state regulation, extra-legal DOMs were travel agencies that doubled as employment agencies.[67] Filipinas entered Malaysia on social visit passes, and proceeded to work illegally. In rare cases, employers could and did petition the Immigration Department to change their foreign servants' immigration status from that of a visitor to a worker.

The illegal route was and continues to be a more life-threatening way by which some Indonesian women contract with *taikong* or illegal labor brokers (who bypass all bureaucratic channels involved in the migration process) to bring them to Malaysia.[68] The illegal route or *jalan bawah* (underground road) entails long bus rides (generally in the middle of the night) from the interior of Java island, for example, to the coastal areas where migrants travel by boat across the ocean to the west coast of Peninsular Malaysia. Migrant women are sold (*jual*) by *taikong* to employers to repay their passage.[69] It may take months, or even a year or more, before the women repay the debts incurred from their passage, during which time they receive no wages.

The Philippine Ministry of Labour, the Indonesian Ministry of Manpower, the Malaysian Ministry of Human Resources, and the Immigration Department regulate DOMs as a way to curb illegal migration, and to prevent the loss of revenues to the state and legal DOMs.[70] Legal DOM fees for services provided to employers and domestic servants, are determined by the labor market. Filipina and Indonesian women respectively pay between RM1000-RM2000 and RM800-RM1500 to DOMs in the labor-sending states for processing travel and work documents. Many migrant women would borrow money or mortgage farm land and houses to pay for their passage.

In this era of the transnationalization of capital and production, DOMs are the informal banking institutions that finance transnational low-wage labor migration. Philippine and Indonesian DOMs buy the women's debts, which they then sell the debts to their Malaysian counterparts. The latter, in turn, deduct a certain amount from the women's salaries each month until the debts are cleared. Steep interest rates, between 3 to 10 percent per month, are added onto principal loan amounts. Some servants work for nearly six to eight months, if not more, before they actually receive their entire monthly salaries (even then, RM30 may be deducted per month to pay the immigration levy, if the Malaysian employer refuses to pay the fee).

Philippine and Indonesian DOMs prepare biographical data packages for Malaysian employers to peruse before making decisions on hiring migrant women. In one case, a DOM representative showed me a model contract that described a domestic worker's expected household tasks: "The Agency supplies the Maid only as a domestic maid to carry out the normal housekeeping duties such as washing, cooking, cleaning, babysitting, etc., and for no other purpose." The "etc." is precisely that which many foreign female domestic workers are compelled to perform. Included in a biographical data package given to me was a twenty-item questionnaire prepared by the DOM and completed by a Filipina or Indonesian woman. Among the questions were: "Are you willing to work if 50 per cent of your salary is deducted to pay your debt?" and "Are you willing to wash cars?" Some of the questions anticipate the nature of unlegislated domestic service, and expand the tasks required of a household servant to include physical work such as washing cars and cleaning storm drains outside of the house. It can be said that in the 1990s, there is no longer a gender division of labor in domestic service. Many female domestic workers today have and/or will assume the work of male chauffeurs and gardeners in Malaysia.

The legal process of hiring a Filipina or Indonesian servant in Malaysia is as follows. A prospective employer approaches a DOM which, in turn, communicates with its overseas affiliate. The Philippine and/or Indonesian DOMs will forward a completed biographical data package on each domestic worker (health examination, application form, completed survey questionnaire, and photograph) to the Malaysian DOM. The prospective employer reviews all biographical data packages and then chooses a worker, after which DOMs at the sending and receiving ends initiate the processes of obtaining exit and entry permits. State regulations insist that air travel for Filipina women must be contracted with national air carriers such as Malaysia Airlines or Philippines Airlines. Women from the nearby archipelago of Indonesia are allowed to travel by ferry (privately owned companies) or by air (Malaysia Airlines or Garuda Indonesia).

DOMs are responsible for ensuring that Filipina and Indonesian women fulfill the state's health requirement for work in Malaysian households. The following was stipulated in a contract that was given to me: "The medical examination will be held at *approved clinics appointed by the Agency* [i.e., DOM. The emphasis is mine]." Several domestic workers in this study admitted that they paid between RM50 and RM80 for health certifications without having to undergo any medical check-up. Some medical establishments and/or personnel profit from the in-migration of Filipina and Indonesian servants without so much as having seen the women.

Malaysian DOMs charge potential employers between RM2000 and RM2500 for a Filipina servant, and between RM2300 and RM3900 for an Indonesian servant. In 1994, a Filipina servant's salary was fixed at RM500.

POEA had previously set the salary at US$250 (or, approximately RM725) but DOM representatives argued that employers were refusing to pay the POEA-determined salary.[71] The "compromise" was RM500. Since the Indonesian state had yet to propose a base salary for Indonesian female domestic workers, DOM representatives insisted that Indonesian women's salary of RM300–330 per month be determined by "the market."

The relatively higher agency fees incurred in hiring an Indonesian woman were explained by representatives of several DOMs: "[B]ecause the Indonesian salary is less," and "We are buying them to tell you frankly." The logic is reversed in these cases: since employers pay less per month for Indonesian domestic servants, then DOMs are compelled to charge higher fees as self-compensation for the difference between Filipina and Indonesian women's salaries. One DOM's method of profit-making involved collusion with a potential employer. I was told the following in a telephone conversation: "Give RM2500, and also RM1400 for 'company fees.' So, altogether it is RM3900. You see, the RM1400 you get back from the maid. You deduct RM100 every month from the maid. Her basic salary is RM300 per month, so you just give her RM200, OK? I can give you two months extra, *so she'll work 26 months for 24-month pay* [emphasis mine]."

DOM-employer interactions are shaped by the use of specific language that makes the entire process of hiring a domestic worker similar to that of purchasing a product. I spoke with representatives of several DOMs just before the Raya holiday (*Hari Raya Puasa*) in which there was a rise in demand for Indonesian servants. Three DOM representatives respectively told me the following:

> I am out of stock this month, why don't you go for a Filipina?

> Call back in a few days, I'm working with the agency over there to replenish my supply.

> Oh my god, Christine! I'm so sorry. . . . I didn't forget you—lah. It's just because my people over there keep promising that I'll get a few soon. They don't know how to do business, you know or not? If they promise to give me the supply, then they must do so—lah. If they cannot, they must let me know in advance because I have customers waiting. OK, why don't you call my friend, maybe she'll help you. I'm so sorry.

Lani, a Filipina servant who operated a hawker's stall on her rest days (two Sundays a month) outside a church, said to me, "It's common sense, don't you know? If you open a business, the first thing is to make money. Look at me, I'm doing it also. But I'm different because I'm selling this [she points to magazines, soap, make-up, food, and so forth.]. *They* [DOMs] *are selling us* [emphasis mine]."

The business metaphor of exchanging goods for cash and profit is shaped by and shapes the way in which DOMs and employers relate to foreign domestic workers. Of interest is what happens when an employer does not like her "product." No DOMs offer refunds. Rather, they have what amounts to an exchange policy. Most offer a three to four month "probationary period" (according to several DOMs) in the event that an employer and an employee are not compatible. Beyond that, some DOMs do not provide any alternatives, while others encourage employers to send the servants back to the DOM for counseling, or in one case, "reeducation." I was told by a client (employer of a Filipina servant) of the particular DOM that "reeducation" meant an overnight stay at an agency house wherein the servant would be instructed to look down and away from the employer if and when the latter reprimanded her (regardless of the circumstances, the servant would always have to apologize to her employer).[72] A DOM representative could and would "slap" the migrant woman if she was sent back to the agency house for stealing her employer's possessions, or having sex with male household members.

DOMs encourage employers to perceive and treat foreign female domestic workers in specific ways. In the aftermath of the state's 1991 deportation threat, and heightened public discourse on the illegal/immoral sexual activities of Filipina and Indonesian servants, at least half of the twenty DOMs that I interviewed told their clients to give the domestic workers (with legal work permits) RM10–30 in lieu of a rest day away from the workplace. Representatives from three DOMs respectively advised me to treat my prospective servant in the following manner:

> Why let the girl out? Once a month is OK, but she doesn't really need a day off because she's staying in your house. And if she gets sick, take her to the doctor.

> Don't let your girl use the phone, and don't let her out of your house. It'll be better for you—lah.

> OK, I'll tell you the conditions. Keep her SPLP [restricted passport for exclusive travel between Indonesia and Malaysia], don't let her go to *pasar malam* [open-air night markets], and open a bank account for her and put her salary there, don't give it to her.

At best, DOMs construct Filipina and Indonesian domestic workers as children incapable of making decisions or as untrustworthy foreigners. At worst, DOMs construct and treat the women as commodities that are sold for profit. Aside from the nouns of "maid" and "servant," representatives of Chinese (Cantonese-speaking) owned and operated DOMs referred to the women as "girls" and "*mui tsai.*" DOM representatives and many Chinese employers' choice of the nouns "girls," and "*mui tsai*" reinforces the perception that adult migrants are children who do not have any rights, and who cannot not be trusted. Indonesian women and Filipinas respectively were called "*yan lay mui*" and "*bun mui.*"[73]

The *mui-tsai* system, as previously discussed, originated in China and was transplanted to Malaysia during colonial rule. Presently, Chinese-operated DOMs and Chinese employers' references to Filipina and Indonesian women as girl-slaves resurrect a feudal institution and attendant social relations. The following chapter examines in greater detail the ways in which some employers treat foreign female domestic workers as nothing more than slaves or personal property.

It should be noted that not all DOMs perceive workers this way and treat them in a dehumanizing manner. Representatives from at least two DOMs insisted that they occasionally called their servant-clients to check if the women needed advice or help in adjusting to a foreign environment. DOMs, in any case, play a major role in the maid trade. Their existence and profit margin depend on their ability to supply Malaysian demands for foreign female domestic workers.

Foreign Female Domestic Workers

Approximately 85 percent of 136 Filipina and Indonesian domestic workers in this study were young, single, and respectively came from rural areas of South and Central Luzon island in the Philippines, and the island of Java in Indonesia. Contrary to a 1988 study conducted on Filipina domestic servants, almost 90 percent of Filipina respondents (80 out of 89 Filipina women) in this study only had a secondary school education.[74] Also, unlike a more recent 1992 study on Indonesian servants, 90 percent of Indonesian respondents (42 out of 47 Indonesian women) in this study were single.[75] The discrepancies in age, marital status, and education level between respondents in my study and that of the other two studies conducted on foreign servants in Malaysia point to a growing belief among DOMs and employers that inexperienced young single women are easier to train and control than married or older women with more life experience. The advice of one employer to her friend who was agonizing over the selection of a foreign

worker best captured the general sentiment of employers on the most suitable and productive servants: "Get them young, get them stupid, and train
them."[76] Prior to migration, rural Filipinas farmed land with their families,
while their urban counterparts worked as office clerks, street hawkers, school
teachers, and nurses. Indonesian women, most of whom only received a primary school education, either were farmers ("*kerja kebun*") or were not
employed ("*duduk dirumah saja,*" "*tak buat apa-apa,*").[77] The two exceptions were an Indonesian university student who had to leave school because
her father passed away; and a government worker in Jakarta who filed a sexual harassment complaint against her male superior, only to lose her job
shortly afterward.

Married Filipina and Indonesian women's reasons for migration stemmed
from the need to escape socioeconomic powerlessness.[78]

Amy: My husband has many girlfriends and he doesn't care about the children and
       me any more. So I took the children to his mother's house and asked her to
       take care of them while I came over here to work.

'Bu Yati: My husband left us because he could not find a job to support his family
       [the bank repossessed his land when he could not service his loan]. I don't
       know where he is now. My cousin told me that I could find work here so I
       borrowed money to pay the *taikong*.

Renaldo: [Husband] drank a lot of alcohol. He would always beat me. I was very
       tired of it. His mother used to scold me because she said that I did not take
       care of him properly. How can I take care of him if I have no money and he
       doesn't give me any money.

Yas: He only cares about himself. He doesn't care about his parents who are get-
       ting old. He doesn't care about me. I have no choice. My children have to eat.

Married respondents' reasons for migration are revealing of the consequences of capitalist and/or patriarchal oppression.[79] In the case of 'Bu Yati,
capitalist expansion dislocated and disrupted rural social relations, in part,
by undermining her husband's ability to care for his family. A consequence
of the practice of patriarchal ideology helped to delimit how and why
Renaldo (whose mother-in-law failed to empathize with her problems), felt
that she had no other alternative but to migrate in order to escape shame,
humiliation, and poverty.

Single migrant women cited two major interrelated reasons for working in
Malaysia: higher pay and a more "comfortable" life. A comfortable life continues to be the picture largely conjured by DOM representatives in labor-
sending states who travel to villages and urban squatter settlements with

promises to the women that they will be working in wealthy households complete with "nice" employers and the latest modern amenities. As discussed shortly, some foreign female domestic workers reinforce this picture.

Filipina and Indonesian domestic workers insisted over and over again that DOMs were proficient in the art of lying to potential migrants and their families. Three Filipina servants said:

> *Mathilde:* They come and tell us . . . give us so much sweet talk . . . [Y]ou can have a good life and a very nice life overseas, good pay, television, videorecorder. . . .
>
> *Ruth:* They told me fantastic stories about making money. . . . They [stories] are not true. Deduct this, deduct that. . . . [A]t the end, no more money in my pocket.
>
> *Angelina:* They are all the same, they cheat and they lie. They will do and say anything to make money.

Mathilde and Angelina added that:

> *Mathilde:* Agency staff holds your neck. They pick you up at the airport, take your passport, and you don't see it anymore until you leave the country.
>
> *Angelina:* I'm not afraid of my employer. I'm afraid of the agency. They hold your passport.

Contrary to state regulation which insists that foreign female domestic workers retain possession of their legal travel documents, DOMs keep the women's passports (for Filipina women) and *Sijil Perjalanan Laksana Paspot* (for Indonesian women) as insurance against women who run away from their employers (presumably to prostitute themselves, or to work for different employers).[80] Contractual relations between employers and DOMs stipulate that either the agency or the employer retains the servant's legal travel document: "The Client is to ensure that all the maid's documents is [sic] in safe custody and to be kept at all times by the Client."

Malaysian employers also did not escape the domestic workers' criticisms. Ami, an Indonesian servant, was so disillusioned with her working environment that she made a promise to herself to forbid her younger sister to work in Malaysia: "I will never do this again. I will not renew my contract. I told my cousin [who was on his way back to Indonesia] to tell my mother that my sister must not come here to work as a servant [*pembantu rumah*]. I will make sure that she does not come over."[81]

Unlike Ami, most foreign domestic workers are not known to convey their negative experiences (dealing with DOMs and employers) back to their friends and/or family members in Indonesia or the Philippines. Ami and Margaret (a Filipina servant) reasoned that the servants would "lose face" if they did so. Caridad Tharan, a counselor and an activist for Filipina servants' rights, argues that:

> The desire to belong to the "in" group of *balikbayan* or the *maka*-abroad is strong. It means attaining a certain status or prestige among village folks and countrymen as a whole . . . He or she is someone who after a year or two of work overseas comes back with a stereo, video recorder, gold jewellery, imported food, apparel and household goods, etc. Hence, translating this image into a reality becomes a goal among many of the maids.[82]

The continuing out-migrating stream of Filipina and Indonesian female domestic workers contributes to sustaining the economic livelihood of their families and/or to conspicuous consumption. More than 90 percent of the women in this study remitted a portion of their salaries, anywhere from one-fifth to one-half of monthly earnings—whenever possible—to their families back home.[83] The most frequent avenue of remittances was that of family (especially in the case of Indonesian servants) or friends who were on their way back home. Interviewees said that remittances were used to purchase anything from construction costs for housing, to basic necessities (food and clothing) and the most modern consumer items such as cameras and compact disk players.

"Economic Soldiers, Commodities, and Prostitutes": Contemporary Representations of Foreign Female Domestic Workers

Since the 1970s, the global move to encourage open markets and free trade for manufactured goods also has come to involve the creation and maintenance of open markets for foreign migrant labor. Analysis of the Malaysian-Philippine-Indonesian maid trade illustrates the manner in which the market for female domestic workers in Southeast Asia is constructed and maintained by states and key nonstate actors.

The Philippines and Indonesia establish agencies to oversee the out-migration of their female nationals. Labor attachés of diplomatic missions in Malaysia monitor and report Malaysian demands for domestic workers back to the home country. DOMs that are licensed by labor-sending and labor-receiving states assume the responsibility for supplying servants to Malaysian employers who, in the context of unlegislated domestic service, buy not only the services but also the persons of Filipina and Indonesian domestic workers.

Analysis of the migratory and consequent employment mechanisms of foreign domestic workers explains how and why the women are dehumanized as they leave their home countries to work in Malaysia. For the different actors in the Malaysian-Philippine-Indonesian maid trade, the social construction and representation of domestic workers as economic soldiers, commodities, and/or prostitutes are effective in obfuscating, and paradoxically, morally legitimizing the demeaning ways in which the women are treated. Phrased differently, while I (and, to be sure, many Filipina and Indonesian servants) would argue that various aspects of the transnationalization of migrant female domestic workers are morally reprehensible, state and nonstate actors in the maid trade would insist that their policies and actions in fact are morally sound.

The Philippine and Indonesian attachés' statements portray migrant women as economic soldiers deployed to battle personal and national economic problems. Men do not qualify to migrate as servants because they do not possess women's perceived natural ability to wield brooms, mops, and dish sponges.

Labor out-migration policies demonstrate how the Ricardian concept of comparative advantage has come to intersect the gender ideology of housework as naturally women's work in an era of open markets and free trade. Labor-sending states export what is perceived to be their comparative advantage, i.e., female domestic servants. To borrow a phrase from Ferdinand Marcos's speech on the Philippine state's policy of promoting overseas employment in 1983, female domestic workers indeed are the "new heroes" of the emerging new world order which is to be constituted primarily from harmonizing gendered national economies with regional and global economies.[84] In this context, it is no wonder that labor-sending states are not effective in addressing the exploitative migratory mechanisms, or the conditions in which foreign female domestic workers exchange labor for wages since their continued out-migration is premised on the greater good of the labor-sending states, economies, and societies.

In spite of reports that document abuse, labor-sending states justify the continued out-migration of female nationals on the grounds that such a policy facilitates migrant women's ability to be gainfully employed as it relieves the political, economic, and social pressures of restructuring national economies. In sum, labor out-migration policies are expected to help peoples to pursue the good life as defined and promoted by neoliberalism. Other free market institutions, such as commercial banks that handle migrant remittances, transportation corporations, and medical institutions that provide health certificates, can only accrue economic benefits from the maid trade.

The perception, attitude, and behavior of DOMs are even more destructive in the sense that Filipina and Indonesian female domestic workers are spoken of and treated as "goods" that are sold, bought, owned, out of stock, or that need replenishing. This particular metaphor of domestic workers as commodities legitimizes and sustains the construction and treatment of Filipina and Indonesian domestic workers as inanimate objects that are traded on the transnational and national markets.

The complicity of labor-sending and labor-receiving states in this process cannot be denied since state agencies are responsible for licensing and regulating (or not) the conduct of DOMs. The absence of bilateral agreements between states, combined with the labor-receiving state's refusal to extend legislative protection to domestic workers, essentially give DOMs the *carte blanche* to conduct business as deemed appropriate. DOMs in this study not only justify their high brokerage fees as compensation for the time and effort expended in ensuring an uninterrupted supply of domestic workers, but also freely dispense advice to employers on how to manage foreign servants. Denying servants the right to keep their travel documents, rest days, telephone privileges, and so forth are not considered abusive behavior. Rather, DOMs and employers perceive their actions as morally acceptable since they conceivably prevent servants from interacting with criminal elements in society.

In postcolonial Malaysia, state authorities opened the immigration gates so that Filipina and Indonesian domestic workers could subsidize the labor force participation of working- and middle-class Malaysian women. This is especially important in a social context in which many male employers are known to refuse to assume their share of the responsibility for performing domestic labor, while the state elite are unprepared to encourage the middle classes to use childcare centers and/or to hire day or part-time domestic workers. Official regulation of the in-migration and employment of foreign domestic workers is part of the strategy of consent that constructs the boundaries of the Malaysian middle classes, and that persuades the middle classes to pursue a particular version of the good life characterized by the consumption of goods and services, including commodified foreign female domestic workers supplied by the transnational maid trade.

The ever-increasing numbers of Filipina and Indonesian female domestic workers have prompted state authorities to circumscribe the movement

124   THE MAID TRADE

and activities of foreign servants in public space. Malaysian public discourse that constructs foreign servants as criminals, particularly as prostitutes, is legitimized by, and legitimizes the official policy of public surveillance of foreign female domestic workers. The control of Filipina and Indonesian servants is seen as necessary for the greater good of Malaysian society *and* foreign domestic workers.

In the following chapter on employer-domestic worker relations in the household, I ascertain further how and why the interplay between negative public discourse of foreign servants, and the uneven distribution and exercise of power inherent in unlegislated live-in domestic service, reinforce public and private notions that Filipina and Indonesian domestic workers are objects to be controlled and/or used as employer-owners so pleased. Filipina and Indonesian servants however are not passive recipients of abuse. They respond in a variety of ways that challenge employers' perceptions and consequent treatment of foreign women as lesser humans.

Notes on the Epigraphs

(In order of appearance): Fernand Braudel, *Afterthoughts on Material Civilization and Capitalism*, trans. by Patricia M. Ranum (Baltimore: Johns Hopkins University Press, 1977), p. 63; Cynthia Enloe, *Bananas, Beaches and Bases: Making Feminist Sense of International Politics* (Berkeley: University of California Press, 1989), p. 196.

Some Scenes from Everyday Life in Kuala Lumpur

(Top) Proprietor of a roadside market displays her wares; (bottom) Filipinas buying miscellaneous goods and food from roadside businesses setup by compatriots.

Photos by the author.

Some Scenes from Everyday Life in Kuala Lumpur

Filipina lights candles.

Photo by the author.

Some Scenes from Everyday Life in Kuala Lumpur

Malaysian vendors in an open-air market, east of downtown
Kuala Lumpur.

Photo by the author.

CHAPTER 5

Infrapolitics of Domestic Service: Strategies of, and Resistances to, Control

A maid has to be trained and initiated into the running of your household. . . . Once [sic] of the major problems people face is on the treatment of domestic help. Are they to be treated as equals? I would be inclined to say NO! The relationship is similar to a managing director and his chauffeur.
—Mrs. T. D. Ampikaipakan, "Social Etiquette" Columnist of The *Star, 1993*

Sometimes I tell her [employer] not to scream at me. I have ears, I am not deaf. Last time, she used to scold me, but now, no more. I told her that I am good at doing my work. I am proud of my work. If she tell[s] me to do something, she only tell[s] me once and I do it. I told her, "Don't follow me around and check on my work. What I steal your things for? If I want to steal, I will be a thief, OK? Not a maid!"
—"Louisa," a Filipina domestic worker in Kuala Lumpur, April 1994

Filipina and Indonesian servants' working relations and conditions in the 1990s are markedly different from Chinese *amahs* of the past. Neither state authorities nor employers prevented *amahs* from reconstructing their social networks of *chi mui* ("sisters") in Malaya. Ethnoreligious proximities of many employers and *amahs* also shaped employer-domestic worker relations: informal rules of interaction checked employers' exercise of power and control in the household.

Today, Filipina and Indonesian servants have neither the freedom to move about in public space nor the mutual understanding with their employers (even when some are from similar ethnoreligious backgrounds) about informal or unwritten rules of conduct. State authorities' raids on public places that are frequented by foreign female domestic workers, and press coverage of arrests of illegal and legal foreign domestic workers who engage in illegal activities, exacerbate the already unequal distribution and exercise of power in employer-servant relations.

In the attempt to prevent legal problems that can and do arise from hiring Filipina and Indonesian servants who are accused of committing illegal/criminal acts on their rest days, Malaysian female employers become supervisor-spies in the private-domestic domain. The interplay of public and private surveillance reinforces the notion that Filipina and Indonesian domestic workers are objects to be controlled rather than workers who exchange domestic labor for wages.

The social construction of foreign female domestic workers as criminals at best, and as objects as worst, portrays a picture of Filipina and Indonesian women as passive victims powerless to challenge or to change the perceptions, attitudes, and behavior of employers. Several important questions arise from such a picture: How do the domestic workers perceive their relationship with employers and even with the Malaysian public? Can and do the women challenge incidences in which they are mistreated and abused by their employers, and also the overall negative representations of their presence in society? If so, how?

This chapter presents an analysis of employer-servant relations from the perspective of the infrapolitics of domestic service. Infrapolitics denote the politics of marginalized or subordinate groups such as peasants, slaves, and servants.[1] Normally, infrapolitical activities are not openly expressed, mainly because of existing power imbalances that inhere in the dyadic relationships of the master-slave, landowner-peasant, and employer-domestic worker.

It is important to emphasize that infrapolitical activities are not defined only by the subordinate party's challenges to the conditions under which labor is exacted by the dominant party. Rather, infrapolitical activities embody contestations over the processes of identity construction, of which the symbolic and material dimensions of class are intertwined with gender, race-ethnicity, religion, and nationality.

Analysis of the infrapolitics of subordinate groups involves identifying and juxtaposing what are called the "public" and "hidden transcripts." In the case of domestic service, the public transcript refers to the ways in which employers overtly establish their superiority within and beyond the workplace, and servants' subsequent manifest acts of deference/subservience/acquiescence. It is the story of domestic service narrated from the perspective of the dominant party: "The public transcript is, to put it crudely, the *self* portrait of dominant elites as they would have themselves seen."[2]

In my conversations with employers, and also my observations of employer-servant relations, I find two key interrelated characteristics in the public transcript of domestic service in Malaysia. First, the employment and supervision of foreign female domestic workers facilitate the construction of middle-class identity in the domestic domain. Second, and within the context of negative public discourse and various punitive measures of the Immigration Department, employers have assumed uncritically the role of domestic spies of foreign servants. Certain types of employer-related abuse result from the combination of employer supervision and surveillance of Filipina and Indonesian servants.

The hidden transcript consists of what the domestic workers say and do beyond the realm of the public transcript. It is Filipina and Indonesian domestic workers' version of how and why they are treated in particular ways, and their responses to employers' behavior. Inherent in the hidden transcript of domestic service are the infrapolitical activities of servants, or "forms of disguised, low profile, undeclared resistance" carried out singularly and collectively by Filipina and Indonesian women who are denied legal protection and rights as workers and as human beings.[3]

The chapter begins with a brief discussion of conceptualizing domestic workers as political actors. This is followed by an examination of key characteristics of the public transcript of domestic service. In the final section, the hidden transcript is made visible and analyzed, i.e., Filipina and Indonesian servants' responses that attempt to redefine, successfully and unsuccessfully, the material and symbolic conditions in which they perform paid reproductive labor.

Maids as Political Actors?

Mainstream political theorists since the Aristotelian era conceptualize and legitimize the conduct of politics, a key dimension of social life, as an activity located solely in the public domain. In classical political philosophy, the public domain that embodied political space, life, and activities was reserved for men whose civil-political rights were constituted by and constituted their ability to move freely between the public and private/domestic domains.[4] In this class-based and gendered schemata, women were constructed and segregated in the domestic domain as nonpolitical persons whose roles and status were predetermined by their capacities to reproduce and nurture future generations.

Even in modern times, with the granting of suffrage to women in Europe and North America, the notion of what constitutes politics and who can be political actors depends on the public-private distinction. The underlying assumption is that men are always political actors and that women, only when they act in public space—i.e., like men—can be political actors.[5]

In postcolonial Malaysia, state structures support the political participation of Malaysian men and women in public space and activities (whether it is "public" narrowly defined as the legislative arena, or "public" broadly conceptualized to include participation in the formal economy). Nevertheless through acts of omission and commission, foreign female domestic workers are not recognized and treated as political actors. While labor unions remain the major avenue of formal political participation for workers in many countries of the world including Malaysia, state authorities prohibit all categories of migrant or "guest" workers from participating in organized labor. In 1993, a representative of the Johor state government said that, "If workers insist on forming unions to represent their interests, employers can refer the matter to the Immigration Department or the Home Ministry for further action."[6]

The irony, in the case of foreign female domestic workers, is that the state's ban on the unionization of migrant workers is moot since labor legislation does not even consider servants as workers. Filipina and Indonesian servants in Malaysia, indeed, are victims in the sense that they cannot act in ways that we have come to expect of workers who express their grievances via formal political channels, and who physically, and at times forcibly or aggressively, renegotiate power relations in the workplace by participating in collective action such as strikes.

We cannot assume, however, that all domestic workers are powerless to redefine employer-employee relations, hence they succumb to the dominative and exploitative aspects of unlegislated domestic service. The denial of civil-political rights does not necessarily preclude the fact that foreign female domestic workers can be political actors who engage in different forms of resistance that challenge or renegotiate employer-employee relations. James C. Scott warned of the consequences of retaining a narrow conception of political action as organized action that overtly challenges the rule of dominant elites:

> So long as we confine our conception of the political to openly declared forms of resistance, then we are driven to conclude that subordinate groups essentially lack a political life or that what political life they do have is restricted to those exceptional moments of popular explosion. Unfortunately, to believe so is to miss the immense political terrain that lies between quiescence and revolt and that, for

better or worse, is the political environment of subject classes. It is to focus on the visible coastline of politics and miss the continent that lies beyond.[7]

Naomi Abrahams offers a reconceptualization of political action that takes into account the sets of everyday social relations in which occur the construction, exercise, and challenge to power in its material and non-material dimensions.

> The activities of daily life provide vast and important dimension to power relation processes in which significant, yet invisible political action occurs. . . . *[P]olitical action is defined as a form of human behaviour that involves the negotiation, alteration, or retrenchment of social values and resources* [italics mine]. Resources include, but are not limited to money, time, space, prestige, and deference. Values refer to the sets of expectations and beliefs which organize and inform a definition of the situation.[8]

This reformulation of political action transcends the notion that political space and activities are exclusively associated with the formal conduct of governance. Since any set of social relations that involves covert and overt (re)negotiation of power qualifies as political action, then the participants should be considered political actors.

Within the context of everyday life, the household is a political arena.[9] Especially in the performance and consumption of paid reproductive labor, the values and resources of employers—not domestic workers—dominate the conditions under which wages are exchanged for housework. The many ways in which employers establish their superior or dominant status, together with the domestic workers' responses, will be informative of the infrapolitics of domestic service in which Filipina and Indonesian servants challenge the unequal distribution and exercise of power in the household.

"Love to Hate Them, Hate to Love Them": The Public Transcript of Domestic Service

The public transcript of domestic service in Malaysia is dominated characteristically by the self-portraits of female as opposed to male employers. In spite of the growing "liberation" of Malaysian women in public space and activities (e.g., increases in the number of women in politics and business), they remain responsible for running the household.[10] Increasingly, middle-class women—whether or not they work beyond the home—are able to transfer the more laborious household tasks to foreign female domestic workers. In this study, only two out of sixty-eight employers were full-time homemakers. The employment of Filipina and Indonesian servants transforms middle-class Malaysian women into household supervisor-managers.

Significantly, the identity construction of the middle-class household supervisor-manager is one of two key self-portraits of female employers. As we will see later, the mass influx of foreign domestic workers in the country, coupled with surveillance of their movement in public space by state authorities, also engender self-portraits of middle-class female employers as domestic spies.

The Middle-Class Household Supervisor-Manager

Studies of women's relations to global, regional, and national capitalist development show that the expansion of capitalist social relations of production has different effects on the performance of reproductive labor in different social classes.[11] In relative terms, while working-class women confront the double burden of working within and beyond the house, middleclass women in advanced industrialized and industrializing societies are able to employ servants to relieve them of the more labor-intensive aspects of housework. Since a middle-class family generally can afford to hire only one servant, the employment of domestic workers by middle classes all over the world has changed the traditional master-servant relationship that prevails among aristocratic households in which servants at the bottom of the servant hierarchy are supervised by servants at the top who, in turn, answer directly to the master.

Scholars of late-nineteenth- and twentieth-century domestic service in the West argue that the mass employment of servants transforms middleclass women into household managers responsible for directing and evaluating the performance of their hired help. Inherent in the supervision of domestic workers are the processes by which occur the construction of middle-class identity.[12] In the United States and Latin America, middle-class female employers have been known to purchase linguistic/verbal, nonverbal, and spatial deference from their servants:

> The wife-servant relationship is founded on contradictions, and in order to keep the servant in her place, a host of mechanisms are often utilized to signal class differences. Through speech patterns, voice tone, obligation to wear a uniform, prohibition on eating certain foods, locking her in the house when the wife leaves, locking her out of special cupboards, disapproving of phone calls and visits, and by providing humble and sparsely furnished quarters, the wildly conflicting cur-

rents of personal intensity and cold disinterest found in many employing house-holds are kept under control.[13]

In postcolonial Malaysia, deference also has become an important aspect of the construction of middle-class identity.

Employer Purchase of Deference.   Encouraged by DOMs, Malaysian male and female employers instruct foreign domestic workers to address them respectively as "Sir" and "Mum." Employers, on the other hand, call their employees by the latter's first names.

Interviews in Malaysian employers' homes reveal the extent to which their children learn to use particular words to establish social superiority over servants. As Aishah, a Malay employer insisted, "I want my children to tell the maid what to do, and not have the maid tell my children what to do." Indeed, young children do "instruct" domestic workers. In one particular interview, while I spoke with a female employer in her living room, her seven-year old daughter told the servant to dig a hole in the garden so that the child could plant her chili seeds. All of a sudden, we heard the servant scream in pain. When we went out to the garden, we saw the young child hitting the servant with a small gardening spade. The child kept saying "Stupid, stupid, stupid. Mommy, look she is so stupid. I told her not to put water there. She didn't listen to me." The servant, who was kneeling on the earth, could only use her hands to shield her face against the child's spade.

During an interview with another female employer, her two sons, who had just returned from soccer practice, sat with us at the dining table and discussed different ways to draw comic book heroes. The older son (twelve years old) asked the servant, who was cooking lunch in the kitchen, to go upstairs to get his coloring pencils. She told him that she would do so as soon as she had finished cooking. He belligerently said, "I want it now. Are you *bodoh* [stupid]?" The servant stopped what she was doing and went upstairs to get his pencils.

In both instances, the mothers failed to reprimand their children. The for-eign domestic workers remained silent. These employers' behavior reinforces the socialization of their children into a particular kind of middle class-hood which expects women to be responsible for housework and legitimizes the attitude that foreign domestic workers do not deserve to be spoken to or treated with respect.[14]

Nonverbal deference in the household is equally distinctive. Filipina and Indonesian servants are instructed by DOMs and certain employers to look down at the ground when they are addressed by their employers; never to maintain eye contact with their employers; and to speak only when employers ask them questions. The more fortunate servants are considered pseudo-kin, or at the very least treated as strangers by the employing families. The less fortunate servants are invisible to employing families until and unless it is time to serve family members. These nonverbal acts are not at all dissimilar from that which Pamela Horn ascertained in the domestic worker class of the Victorian era in Great Britain.[15] Conceivably, Malaysian employers' expectations of such deference reflect a particular instance in which there appears to be little difference between the postcolonial and colonial mindset. It can be argued that the pursuit of modernity, as far as these employers are concerned, is synonymous with emulating the demeanor and Victorian values of their former colonial masters.

Foreign domestic workers in upper-middle-class Malaysian households have been known to wear uniforms that are patterned after those of European female servants: black dress or blouse and skirt, white aprons, and caps.[16] Paradoxically, uniformed servants in wealthy households may be slightly better off, in some instances, than their counterparts in middle-class households. Since wealthy families are able to employ several servants, no one servant is made to perform all household tasks. Although the uniforms mark Filipina and Indonesian women as "maids," nonetheless the women retain some notion of their status as human beings (of a lower class than employing family members, to be sure).

Employer purchase of spatial deference can be seen readily in public space and in employers' homes. Servants who accompany their employers on trips to shopping malls inevitably carry babies and/or bags while their employers freely peruse consumer goods. In country clubs, servants have the thankless responsibility of ensuring that young children abide by the clubs' swimming regulations while their employers relax with a game of golf, and/or chat with friends by the poolside.[17]

Servants' bedrooms in employers' homes are located on the ground floor of two story link or row houses. The allocation of living space in which employers occupy the upper floor while migrant women live on the ground-level, is a manifestation of power relations. Servants have little to no privacy: nearly all of the women interviewed said that while they were required to knock before entering any bedroom other than their own, employers failed to reciprocate. The less fortunate are not even allocated bedrooms. Instead, they are made to sleep in storage rooms with no ventilation or even along corridors outside kitchens. When employers' entertained guests in the home, the domestic workers were expected to remain in the kitchen and emerge only to serve meals.

From my field research, I discerned two additional ways in which employers purchased deference, i.e., by amplifying the faults of other employers, and by giving material gifts. Amplification of other employers' faults is most apparent when an employer shows her servant newspaper articles on the abuse of foreign domestic workers to reinforce, in the migrant woman, an appreciation for the conceivably decent and humane ways in which she is treated by her employer. In separate interviews conducted with Melina, Latifah, and Suet Ling, the three employers respectively described the way they used such articles:

> I cut out that article [on how a servant was punched and slapped by her employer] and told her to read it. I reminded her how lucky she was that we were so nice to her.

> I keep the newspapers [on abuse] so that when she doesn't behave properly I will show it to her.

> I gave her the papers and told her, "I treat you well, you should be grateful."

Whereas an employer's act of "sharing" newspaper articles with her servant carries an implied threat, the act of giving gifts to a servant appears to be an objectivation of the employer's sense of gratitude which, at the same time, "euphemizes" her superior economic status.[18] Swee Ping, a middle-class informant insisted that European and Malaysian employers had different motives for giving material gifts to domestic workers. She said to me while we were at an antique store selecting furniture for her friend Grace: "Come on, Christine. We all know why the Europeans do it. Do you really think that they care about their maids? They just want the maids to stay out of their way when they are in the house." Swee Ping's remarks implied that although some Malaysians abused their foreign domestic workers, Europeans couched their demeaning superior racial and class attitudes toward servants in material gifts. Grace, having heard Swee Ping's argument, quickly tried to explain why her husband Bill, a British expatriate, wanted her to buy presents for the Filipina servant. She said, "Bill tells me to get her whatever she wants so that she can be 'out of our hair.' It is difficult, you know-lah, having a stranger in the house. There is no privacy. She knows everything about us."

A brief discussion of an aspect of the hidden transcript (i.e., what domestic workers say and do in the absence of their employers) will help to illustrate how receiving gifts from employers allow Filipinas to rank their employers according to race. Over the course of an informal group discussion in a Kuala Lumpur shopping mall, several Filipina servants debated the virtues and vices of their employers. A group of servants who worked for European expatriates argued that their employers were better than Malaysians because Europeans provided their servants not only with clean and well-ventilated bedrooms (some servants even boasted of having air-conditioners in their rooms), but also television sets and videocassette players:

> *Catherine:* I hope you don't mind because I have to tell you, Christine. Chinese employers are very stingy. Please don't be offended because you are Chinese, but you are different from them [employers].
>
> *Louisa:* Why do you talk like that? She cannot be like them. [Louisa parodies her female employer in the manner in which her employer tries to apply eyeliner while conversing in a high squeaky voice to her husband]
>
> *Catherine:* The Chinese, they are very stingy. They never give enough food to eat, always complain. . . . [Y]ou can't do this, you can't do that.
>
> *Louisa:* All employers are good and bad. Do you think Europeans are better?
>
> *Catherine:* Of course, my employer [British] gives me air-con [air-conditioning unit in the bedroom], TV, and today she says she's going to buy a VCR so that I can watch videotapes.
>
> *Angelina:* Yes, my employer [Australian] rents videotapes for me to watch at night.
>
> *Louisa:* Think! Why she buy you all these things? Use your brain! She tells you not to come out of your room unless she calls you, am I right?
>
> *Catherine:* [nods her head]
>
> *Louisa:* You see, not all employers are good. Some Europeans are also bad. They want us to stay in the room, so they buy us TV. My former employer was British. OK, they buy for me, I accept!

Louisa chided Angelina and Catherine for failing to understand the reasons underlying the largess of some European employers. From Louisa's point of view, the gifts were acceptable so long as Filipinas acknowledged that the purchase of privacy was a key motive of European employers.

Malaysian employers in this study who gave gifts to foreign domestic workers did so simultaneously to express their gratitude and to purchase obligation. I was present when Emily, a Chinese employer, gave her Indonesian servant a 22-karat gold chain, a roundtrip ticket to Indonesia for two weeks, and new clothes in celebration of the 1994 Chinese New Year. The domestic worker was visibly ecstatic when she received the gifts. After the servant left the room, Emily looked at me and said, "The way to keep them in line is to make them obligated. I give her presents, she works hard for me."[19]

Receiving gifts obligates the domestic worker to her employer, and subsequently increases the employer's expectation of a particular kind of reci-
procity. If and when a servant fails to fulfill the other half of this unwritten
social contract, the employer may experience feelings of anger and/or
betrayal. Jane, whose first foreign domestic worker suddenly decided to
quit, described her response:

> Unlike my other friends, I refused to deduct from her salary. Rita worked for two
> years and kept to herself. She never had the bad habits of the others, like going
> out late at night, talking on the telephone, having visitors. My sons were attached
> to her but she was always so detached. It seemed like she didn't want to get too
> close to them. And now, I understand why. Two weeks before she left, she started
> to act strange. She finally said that she wanted to work for herself, open a
> hawker's stall. I felt so betrayed. I was always good to her. I bought her clothes,
> gave her days off. I took her everywhere. All she had to do was to pay for her own
> toiletries. She knew everything about my life and lifestyle. She knew all of my
> friends. She knew my schedule. She remembered what I liked and didn't. When
> she left, I felt angry and betrayed–all mixed up feelings. I treated her like she was
> my younger sister.

Jane expected Rita to reciprocate her kindness by staying with the family
rather than leaving Jane to start her own business. At the very least, Jane
expected Rita to have been more forthcoming with her decision to leave the
household.

Implicit in the different ways employers purchased deference and obligation is the establishment of social distance and status between employers
and foreign servants. There also are other ways in which middle-class identity is constructed.

Civilized Employers Versus Backward Maids   Key studies of domestic service
in the West, particularly in the United States, demonstrate that the history
of slavery, industrialization, and concomitant changes in immigration patterns have allowed white female employers to purchase status from African-
American, Japanese, Chicana, and Caribbean female servants.[20] Upper
and/or middle-class identity construction of white employers as more educated and presumably more civilized occurs in juxtaposition to that of nonwhite working-class women of color as backward servants.[21]

In postcolonial Malaysia employer-domestic servant relations are somewhat more complex. On the surface, a central issue does not appear to be the
different ethnic backgrounds of employers and employees. One legacy of
precolonial and colonial migration and settlement throughout Southeast

Asia is that contemporary Malays are the ethnic cousins of many Indonesians and Filipinas, and the same can be said (to a lesser extent) of the relationship between some Chinese and Filipinas.[22]

Rather, it is the specific nationality of the servant and concomitant ascribed traits, which help facilitate employer construction of social status. Paradoxically, the employment of a servant from either the Philippines or Indonesia has the potential to resurrect and reaffirm what the British constructed in colonial Malaya, i.e., Malays : Chinese = poor : rich = low : high social status.

In the particular group of middle-class employers with whom I spoke, I find that there is an emerging distinction between those who hired Filipinas and those who hired Indonesian women. Malaysian employers (much like European employers' perceptions of "Hylam Boys" and "Klings" during the colonial period) perceived Indonesian women as less educated and less hygienic than Filipinas. In short, Indonesian women were unceremoniously given the title of "backward" maids. Below are some of the justificatory statements from employers who hired Filipina rather than Indonesian servants.

> No Indonesians! They give you the idea that they are always going to run away. No doubt they are cheaper, but you hear so many stories of them stealing things . . . a lot of stories. It is not worth it [to employ Indonesian domestic workers]. Better to know the devil than not to know what it's all about.

> Indonesians are dirty, they steal. Filipinos are arrogant but they are better than Indonesians.

> Indonesians can't be trusted and they are so dirty.

> They [Filipinas] can speak English and help my children with their homework.

> Filipinos are better educated and know how to behave properly.

> I prefer a Filipino [sic] girl even though Filipinos are fussy because they are educated. The white people have spoilt them.

> Those who get Indonesians are damn stupid because they [Indonesians] are so lazy and dumb.

> Very simple. One word. Hygiene. Filipinos are more hygienic.

Employers' belief that Indonesian servants are less modern, or conversely more backward than Filipinas is fueled by the fact that Filipinas have higher levels of education and are paid higher monthly salaries than their Indonesian counterparts. Most Filipina servants I encountered had attained at least a secondary school level education, while Indonesian servants, who came mainly from rural areas, had received at best a primary school level education.

Many rural Indonesian women's unfamiliarity with performing modern housework reinforces employers' negative perceptions of this group of foreign servants. The mutual desire of employers and DOMs to find young and inexperienced domestic servants has led to the increasing selection and in-migration of Indonesian women from the remotest villages wherein some women were barely exposed to modern utilities, let alone a modern lifestyle, prior to migration. From a DOM's perspective, the younger and less experienced the servant, the less likely she is to run away from her employer and in the process cause financial and legal problems for the DOM. From the perspective of some Malaysian employers, the younger and less experienced the domestic worker, the more likely she is expected to accept her subordination in the workplace.

While the in-migration of rural Indonesian women may solve employer demands for docile servants, women who neither are exposed to modern housework prior to migration nor formally trained to perform modern housework can cause different types of problems for employers. Meena, an Indian employer who hired her first Indonesian servant six years ago, described her experience:

> I went to a flat to get her. I was horrified. The stench and the dirt. Must have been at least 20 men and women in the one bedroom flat. They had just arrived by boat. E was a "*kebun* [farm] worker" in Indonesia. She knew absolutely next to nothing about housework. She had never been in a car. When we drove her back [to the house], she puked all over the back seat. Then she was shocked at the size of her bedroom. To make matters worse, she didn't know how to switch on the light. I came back and saw her sitting in the dark. Oh, and then the phone. When it rang, you should have seen her face the second she heard a human voice at the other end! She also didn't know how to use the taps on the sink. That night, we had to go out to a dinner function. . . . I had no choice but to put food in her room and lock her inside until we came back. . . . Christine, she didn't even know how to use the toilet. She'd do her business by squatting on the floor with the door open. I had to say something to her, you know, because of my two boys. Can you imagine? Headache, only.

Meena reasoned that locking the Indonesian woman in the bedroom that night was the only way to prevent unforeseen problems that could and did arise from hiring foreign domestic workers who had had no prior experience living and working in modern middle-class households.

Indonesian women who had not been trained to perform modern house-work posed potential threats to themselves and the employing families. Rose, a Chinese employer, was animated in her narrative on the "back-wardness" of her first foreign servant, an Indonesian woman:

> She was so stupid. Aduh! She nearly killed us. I asked her if she knew how to use the gas stove, and she said yes. She switched on the gas, and then went to do some-thing else. I don't know how long the gas was on before she came into my room and asked me to follow her into the kitchen. She held a matchbox and started striking a match while she asked me if this was the way to light the stove! I tell you, no more of this-ah! One morning, I walked into the kitchen and the whole place was like a sauna. Guess what I saw? One egg bobbing in the *kuali* [wok] . . . she was boiling one egg in a *kuali*-full of water! Give me a Filipino girl anytime.

Some employers can and do perpetuate a self-reinforcing cycle of frustra-tion in that while they demand trainable servants, they also expect servants to know how to perform modern urban housework without additional instruc-tion. As a result, the choice of a Filipina over an Indonesian woman not only symbolizes an employer's refusal to devote time and effort to "modernize" the foreign servant, but subsequently elevates the employer's social status in rela-tion to other members of the larger group of Malaysian employers.

In this study, the majority of Malaysian employers of Filipina domestic workers were non-Malays: 26 out of 36 Chinese employers, 7 out of 13 Indian employers, 3 out of 3 employers of mixed descent (two were of Chinese-Indian descent and one was of Malay-Indian descent), and 3 out of 16 Malay employers. The sample size of 68 employers does not allow for a more definitive statement here with respect to whether Indonesians were and/or are employed mostly by Malays in Malaysia.

Non-Malay employers of Filipina servants in this study believed that Malays hired Indonesian servants because of cultural, religious, and lin-guistic similarities, *and* that Indonesian women's salaries were lower than that of Filipina servants. All sixteen Malay employers agreed with the first reason. According to Aishah, "In Muslim households, Indonesian maids are usually preferred because of similarities in our cultures."

The Malay employers, however, objected to the second reason, which implied that they could not afford to pay the higher salaries of Filipina ser-vants. Some Malays who employed Indonesian domestic workers did so to prevent real or perceived criticisms from the Malay community. They rea-soned that if they were unencumbered by the expectations of kinfolk and/or state authorities, they would hire Filipina servants instead. For example,

Latifah said that "A lot of my friends in the civil service pick Indonesians because of religion . . . to save others from criticizing them. It's not so much the cost." Khatijah explained that she employed an Indonesian as opposed to a Filipina domestic worker because of her mother-in-law's objection to a Christian servant in the household: "I got an Indonesian maid only because of my mother-in-law. I didn't want to hear her harass me because the maid eats [pork]. Given a choice, I'd prefer a Filipina girl. Indonesians always say that they have to *balik kampung* [go back to their villages] or wherever they go on their day off, and who knows what they do."

Out of the group of sixteen Malay employers, the three who hired Filipina servants assured me that there were no explicit or implicit barriers to Malay employment of Filipinas. Yasmine, one of the three Malay employers, insisted that she and other Malay employers chose Filipina servants because the women were more hardworking and they also were of great help in tutoring Malay children to read and write English.

Implicit in non-Malay and Malay employment of Filipina servants in this study is the understanding that employers were willing and able to pay higher wages for more "civilized" foreign domestic workers. Whereas the majority of Malay employers in this study preferred or felt that they had to employ Indonesian women because of cultural, religious, and linguistic considerations, Latifah and Khatijah's comments suggested that some would disassociate themselves from the community of lower status employers of Indonesian servants so long as the act of employing Filipinas did not result in familial or social sanctions.

In this study, the majority of non-Malays employed Filipinas. Given the hierarchical ranking of foreign servants, there is the unstated assumption among employers that "less wealthy" Malaysians can only employ Indonesian servants. Included in this group of less wealthy employers are Malays. Paradoxically, the state's earlier insistence that only Malays could employ Indonesian-Muslim servants encourages the perception that middle-class Malays are less well off than the non-Malay middle classes. Further research has the potential to ascertain, in greater depth and with more clarity, the ways in which specific intersections of nationality-religion-ethnicity-class-gender in Malaysian employment of foreign domestic workers shape emerging middle-class subjectivity and intersubjectivity.

Employers' ranking of domestic workers according to nationality has affected how Filipina servants perceive their Indonesian peers. Although the example I am about to cite is more appropriate for the section on "hidden transcripts," I have elected to include it in the discussion of the public transcript in order to illustrate the extent to which some foreign female domestic workers, in the absence of their employers, can strengthen certain aspects of the public transcript.

A group of Filipina servants in a church reinforced their employers' social status (and, by extension, their own status within the larger group of foreign domestic workers) when they asked me to tell them what nationality of servant I would choose, if and when I decided to employ a domestic worker. When I appeared noncommittal, they said:

> *Salbi:* Please don't get an Indonesian maid because they are not skilled. They don't know how to clean the house and they also steal. We are better.
>
> *Esther:* Indonesians are very lazy and dirty. They never wash things properly. Also, they are not good at cooking.
>
> *Lani:* You want to employ an Indonesian girl? What can she do? They are very stupid, do you know?

It is important to emphasize that none of the Filipina servants above had spoken to or worked with Indonesian servants. Rather, their impressions of Indonesian servants were formed largely from newspaper articles and conversations with their employers. By arguing that they were more capable than Indonesian women in performing housework, the Filipina servants affirmed the rank order of foreign domestic workers that had been constructed by their employers.

Given Filipina servants' desire to distance themselves from Indonesian women's constructed identity as lazy, ignorant, and criminally oriented servants, the possibility of solidarity between the two groups of women may be contingent on Filipinas' ability to challenge the public transcript that has created hierarchical categories of servants according to nationality. Even so, Filipina and Indonesian servants first must be able to overcome the language barrier that divides them since Filipinas are proficient in English while most Indonesian women arrive in Malaysia speaking *Bahasa Melayu* (Malay language) and/or different Indonesian dialects. The hierarchical ranking of servants; the socially isolated occupation of domestic service; and linguistic differences among foreign domestic workers assure state authorities, DOMs, and employers that Filipina and Indonesian women cannot readily organize to demand their rights.

Thus far, it can be said that the public transcript of domestic service offers a relatively benign picture of employer-servant relations. However, in their efforts to reinforce social and economic superiority, middle-class employer-supervisors resort to more negative methods of supervision and control that are perpetuated by the absence of labor legislation.

Dehumanizing the Hired Help   In individual interviews, Suet Ling, Susan, and Janet respectively explained why they would verbally reprimand their servants:

> You have to scold her even if she does things right, just to remind her who is boss . . . so that she doesn't get the wrong idea that she can step all over us.

> I don't like it but I have to scold her now and again. I know that she pretends not to hear, so I shout louder.

> You are like a manager, reward when they do well, punish when they fuck up. You know, like that experiment, what is the name, Pavlov?

Verbal reprimands function not only to correct servants' mistakes, but also to reinforce employers' higher social status. Scolding episodes transform into physical assault when servants inadvertently fail to meet, or even at times purposely reject their employers' expectations of particular behavioral and attitudinal postures (see section on hidden transcript). I was told by Filipina and Indonesian servants who had worked in Malaysia for a year or more that women with barely a few months of work experience in Malaysia would respond with tears to employers' physical assaults. A Filipina servant said that she would "go back to my room and cry," whenever her face was forcefully graced by her female employer's palm.

In some cases, employers went so far as to make the final decision on when a servant was allowed to retire for the night. One evening, while I was visiting her family, Sally asked her servant to bathe her young children. As Sally and I talked, I saw the domestic worker walk up and down the stairs several times, catering to the children's demands. Sally's husband, who was watching television, said to the servant, "I'm calling you now, come down at once." He asked her, "Hey, my daughter is sick, where's the medicine?" The domestic worker replied, "Sir, she already ate the pill." As the servant turned to walk away, he looked at me and said loudly, "They give you headaches. Some of them are so stupid!" Later that evening, the couple invited me out to dinner. While we were at a neighborhood coffee shop, I reminded them that the domestic worker had not had any dinner, and suggested that the couple buy food for her. Both the husband and wife fell silent. When we went back to their house, the husband said to the servant who was standing quietly outside her bedroom, "You can go to sleep now."

The couple's refusal to buy dinner for the domestic worker reflects a key contradiction in contemporary live-in domestic service in Malaysia. Employing families expect to be served at all times of the day, but they resent having to provide servants with board and lodging, in addition to wages. Consequently, some employers resort to a daily meticulous inventory of food in the refrigerator, much like how May Lan and Sandy responded to servants who ate food from the refrigerator (see chapter 4). Yet, no employer in this study even considered hiring day or part-time workers, partly because of the latter's work schedules.

Employer complaints ranged from migrant women who consumed too much food at employer's expense, to the length of time taken in performing household tasks. On separate occasions, three employers Sharifah, Susan, and Vivien, respectively had the following to say about their employees:

> Oh my goodness, she is so lazy. She takes how many hours to clean the first floor, you won't believe.

> Of course she [domestic worker is Indonesian-Muslim] can pray. But I tell her, "Remember, *sembahyang* [pray] on your own time." I cannot afford to let her pray on my hardearned money. I tell you, they [servants] are too much sometimes.

> This batch of Filipina maids is not like the pioneer batch [in the mid to late 1980s] because they want to bathe with hot water, good taste in clothes, cannot sleep without mattress, cannot walk in the house without slippers. She asked me to get her slippers so that she could wear them in the house. I asked her what was wrong with her feet. She stopped asking for slippers.

Narratives that construct migrant women as inherently lazy and/or demanding simultaneously represent employers as hardworking and reasonable. Implicit in the narratives are employers' justification for making servants work longer hours, pay for their own food, and so forth.

The Malaysian state's refusal to legislate domestic service has the effect of transferring the responsibility of determining work relations and boundaries to employers and foreign domestic workers. The task of delineating the conditions in which labor is exchanged for wages at best is extremely difficult since Filipina and Indonesian women not only work in their employers' houses, but are also required legally to reside with their employers. The work environment then is dominated by the wage-paying party. The material and symbolic aspects of the public transcript of domestic service reveal how middle-class identity is constructed in the domestic domain, and implicitly, employers' conceptualizations of what is *not* just or fair in the exchange of wages for labor.

Today, the abusive aspects of employer-domestic worker relations are exacerbated by the consequences of the state's policy of circumscribing the activities of Filipina and Indonesian servants in public space.

Female Employers as Domestic Spies

While state agencies such as the Police and Immigration Departments, together with newspaper reporters conduct surveillance of foreign servants beyond employers' homes, the surveillance of servants in the domestic domain largely remains the responsibility of female employer-supervisors. The state deftly enlists middle-class female employers as spies in the domestic realm via measures that are implemented by the Immigration Department.

The Immigration Department will confiscate DOMs and employers' deposits of bond money (required by law) if foreign domestic workers are detained by the police for criminal activities, or if the women run away from their workplace. In addition, the annual levy of RM360 paid by an employer or a servant will be forfeited should either party decide to terminate the work contract early.[23] The Immigration Department explains the official rationale for these punitive measures: "We want to discourage maids from running away from employers or employers dismissing maids at their whim."[24] These measures introduced to curb illegal activities of foreign servants, and employer abuse, have had negative repercussions on migrant women's lives instead.

A key consequence is that foreign servants either continue to suffer abuse or risk deportation by running away from abusive employers. Nevertheless, in my conversations with Malaysian employers, taxi drivers, grocers in farmers' markets and retail shop owners, it is believed that Filipina and Indonesian servants run away to become prostitutes in order to earn more money.

The press has played a major role in shaping negative public perceptions of foreign domestic workers by printing sensationalized articles of police arrests and, in the process, identifying certain public places as sites of prostitution involving Filipina and/or Indonesian women. As Azizah Kassim writes in the case of Indonesian migrant workers, "The local population has had limited or non-interactions with the Indonesians, and thus press coverage of the Indonesian immigrant issue was seminal in setting the tone of public opinion and shaping individual responses and reactions to the Indonesians."[25]

Newspaper articles help constitute what are called the "sexploits" of Filipina and Indonesian domestic workers. Sexploits are transmitted via employers' social networks, in person, or on the telephone.[26] Repeatedly over the course of field research, informal discussions by employers and their friends in homes, restaurants, country clubs, and so forth, would center on sexploits. In employers' houses, sexploits were discussed openly by Malaysians in the presence of the employer-host's servant as if she either did not exist or could not understand the conversation.[27]

During a dinner party in the home of a middle-class informant, a group of three middle-class employers swapped sexploits while the host's foreign servant walked back and forth from the kitchen carrying plates of food.

> *Lily:* Yoke Fong has a maid from the Philippines. She hired her to take care of the house and the children. And, she would tell us how good the maid was—the girl changed her [Yoke Fong's] sheets in the master bedroom everyday! Imagine sleeping on fresh sheets every night! One day, Yoke Fong went to work without her briefcase and so she drove home to get it. She went to her bedroom and found the maid in bed with a stranger. The girl used her house as "sex for service!"
>
> *Yasmine:* Oh yes, and do you know the story of this woman who found her maid in bed with her husband? God, she fired the maid on the spot. Aduh, you know what the maid said to her? "I slept with your son too!"
>
> *Janet:* You see, how can you trust them, ah? Even though they are good, you'd never really know. Like my maid, when she first came, she cried for six weeks nonstop! I'm not joking-lah! I swear! I asked her what was wrong and she said that she was homesick . . . missed her children or something like that. How the hell would I know if she's lying or not?

A key moral in these tales of sexploits is that foreign domestic workers, even those who appear to diligently perform domestic labor, cannot be trusted.

At another female employer's house, her husband Greg described to his guests what had happened to a colleague from his workplace:

> Hey, my friend from work came home one day and found the house completely dark [wife and children were in London]. The maid left a note on the table to say that she couldn't take it anymore. Then his next maid, oh boy, she was weird. For a while they kept hearing the front door open and close in the middle of the night. Then one night, he decided to go downstairs and investigate the strange

noise. He saw her [servant] at the door, smiling at him. He turned around and saw a pair of men's black shoes underneath the living room drapes. He pulled the drapes back and found a man hiding behind the curtains!

The issue of foreign domestic workers' (alleged) sexual misconduct was accepted by fellow discussants, Melina and Sandy, as key reasons for employers' need to be more restrictive of the servants' movement and association with peoples beyond the domestic domain.

> *Melina:* What to do? You want to be nice and if you are, they climb all over your head. If you are strict, then they say you are bad. Christine, write this down. I want you to write this down: "You love to hate them [foreign female domestic workers] and you hate to love them." This is how we feel about them. Have you written it down? Good . . . we are not monsters. Eh, remember, don't use my real name. Promise me ah, you know what I mean?
>
> *Sandy [nodded her head in agreement]:* I tell my friends, don't give the maid too much freedom and face. If they do, then *habis*-lah [lit: "finished/gone"]. We should not grovel. Oh, and don't be too friendly. Familiarity breeds contempt.

Melina's phrase, "love to hate them, hate to love them," neatly captures employers' sense of distrust in dealing with foreign domestic workers.

Sexploits that were discussed by employers and their friends did not usually refer to the behavior of the conversants' employees. Rather, the servant in question always worked for an employer's friend, or a friend's friend. To be sure, sensationalized newsprint articles contribute to the potency of the stories. Regardless of the degree of truth, sexploits were perceived by conversants as real events that occurred in the lives of their friends or fellow Malaysians. Sexploits heighten employers' fear over the possibility of foreign servants contracting sexually transmitted diseases and, in turn, infecting members of the household.

A subtext of most, if not all the stories, is a potential threat: foreign domestic workers might engage in sexual relations with female employers' husbands. For example, when Rosa mentioned to her female employer that her male employer was looking at her in a "strange" manner, she was instructed to keep out of his way: "I told mum about it. She told me to stay in my room or the kitchen if she was not home. I cannot go to the living room to clean when he is the only one at home." Lin, an Indonesian domestic worker whose male employer consistently reminded his wife to treat her with more respect, said "Mum is jealous because when she scolds me, sir always sides with me. Sometimes when she goes overseas, he takes me shopping and buys me nice things [e.g., clothes, accessories]." Significantly, Lin's statement identifies the female employer as the more abusive party.

The interests of female employers and state authorities converge with respect to the presence of Filipina and Indonesian domestic workers in Malaysian society. Middle-class employers' individual and collective fear over the perceived sexual and criminal tendencies of all foreign servants, and the potentially punitive legal consequences, have become a key rationale for severely curtailing Filipina and Indonesian the servants' ability to interact with peoples beyond the workplace. In an interview at her home, Maimunah repeated the advice that she gave to her friends who also employed foreign servants: "The way to keep her in line is not to let her out of the house, always keep her in sight. Don't let her use the phone. Really, never let her out unless you have to."

The "disease" metaphor was prevalent in many employers' rationale for denying their servants access to the world beyond the four walls of the home: "Don't let them be contaminated. Don't let them out to learn bad habits from outsiders"; "less getting together, less trouble"; "I don't want my girl getting bad ideas from other people"; and "I drive her to church and wait for her. I want to see that she doesn't mix with bad company." In the first few weeks of my field research, I quickly discovered that some employers were not enthusiastic, to say the least, about allowing me to speak with their servants. One irate employer said to me: "What you need to know about my maid, I will tell you. I don't want her talking to other people. You read the papers . . . so many stories about how they are prostitutes and criminals."

Employers' surveillance of domestic workers extends to monitoring phones and relying on their children and their neighbors to assume the role of substitute spies. During an interview in Khatijah's office, Janet and Khatijah shared with me their strategies for checking on the servants. Khatijah taught her eleven year-old son to report on the behavior of the servant in her absence ("My son told me the other day that she was on the phone for hours"), while Janet telephoned her house intermittently during the work day to ascertain if the domestic worker was busy performing housework or merely chatting with a compatriot over the telephone ("I will call back to my house to see if the line is busy and for how long.") An Indian employer, Prithiva, depended on her close relationship with an elderly neighbor who would visit her house several times during the day just to ensure that the foreign servant did not use the telephone or entertain guests.

At a church in Kuala Lumpur, I was privy to a conversation between two Filipina servants that confirmed a neighbor's role:

Patricia: Sometimes there is not enough food to eat [in the house].
Elba: If you are hungry, go outside and buy food. How can you work if you are hungry?
Patricia: I am scared that the neighbors will see me and tell her [female employer] that I went out of the house.

Here, the strategy of delegating neighbors as spies is functionally abusive since Filipina and/or Indonesian servants who, out of hunger, leave the workplace to buy food will risk punishment.

In the above cases, employers' intent is to protect foreign domestic workers from outside criminal influences. However, the methods of surveillance and control prevent servants from learning their contractual rights to a certain number of rest days and wage levels. Rose, who sat in her office at a state agency as we spoke admitted that, "Yes, I *pakat* [plot] with my friends. I don't tell my maid how much others are getting paid because she'll only ask for more." Melina, in a flash of introspection, empathized with domestic workers by saying to her friends and me that, "You know-lah, the servant mentality—forever asking but always forgetting to return the favor. Just like us when we work. We ask for better hours, benefits, raises, but we don't want to give in return."

Taken as a whole, employer purchase of status/deference/obligation coupled with other methods of control and surveillance constitute middle-class women as modern, clean, trustworthy, and hardworking, while Filipina and Indonesian servants are constructed as more or less backward, dirty, untrustworthy, and lazy. Some scholars argue that domestic service, especially in the West, is an institution that facilitates the modernization of rural/Third World women or women of color.[28] This view is expressed by Janet, who believed that, "If I don't do anything else, let the satisfaction be mine that I helped to uplift the life of another woman. Why some women are so backward, it's not through any fault of theirs or mine."

However, Malaysian women such as Emily, Meena, and to a lesser extent, Janet, are exceptions in a group of employers whose relationships with Filipina and Indonesian servants were characterized mainly by the perceived need to find better or more effective modes of control. For example, Vivien said that, "I teach my maid to better herself. . . . I don't want her to stay a maid forever." Yet, she would refuse her servant's request for house slippers in which to work, a mattress on which to sleep, and so forth.

The growing trend of employing Filipina and Indonesian domestic workers in Malaysia tells us more about how middle-class employers and their children, rather than migrant women, are socialized into the modern urban middle-class lifestyle. Within the context of unlegislated employer-domestic worker relations, and the manner in which Filipina and Indonesian servants are treated and portrayed by state authorities and the press, the public transcript of domestic service reveals and encourages a troubling trend of employer-related emotional, physical, and at times, sexual abuse of Filipina and Indonesian domestic workers.

Every employer in this study argued that she did not abuse her servant. Abuse was defined in terms of rape and extreme physical assault (e.g., punching or kicking the servant). Many employers' refusal to provide rest days, adequate sleeping accommodations, structured work hours, and so forth, was justified instead from the perspective of protecting their servants from criminal influences, or that servants were lazy and stupid. Every employer believed that she had been "taken advantage of" at one point or another by domestic workers.

Employers who insisted on monitoring and circumscribing servants' behavior and activities, then had to take the time and effort, for example, to check the refrigerator; drive Filipina servants to and from Sunday church services; reprimand for the sake of reinforcing the idea of "who's the boss"; and telephone home whenever they leave their houses for more than a few minutes. To be sure, the negative aspects of employers' relationships with Filipina and Indonesian servants dehumanize not only the oppressed/servant, but also the oppressor/employer. Of importance to note is that the oppressor in most instances is identifiably the female as opposed to the male employer.

As discerned, the public transcript of domestic service mainly tells the story of the processes in which female employers construct and impose social and economic superiority over foreign domestic workers. In this version of domestic service, Filipina and Indonesian women seemingly acquiesce to work conditions and environments that denigrate their labor and persons. Nonetheless, the women may and do resist middle-class construction of their identity as lazy, stupid, dirty, and/or sex-hungry servants—ascribed traits that are considered undeserving of humane treatment: "[Subordinates] obey and conform *not* because they have internalized the norms of the domestic servant but because a structure of surveillance, reward, and punishment makes it prudent for them to comply."[29] The record of Filipina and

Indonesian domestic workers' responses can be found in what is called the "hidden transcript."

Hidden Transcript of Domestic Service

In metaphorical terms, the public transcript of domestic service is a theatrical performance that is produced and directed by employers (aided indirectly by state authorities). Backstage, "beyond the direct observation by powerholders," is a hidden transcript, in which can be found the different ways that Filipina and Indonesian servants reject the social codes of conduct or parameters established by their employers and even the Malaysian public.[30]

Identifying and examining the hidden transcript involved mostly off-stage conversations with domestic workers at "informal assemblages" such as churches, shopping malls, and discotheques.[31] Many employers' refusal to give servants rest days, then, is due partly to their fear of servants coming together to exchange stories of employers' lifestyles, contractual rights, and alternative ways to generate income (e.g., selling their bodies or setting up illegal food/hawker stalls).[32] Indeed, at the informal gathering places, Filipina and Indonesian servants shared with their friends information on a variety of topics ranging from ways to cope with abusive employers and gossip about employing families, to identifying retail shops with the latest fashion items on sale.

Slaves in the Household

The slave (*hamba*) metaphor dominated Filipina and Indonesian women's narratives on the many ways in which they were treated by their employers. Late one morning after a Sunday church service, a group of six Filipina servants who saw me talking with a Filipina informant eagerly joined our conversation about their working conditions.

Felicitas: We are human. We have the same kind of heart and body, why do they treat us like we are not human?

Auntie [Felicitas' aunt]: I swallow only because of money. If you have a brain, you must know that you have a human right to fight. She cannot pay me RM500 and then treat me like a slave.

Lourdes: They get my blood, you know, for the medical exam [she demonstrates with her fingers the many "inches" of blood that were taken from her]. When you take my blood, how can you treat me like a slave?

Maria Rosa: See, they don't think we are human. We are like slaves to them. They take our sweat but they don't give us respect.

Ruth: Chinese employers are very bad. Big house, big car, big wallet, but they give us nothing. Only want to use us like we are slaves.

Pilar: Do I look like a slave? Please tell me why Malaysians treat us so badly?

At a farmer's market, Subaidah complained to her friend, Kak Tin, about the way she was treated by her employer.

Subaidah: I wake up at 5 a.m. and work sometimes until 1 a.m. No time to rest at all. She [employer] scolds me when I sit down. She scolds me when I cannot quickly finish my work. How can I do it if the children always tell me to get this and get that? I only eat rice with gravy, and I am always hungry. I am like a slave [she starts crying].

Kak Tin: No, no. You are like garbage [*sampah*], worse than a slave! [Subaidah wipes her eyes and then laughs. The two women go onto plan Subaidah's "escape" from her employer]

Foreign domestic workers' rejection of the degree of dehumanization that inheres in the exchange of wages for housework in Malaysia is captured in the frequent use of the slave metaphor. As Judith Rollins writes in the context of domestic service in Boston:

This knowledge of their [servants'] powerlessness as a group combines with their inability to express their outrage to those who have caused it, form the basis of the deep and pervasive *ressentiment* in the women I interviewed. The presence of such *ressentiment* attests to domestics' lack of belief in their own inferiority, their sense of injustice about their treatment and position, and their rejection of the legitimacy of their subordination.[33]

Filipina and Indonesian servants in this study, however, expressed their outrage in distinct, and at times culturally specific ways. It is via their narratives that we come to understand how they perceive their subordination, and why they respond as they do.

Labor of Love, Labor of Sorrow

To reiterate, Filipina and Indonesian women alike who had worked in Malaysia for only a few months tended to cry in response to situations in which they either were denied food, rest, or were verbally abused (and/or physically assaulted) by their employers. Juanita, a Filipina who had worked merely four months as a servant, said to me while she watched over her employer's children in a neighborhood playground: "I didn't pay attention when I was ironing because the baby was crying so loud. Sir scolded me because I made a hole in his shirt [she uses her hands to show the width of the iron-burn]. But mum was worse. She wouldn't stop calling me stupid, and she said that she would deduct from my salary. I went back to my room and cried."

Similar to the previous point made by the Indonesian domestic worker Lin, Juanita's statement also reveals that female employers are more abusive than male employers. Men become, by default, the lesser evil of employers since women unequivocally are assigned the responsibility for supervising foreign domestic workers.

The responses of Indonesian servants with Malay employers were particularly interesting. They expected Malay employers to treat them like family members since many Malays may be and are the ethnoreligious cousins of Indonesians. Put differently, Indonesian servants' references to parental or kin bonds emerged only in narratives of Malay employers' actions toward them. This phenomenon conforms to the findings of Jean Taylor and Kathy Robinson's respective studies of domestic service in Indonesia. Taylor and Robinson argue that paid reproductive labor mostly is perceived by employers and domestic workers through the schemata of kin relations rather than work relations.[34]

In the case of Indonesian servants with Malay employers, the former framed their narratives in familial terms because of ethnoreligious proximity to Malays. The narratives reflected the women's horror upon realizing that shared ethnoreligious heritage between Malays and Indonesians did not prevent mistreatment and abuse at the hands of Malay employers. Ibu Nin, an older Indonesian woman who had run away recently from her physically abusive Malay employers, cried as she said that, "We [Malays and Indonesians] are one nation/race [*bangsa*] of peoples. I never thought that they'd mistreat me the way they did. Yes, the Chinese are bad, but not as bad [as the Malays]." One day, in her female employer's absence, Lijah climbed over the metal fence at the back of the house and told me as I was standing in the alley what she said to her employer after she had been reprimanded with harsh words: "Why do you treat me this way? I am also human. You are high [*tinggi*], and I am low [*rendah*]. From young until now, my own parents don't scold me this way. Why do you do this to me? I work very hard for you."

Susanti, who was introduced to me by a baker at a farmers' market, narrated her experience in a similar manner. She described what happened one day when she went grocery shopping with her female employer.

My employer, daughter of a *Datuk* too, scolded me outside the supermarket. . . . [*Datuk* (similar to the British version of "Sir") is an honorary title that is awarded by the *Agung* (king) or *Sultan* to Malaysians for exemplary service to the country, e.g., *Datuk* Michael Chan or *Datuk* Ali Shafie.] She used bad words like "bastard," "stupid dumb-dumb," "*puki mak*" [to have sexual intercourse with her mother], "chicken backside." She didn't think I knew some of the English words. I told her to watch her mouth in public but she got angrier. I was ashamed [*malu*] since it took place in public. She is not well brought up by her parents. No manners.

Nursiah, whom I interviewed while we walked back to her employer's house, was extremely insulted after her employer's son degraded her by performing an obscene act with his fingers. She said, "I do not believe how ill-mannered Malays are. My own mother would have slapped me if I did that. She [employer] didn't say anything to him." Nursiah's friend Sri, proceeded to describe an incident in which her Malay employer, in a fit of anger over the way Sri washed certain clothes, told Sri that she hoped Sri would be sexually assaulted by men. Sri responded to her employer's words in the following way: "I told my employer, 'You have father, I have father. You have mother, I have mother. You have two hands and feet, I have two hands and feet. Why do you speak to me like this? Am I not human? I am mother's and father's daughter."

Filipina servants, on the other hand, approached domestic service specifically from the perspective of contractual work. Eva, a Filipina servant who sold miscellaneous consumer goods (such as Philippine magazines, soap, and candy, that were imported by a DOM representative without the knowledge of the DOM's owner) to her compatriots at church, stated that "We have contracts. We show the employer the contracts. They cannot do anything to us. We will tell the embassy. We can read. We know the law." This small measure of potential protection that the embassy could offer was criticized greatly by a fellow servant Lita, who replied, "The embassy? They cannot do anything. They don't care. You go now and see what they'll do for you? Nothing! If I have a problem, I won't go there." When I asked Lita what she would do instead, she replied, "Hah, so many things. You want to know? What are you studying? To be a professor? Then you must be smart. You go and see! Do you like living in America? When will you go back there?"

Lita, who had just met me, was not sure if I was an undercover immigration officer or a DOM representative who was interested in finding out what foreign domestic workers said and did on their rest days. Feeling uncertain of my identity, she refused to divulge information that she thought would be harmful to her and her compatriots. Lita quickly shifted the focus of the conversation since she was not prepared to tell me how the women resisted their subordination.

Lita's statement, "Then you must be smart. You go and see!," elicits a key issue that confronts many researchers of live-in domestic service. What is the most accessible and unobtrusive way in which to observe employer-employee relations? The period of field research for this study was not conducive to a length of uninterrupted observation of employer-employee interactions because of employers' fear of publicity and the exposure of foreign domestic workers to strangers who conceivably could incite employer-employee contestations over work conditions. At any rate, what emerged from a period of field research characterized by shopping, having meals, and conversing with foreign domestic workers who waited for public transportation or who shopped for groceries at farmers' markets, were the women's narratives. The narratives recorded Filipina and Indonesian women's efforts to redefine the conditions in which they performed paid reproductive labor, including challenges to the identities that were constructed for them by the public transcript.

Verbal and Nonverbal Infrapolitical Activities

Defiance   Louisa, who contributed to one of the epigraphs in this chapter, appealed to her employer's sense of *logos* (logic/reason), albeit with a sarcastic tone of voice. Reminding her female employer that she was a domestic worker, not a thief, she added that it therefore would not be necessary to follow her around the house. Louisa said to me that her words had succeeded in altering her employer's behavior toward her. Ever since that incident, she had been free to perform housework without close supervision.

Other servants' challenges to their employers' behavior and attitudes were less successful in redefining employer-employee relations. In fact, some of the challenges reaffirmed the public transcript of domestic service:

> The appearance that power requires are, to be sure, imposed forcefully on subordinate groups. But this does not preclude their active use as a means of resistance and evasion. The evasion, it must be noted, however, is purchased at the considerable cost of contributing to the production of a public transcript that *apparently* ratifies the social ideology of the dominant.[35]

To put it simply, an employer at a certain point may overtly insist that her foreign domestic worker behave in a deferential manner. The servant then expresses deference in a way that challenges her employer's authority. The consequence of the act, in some cases, may very well reaffirm the employer's negative perception of foreign domestic workers. For example, Mira, a Filipina servant, told me the following while we were at an afternoon discotheque patronized by Filipinas:

> She [employer] scolded me for hanging clothes the wrong way. I did not know how she wanted the clothes to be arranged [on the clothes line in the garden]. She said to me, "Do you understand?" OK-lah. I said "Yes, mum!" [much like a foot soldier reaffirming the command of his sergeant] She slapped me, you know! My employer slapped me! I kept saying "Yes, mum!" until she went back into the house.

Ami, an Indonesian domestic worker who was barely five feet tall, described to me as we waited at a bus-stop, her defiant stance toward her former employer after having been slapped because her employer had not liked the way her instructions had been carried out: "When my employer scolded me, I just looked at her. She told me not to look at her, so I looked at the piano [Ami smiles out of the side of her mouth]. Then, she got angry and slapped my left cheek. God be my witness, I slapped her back and I quit my job."[36] In both instances, the servants' actions could well have reaffirmed employers' insistence on greater forms of control.

At a restaurant, three Filipinas who sat at a table adjacent to the one Louisa and I were sitting at, had the following to say about a compatriot who killed her employer's baby in 1990.[37]

> *Priscilla:* If they treat us better, we wouldn't do it [kill the baby]. They treat us like animals, so we act like animals.
> *Imelda:* My employers think I am stupid. I let them think I am stupid so long as I get my salary.
> *Carlita:* How much money do you think you can get? RM500, deduct RM30 for levy, deduct RM150 for your debt, and each month you get RM320. Then you buy things and you send money back. You save no money. You stupid!

Imelda's statement illustrates the extent to which employers can and do dominate work relations and environments: some servants find themselves having to perform acts of self-deprecation in order to receive the wages that are legally due them in the first place. As Carlita implied, the strategy of confirming employers' belief that foreign domestic workers are less intelligent, ultimately, is counterproductive if the women fail to accumulate savings. In many cases, they are not able to save much money after paying off debts (e.g., debts incurred in employment application fees and passage to

Malaysia), buying the latest imported consumer goods, and remitting portions of wages back to family members.

There is, however, a financial avenue in which some get even, so to speak, with their employers.

"Immunizing" Employers   In return for the uncompensated labor that is extracted by their employers (e.g., working well into the evening), foreign domestic workers may consistently use their employers' telephones to call friends and/or families overseas. Some employers' telephone bills have been known to exceed RM1000 per month. In one case, a Filipina servant was overheard telling her friend that she had slowly "immunized" her employer to expect high telephone charges by gradually raising the charges on monthly statements from the telephone company.[38] Employers who are shocked by exorbitant monthly telephone bills, and/or employers who know of others who have had this experience, lock the telephone or call home intermittently to check on servants' activities. The women's infrapolitical acts of defiance reinforce the public transcript of domestic service since they behaved in ways that employers, rightly or wrongly, have come to expect of foreign domestic workers.

Performing the Unexpected   Sometimes, Filipina and Indonesian servants' acts of resistance are spontaneous, while the responses of others are planned. At the same afternoon discotheque in which I interviewed Mira, two Filipina servants respectively shared with me the different ways in which they curbed what they considered were excessive demands of their employers. Renaldo performed a caricature of her female employer's reaction to her spontaneous performance as she narrated the incident.

> Once I got a fever and my employer said to me, "You must continue to work." I felt so dizzy and she scolded me for washing the plates so slowly. So, I dropped the plates. They just fell out of my hands. She told me to go back to my room and sleep. She picked up the broken plates like this [the servant performed an exaggerated version of the way in which her employer held her rheumatic-ridden hips as she slowly bent down to pick up pieces of plates].

Teresa, on the other hand, took advantage of her employer's sense of gratitude.

> My employer likes me because I take good care of David [baby]. A few weeks ago, she told me that she didn't know what to do if I went back to the Philippines. I waited a few days and I told her, "Mum, I cannot iron anymore. My wrist is swollen." She told me that she would take me to the doctor. I said, "No need. My

doctor in the Philippines already said that if I use my hand too much, it will hurt"
[Teresa laughs]. She employed an Indian woman to iron three times a week.

Renaldo and Teresa narrated their experiences in ways designed to affirm
their intelligence—contra the public transcript in which foreign domestic
workers were represented as stupid or backward.

It should not come as a surprise that domestic workers' narratives almost
always identified female employers as the abusers. The mutually reinforcing
practices of public and private patriarchy that assign Malaysian women the
primary role of homemaker then also constitute the women as the primary
abusers of foreign female domestic workers.

Filipina and Indonesian servants' narratives revealed an unstated threshold that governed their responses to verbal abuse by female employers.
When employers traversed this threshold with foul language and/or gestures, some women could and did respond immediately and in distinct
ways, regardless of the consequences.

On the second day of a week-long Chinese New Year celebration, Ruth's
employer held a dinner for her husband's colleagues. In the kitchen, the
female employer used a series of Cantonese expletives to reprimand Ruth
for forgetting to place cognac glasses on the dining room table. Ruth, who
had worked in Kuala Lumpur for nearly one and one-half years, understood
the meaning of the words and reacted in a way that caused her employer to
apologize for the previously crude behavior. In the presence of six other
Filipinas, Ruth described the incident.

> In the kitchen, she said she was going to do something to my mother [gestures
> with her hand], and she told me to suck you know [she demonstrates with her lips]
> . . . I am too embarrassed to say it! How can she even think like this? When she
> told me to bring the soup bowls to the table, I bring one at a time because I was
> very angry. All of her friends saw me do it. Yes, she was embarrassed. What do you
> think her friends would say if they knew what she said to me? Why she treat me
> like an idiot, I don't know. After that, she said to me, "Please can you bring all the
> bowls at once?" She said nicely, so I brought out all the bowls. She dare not treat
> me like a fool anymore because I will embarrass her in front of her friends.

Pilar added to Ruth's narrative by describing how she had threatened to quit
when her female employer verbally insulted her.

> My employer scolded me for waking up at 6.30 a.m. instead of 6 a.m. She fol-
> lowed me into the kitchen and scolded me. She scolded me so hard, I felt dizzy
> and fainted. She pulled me up from the floor and scolded me some more. So

many bad words like "fuck up" and "bitch." I don't know why she scold me when I do everything for her. I went to my room and packed my bag. She was scared and asked me not to leave. I carried my bag to the door, and she stood in front of me. Then, she fell to her knees like this [Pilar demonstrates] and said sorry. So I didn't leave.

Ruth's and Pilar's nonverbal responses indirectly questioned the conduct, hence authority of their respective employers. The result in both cases was capitulation on the part of the dominant party.

In the public transcript, foreign domestic workers' performances are filled with acts of deference (in most cases, at least). In the hidden transcript of domestic service, employers are ridiculed with lewd jokes and performances of exaggerated body movements. These private performances in the presence of compatriots and/or in my presence allowed the women to reconstitute a sense of dignity that was denied them by employers. To be sure, the performances revealed strategies of coping with employers.

Susanti continued to describe her work experience to me while she picked out the freshest fish in the farmers' market for her employer.

> She came home drunk at 5 in the morning. I was so worried. Earlier, she didn't tell me where she was going. I didn't sleep all night. I kept her dinner on the table and all of her cats refused to eat because she wasn't there. She came home and started yelling at me. I was angry but I told her I was afraid that something had happened to her. She yelled at me some more. It was so loud. I am sure people outside the house could hear her. I went to her room and threw out all of her clothes . . . What did she say to me? Nothing. She fell on her bed and went to sleep. The next day, she woke up and told me to get her Panadol [similar to Tylenol] because she had a headache. I purposely made a lot of noise . . . switched on the radio very loud in the kitchen so that she could hear upstairs. She gave me money and told me to go shopping. Weekends are the best times to earn extra money.

Rusiah, who had started work recently as a waitress, explained why she quit her previous job:

> [My employer] saw me talking to the neighbor. We were only talking about cooking *rendang* [Malay version of dry curry]. She parked the car, got out and pulled me by my neck [she demonstrates]. The neighbor saw her do it. She didn't give me face. I went back to the house and told her I was leaving. She said no, and locked the gate. She put the key in her pocket. She came to my room and banged on the door. She screamed like a crazy woman. I opened the door and said, "What do you want? You want to look at me, yes?" So, I switched on all the lights in the house, opened all the windows and doors and took off all my clothes. I shouted

to the neighbors, "Look! Look! I have no clothes on!" I am her twenty-eighth maid in two years. Most left after one to two weeks. I stayed for eight months. My brother [who worked in the construction industry] came to get me and he arranged to change permits so that I can work here [in the restaurant].

Minah, her Indonesian friend who worked for a Chinese family, added:

> When I first arrived in Malaysia, my employer scolded me all the time. I cried. Then my friend [she looked at Rusiah] told me [over the telephone] to smile sweetly. So I smiled sweetly every time my employer scolded me. My employer said to me, "I give up. How can I scold you when you smile all the time?" She [employer] told her friend that I bring the family prosperity because I smile so much. She [employer] even struck big when she bought *empat ekor* [four digit lottery number].

Susanti's and Rusiah's narratives constructed middle-class female employers as unreasonable, if not psychologically unstable household supervisor-managers. Even though Susanti successfully devised a strategy with which to deal with her employer, Rusiah was left with little option but to quit her job. Perhaps, *Fortuna* had a hand in Minah's good working relationship with her employer. What was important for Minah's sake was that the simple act of smiling became a successful coping strategy.

Filipina and Indonesian servants who have telephone privileges, rest days, or who are asked to run errands beyond their employers' houses, are able to share their work experiences with one another. The implication is that those who are prohibited from leaving their employers' houses and/or from using employers' telephones, are completely isolated and defenseless. However, some Indonesian domestic workers challenged their confinement in culturally specific ways.

Fasting   Indonesian servants who were kept in employers' houses with no possibility of rest days, could and did draw on the Muslim practice of "fasting" to protest their lack of rights. In fact, it was reported that during the 1991 state threat of deportation, many Indonesian domestic workers abstained from eating to protest the state's policy of deporting all illegal Indonesian domestic workers.[39]

During an interview with Sujanti in her employer's house (her employer had just left for work), she told me that she had not eaten anything for the last few days. I asked her if she was given enough food to eat, and she nodded her head. I then asked her why she had not eaten anything since the fasting month (*Hari Raya Puasa*) had long ended. She shrugged her shoulders and looked at me directly without saying a word. A few days later, I was told by her female employer's neighbor that:

> She [female employer] doesn't treat her servant well at all. She works the girl like a bull. She's really cruel. Who could work for her? The girl is always up at 5 every morning. I see her outside hanging clothes in the morning and she works nonstop until 10 at night. Sometimes we see her washing their cars late at night. And, when he [female employer's husband] comes home late, she scolds the girl. We can hear.

I do not fully know what happened to Sujanti, except for the fact that approximately two weeks after the interview, she was sent home to Indonesia.

Siti, an Indonesian servant of a Chinese employer in this study, was sent back to the DOM immediately when she refused to eat. The employer said to me, "She'll wash two dishes and go back into her room to cry. Every time I spoke to her, she would cry. You know, this is not the right way to treat me. Then, she refused to eat. She wouldn't eat anything. I was so scared. I called the agent, and he came and took her away."

Siti's hunger strike had frightened her female employer, and consequently took her away from a work environment in which she was prohibited from leaving the house; she was not allowed to send or receive mail from Indonesia; and she had not been paid any wages for the first six months of her work tenure. Later, I was informed by an Indonesian servant in the same neighborhood that Siti had been placed with another family, and that on her rest days, she would return to visit her compatriots.

Use of Bodily Fluids   Another form of nonverbal infrapolitical activity is some foreign domestic workers' use of bodily fluids to contaminate their employers' possessions. A female employer in this study told me that her servant had accidentally cut her finger while chopping vegetables, but that she had refused to put a Band-Aid on the wound. Instead, the female employer found bloodstains all over the clothes that her servant ironed shortly after cutting her finger: "I gave her the Band-Aid and told her to wash her finger before putting it on. The stupid girl didn't do it. There were bloodstains on every piece of clothing. I tell you, the girl is stupid. What to do?" Yet, the "girl" was not stupid enough since the female employer would ask her to help the seven year-old daughter with her school homework.

I discovered by accident that Lita, the Filipina servant who previously argued that the embassy was ineffective in resolving employer-employee disputes, used her menstrual blood to change her employer's behavior. One day, during an interview with one of the female employers in this study, I was pleasantly surprised to see Lita walk out of the kitchen. Her employer had just finished complaining about what had happened the day before. She had seen trails of blood all over the house, and upon further inquiry, discovered that Lita was on her menstrual cycle. The female employer went out, bought sanitary pads, and asked Lita if she knew how to use them. Lita answered in the affirmative but she refused to use the pads. In any event, Lita was made to clean up her own blood.

As Lita walked past her employer and me, the employer loudly said that, "*Bun Mui* [lit: Filipina *mui-tsai* or girl-slave] are as dumb as the Indonesian ones." Unfazed by the comment, Lita looked at me and smiled as if to congratulate me for having solved her puzzle.

The female employer had failed to decipher Lita's symbolic message. Lita was neither backward nor stupid especially since she had worked as a nurse's aide in Manila prior to her job as a domestic worker in Malaysia. Even though Lita was forced to clean up her blood throughout the house, she successfully redefined the conditions in which her employer demanded her services. As Lita walked toward the staircase, the employer said, "Lita, put the clothes basket on the staircase. I will put it away later. You go back and rest." The employer then said to me, "Aiyah! No more blood on my floor and bedroom please. So dirty. Better let her rest, take it easy."

Another case involving bodily fluids in an infrapolitical act occurred one afternoon when I interviewed an employer in her home. Midway through the interview, the employer told me that she had to take her daughter to the music school. Instead of asking me to leave with her, she told me to wait in her house and offered me lunch that the servant had prepared earlier. She said, "Yati is an excellent cook. She is the best maid I've employed so far. I'll ask her to prepare a plate for you."

After the employer left the house, Yati set the table and brought out the food. She served me and then sat down to chat with me. She said that in the beginning she had had a difficult relationship with her female employer. Yati explained why:

> She [female employer] used to say that my cooking was not good enough. I would tell her to "cook it yourself, then you will like it better." She told me that people with big mouths would get hurt. So, I put saliva [*air liur*] and *hoisin* [oyster sauce] in the chicken stew, just the way she likes it. . . . I tell her that it is a special recipe. She eats, her husband eats, the children eat, I also eat. You see, she doesn't say my cooking is bad anymore. I am a very good cook. Next time I make

kangkung with *belachan* [or *sambal kangkung*, i.e., vegetables cooked in shrimp chili paste] you should come by. It is very good.

According to various versions of Malay folk wisdom, the recitation of certain mantras while adding one's saliva to food prepared for others ensures that those who consume the food will behave in ways advantageous to the cook. By the time Yati told me the story of how she had convinced her employer that she was a skilled cook, I had already finished my meal. Nonetheless, I graciously accepted her invitation but my research schedule ultimately did not permit me to return to her employer's house for another meal.

In the examples above, Filipina and Indonesian domestic workers engaged in individualized infrapolitical activities that altered one or another aspect of employer-domestic worker relations. The most common and final act of protest is the phenomenon of "run away" foreign servants. Contrary to the belief of state authorities, the press, and employers, Filipina and Indonesian domestic workers in this study insisted that those who ran away did so to escape their abusive employers (see the examples of Subaidah and Ibu Nin).

Dress by Design: Redefining the Identity of the Maid   Filipina servants especially were sensitive to, and critical of, Malaysian discourse that associated all foreign domestic workers with sex-for-sale acts. Ironically, as Filipinas attempt to dress and act in ways that disassociate them from their status and image as servants, the different apparel and demeanor have had the effect of reinforcing the negative perceptions of the Malaysian public. This specific form of resistance strengthens the public transcript of domestic service in which Malaysian employers and the public believe that most, if not all, foreign servants would become prostitutes if given the opportunity to do so.

On their rest days, some Filipina and Indonesian women can be seen clothed in full length dresses or skirts/jeans and blouses while they mingle with their friends at churches, farmers' markets, shopping malls, and bus and taxi stands. Others make it a point to wear lycra pants, tank tops, and high heels. Salbi's friend, who was among a handful of Filipina domestic workers selling toiletries and other goods on the property of a church, turned to me and said, "See, look around you. We do not dress like maids. We dress like we work in the office. Very good, huh?" Servants who are given rest days by employers perfect the art of distancing themselves from their image as "maids": some women go to beauty salons to perm their hair and manicure their fingernails, while others proudly exhibit their various pieces of pricey jewelry.

At a dinner in a fast-food restaurant with a group of Filipina domestic workers, Amy complained that her employer had given her an ultimatum: either she cut her long nails painted fire-engine red or the employer would terminate her contract. Amy told us, "I am not going to cut my nails. She [employer] doesn't like it because she says that my nails prevent me from washing clothes properly. Who says so? I do my work like any maid. She told me also to wear jeans when I work. Why should I wear jeans?" Rosa, her friend responded, "How can you sweep the floor and clean the toilet looking like this? [Amy was wearing a short, tight skirt and a V-neck tank top]" Amy answered, "No big deal."

The conversation shifted to psychological tests that foreign domestic workers must pass before they are given their exit and entry permits. Amy described the test: "It is in English and Tagalog. So many questions to answer. There is a picture of a man and a woman, and they ask us to describe . . . [D]raw the hair and draw the clothes. Describe in ten words."

Nancy who had been relatively quiet, gestured with her fingers. Rosa responded by saying, "Oh, Nancy just wants to sell her *puki* ["vagina" in colloquial Malay]." In an attempt to pacify Nancy, who was visibly upset by the comment, Amy said: "She [Rosa] just made a joke. Nancy is not like them [pointing to two Filipina domestic workers who had just walked past our table wearing body hugging clothes]. They do this [prostitute themselves] on Sunday to earn extra money. But we are not like them." The majority of the foreign domestic workers with whom I spoke, indeed, were exceedingly conservative in their views of sex with Malaysian men. Most of the women resented the Malaysian public's belief that all foreign servants are sexually immoral women.

Foreign domestic workers who date Malaysian men also run the risk of being labeled as prostitutes. Renaldo and "Soon" tried to explain the decision of some compatriots who were in relationships with Malaysian men. ("Soon" was the nickname that the servant's friends gave her because she would always tell her Malaysian male suitors at the church that she would decide soon if she was interested in dating them.)

> *Renaldo:* Men sweettalk, already they [servants] give everything. But sometimes, you can't blame them. They are homesick and also "home sex" [she laughs]. They are human, just like everyone else.
>
> *Soon:* Some Filipina maids want boyfriends because of the call of nature. It is very hard to control the call of nature.

The combination of public and private surveillance of foreign female domestic workers in Malaysia has had the effect of simultaneously dehumanizing and sexualizing Filipina and Indonesian women. From this perspective, there is little room left for many to perceive foreign domestic workers as women with real emotions, feelings, hopes, and dreams. While male migrant workers are given relatively unrestricted movement in public space, the policies and actions of state authorities, employers, and DOMs, consistently try to strip Filipina and Indonesian domestic workers of "the call to nature," and other expressions that afford some sense of comfort and belonging to humanity. It is the hidden transcript, as discussed, that records Filipina and Indonesian domestic workers' struggle for self and group validation.

The Bleak Future

The hidden transcript of domestic service that can reveal foreign servants' responses to the material and symbolic domination of their employers is shaped mostly by the structure of work environments established indirectly by state authorities, and directly controlled by employers. Taken out of context, foreign domestic workers' responses, e.g., foot dragging, feigning illness, smearing employers' possession with blood, and dressing and acting differently on their rest days, may appear trivial and inconsequential. If Filipina and Indonesian women's verbal and nonverbal infrapolitical activities are considered within the boundaries of what acts are and are not possible in unlegislated work environments that retain the remnants of slavery, then foreign domestic workers are political actors who attempt to renegotiate employer-employee relations in the household in particular, and the Malaysian public's perceptions of foreign servants in general.

The overall effectiveness of foreign servants' infrapolitical activities remains questionable. In some instances, infrapolitical activities that sought to change employer-constructed identities and working conditions further strengthened negative representations of foreign domestic workers in and by the public transcript. Within the existing political and economic contexts of Malaysian society, the women's efforts to demonstrate that they are not dishonest, backward, lazy, and/or sexually-depraved foreign servants, can and do backfire. Presently the identification of informal assemblages as places that nurture covert or clandestine activities of foreign domestic workers have led to raids by state authorities (in search of illegal migrants and/or illegal migrant activities), and many employers' refusal (at the behest of

DOMs) to give servants rest days or even the right to make and receive telephone calls. The fate of informal assemblages appears precarious, and by extension Filipina and Indonesian domestic workers' ability once or twice a month to meet with their compatriots and regain some sense of validation as human beings who are deserving of friendship, respect, and dignity.

Contradictions emerging from the Malaysian state's quest for social stability in the growing presence of foreign migrant workers, and middle-class women's need for relief from housework, are not without negative repercussions on the lives of Filipina and Indonesian servants. In the next chapter, which provides a closer analysis of middle-class demands for paid reproductive labor, I discuss how and why there is an overall absence, or lack of urgency, in the official and middle classes' acknowledgment of the need to stem employer-related abuse of foreign female domestic workers.

Notes on the Epigraphs

(In order of appearance): Mrs. T. D. Ampikaipakan, "Social Etiquette" Columnist of The *Star*, November 15, 1993; Author's interview with "Louisa," on April 10, 1994, Kuala Lumpur.

CHAPTER 6

Modernity Via Consumption: Domestic Service and the Making of the Modern Malaysian Middle Classes

What I mean may be put into the form of a question, I said: Are dogs divided into hes and shes, or do they both share equally in hunting and in keeping watch and in the other duties of dogs? [O]r do we entrust to the males the entire and exclusive care of the flocks, while we leave the females at home, under the idea that the bearing and suckling of their puppies is labour enough for them?
—Plato, *Republic*, circa 380 - 370 B.C.

A woman who has a head full of Greek, like Mme. Dacier, or carries on fundamental controversies about mechanics, might as well have a beard.
 —Immanuel Kant, *Observations on the Feeling of the Beautiful and the Sublime*, 1799

Toward the end of the NEP period, persistent demands for live-in domestic workers led to the formal reopening of the immigration gates and the implementation of rules governing Malaysian employment of Filipina and Indonesian servants. Their mass employment comes at a cost both to the women and middle-class female employers. As ascertained in the previous chapter, many female employers in this study failed to question the ways in which capitalist development mediated through the patriarchal-ethnic lens in Malaysia shape their lives and obscure the sociomoral consequences of their relation to foreign domestic workers.

While extreme cases of physical abuse are sensationalized by the newsprint media, the relatively less abusive aspects of employer-foreign servant relations have not received much attention.[1] Long work hours, no rest days, inadequate nutrition, and verbal harassment have become routine among servants in some middle-class households. This is not to say that no Malaysians are concerned with employer mistreatment and abuse of foreign servants. To be sure, NGOs are involved actively in counseling abused foreign servants, and lobbying the state for foreign migrant workers' rights. Nonetheless, such voices on behalf of Filipina and Indonesian domestic workers barely have been able to challenge the general public and private apathy toward foreign servants' working relations and conditions.

In this chapter, I argue that employers and the public-at-large have been able to ignore Filipina and Indonesian domestic workers' plights because of the ways in which interests of the state elite and the middle classes have converged. For the Malaysian state elite, contemporary domestic service helps socialize the middle classes in general and women in particular to specific kinds of social relations and organizations deemed necessary for the future of society and country. The employment rules encourage the middle classes' adoption of the nuclear family form for specific normative and political economic purposes.

From the perspective of the middle classes, not only are foreign servants substitute homemakers but they also are symbols that construct and maintain social status. In short, the in-migration and employment of Filipina and Indonesian domestic workers have become a major part of the state elite and the middle classes' pursuit of a shared vision of modernity that defines national and personal progress, in part, with the ability to purchase, consume, and display goods—including that of commodified Filipina and Indonesian female servants.

This chapter begins with a discussion of the Malaysian state's juridical-legislative relation to middle-class women, especially in reference to the implementation and intended consequences of the 1984 National Population Policy (NPP). The NPP was a policy that overtly encouraged women to have more children in order to meet the projected labor demands of the twenty-first century. In this section, I revisit the employment rules to show how and why contemporary domestic service has been coopted as one of the state's "educative" institutions.

State involvement in the changing form and content of contemporary domestic service has, as one of its key objectives, the middle classes' adoption of the nuclear family form. In the midst of the politics of socioeconomic restructuring, the nuclear family becomes the site of and for the reaffirmation of the state's normative position vis-à-vis Malaysian women. The family rule, which allowed only married couples with children to employ foreign servants, was used as leverage to redomesticate Malaysian women.

The middle-class nuclear family form also has a perceived distinct political-economic advantage for development in Malaysia. Members of the nuclear family are expected to encourage the expansion of the capitalist market economy. Family members, especially in urban areas such as Kuala

Lumpur, increasingly rely on the capitalist market as opposed to the community or extended family members for the provision of goods and services. Chapter 4 demonstrated that key among the services offered by the capitalist market economy in Malaysia is that of foreign migrant women's domestic labor.

A major reason for the middle classes' employment of foreign domestic workers is the lack of childcare support for mothers who work beyond the home. The question, however, arises as to why Malaysians who turn to the capitalist market for the supply of domestic labor would elect to hire foreign servants instead of sending their children to creches or childcare centers. Female employers' decision to do so is shaped by the prevailing Asian patriarchal belief that the performance of housework is women's work, and that the women negotiate this constraint by transferring the responsibility of domestic labor to Filipina and Indonesian women who work under their supervision.

The contemporary institution of domestic service in Malaysia is indicative of more than the issues of which gender, what social class, and what nationality ought to perform paid reproductive labor. Interviews of Malaysian employers revealed that the presence of a foreign domestic worker in a Malaysian household is considered a significant symbol of a family's achievement of "middle class-hood." Put simply, the middle classes' consumption of Filipina and Indonesian women's domestic labor is considered by Malaysian Malay, Chinese, and Indian employers alike as a key way to construct and maintain social status in an age of rapid social change.

The last part of this chapter locates Malaysian demands for servants within the context of the middle classes' consumption of goods and services. I examine the public and private (namely the advertising industry) sectors' role in promoting consumption-oriented lifestyles for Malays and non-Malays from the middle classes. In the schemata of what I call "modernity via consumption," the social construction of Filipina and Indonesian servants as a symbol of distinction between the middle and working classes, and also as commodities, obfuscates the notion that foreign domestic workers are women who deserve to be treated with respect and dignity, and who have a right to legal recognition and protection as workers.

The National Population Policy: Redomesticating Malaysian Women

Midway through the period of the NEP, during which Malaysian women enjoyed greater education and employment opportunities, a specific policy was introduced that attempted to redomesticate Malaysian women from specific social classes. In 1984, Prime Minister Dr. Mahathir Mohamad announced the National Population Policy (NPP)—the state's plan for a population of 70 million in 115 years (the population in 1984 was 12.6 million).[2] As a result, the Malaysian state appeared to overtly shift to a pronatalist position when most of the developing world was struggling to search for more effective means of controlling population growth.[3]

The NPP is a continuation of the gendered ideological basis of state power. The real and perceived requirements of export-oriented development have made this only more salient. The gendered ideological basis is discerned most readily by the law and its implementation.

The Malaysian state's juridical-legislative dimension constructs rules that regulate relations within civil society. Among the rules are those that define the formal status and roles of women.[4] Malaysian women, unlike their Western counterparts, won suffrage at the same time that society achieved independence from colonialism: female citizenship was necessary for the perception of and the claim to a newly born or liberated nation of Malaysians.

In spite of women's suffrage, men remained in the eyes of the law as the more legitimate gender possessor of civil-political rights.[5] At the outset, Malaysian women's right to vote in 1957 was synonymous with the formal recognition of women as legitimate citizens. However, for at least five years after independence in 1957, the postcolonial state refused to grant citizenship to children born in Malaysia if the only parent with Malaysian citizenship was the mother.[6] Children born to families in which only the father was a citizen, however, were automatically granted citizenship.

Although the Federal Constitution was amended in 1962 to recognize Malaysian women as bearers of citizenship, there remains the belief that men, not women, are the legitimate bearers of citizenship. Presently, Article 23 Clause (1) of the Federal Constitution permits anyone who is twenty-one years old and above to renounce his/her citizenship.[7] Nonetheless, Article 23, Clause (3) allows a sixteen-year old woman to renounce her citizenship if she marries a non-Malaysian citizen. This rule is based on the assumption that if and when a Malaysian woman marries a non-Malaysian citizen, she would want and would be expected to adopt her husband's citizenship.

The basis for the Federal Constitution's construction of Malaysian female citizenry can be traced to the classical liberal conception of gender and gender rights in the state-society divide. I neither argue that Malaysian Malay, Chinese, and Indian cultures were/are not patriarchal in their conception of women's rights, roles, and status, nor do I intend to make "strawmen" of Western/British state and culture. The point that I wish to impress here is that the construction of the modern Malaysian state apparatus was modeled after that of its colonial master. In other words, the "import" of a foreign form of state must necessarily include the "import" of different ideas and ways of organizing social relations and institutions. This does not mean that indigenous or "traditional" forms of social institutions were static prior to, or discarded at the imposition of, foreign structures. Rather, the Malaysian politico-bureaucratic elite chose to focus on restructuring some dimensions of imported institutions at the expense of others. A key dimension left somewhat intact is the conception of women and the family as "natural," hence free from state intervention.

According to the classical liberal framework, the state is the guarantor and protector of citizens' possession and expression of civil-political rights. Social relations and organizations in public space are believed to be characteristic of, and dependent on, the exercise of instrumental rationality. Of the two sexes, men are constituted as the gender possessor of instrumental rationality since they must and do freely move between the public and private-domestic domains.[8]

The private or domestic domain is a distinctly unremunerated work domain characterized by expressions of love and comfort, rather than instrumental rationality.[9] As such, the institution of the family is conceptualized as a nonpolitical "natural" unit of social organization.[10] Women, by virtue of their capacity to bear children, are located exclusively within the domestic domain wherein their identities are the product of two interrelated processes: women are ascribed expressive/affective rationality as opposed to instrumental powers of rationality, and concomitantly, their preordained role is to provide emotional comfort and reproductive labor.

Taken to its logical conclusion, women are perceived as incapable of possessing and exercising civil-political rights. They enjoy civil-political rights only by association with their husbands and fathers.[11] The liberal construction of women's roles and status is epitomized or embodied in the rise of bourgeois society in the West, i.e., concrete manifestations of the theory of gender relations and family life.

In the case of postcolonial Malaysia, key legacies of British colonialism are assumptions that inform the juridical-legislative construction of women's formal roles and status. Women's legal rights are grounded in the belief that they are, above all else, primarily wives and mothers in charge of the domestic domain. Left unacknowledged in the liberal framework is that implicit in

the state's construction of women's rights is the regulation of gender relations. Critical feminist theorists today argue that the liberal construction of
women's identities as wives and mothers has to be maintained consistently
by legislation and policies "pertaining to the family, population, labor force
and labor management, housing, sexual behaviour and expression, provision
of child care and education, taxation and income redistribution, and the creation and use of military forces."[12] That is, legislation and policies on a variety of aspects of social life surreptitiously maintain women's status and roles
primarily as wives and mothers.

Particularly in the realm of Malaysian employment legislation, the concept
of equal pay for equal work does not exist. The assumption is that if women
venture to work beyond the home, then they are expected to do so only temporarily. While the Federal Constitution prohibits religious and race discrimination, it does not protect women against sex discrimination. As late as 1994,
the issue of sex discrimination in employment practices remained unaddressed by the state.

Personal income tax legislation constitutes and legitimates male social
and economic control within a nuclear family unit. The Income Tax Act
1978, Clause 53, Section 45, allows a Malaysian woman to file her income
tax return separately from her husband *only if* her income is derived from
a recognized and registered profession (medicine, law, architecture, and so
forth). In this case, middle-class women benefit from the legislation so long
as they are engaged in a profession that is recognized formally by a community of peers and by the state.

The invisible contribution of women within the domestic domain is
superimposed on to women who work alongside husbands in building
family businesses. A Malaysian woman is not permitted to file separately
if her income is derived from services rendered to a business owned by
her husband.

The state penalizes families in which women are the sole breadwinners,
while rewarding families in which husbands work outside the home while
their wives either perform housework, or employ others to do so. Sections 47
and 48 (1) of the Income Tax Act 1978 respectively prohibit working women
who file separately from their husbands to claim deductions for nonworking
or unemployed husbands or for wages paid to childcare providers. Put succinctly, a husband is allowed to claim deductions for nonworking wives and
for childcare, whereas a wife who works beyond the home is prohibited from
doing so.

Arguably, middle- and upper-middle-class women can afford not to participate as workers in the formal economy. Increasingly however, many middle-class women are compelled to work beyond their homes either because of the personal desire to pursue careers, and/or the need to maintain the ability to pursue modern urban lifestyles. The NEP did not plan for women to be more than temporary workers in the economy. Zainab Wahidin argues "That Malay women received the benefits of the NEP is accidental for there was no explicit recognition in the policy that Malay women's participation were equally important in the restructuring of occupations."[13] When the state planned FTZs, it was assumed that TNCs would hire Malaysian (especially Malay) men.[14] When TNCs preferred female workers instead, the Federal Industrial Development Authority (FIDA) produced a brochure promoting women's "natural" skill in assembling computer chips. The brochure read, "The manual dexterity of the oriental female is famous the world over. Her hands are small and she works fast with extreme care. Who therefore could be better qualified by nature and inheritance to contribute to the efficiency of a bench assembly line than the oriental girl?"[15]

By the late 1970s, approximately 80,000 Malaysian women (from all ethnic groups between the ages of 16 and mid-20s) worked in TNC-owned factories.[16] Gradually, public discourse on the consequences of young women's, especially Malay women's, newfound social and economic independence from men was framed in terms of the declining standards of female morality. The infamous *Minah Karan* metaphor emerged in public discourse to symbolize the perceived sexual liberation of all female factory workers.[17] Women's economic independence would be conflated with declining sexual morality.

What little social and economic progress that Malaysian women achieved during the 1970s did not go unchallenged. The image of sexually "loose" female factory workers in a development era in which family planning programs were pursued actively while the marriage age increased and fertility rates decreased linked Malaysian women's growing socioeconomic independence to the size of the future Malaysian workforce.[18]

Within the Malay community or the numerically and politically dominant ethnic group, women's independence became synonymous with Malay men's sense of real or perceived loss of social and economic control over their womenfolk.[19] The 1970s Islamic movement, in part, provided men with a legitimate avenue for reasserting their control over Malay women. The state's 1980s Islamization program would reinforce further the images of the ideal

Muslim wife and mother. As Aihwa Ong writes, "The call for a strengthening of the Malay race required women to adhere to a stricter Islamic version of male authority and of women's roles as mothers and wives."[20]

Scholars of Malaysian women in development identify two key consequences of women's newfound socioeconomic independence. On the one hand, Malaysian men's belief that women were more sexually approachable meant that working women confronted increased incidences of verbal and sexual harassment from men in public space. Rural and urban Malay women began to wear the veil, not only as a symbol of religious purity, but also for protection against harassment.[21]

On the other hand, some Malay men began to forego the Islamic marriage contract that constitutes men as the responsible party for the economic support of the family. Aihwa Ong reported that wives of the Malay rural elite (UMNO members) petitioned the state to require husbands to pay their wives monetary "allowances." She argued that the petition was not a reflection of marxist-feminist demands for "wages for housework." Rather, Malay women insisted that their husbands fulfill the traditional male role since "land scarcity, widespread female wage labor and secularization in many cases reduced men's customary obligation to be the sole supporters of their families."[22]

The state's solution was to reinforce women's roles as mothers and wives while laying the groundwork for a larger population and workforce that could support the labor demands of export-oriented development. In 1984, the NPP was introduced and incorporated into the Fourth Malaysia Development Plan:

> Recognizing that a larger population constitutes an important human resource to create *a larger consumer base with an increasing purchasing power* [emphasis mine] to generate and support industrial growth through productive exploitation of natural resources, Malaysia could, therefore, plan for a larger population which could ultimately reach 70 million.[23]

The NPP was formulated under the assumptive equation of more babies=more workers=more purchasing or consumptive power=more development. It was acknowledged then that the modernity project could not be fully realized unless Malaysian women strengthened their role as reproducers of the future Malaysian workforce.

To reflect the new pronatalist position, the National Family Planning Board was renamed the National Population and Family Development

Board. The following incentives were given to Malaysian women to have more children: extended paid maternity benefits to mothers for their first five children (as opposed to the first three children); and income tax deductions or "child relief" was raised for the third, fourth, and fifth child.[24]

It has been posited that the NPP was the official response to Islamicist assertions that women no longer were fulfilling their traditional roles as wives and mothers.[25] This perspective is only one part of the larger picture. Rather, it was the confluence of Islamicists' demands, and planning for the expansion of export-oriented development, that finally brought the state's gendered basis to the foreground as embodied in the NPP:

> Indeed it [the state] could not offer any explanation as to how the figure of 70 million was to be achieved in 115 years by women having five children each. At the present growth rate of 2.2 percent, Malaysia's population would reach 70 million in 71 years (i.e. in 2051) or 117 million in 115 years . . . *Numerical juggling notwithstanding, it is quite clear that the Prime Minister's message is that he wants a rapid increase in the country' population and that is to be achieved by an increase in fertility rates* [emphasis mine]. The best official rationale for this is that for Malaysia to become a great society (presumably like South Korea and Japan), it will require a policy of heavy industrialization. This, in turn, requires a large population to provide both the labour force as well as the domestic market for industrial products.[26]

We know that the juridical-legislative dimension was gendered in its modern inception. The next logical question is, "Which class(es) of women is the realistic target of the NPP?" Prime Minister Dr. Mahathir Mohamad would identify women from the middle and upper-middle-classes as the primary target groups. One newspaper quoted him as having said in 1984 that, "Women whose husbands could afford [five children] should stay at home to raise their families." Another newspaper quoted him in a slightly different way: "In a situation where there may be unemployment, it will be good for the girls to have babies and let *others* [emphasis mine] be employed."[27]

The latter message was that women should not compete with men in the job market during times of economic downturn/crisis. The former message would encourage women from the middle and upper-middle classes to stay home and have children in preparation for a larger population and workforce that would bolster export-oriented development by bringing about "a larger consumer base with an increasing purchasing power."

It became clear during the mid-1980s that the economy eventually would confront labor shortages in the twenty-first century if the initial policy of limiting population growth was not reversed. Hence, the pronatalist

NPP was expected to increase the national birth rate by encouraging women to bear more children, and at the very same time, to quell the complaints of Malaysian men in general, and Islamicists in particular.

Since then, rapid economic growth has facilitated the in-migration of foreign workers *and* made explicit the need for Malaysian women from all classes to work beyond the home: by the early 1990s, the unemployment rate had declined to approximately 3 percent (see table 2.9).[28] Today, the Malaysian economy requires Malaysian women's active participation along the productive and reproductive dimensions. In her keynote address at the 1993 International Strategic and International Studies' National Conference on Women, Minister of National Unity and Social Development Datuk Seri Paduka Napsiah Omar best summarized the state's position toward women.

> But, however much we would like to rest on our laurels as a nation, the needs of the country remains our imperative. Women, the country needs you! In our effort to achieve the very realistic socio-economic target, as set out by Wawasan 2020, we have come across one enormous problem. *Our successes, we find, have left us with a labour shortage . . . Now we have to lay the groundwork of our future with a population of 18 million* [emphasis mine]. With a gradually aging population— also due to another success, good health care—our labour shortage will be exacerbated. It is only reasonable therefore that the government looks to its women as a reservoir of ready labour . . . *It then becomes obvious where and to whom we must turn. It is to our women* [emphasis mine]. But women are already burdened with the reproductive role. We reproduce society not only physically but socially. We are the nurturers. Should that the national interest be given its due priority, women must now bear the full brunt of the economic burden, too.[29]

She exhorted women to assume their responsibility to economy and country by having children and by participating in the labor force.

In the early to mid 1980s, the NPP was expected to encourage women to stay home and reproduce and nurture future generations of Malaysians. Today, the state and the economy require women to bear children *and* to work outside the home. These messages seem contradictory only if we fail to take into account the underlying capitalist-patriarchal construction of women as appendages to men.[30] So long as women are located in and constructed as the gender in charge of the domestic domain, then their participation in public space and activities is required only in times of political and economic challenges. Modern history of the developing world in general, and Malaysia in particular, abounds with examples of women's participation in nascent nationalist movements against colonialism, only to be relegated to the domestic domain after independence.[31] The state's modernity project of Vision 2020 entails a greater emphasis on women—specifically the middle and upper-middle classes—in their capacities simultaneously as mothers and workers.

In addition to legislative changes designed to encourage women to have children, what other state benefits are there for middle-class women to do so, especially since the issue of who performs childcare and housework could prevent some, if not many, middle-class women from working beyond the home? According to the family rule governing the employment of foreign domestic workers, only married couples who earn a certain combined level of annual income, and who have children, legally qualify to employ Filipina and Indonesian domestic workers.

The gendered state apparatus is not interested merely in middle-class women having more babies per se, but that women reproduce the future workforce within a family structure that is acceptable. Only the middle classes (and upper-middle classes) who have nuclear families then are rewarded with state approval to employ Filipina and Indonesian domestic workers.

The income and family rules construct a middle-class nuclear family in which women's roles and identities as workers, wives, mothers, and supervisor-spies of foreign servants are emphasized simultaneously in their service to the country and family. Given the level of entrenched public patriarchy in Malaysian society, the employment rules cannot but function to reinforce the state's normative position vis-à-vis Malaysian women. Specifically, the interplay between the socioeconomic implications of the NPP and the state's employment rules has the effect of what M. Jacqui Alexander, in a different context, identifies as the gendered state's effort to "redraft morality."[32]

To be sure, the family rule insists that middle-class women who can be relieved socially and legally from performing housework are those who practice the patriarchal construction of the family. Inevitably, the state assumes a harsh and punitive posture toward those who require domestic help but who, for one reason or another, fail to meet this requirement.[33] Middle-class women and men who choose to remain single or who are single parents; middle-class couples who do not have children; and the elderly who do not have young children living with them are excluded, in theory, from the exclusive community of legal employers of foreign domestic workers. In practice, Malaysians in any of the above categories are able to employ Filipina and Indonesian servants by way of creative, DOM-initiated solutions (see chapter 4).

Aside from the intent to redraft morality, the choice of the nuclear family form is premised on a specific political economic rationale. The rest of this chapter discusses how and why the persons and labor of foreign domestic workers are indispensable in encouraging the expanding Malaysian middle classes to pursue a particular vision of modernity that strengthens export-oriented development and maintains social stability in the multiethnic society.

Creches or Foreign Maids?:
Middle-Class Family and the Privatization of Social Life

Feminist scholarship of household relations continues to demystify or deconstruct the family by arguing that it is not merely an institution filled with love and care.[34] Rather, the family in its various forms cannot be adequately understood without examining the relationship between the (patriarchal) state, capitalist development, gender division of labor in the domestic domain, and/or prevailing interracial/interethnic relations. Succinctly put, it is argued that changing family forms, which accompany the shift in production from within to beyond the domestic domain, are consequences of capitalist expansion mediated through patriarchal and/or racial-ethnic ideologies.[35] The capitalist-patriarchal (and/or racialized-ethnicized) state is identified as a facilitator of changing family forms via social legislation and policies.[36]

It is appropriate to warn the reader, at this point, that in the following discussion on the Malaysian state's relation to the family, there will not be an analysis of ethnicity per se. I am aware that feminists of color have critiqued the scholarship of feminists such as R. W. Connell who, in the discussion on state-family-gender relations, fail to integrate or deal with the dimensions of race and/or ethnicity.[37] While I agree that race and/or ethnicity are important dimensions in understanding the political economy of many countries of the world, I argue that in the context of the family rule, which encourages the middle classes' adoption of the nuclear family form, ethnicity paradoxically is not key to the state's relation to female employers in Malaysia.

An argument can be made that within the context of interethnic relations, the NPP could be and was implemented with Malay women in mind: i.e., to increase the Malay population relative to non-Malays. Even so, the "family" rule that normalizes Malaysian employment of foreign domestic workers within the nuclear family form *applies to middle-class women from all ethnic groups*. It is in this sense that the Malaysian state is gendered without regard to ethnicity. As discussed later, the state's ethnic-blind policy vis-à-vis the Malaysian nuclear family is part of the efforts to overcome ethnic differences in the construction of a modern Malaysian family.

State regulation of Malaysian employment of Filipina and Indonesian servants has coopted contemporary domestic service as a key educative institution to socialize employers into a particular kind of middle class-hood. Of the different family forms, the nuclear family is considered the most appropriate organization of modern social life that facilitates the development of capitalist market economies.[38] As Janet W. Salaff points out in her study of the family and the state in Singapore, "By changing the source as well as the distribution of resources, the state economic and social policies restructure the fabric of community and family life. Peoples not only become more closely integrated into a national market economy, they also enter deeply into the capitalist culture."[39]

Salaff further writes that, "As members of households become directly linked to the market economy as consumers, debtors, and pensioners, wider ties to the local community based on mutual aid are weakening. At the same time, these exchanges stimulate the market economy and empower the state."[40] Contemporary capitalist development in Singapore is revealing of the extent to which the state is involved in what can be called the "privatization of social life" in which families are encouraged to turn to capitalist markets for the provision of goods and services.

Similarly in Malaysia, the processes of privatizing social life at the level of the household occur in conjunction with economic privatization at the national level, in which the state appears to disengage from the economy by selling major industries to privately owned corporations that, in turn, offer manufactured products and services to the peoples. A key difference is that while economic privatization at the national level is premised on addressing economic inefficiency in state-owned and controlled industries, the privatization of social life in the form of the nuclear family is premised on the real or perceived need to mold society in a manner that is conducive to bringing about and normalizing capitalist social relations and lifestyles.

The family rule governing Malaysian employment of foreign female domestic workers embody the assumption that the nuclear family is the most appropriate and "natural" form for socializing the Malaysian middle classes—regardless of ethnic, religious, and cultural differences—into a modern urban capitalist lifestyle. In the absence of alternative resource avenues that could be and were provided by extended families or households in the past, middle-class family members rely on the capitalist market for the provision of services. This level of dependence on the market increasingly is reflected in middle-class women's demands for household help. The phenomenon of Filipina and Indonesian domestic workers in Malaysia, and the structure and processes of the Malaysian-Philippine-Indonesian maid trade, are telling of the degree to which the transnational migrant domestic labor market has become a major provider of "privatized" childcare services.

The question arises as to why Malaysian women would elect to employ foreign servants rather than contract with formal or informal childcare centers/creches. After all, the growth of childcare centers also could be seen as an indicator and a factor in the expansion of the capitalist market economy.

None of the female or male employers in this study had ever considered sending their children to creches. Ostensibly in a multiethnic society, childcare centers may be a problem for Muslim families because of the potential for Muslim children to be exposed to "*haram*" or unclean food. Melina was the only one out of all the employers interviewed who either mentioned or implied that middle-class Malay families refuse to use creches for this particular reason: "I'll tell you why, Christine. Guaranteed, if it's [a] Chinese [managed creche], then there'll be pork. . . ."

If most of the employers did not consider ethnoreligious differences as a mitigating factor in the use of childcare centers, then what are the underlying structural reasons for the absence of the middle classes' support of creches? Until recently, the state did not consider promoting creches as an alternative avenue of childcare for working mothers per se. Even during the 1970s decline in the supply of domestic servants, state agencies did not respond by establishing childcare centers at the workplace.[41] In an interview conducted at her workplace, Rose a mid-level state bureaucrat who employed a foreign servant, reasoned that there are "too many constraints [she looks up]. They are men upstairs making the decisions."

Three interrelated reasons emerged from my field interviews of middle-class women who refused to send their children to childcare centers. The women were concerned for their children's welfare while in creches; they wanted to be relieved from the more laborious aspects of housework; and they considered creches as institutions traditionally favored by the working class. Although the Malaysian state recently passed a series of legislation to upgrade existing formal creches and to regulate informal neighborhood creches, female employers' fear of creches as breeding grounds for disease and abuse inevitably affected their decisions.[42] Over lunch at a country club, an educator and a corporate consultant, respectively said:

Jane: I don't want my kid picking up diseases and getting into accidents.

Karen: It [creche] is not popular in this part of the world. You never know how they'll treat your children. Centers must be professionally run. I don't want any accidents with my children.

The perception of creches as unhealthy and dangerous places for children is not the only or even the most significant reason for the employment of foreign domestic workers. The choice of Filipina and Indonesian servants over creches also is related to middle-class women's responses to the practice of Asian patriarchy in the domestic domain.

Most certainly, a key consequence of the state's modernity project for many Malaysian women is the promise of the freedom of choice. Expanded education and employment opportunities encourage women from the middle classes to realize their potentials beyond the four walls of the home. Nonetheless, the practice of private patriarchy continues to characterize household relations.

Regardless of different class, ethnic, and religious backgrounds, most Malaysian women are held responsible for the performance of housework and childcare.[43] Studies of professional women's withdrawal from the labor market find the major reason to be women's lack of alternative avenues for childcare services.[44] Conversely, women's ability to secure domestic help have allowed mothers to remain in the workforce while increasing the quantity and quality of time spent with children.[45]

Husbands of female employers in this study did not perform domestic tasks such as bathing young children, cooking meals, cleaning bathrooms, or washing and ironing clothes. During an informal social gathering in an employer's home, Greg and his friend Sunny unabashedly announced, in front of their wives, their respective aversion to performing housework.

Greg: I won't do the work. After a full day at the office, all I want to do is relax and eat dinner.

Sunny: If you want a hassle free lifestyle, get a maid to live in so that you can have her do all the stuff that you don't want to do yourself. If you want to do everything and don't have enough money, then it's easy for you, don't get a maid!

Over the course of dinner at the house of a middle-class Indian couple, Joseph, Prithiva, and one of their guests had the following to say about childcare:

Prithiva: Look, you put the child in kindergarten and pick him up after work—
sounds good, right? But who'll do the housework: iron, cook, and clean?

Joseph: Don't look at me, dear. I'm not going to do it. Why break your back when
you can pay someone to do it?

Bee Lan: We are mortgaged to our heads. But it is worth it to get a maid . . . allows
us to enjoy life a bit more.

Enhanced purchasing powers of middle-class couples allow husbands such as Sunny and Joseph not to do any housework, while maintaining their expectations that domestic labor is and should be performed by the women in the household.

The employment of foreign domestic workers reinforces the patriarchal assumption and definition of who-is-supposed-to-do-what-in-the-home. Equally significant, the presence of a foreign domestic worker allows some female employers to reason that their husbands' refusal to perform housework is *biologically programmed and not socially constructed.* At a different informal group discussion organized by Melina in her house, three professional women (a Malay doctor, a Chinese accountant, and a Chinese *remisier*) laughed when I asked if their husbands helped to care for young children, cleaned bathrooms, and so forth. One of them said, "Christine, you must know the Asian mentality: men just sit back and *goyang kaki.*"[46]

Male employers' refusal to perform housework was most evident during the course of an interview with Eileen, a Chinese female employer. Eileen and her husband had different expectations of the division of household tasks. As Eileen and I conversed in the dining room, her husband who was sitting in the living room barely fifteen feet away from the kitchen door, raised his voice to ask the foreign servant to bring him a cup of tea. While the servant waited for the water to boil, he looked at me and said, "I'm so sorry, she's extremely lazy." Minutes later, Eileen got up, went into the kitchen, and personally prepared tea for me so that the servant could finish washing the dishes.

The husband's behavior conveyed the impression that the presence of a domestic worker in his home meant that he need not and should not have to get up, walk to the kitchen, and pour himself a cup of tea. Eileen, on the other hand, perceived the employment of a foreign domestic worker as a way to assist in the performance of household tasks that, according to tradition, is women's responsibility.

It can be argued that marital or familial discord could surface easily as a result of male employers' refusal to perform their share of housework while female employers have to balance the demands of working beyond the home and taking care of the family. However, middle-class families with dual income earners in an era of the transnationalization of migrant domestic labor have lessened female employers' household chores without any major changes in husbands' expectations for well-kept homes. Significantly, middle-class women such as Eileen, who employ foreign domestic workers, can safely realize the image of the modern liberated woman without necessarily challenging their husbands' patriarchal attitudes toward the performance of housework.

Even so, Malaysian men, who wish their wives to adhere to their traditionally ascribed domestic roles, are hardly unaware that women in increasing numbers are transferring their household responsibilities to servants.[47] The following are excerpts from a newspaper survey of Malaysian men's opinions regarding working mothers' employment of servants:

[Women] should not leave the family to others.

It might be more economical for the wife to stop working than for her to work outside the home to have another source of income just to be able to afford household help.

It would not be good for your child, your own flesh and blood, to be inclined towards an outsider.

Because of my career, we were always on the move. I feel that because my wife took care of the children all by herself, my children were loyal to her throughout their childhood, helping out with chores. I think children who grow up in families where their mothers take care of them, develop a stronger bond with their mothers. They understand how mothers do so much for them.[48]

Middle-class wives' demands for and consequent employment of foreign servants can be read as a kind of indirect "challenge" to Asian patriarchy. Nonetheless, it is a challenge that succeeds in reinforcing the belief that domestic labor is women's work since the substitute homemakers are women, not men.

The third reason why female employers prefer domestic workers to creches concerns their efforts to maintain social status. The employers considered creches to be the traditional childcare institutions of and for the working class, while wealthier families employed *amahs*. Meena, the owner-manager of a travel agency, stated the issue bluntly: "Creches bring up the connotation of lower class, like one step behind the middle class. You see, only secretaries and primary school teachers send their children to childcare centers. Why the hell would you want to send your child to someone else's house for a whole day? It's low status and demeaning."

Well-intentioned state policies perpetuate the middle classes' association of creches mostly with the childcare needs of the working classes. In 1991, the Minister of National Unity and Social Development offered financial aid to nonprofit organizations that provide childcare services to poor women: "We hope to encourage voluntary organizations to provide such facilities for working women who cannot afford to engage a babysitter or a maid."[49] The assumption is that those who are able to afford domestic workers will naturally reject childcare centers. Consequently, there does not seem to be the need to encourage middle-class women to utilize state-licensed and regulated creches.

Today, factory shift hours have been restructured to lessen the childcare woes of working-class mothers: women can work the evening shift from five to eleven o'clock, while their husbands are asked to care for the children. Seen from a more critical perspective, the state's policy is designed to strengthen capital accumulation by ensuring an uninterrupted supply of low-wage female labor for factory work. By 1995, it is expected that creches will be established throughout low-income neighborhoods to cater to the needs of working mothers.[50]

State solutions for working-class mothers ironically reinforce middle-class mothers' perceptions that creches are for those who cannot afford to employ servants. Representatives of formal and informal creches in Bangsar and Ampang Jaya confirmed that their clients mostly were lower ranked civil servants, primary school teachers, street hawkers, and tailors.[51]

Dual-career middle-class couples' combined income allows husbands and wives to purchase and consume Filipina and Indonesian women's labor. Foreign servants not only leave women from the middle classes free to pursue careers and other more leisurely and pleasurable responsibilities (e.g., helping children complete their homework) in the home, but also meet many of their husbands' needs (such as having freshly ironed shirts and cooked food on demand).

Latifah, a Malay employer, who worked with Rose in the same state agency, succinctly expressed most of their fellow employers' rationale for hiring live-in servants: "Even if they put one [childcare center] here [place of work], I must have a maid at home to clean the house so that I'll have more time with my husband and children." Rose agreed and added that, "If I'm not working, I'll still need a maid. Let me tell you why . . . poor bones-lah! I'm getting old [mid-40s]. I don't mind cooking but washing toilets, scrubbing floors? Forget it-lah! [She pointed to her legs.] Diseases of the rich [hearty laughter]." Foreign female domestic workers are a solution to the "diseases of the rich," in that Filipina and Indonesian women perform domestic labor while reflecting employing families' achievement of middle class-hood.

State policies on creches and the employment of foreign domestic workers reinforce middle-class nuclear families' dependence on the transnational migrant domestic labor market. Female employers' choice of foreign servants over other forms of childcare frees working mothers from housework and simultaneously symbolizes Malaysian families' achievement of middle class-hood. The latter point is of extreme importance in the ability to understand the middle classes' attitudes and behavior toward Filipina and Indonesian domestic workers.

Malaysian demands for and consumption of foreign servants' labor have become an inextricable part of efforts by the state elite to bring about middle-class lifestyles commensurate with the requirements of export-oriented development, especially the expansion of capitalist markets. I now turn to an exploration of the state's relation to the expanding middle classes, i.e., how the state elite and the advertising industry promote consumption-oriented lifestyles of the middle classes that are supposed to reflect progress toward modernity.

Two major consequences emerge from the middle classes' pursuit of modernity via consumption. First, is the conflation of employing Filipina and Indonesian domestic workers with consuming and displaying material goods. Within this context, there are employers who fail to reflect on or worry about the servitude of their foreign domestic workers. Second, interethnic relations take on a new political dimension. The potential divisiveness of ethnic, religious, and cultural differences within the growing community of the Malaysian middle classes—who constitute some of the state's major social forces—increasingly appear to be peripheralized by emerging lifestyles of the middle classes that privilege acts of consumption as symbolic of having achieved middle class-hood.

Material Consumption and the Pursuit of Distinction

The poor are important. And look, look, even if we redistribute everything, and it's spread so thin that we're all poor—that's good. Consider the culture we poor have invented—vegetarianism and fasting, pencil sketches, pottery, singing without instruments, mending, saving and reusing things, quilting patchworks . . . and kung fu, which doesn't require expensive sports equipment. Oh, let's value the poor, who in a way are all of us.

—"Uncle Bun," in Maxine Hong Kingston's *China Men*, 1977

Societies currently experiencing rapid industrialization offer unprecedented opportunities to examine the relation of different social classes to capitalist development. Theoretical literature on social class in general reflects the codification of a wealth of intellectual endeavors undertaken by Marxist and Weberian scholars who respectively attempt to offer the definitive perspective in analyses of class stratification.[52] Although Marxist and Weberian analyses of class stratification are markedly different, there is an underlying common assumption.

Classes are assumed to be identified easily or preconstituted in the social structure respectively because of production or market relations. Ironically, in spite of different ideological and methodological orientations, the "middle class" is conceptualized in the center of the capitalist-proletarian distinction, or the upper-lower class divide. Whether or not the middle class is more or less permanently situated in the center of this divide is a related but separate issue.[53]

Contemporary intellectual debates among class theorists point to a possible convergence of structure and agency in class theory as Neo-Marxists grapple with the role of human agency in class formation while Neo-Weberians admit to the importance of structural constraints in determining life chances.[54] Class theorists from both perspectives are beginning to acknowledge that class formation involves the material *and* the symbolic dimensions—i.e., the simultaneous processes of establishing interclass material and symbolic distinctions, and intraclass subjectivity.[55] Pierre Bourdieu describes these processes as "the pursuit of distinction," i.e., the construction of distinctive lifestyles:

> [B]ecause social agents are capable of perceiving as significant distinctions the "spontaneous" distinctions that their categories of perception lead them to regard as pertinent, it follows that they are also capable of intentionally underscoring these spontaneous differences in life-style by what Weber calls "the stylization of life" (*die Stilisierung des Lebens*). The pursuit of distinction—which may be expressed in ways of speaking or the refusal of misalliances—produces separations intended to be perceived, or more precisely, known and organized, as legitimate differences, which most often means differences in nature ("natural distinction").[56]

Of particular interest to this study are the following questions: How do members of the expanding Malaysian middle classes distinguish themselves from other classes? In what ways do the state and private sector capital facilitate the middle classes' pursuit of distinction?

The above questions are relevant to the extent that the institution of domestic service is coopted by the state elite to police the form and content of the expanding Malaysian middle classes. Analysis of contemporary domestic service in Malaysia demonstrates how the state is involved actively in constructing an "imagined community" of the urban middle classes with distinctly consumption-oriented lifestyles.[57] As discussed, the middle classes' pursuit of modern consumption-oriented lifestyles encourages, if not legitimizes, an overall desensitized attitude toward Filipina and Indonesian domestic workers—an attitude that dehumanizes them.

Rules governing Malaysian employment of foreign domestic workers were implemented during a period of rapid social change that was brought about by the perceived exigencies of ensuring stability in a multiethnic society while attempting to capture transnational capital and markets to fuel rapid industrialization. Specifically, the income rule was responsible for objectifying the material boundaries of the expanding middle classes to indirectly address criticisms that development had not benefitted Malaysians, especially Malays. The family rule today is charged with promoting the form of the nuclear family—irrespective of ethnic, religious, and cultural differences—as the norm for the Malay and non-Malay middle classes.

The assumption widely held among the middle classes that modernity can be achieved via consumption already is discernible in the mutually reinforcing processes of dehumanizing and commodifying foreign female domestic workers. According to employers in this study, membership into middle class-hood depended on three major factors: a certain annual household income level (between RM24,000 and RM50,000); a white-collar occupation and/or university-level education; and "lifestyle." Lifestyle was defined further as having traveled overseas or having knowledge and appreciation of different cultures and peoples; ownership of a house or a condominium; and ownership of an imported car(s), the latest consumer items (such as computers and laser disc players); and the presence of a live-in servant.

For both the Malay and non-Malay middle-class employers in this study, the key defining feature of a modern middle-class lifestyle is the ability to consume or display what their income permits.[58] Middle-class consumption of goods and services offered by the capitalist market is facilitated and reinforced by the fact that all of the sixty-eight employers in this study lived in nuclear families. Employers' parents and/or in-laws either lived in different neighborhoods in Kuala Lumpur, or in other states in Malaysia.

In spite of differences in ethnic, religious, and cultural backgrounds, Malaysian employers' definitions of middle class in general, and lifestyle in particular, were relatively similar. Implicit in employers' conceptualization of the modern middle-class lifestyle was the privileging of physical comfort and concomitant aesthetic appreciation and display of material goods over the more traditional and conflictual issues of ethnic, religious, and cultural differences that have been used to construct identity. In this study, Melina a Chinese female corporate executive, was the only one out of sixty-eight employers who emphasized ethnic differences in her narrative of the lifestyles of the Malaysian middle classes:

> For Malays, it's the car they drive, where they live and what kind of house they live in. The women are always so well bedecked. But they have no base, they are not solid. . . . What I mean is that the government pampers them so much that if the government stopped helping them, they simply couldn't survive. Ask any Malay, and he'll tell you, "*style mesti ada, duit tak apa*" [it doesn't matter if one doesn't have money, one must have "style" over and above all else]. I'm telling you what is fact. My Malay friend [ ], he drives a Jaguar, lives in a nice house, but he can't even give us his share of RM5000 so that he can join us in setting up the business I told you about. . .

The Malay-dominated state's refusal to abrogate officially the ethnic specific aspects of the overall development policy fuels the perceptions of non-Malays such as Melina who believe that Malays, by virtue of their ethnic background, are given *carte blanche* entry into the imagined community of the middle classes. It is believed that Malay conceptions of middle classhood are characteristically stylized or formulaic, i.e., ownership of imported cars, modern houses, designer clothes, and so forth. Significantly, non-Malay employers are not much different than their Malay counterparts in the pursuit of consumption-oriented lifestyles.

The NEP, to be sure, was an affirmative action program that privileged Malays in most aspects of social life. Even though the NEP's successor, the NDP inherits this legacy, official rhetoric in the 1990s vacillates between, or is confronted increasingly by, the perceived need to continue to cater to Malay demands for state trusteeship on the one hand, and the necessity of downplaying ethnic differences and of instilling the value of economic competitiveness in the multiethnic society on the other hand. According to Prime Minister Dr. Mahathir Mohamad:

> In particular, the Bumiputeras are still far behind other races in business, especially in the commercial and industrial activities which, with the emphasis on industrialization, constitute the growth sectors of the economy. In continuing these efforts, the government realizes that it is essential to pay more attention to the qualitative aspects of Bumiputera participation as these have been given less emphasis in the past . . . It is time the Bumiputeras cease to expect to do business only with the government. They must go fully into the marketplace to compete. The contracts and the sales must be with the public. It is not impossible to reduce their dependence on government contracts.[59]

Given the history of real and perceived interethnic contestations, it is not surprising that embodied in the development path are the dual processes of state production of similarity and difference. Development involves all Malaysians regardless of ethnic background. Yet, development structures, institutions, and processes institutionalize preference for Malays. In the same vein, the state constructed rules of inclusion and exclusion into the imagined community of middle-class employers of Filipina and Indonesian domestic workers. Within this group of employers during the 1980s, there had been a lower income qualification level for Malay employers.

Nonetheless, state production of similarity—i.e., to deemphasize ethnic, religious, and cultural differences—increasingly is stressed in the path of export-oriented development that, according to plan, will create a developed Malaysian society by 2020. For the employers of foreign domestic workers in this study, their ability to live distinctly materialistic lifestyles binds them into an imagined community of the consumption-oriented Malaysian middle classes.

This is not to argue that ethnic, religious, and cultural differences are overcome completely with the structures and processes of export-oriented development. Rather, within the context of enhanced consumption of goods and services, Malay and non-Malay middle-class employers exhibit a degree of commonality that characterizes the lifestyles of the modern urban middle classes. This is what appears to be encouraged in an effort to downplay interethnic contestations that, rightly or wrongly, have been identified as one of the consequences of the ethnic-specific NEP.

While the family rule encourages middle-class dependence on the capitalist market for the provision of goods and services, the task of reinforcing the middle classes' pursuit of modernity via consumption primarily is left to the mass media, in particular the advertising industry.

Advertising Modernity

The contemporary transnational integration, consolidation, and expansion of media/information corporations facilitate the dissemination of particular images that reflect preconceived notions of modern lifestyles.[60] The expansion of open markets and free trade has allowed members of the Malaysian middle classes to be "cosmopolitans at home" without the need even to travel outside of the country.[61]

> [T]he distribution of the electronic capabilities to produce and disseminate information (newspapers, magazines, television stations, film production studios, etc.) . . . are now available to a growing number of private and public interests throughout the world; and to the images of the world created by these media. . . . What this means is that many audiences throughout the world experience the media themselves as a complicated and interconnected repertoire of print celluloid, electronic services, and billboards . . . the more like they are to construct 'imagined worlds' which are chimerical, aesthetic, even fantastic objects, particularly if assessed by the criteria of some other perspective, some other 'imagined' world.[62]

It should be noted that the state maintains control over the mass media in the sense that the investment arms of major mainstream ethnic political parties such as the UMNO and the MCA own and control most major newspapers and even TV3, which in 1994 was the only commercial television station.[63] A slew of restrictive legislation such as the Printing Presses and Publications Act 1984 are used to regulate print media content.

I wish to stress that the advertising industry is not the primary target of restrictive legislation on the mass media. Such legislation is designed mostly to control the production and dissemination of information that is considered seditious.[64] For example in 1986, the *Asian Wall Street Journal* was banned for having published an article that reported bureaucratic corruption in a state-owned corporation.[65]

The fact that mainstream political parties, especially UMNO, exercise substantial control over the mass media indicates state involvement in encouraging local and transnational capital to promote a consumption-oriented lifestyle for the middle classes. Prime Minister Dr. Mahathir Mohamad, speaking at the opening of Kuala Lumpur's Sogo Pernas Department Store (the largest department store in 1994, in Southeast Asia), said that large-scale shopping centers offering "quality goods catering to the middle and upper income groups . . . [represent] another step in the standard and way of life which the people could expect with development."[66]

Implicit in the modernity project of creating a developed society by 2020, is the conflation of development with enhanced material consumption in spite of or indeed because of ethnic, religious, and cultural differences. The advertising industry, to be sure, readily assumes the responsibility for constructing and reinforcing the pursuit of modernity via consumption. Today, billboard, magazine, radio, and television advertisements in Kuala Lumpur promote yachting and golfing in privately owned recreational clubs as acceptable and expected middle-class leisure activities.[67] Culture industries'[68] promotion of modernity in terms of what one consumes and exhibits or displays at the very same time (clothing, vacation, food, automobiles, and so forth), shapes the lifestyles of the modern urban middle classes.[69]

The role of advertisements in encouraging the middle classes to pursue modernity via consumption was made explicitly clear to me during the course of the February 1994 Chinese New Year celebrations. Swee Ping a middle-class Chinese informant, invited me to a dinner at a hotel restaurant in Kuala Lumpur. There, she introduced me to her eleven guests as a friend who had recently returned to Malaysia to conduct research on foreign female domestic workers. Eager to ensure an uninterrupted flow of conversation, Swee Ping sat me next to Jonathan, a European expatriate who was an upper-level management executive in one of the largest and most successful transnational advertising corporations in Kuala Lumpur.

During my conversation with Jonathan about different approaches to advertising consumer products, he mentioned that the average monthly income of a Malaysian family was approximately RM1000. More importantly, he quietly asserted that a middle class did not really exist in Malaysia. I can only assume that it was out of his fear of eliciting the wrath of fellow dinner guests, all of whom were professional/credentialed Malaysians.[70] I asked him if his perception was related in any way to the average income level of Malaysian families that he had stated earlier. He assured me that the definition of middle class depended on more than just income level. Accordingly, he argued that "psychographics" or the analysis of consumer values, beliefs, and attitudes, were at least as important in identifying the middle class. I pursued the matter further by asking him if he meant that on the basis of his corporation's research of Malaysian psychographics, he had then come to the conclusion that the middle classes essentially were nonexistent in Malaysia. And, if that was the case, what classes of Malaysians were the target group of advertisements that promoted consumer products such as imported cars, mobile handphones, country/golf club memberships, college savings insurance schemes, and Malaysian-British/American/Australian/Canadian college twinning programs?[71] The advertising industry executive laughed and said, "This is why you [Malaysia] need us!"

Middle-class Malaysian emulation of the model of modern urban lifestyle that is promoted by the advertising industry, and that commodifies social life by emphasizing material consumption, can and does take the form of wearing designer clothes, drinking particular brands of imported beer, driving European manufactured cars, pursuing certain kinds of recreational activities, and so forth.[72] In my interviews with at least fifty of the sixty-eight employers, there were discussions of the latest European fashion, the best model of European manufactured automobiles, and even different kinds of Western consumer products to import for sale to the middle classes. Implicit in such discussions was the manner in which middle-class employers, with the help of culture industries, construct and legitimize consumption-oriented modern urban lifestyles in a rapidly industrializing country.

In the last few years, print advertisements have played a key role in inducing the middle class to purchase social status by joining private multiethnic country or recreational clubs that have been established in major cities throughout Malaysia. Membership in these clubs depends on the applicant's ability to pay one-time application fees that cost several thousands of Malaysian *Ringgit* (aside from monthly or annual membership fees), and occupation and lifestyle (e.g., professional and social affiliations). The middle classes in Malaysia, then, have their own recreational organizations and methods of recruitment that deny entry to those who fail to possess and/or exhibit the material and symbolic distinctions expected by and of the middle classes.[73]

These country clubs provide stickers or membership "badges" that are adhered to front windshields of automobiles, thus, readily identifying the owner's club and social class affiliation.[74] Indeed, I conducted several interviews at various country clubs because the employers insisted that their clubs offered a more private and comfortable environment in which to converse.

Affiliates of country/sporting clubs throughout Malaysia allow for cross-membership, and consequently club members are able to work actively to construct an imagined community of members who are bound by an ethos of exclusivity. Print media advertisements help to constitute and reinforce the image of exclusivity offered by country clubs while simultaneously encouraging or "calling" for potential members. The same can be said of advertisements in all form of media that sell to the middle classes the idea that the best way to pursue a distinctive lifestyle is to purchase, consume, and display high-quality foreign/Western manufactured goods.

Jomo Kwame Sundaram suggests that the consumption of Western cultural products is encouraged particularly because Western culture is the "lowest common denominator" in a culturally contentious multiethnic society:

> Official reluctance to accept non-Malay ethnic cultures has ironically allowed vulgar imitations of imported Anglo-American culture to emerge as the lowest common denominator of Malaysian cultural life. The earlier emergence of shared cultural elements has been taken over by 'nonsensitive' western cultural hegemony dished out by the state controlled mass media.[75]

Western cultural products are the most viable and readily available solution to balancing the demands of, or mitigating contestations between Malays and non-Malays, especially the Chinese, over the degree of each ethnic group's symbolic representations in the multiethnic society.

My field research supports Jomo's point. In interviews of individual employers and also informal group discussions organized by several employers, Malays and non-Malays insisted that fishmongers, food stall operators/street hawkers, and other participants of the informal economy were not legitimate members of the middle classes primarily because of different occupations (e.g., the manual-nonmanual distinction), and consequently lifestyles.

Over dinner at the house of an Indian bank executive, guests talked about the difference between a fishmonger and a corporate executive. The host, Joseph, argued that a fishmonger "acts and thinks in a different way, even though he can buy out most of us if he wanted to [meaning that the fishmonger rarely, if ever, pays his personal income tax, thus he would have more liquid and fixed assets than most of the respondents in the room]." His wife Prithiva an orthodontist, and their friends Bee Lan, a Chinese female accountant, and Din, a Malay businessman, laughed when Joseph used crude verbal and nonverbal gestures in his caricature of the fishmonger.

Prithiva supported her husband's argument by giving us additional information about the fishmonger's lifestyle. She said, "Do you know or not, 'Ah

Chun' the fishmonger at the market has enough money to send his son to Australia for further studies? They have so much money but you'd never know it by looking at them. I bet that if you go to his house, it'll [the house] look like a poor man's house. He doesn't even own a car!" Prithiva, pokes fun at members of the informal economy who may have the purchasing powers of the middle classes, but who cannot or choose not to pursue the middle-class lifestyle characterized by the appreciation and consumption of high-quality consumer goods—not to mention foreign female domestic workers' labor.

Operators of grocery stalls in farmers' markets, on the other hand, perceived white collar workers or professionals like Prithiva, in a very different light. Mrs. Lim, who sold baked goods at a farmers' market in Kuala Lumpur, said the following to me after a man and a woman who were dressed in business suits haggled with her over the price of banana bread. They criticized Mrs. Lim for wanting to make a fifty-cent profit on the sale. As the couple walked away from the stall, she said to me:

> I'll see when they'll come crashing down. Think they wear western suits, work in big office, buy BMW, use *tai kor tai* [colloquial Cantonese for cellular handphone], and they own the place? Hah, sooner or later they'll fall. Arrogant bastards. Who do they think they are? We earn our money with our sweat and blood. What do they do? Sit down all day until they have no backside . . . and no backbone!

Mrs. Lim critiqued what she considered as white collar professionals' real and perceived penchant for consuming or collecting material symbols of social status—especially high-end western consumer products—while denigrating those who would not or could not do so. Uncle Tan, the owner of a coffeeshop in Kuala Lumpur's business district, had a similar view of white collar professionals who patronized his shop during lunch hours.

> I honour them by calling them *si tau* [boss]. So long as they come to spend money, I don't care. But I will tell you now, they are nothing like the *si tau* of your grandfather or father's generation. These people have no values. They always want more for their money. They don't realize that we have to make a living too. They buy expensive clothes from America, from London . . . but they don't want to pay 60 cents for a cup of coffee. What kind of people are they?

Implicit in Uncle Tan's comments was the notion that middle-class values and morals have not kept pace with their increased earning powers. It is this lag that reveals one consequence in which export-oriented development can shape the consciousness of the expanding middle classes.

The Malaysian state encourages and reinforces the middle classes' construction and maintenance of status via the consumption of goods and services. For employers of foreign domestic workers, the income rule clearly delineates the material boundaries of the middle classes. Within these boundaries, the state elite and local and foreign capital promote the middle classes' construction of status and identities in the form of modern lifestyles that are characteristically shaped by new patterns of consumption. Enhanced middle-class consumption of goods and services is key to the production of similarity in the pursuit of modernity. By selling lifestyle images, the advertising industry helps construct an imagined community of consumption-oriented middle-class Malaysians.

Arguably, there is nothing insidious about the expansion of capitalist markets that bring to peoples different choices and presumably higher quality consumer goods and services. However, the middle classes' employment of foreign female domestic workers occurs within a context in which acts of consumption are promoted and valued as symbolic of personal and national progress. In this context, the in-migration and employment mechanisms that dehumanize and commodify foreign servants, together with negative public perception and discourse, then can and do legitimize the conflation of hiring foreign servants with owning the women.

Contemporary domestic service has become an indispensable part of the state elite's strategy of consent. State involvement in Malaysian employment of foreign domestic workers inculcates Malaysians into new forms of social relations and organizations that strengthen the growth of the capitalist market economy, and that ensure social stability in the multiethnic society. In the context of the global expansion of neoliberalism, the state elite and the middle classes' pursuit of modernity have come to necessitate and perpetuate premodern aspects of unlegislated live-in domestic service, i.e., the service and servitude of foreign female domestic workers.

Notes on the Epigraphs

(In order of appearance): Martha Lee Osbourne, ed., *Woman in Western Thought* (New York: Random House, 1979), p. 18 and p. 155; Maxine Hong Kingston, *China Men* (New York: Ballantine Books, 1981), p. 194.

CHAPTER 7

Conclusion

The cultivation of those sciences which have enlarged the limits of the empire of man over the external world, has, for want of the poetical faculty, proportionately circumscribed those of the internal world; and man, having enslaved the elements, remains himself a slave.
—Percy Bysshe Shelley, "Defense of Poetry," 1821

Contemporary domestic service in Malaysia is indicative of more than just the performance and consumption of paid reproductive labor. Changes in the profile of domestic workers are not merely a natural consequence of modernization. Rather, contemporary domestic service has become an educative institution through which the state objectifies the material boundaries of the middle classes and, at the very same time, normalizes middle-class adoption of the nuclear family.

It should come as no surprise to discover that the state is involved in shaping the material and symbolic aspects of social life. From the colonial to the postcolonial era, strategies of coercion-repression and consent have been used to arrange and rearrange society. Such strategies have and continue to involve low wage foreign migrant labor.

To develop a natural resource-based export economy, the British encouraged the in-migration of Chinese and Indian workers and proceeded to construct "racial" identities and a division of labor that ensured social order in the midst of the processes of (predominantly European) capital accumulation.

The postcolonial state elite implemented the NEP to redress the colonial legacy that naturalized the association of ethnicities with different economic function and geographic space. The NEP was an affirmative action development program that sought to construct a modern urban professional Malay identity out of the inherited colonial identity of Malays as rural fishermen and farmers. Strategies of coercion, such as quota systems in employment and education, and the transfer of corporate wealth, institutionalized public and private sector preference for Malays, as state agencies became the trustees of redistributed Malay corporate wealth. Public discourse critical of various aspects and effects of the NEP was silenced mainly and visibly by repressive legislation.

My analysis demonstrates that efforts by the postcolonial state elite to rearrange society were not dependent solely on strategies of coercion-repression. By adopting an educative ethos, the increasingly gendered and ethnicized state apparatus has broadened and deepened considerably its involvement in everyday life. A key strategy of garnering consent draws on contemporary demands for foreign female domestic workers to inculcate Malaysians into different forms of social relations and organization that fulfill the objectives of expanding export-oriented capitalist development and maintaining social stability in the multiethnic society.

The larger fields of possible actions and responses that led to Malaysian employment of Filipina and Indonesian servants were shaped, partly, by the history of the state's relation to domestic service—especially the consistent refusal to legislate the performance and consumption of domestic labor. This could only reinforce the patriarchal belief that housework is nonwork, even when it is remunerated. During the colonial era, contestations between European employers and Chinese male servants were solved effectively with the first wave of Chinese migrant female servants during the 1930s.

Unlegislated domestic service in the postcolonial era reflects more than the belief that housework is nonwork. Legislated domestic service in the 1970s would have affected the supply of female workers in factories owned by TNCs. Many Malaysian female servants and would-be servants who were faced with the prospect of performing either paid housework in unlegislated environments or the more structured and relatively higher waged factory work, chose the latter. To be sure, the Malay/UMNO-controlled state could not openly encourage Malay or non-Malay women to be servants since the NEP was premised on uplifting the socioeconomic lot of Malays without appearing, at the very least, to undermine the socioeconomic future of non-Malays. Malaysian demands for servants were quickly filled by the second wave of foreign (Filipina and Indonesian) female servants that resulted from labor-sending states' responses to changes in the global and regional economies.

At the outset, it can be said that the official regulation of Filipina and Indonesian domestic workers' in-migration is necessary to ensure a more orderly movement of "guest" workers in and out of Malaysia. Yet, official regulation meant more than merely processing work permits for foreign workers. A closer analysis of the three key rules—income, religion, and family rules—governing the employment of Filipina and Indonesian servants delineates how and why only certain categories of Malaysians legally qualify to do so.

Rule I, the income rule, stated that a Malaysian family must be able to furnish proof (in the form of a copy the *Borang J* personal income tax return) of a certain level of annual income in order to qualify for state approval to employ a foreign domestic worker. In the 1980s, an annual income of RM50,000 was required to employ a Filipina servant whereas there was no preset annual income level to employ an Indonesian servant. In 1994, the difference between income levels had changed somewhat: RM48,000 to employ a Filipina domestic worker and RM24,000 to employ an Indonesian servant.

During the NEP's second decade and within a context of growing criticism that development had not benefitted a majority of Malays who were the targeted recipients of redistributed and new wealth, the income rule constructed the material qualification for Malay and non-Malay entry into the imagined community of the Malaysian middle classes. The lower income qualification rule for the employment of Indonesian servants, in effect, subsidized the Malay middle classes: Malays were expected to employ Indonesian women who were of similar ethnoreligious backgrounds. This rule allowed the state elite surreptitiously to offer a visible indicator of the NEP's success in expanding the Malay middle classes in particular, and the Malaysian middle classes in general, as foreign domestic workers became public boundary markers of, and for, the Malaysian middle classes.

Prior to 1991, rule II, the religion rule, allowed only Muslims (read: Malay) to employ Muslim (read: Indonesian) servants. The intent was to construct and maintain clear boundary markers within the expanding Malaysian middle classes: Malays would employ Indonesian-Muslim servants while most non-Malays who are also non-Muslims would employ Filipina-Christian servants.

Many non-Malays who had failed to meet the income qualification rule to employ Filipinas began to employ illegal Indonesian servants. The blurring of intraclass ethnoreligious boundaries separating the Malay from non-Malay middle classes, and also the blurring of interclass boundaries (since working-class peoples could and did employ illegal and indentured Indonesian servants), prompted the state authorities to enforce this rule rigorously by searching for illegal foreign servants, and subsequently deporting them. When the Malay and non-Malay middle classes vehemently objected to the proposed deportation of Indonesian servants, the rule was retracted.

Rule III, the family rule, insisted that Malaysians who wanted to employ foreign female domestic workers had to be able to furnish proof of marriage and children. Applications for state approval to employ foreign servants must include copies of personal income tax returns, *and* respective official marriage and birth certificates of employers and their children. This rule, which inculcates Malaysian adoption of the nuclear family form, is premised on achieving two interrelated objectives.

During the NEP period, expanded education and employment opportunities for Malaysian women led to a gradual increase in the marriage age and a decrease in the birth rate. An eventual reduction in the size of the future Malaysian workforce, then, had the potential to jeopardize the official plan to deepen industrialization, and ultimately the success of the modernity project in constructing a developed socially stable multiethnic polity. At the very same time, public discourse centered on the fear among Malaysians, especially men, that they were losing financial and social control over their womenfolk, since many more women were active in the workforce. Malaysian women's new roles and status were perceived to have been achieved at the expense of the socioeconomic future of the country.

A key answer to the dilemma was the 1984 National Population Policy (NPP). Prime Minister Dr. Mahathir Mohamad appealed to women to stay at home, if possible, and have at least five children per family. The NPP had dual objectives: to ensure continued economic growth by increasing the size of the future workforce that would eventually increase the productive and consumptive capacities of the Malaysian economy and society; and to reconstitute Malay and non-Malay women's roles and identities primarily as mothers and wives.

Since the late 1980s, labor shortages require Malaysian women to serve their country in the dual capacity of mother and worker. Today, the family rule encourages women to work beyond the home without having to worry about childcare and housework. Taken together, the income and family rules draw on Malaysian demands for household help to coopt domestic service as a key educative institution of the state.

The middle classes' demands for servants also tell us how contemporary export-oriented development offers Malaysian women new opportunities and new forms of dependence. In spite of, or perhaps because of, additional employment and education opportunities, women remain constrained by the practice of private patriarchy that holds them responsible for house-work. Private patriarchy is reinforced by and reinforces public patriarchy, in which various pieces of legislation and policies on taxation and childcare constitute women from the middle classes primarily as homemakers.

Although Malaysian employment of Filipina and Indonesian servants frees working mothers to pursue careers while maintaining families, Filipina and Indonesian domestic workers are more than substitute homemakers in middle-class families. Just as they are constituted as public boundary markers by the income rule, they are boundary markers in private space as well.

Analysis of employer-foreign servant relations ascertained that Malaysian employment of Filipina and Indonesian women facilitates the construction of middle-class identity in the domestic domain. The transformation of working mothers into household executives is distinguished by the identity construction of middle-class female employers as clean, trustworthy, and civilized while foreign servants are seen more or less as unsanitary, untrust-worthy, and backward. The negative aspects of employer supervision in unlegislated work environments are amplified by state authorities' efforts to circumscribe foreign servants' activities in public space and the consequent public perception of foreign servants as prostitutes and criminals. Many times, employers' methods of control and surveillance can and do result in verbal, emotional, and physical abuse of Filipina and Indonesian domestic workers.

Foreign servants do not passively accept the identities and traits con-structed by Malaysian employers, society, and the state. Filipina and Indo-nesian domestic workers' individual and collective infrapolitical activities challenge and/or renegotiate different kinds of values and the use of resources in the performance and consumption of paid reproductive labor.

The Malaysian modernity project, which promises the middle classes the opportunity to pursue a certain version of the good life, takes an ironic turn that is characterized by the dehumanization of foreign domestic workers and their abusive employers. Fearful that servants will engage in illegal and immoral activities within and beyond the workplace, many female employ-ers deny the domestic workers such basic rights as rest days, rest periods dur-ing the daytime, the freedom to socialize with friends, and decent sleeping accommodations. The caring nuclear family that the state is intent on con-structing in part by way of regulating the in-migration and employment of foreign domestic workers may also prepare the present and possibly future generations of the middle classes to expect women to perform housework, and to perceive and treat Filipina and Indonesian women as little more than foreign servants who can be owned and who must be controlled.

In the 1990s, the political economy of the nuclear family is an extremely important dimension of the modernity project. The expansion of export-oriented development in Malaysia requires changes not only in peoples' relation to the production process, but also in consumption patterns. The model of the nuclear family is considered as the most appropriate structure for socializing members of the expanding middle classes to come to rely on or expect the capitalist market to be the major provider of consumer goods and services. The Malaysian-Philippine-Indonesian maid trade, in which servants are exported and imported like commodities, is an example of the middle classes' growing dependence on the capitalist market.

Malaysian employment of foreign female domestic workers has become a key part in the middle classes' pursuit of distinctive identities and lifestyles, hence modernity by way of consuming material goods and services offered by the capitalist market. While the employment rules construct and legitimize the form (i.e., the nuclear family) in which modernity via consumption is best pursued by the middle classes, the advertising industry helps promote identity construction via the consumption of high-quality goods and services. I found little difference in Malay and non-Malay employers' definition of a middle class lifestyle that is characterized by the purchase and display of material goods, including that of commodified foreign servants as symbols of social status.

Silence over the working conditions of Filipina and Indonesian servants shows how the notion of civilizational progress according to neoliberalism is globalized and, in the case of Malaysia, mediated through the lens of a real or perceived urgency to ensure social stability in a multiethnic society. At issue is not just the simple, compelling, and necessary argument that some foreign domestic workers are mistreated, abused, and should be protected against profit-hungry DOMs and employers who lack conscience. Rather, it is how morality is reworked in a way that naturalizes public and private acceptance of the dehumanization of Filipina and Indonesian women. The state's strategy of garnering consent, which seeks to inculcate different kinds of social relations and organizations (with the objective of creating a new kind of citizenry and a new level of civilization), subsequently appears to be inculcating a certain kind of morality in which the mistreatment and abuse of foreign domestic workers remain largely unproblematized.

Utilitarianism: The Route to a Socially Engineered Modern Malaysian Polity

A dominant social code of conduct has emerged from the mechanisms and consequences of the in-migration and employment of foreign female domestic workers in Malaysia. It is evident in labor sending states' responses to changes in the transnational economy; the opening of the immigration gates; the nature of DOMs that specialize in the supply of domestic labor; and employer-foreign servant relations.

I have shown that the dominant social code of conduct, which extends from the transnational to the household level, reproduces the Benthamite principle of utility. Jeremy Bentham, writing in the Enlightenment era, proposed that the utility or value of an action should be based on a "felicific calculus" of pleasure against pain, i.e., an action is valid and morally good if it is effective in bringing about a particular response that is favorable to the actor.[1]

Approximately two hundred years later and in a different region of the world, the Benthamite principle of utility that is informed by felicific calculus is evident as labor-sending and labor-receiving states and their social forces respond to the expansion of open markets and free trade. From the perspective of labor-sending states, the "export" of domestic workers is a way to maintain, if not increase, foreign exchange earnings; relieve the political, economic, and social pressures of unemployment and underemployment; and improve the skills training of migrant workers. Labor out-migration policies conceivably "maximize pleasure" and "minimize pain" as sending states pursue the "greatest happiness of the greatest number" of peoples: peoples are expected to have less competition in the job market, while female nationals are given the opportunity to work overseas, and the demands of overseas employers are met accordingly.

The utility of labor out-migration policies is conflated with the ethical presumption that the out-migration of domestic workers will bring the greatest good to society and the economy in the labor-sending countries. Despite reports of employer mistreatment and abuse of foreign female domestic workers in Malaysia and elsewhere, labor export policies are morally justified—from a utilitarian perspective—because of the larger and putatively more important political, economic, and social benefits that are elicited from labor out-migration.

From the perspective of the labor-receiving state of Malaysia, the utility of the labor in-migration policy is discerned from the fact that Filipina and Indonesian domestic workers allow working-class and middle-class Malaysian women to participate in the labor force, and ultimately the modernity project. Yet, growing numbers of female and male migrant workers are considered a potentially disruptive force in the multiethnic society. The need to ensure social order in the context of mutual coexistence between Malaysians and "guest" workers becomes the justification for public and private surveillance on foreign female domestic workers. Nonetheles, these two modes of surveillance contribute to negative public perceptions of foreign servants while legitimizing employers' dehumanizing attitudes and behavior toward the women in private space.

Global, regional, and national efforts to encourage open markets and free trade in material goods are matched, today, with open markets and free trade in foreign female domestic workers. DOMs would argue that exorbitant fees are necessary to ensure an efficient and uninterrupted supply of workers. Some draconian measures to control foreign servants are considered necessary to ensure the conduct of business within legal parameters set by the labor-receiving state. Middle-class employers, then, may and do proceed to recoup monies that are given to DOMs and the costs incurred in providing Filipina and Indonesian women with board and lodging, by extracting more labor from and/or refusing to pay monthly wages to the domestic workers.

In each of the above cases, it cannot be argued that the practice of utilitarianism is significantly immoral or amoral since what is of utility, according to the actors, is what is necessarily moral. The policies of labor-sending and receiving states as well as DOMs, and the actions and perceptions of employers, are premised respectively on the belief that the transnationalization of migrant domestic labor, and the modes of public and private surveillance of foreign domestic workers, bring about responses favorable to the respective actors. Morality in these instances is bounded by the dictates of policies and actions that are effective, not so much from the perspective of servants' interests, but from the perspective of the interests to maintain a constant revenue inflow in the form of foreign exchange earnings; an uninterrupted supply of labor; and the social control of foreigners at the household and national levels. Morality is conceived in and exercised on purely utilitarian terms.

As far as the Malaysian state's relationship to capitalist development is concerned, the effort to social engineer a stable developed multiethnic polity is necessary, and even strengthened by the global expansion of neoliberalism. Neoliberalism is globalized on the presumption that open markets and free trade are the most viable routes to local, national, regional, and global development.[2] In the face of this, utilitarianism becomes the practical ideology that conjoins the needs of transnational capital with the state elite's objective of maintaining legitimacy while restructuring Malaysian economy and society.

In 1993 Prime Minister Dr. Mahathir Mohamad said that:

> We have asked the Ministry of Education to *concentrate on manual and living skills rather than on learning too much about history and arts and all that because we are going to have an industrialized society* [emphasis mine]. Fine, if you can have people who can write good novels and all that. We need a few of them, but not too many. . . . We want to actively change the value system. We have devoted RM100 million for this process. We are setting up centres where we will take the people and tell them why this value system is bad and why this is good and why you should practice this value system and not that. . . . We have to explain this thing to them because we cannot expect them to reason these things out themselves.[3]

The Prime Minister's statement confirms the existence of strategies of consent through which the state seeks to construct a different kind of citizenry with "modern" values. Implicit in the proposed emphasis on manual and living skills is that the command of technological knowhow will improve human resource development, thus deepen industrialization and the competitiveness of the economy. The construction and dissemination of technological values, skills, and knowledge are privileged over the critical study and discourse on humanity(s):

> With the transformation of the nation from an agricultural economy to an industrial economy, there will be new demands not only for technical, managerial, and skilled manpower but also for a *labour force that is instilled with the values and culture of an industrialized society* [emphasis mine]. Industrial skill will have to be developed at a rapid pace to provide support for further expansion of the manufacturing industries. While the government will continue to expand and re-oriented [sic] the education and training system, the private sector will be called upon to share a larger burden of training the human resources of the country.[4]

Social engineering in preparation for the twenty-first century involves engineering different values—most notably the value of utility—that undergird peoples' relation to the natural and social environments.[5]

Utilitarianism, however, makes the task of nurturing a "caring" family and society all the more difficult. Already, the dehumanization of foreign female domestic workers in Malaysia indicates that social engineering in this manner comes at a potentially great cost to the individual and collective humanity of the peoples. To build a society fed mostly on a diet of utilitarianism is to build a society that has the potential to be gradually divorced from, or unfamiliar with and unreflective of, the historical struggles that have helped shape visions of what is and is not possible, and what should and should not be permissible in the present and for the future.

The path of export-oriented development that is packaged and promoted by the World Bank and the IMF, and consequently adopted by the state (albeit with a combination of direct and indirect modes of state involvement), is one that hinges on increased production and consumption. Taken to its logical conclusion, sustained consumption is expected to stimulate further innovations in technology that, in turn, enhance the production process. State and private-sector encouragement of the middle classes' emphasis on consumption is indicative of the initial steps in a modernity project designed to undermine or even eliminate real and perceived ethnic, religious, and cultural differences. Indeed, given the state elite's attempts to secure for Malaysian society and economy an advantageous position in the race among states and nonstate actors to attract transnational capital and markets, the need to address the plight of foreign female domestic workers cannot but become incidental to the modernity project.

Prime Minister Dr. Mahathir Mohamad acknowledges some of the contradictions in pursuing a vision of modernity that is shaped by neoliberalism:

> What might you rightly ask, is "a fully developed country"? Do we want to be like any particular country of the present nineteen countries that are generally regarded as "developed counties"? Do we want to be like the United Kingdom, like Canada, like Holland, like Sweden, like Finland, like Japan? To be sure, each of the nineteen, out of a world community of more than 160 states, has its strength. But each also has its fair share of weaknesses. Without being a duplicate of any of them we can still be developed.[6]

In other words, the modernity project can emulate the West and Japan, albeit without generating the myriad of social problems that are perceived to confront them. As if to reemphasize his point, the Prime Minister has been extremely vocal in his criticism of social life especially in the West. He has argued that, "The ideology and logic of materialism have all too easily influenced human society . . . This is a direct result of the impact of Western thought, which fanatically focuses on the material basis of life. Values based on the spiritual, on peace of mind, and on belief in feelings loftier than desire, have no place in the Western psyche."[7]

Paradoxically, the privileging of utilitarianism as a key driving force for the future has had the effect of encouraging rather than discouraging materialism. To restate my earlier point, the expansion of export-oriented development and the success of the modernity project are premised on changes in production *and* consumption patterns and processes.

A belief in feelings loftier than desire is possible when social actors, in their everyday lives, begin to confront the ways in which the principle of utility has become the basis from which to define, perceive, and evaluate one's self and others. Many Malaysian female employers would readily rationalize their abusive behavior toward foreign domestic workers from the perspective of utility—i.e., they justify their behavior from the perspective that it is, for the most part, necessary and effective in bringing about particular outcomes. To deny Filipina and Indonesian servants rest days is to be able to prevent the spread of sexually transmitted diseases and/or legal problems to employers and the workers. Consequently, while the path of export-oriented development improves the standard of living for the expanding middle classes, the various structural forces that shape the in-migration and employment of foreign servants also work to enslave the consciousness of employers.

It is admirable that the modernity project, as pointed out by the Prime Minister, should not be designed to encourage a kind of materialism void of some sense of humanity and dignity. The many different peoples and cultures in Malaysia offer the opportunity to construct an alternative vision of development that need not necessarily sacrifice humanity for material progress and wealth. Yet, economic and social preparations for capturing transnational markets and capital, thus material wealth, threaten to bring about the reverse.

The present global wave to create and harmonize open markets and free trade thrives on and affirms a materialistically oriented social identity and life. For better and for worse, postcolonial states and societies must contend with this: in such a milieu, an acceptance of the covenant of improving living standards, hence quality of life, automatically dictates an acceptance of a reductionist notion of civilizational progress. At the close of the twentieth century, a key challenge remains for all—to strive to build and maintain societies in which "service" is given to humanity, not to capital.

Note on the Epigraph

John Shawcross, *Shelley's Literary and Philosophical Criticism* (London: H. Milford, 1909), p. 148.

Glossary

Malay words used in text:

adat	customary law
air liur	saliva
ayam goreng	fried chicken
Ali-Baba	the symbiotic financial partnership between a Malay (*Ali*) and a Chinese (*Baba*)
Bahasa Melayu	Malay language
balik kampung	go back to the village
bangsa	race or nation
bodoh	stupid
Borang	J J form (personal income tax form)
Bumiputera	sons of the soil
dakwah	proselytizing activities; individuals and/or groups involved in such activities
darah keturunan Kling	descended from Indians
darah keturunan Arab	descended from Arabs
Datuk	honorary title given to Malaysians for service to the country; grandfather
Dewan Rakyat	House of Representatives
Dewan Negara	Senate
duduk dirumah saja	merely sit at home
duit kopi	coffee money; bribe
dulang	tray; *dulang* washing is method of salvaging tin ore
empat ekor	four-digit lottery game
goyang kaki	to sway one's legs (connote laziness)
habis	finished
haram	unclean
Hari Raya Puasa	Raya holiday (Ramadan month)

hamba	slave
hamba orang	someone else's slave
hikayat	stories
jalan bawah	underground road; illegal route
jual	to sell
kafir-mengafir	to be infidel-ized
kangkung with *belachan*	vegetable cooked with shrimp paste (*sambal kangkung*)
konfrontasi	confrontation
kerja kebun	to farm
kuali	wok
Melayu Jati	"true" Malays
Minah Karan	metaphor for a woman who seeks thrills/excitement
mufti	interpreters of Islamic law
pakat	to plot
pasar malam	open-air night markets in neighbourhoods
raja/Sultan	Malay ruler
rakyat	subjects, people
rendah	low; short
rendang	dry curry
sampah	garbage
sembahynag	to pray
style mesti ada, duit tak apa	must have style over and above all else
taikong	illegal Indonesian labour brokers
tak buat apa-apa	am not or did not do much
tinggi	tall; high

Chinese (Cantonese) words used in text:

amah	single, celibate Chinese domestic workers of the 1930s; servant
bun mui	Filipina girl-slave/servant
chi mui	sisters
fong chai	a small room or a flat
Ku Por Uk	old maids' house/grandaunt's house
kung yan	"work people"; workers; servants
mang sui	life's destiny
mui tsai	girl-slave
Po Leung Kuk	refuge for run-away girl-slaves
si tau	boss

sor hei	to comb one's hair into a bun at the back to the head
sui hak	"water guest"; male labor broker
tai kor tai	cellular hand-phone
yan lay mui	Indonesian girl-slave/servant

Other words used in text:

kangany	Indian labor recruiter who also worked in the plantation/estate
Kling	pejorative term for South Indians in colonial Malaya
balikbayan or **maka**-abroad	Filipino returnees from overseas employment

Notes

1. Introduction

1. Throughout this study, the nouns "domestic worker," "domestic servant," "servant," and "household worker" are used interchangeably. The phrases "foreign female domestic workers," "foreign domestic workers," "foreign servants," "Filipina and Indonesian domestic workers," and "transnational migrant domestic labor/workers" also are used interchangeably. Unless specified otherwise, domestic service refers to the category of live-in domestic service, and not to day-work or part-time work.

2. Three of the most prominent nongovernmental organizations are *Tenaganita*; The Gender Project Group at the Asian and Pacific Development Centre; and the International Council on Management of Population Programmes. For discussions of employer-related abuse of foreign female domestic workers elsewhere in the world, see Patricia Weinert, *Foreign Female Domestic Workers: Help Wanted!* Working Paper on International Migration for Employment (Geneva: International Labour Organization, 1991); Asian and Pacific Development Centre [APDC], *The Trade in Domestic Helpers: Causes, Mechanisms, and Consequences* (Kuala Lumpur: Asian and Pacific Development Centre, 1989); *Asian Migrant Forum*, Special Issue: Migrant Workers and Trade Unions, no. 6 (1992): 1–37; *Issues in Gender and Development*, Special Issue: International Migration of Women, no. 5 (1993): 1–39; *Middle East Watch: Women's Rights Project*, Special Issue: Punishing the Victim: Rape and Mistreatment of Asian Maids in Kuwait, 4, no. 8 (1992): 1–44; and Christian Conference of Asia—Urban Rural Mission [CCA-URM], *Asian Labor: Migration from Poverty to Bondage*, Report of the Workshop on Labor Migration, Hong Kong August 9–15, 1990.

3. As stated by the Prime Minister in his speech, "Malaysia: the Way Forward," to the Business Council on February 28, 1991 in Kuala Lumpur, Malaysia. For a full text of the speech, see Ahmad Sarji Abdul Hamid, ed., *Malaysia's Vision 2020: Understanding the Concept, Implications and Challenges* (Petaling Jaya: Pelanduk Publications, 1991), pp. 403–420.

4. *The Star* April 10, 1994.

5. Quoted in Stephen Gill and James H. Mittelman, "Innovation in International Relations Theory: Coxian Historicism as an Alternative Paradigm," Paper presented to the

Eminent Scholar Panel, 1993 Annual Meeting of the International Studies Association, Acapulco, Mexico, March 1993, p. 4.

6. By definition, the concept of social reproduction embodies paid reproductive labor since the performance of many household tasks may and can be transferred to domestic workers: "[Social reproduction] refer[s] to the array of activities involved in maintaining people both on a daily basis and intergenerationally . . includes acts such as purchasing household goods, preparing and serving food, laundering and repairing clothing, maintaining furniture and appliances." (Evelyn Nakano Glenn, "From Servitude to Service Work: Historical Continuities in the Racial Division of Paid Reproductive Labor," *Signs: Journal of Women in Culture and Society* 18, 1 [1992], p. 1).

7. Gary Gereffi and Stephanie Fonda, "Regional Paths of Development," *Annual Review of Sociology* 18 (1992): 424. For excellent review essays of literature of Asian state-society relations in the midst of industrialization, see Robert Wade, "East Asia's Economic Success: Conflicting Perspectives, Partial Insights, Shaky Evidence," *World Politics* 44, no. 2 (1992): 270–320; and Gary Hawes and Hong Liu, "Exploring the Dynamics of the Southeast Asian Political Economy," *World Politics* 45, no. 4 (1993): 629–660.

The perspective of the developmental state is in sharp contrast to two other perspectives on the success of rapid industrialization in Asia: "Magic of the Marketplace" (MM) and the "Confucian Culture"(CC) explanations (see Ruth McVey's introductory chapter in her edited volume, *Southeast Asian Capitalists* [Ithaca: Cornell Southeast Asia Program, 1992]). As Alice Amsden's work demonstrates, the facticity of the neoliberal MM perspective is highly questionable (*Asia's Next Giant: South Korea and Late Industrialization* [New York: Oxford University Press, 1989]). The culturalist perspective as predominantly conceptualized is equally dangerous because of the implication that non-Confucian societies will be destined to a fate of poverty and obscurity. For cultural explanations of rapid economic growth in Asia, see Y. S. Leung, "The Uncertain Phoenix: Confucianism and its Modern Fate," *Asian Culture* 10 (1987): 85–94; Michio Morishima, *Why Has Japan "Succeeded"?: Western Technology and the Japanese Ethos* (New York: Cambridge University Press, 1982); Roy Hofheinz and Kent E. Calder, *The East Asia Edge* (New York: Basic Books, 1982); and Lucian W. Pye, *Asian Power and Politics: The Cultural Dimensions of Authority* (Cambridge: Belknap Press, 1985).

8. Kevin Hewison, Richard Robison, and Garry Rodan, "Introduction: Changing Forms of State Power in Southeast Asia," in *Southeast Asia in the 1990s: Authoritarianism, Democracy and Capitalist*, eds. Kevin Hewison, Richard Robison, and Garry Rodan (Sydney: Allen & Unwin, 1993), p. 4.

9. Representative literature on the coercive-repressive Asian state are Amsden, *Asia's Next Giant*; Ruth McVey, *Southeast Asian Capitalists*; Richard Higgott and Richard Robison, eds., *Southeast Asia: Essays in the Political Economy of Structural Change* (London: Routledge and Kegan Paul, 1985); Frederic C. Deyo, ed., *The Political Economy of the New Asian Industrialism* (Ithaca: Cornell University Press, 1987); and Walden Bello

and Stephanie Rosenfeld, "Dragons in Distress: The Crisis of the NICs," *World Policy Journal* 7, no. 3 (1990): 431–468.

10. Since the 1970s, Asian labor-sending states continue to encourage female nationals to travel throughout Asia, the Middle East, Western Europe, and North America, to work as foreign female domestic workers. See Asian and Pacific Development Centre, *The Trade in Domestic Helpers*; and Weinert, *Help Wanted!*.

11. For the transition from male to female servants in North America and Europe, see Judith Rollins, *Between Women: Domestics and Their Employers* (Philadelphia: Temple University Press, 1985), chapter 1; and Theresa McBride, *The Domestic Revolution: The Modernization of Household Service in England and France 1820–1920* (London: Holmes and Meier, 1976). For analyses of the gender-class-racial dimension of domestic service in North America, see Susan Tucker, *Telling Memories Among Southern Women: Domestic Workers and Their Employers in the Segregated South* (Baton Rouge: Louisiana State University Press, 1988); Mary Romero, *M.A.I.D. in the USA* (New York: Routledge, 1992); Rollins, *Between Women*; Bonnie Thornton Dill, *Across the Boundaries of Race and Class: An Exploration of Work and Family Among Black Female Domestic Servants* (New York: Garland, 1994); Phyllis Palmer, *Domesticity and Dirt: Housewives and Domestic Servants in the United States, 1920–1945* (Philadelphia: Temple University Press, 1989); and David M. Katzman, *Seven Days A Week: Women and Domestic Service in Industrializing America* (New York: Oxford University Press, 1978). For analysis of the gender-class-racial dimension of domestic service in the non-Western world, see Jacklyn Cock, *Maids and Madams: A Study in the Politics of Exploitation* (Johannesburg: Ravan Press), 1980.

Two major studies stand out in their authors' attempts to link transformations in domestic service to changing immigration patterns, hence national and international politics. See especially Evelyn Nakano Glenn, *Issei, Nisei, and War Bride: Three Generations of Japanese-American Women in Domestic Service* (Philadelphia: Temple University Press, 1986); and Cynthia Enloe, *Bananas, Beaches and Bases: Making Feminist Sense of International Politics* (Berkeley: University of California Press, 1989).

12. For discussion on the relationship between domestic service and rural female outmigrants, see Elizabeth Jelin, "Migration and Labor Force Participation of Latin American Women: Domestic Service in the Cities," *Signs: Journal of Women in Culture and Society* 3, no. 1 (177): 129–141; Roger Sanjek and Shellee Colen, eds., *At Work in Homes: Household Workers in World Perspectives* (Washington D.C.: American Anthropological Association, 1990); Ximena Bunster and Elsa M. Chaney, *Sellers and Servants: Working Women in Lima, Peru* (New York: Praeger, 1985); M. Palabrico-Costello, "Female Domestic Servants in Cagayan de Oro, Philippines: Social and Economic Implications of Employment in a Pre-Modern Occupation, in *Women in the Urban and Industrial Workforce: Southeast and East Asia*, ed. Gavin W. Jones, Monograph no. 33 (Canberra: Development Studies Centre, The Australian National University, 1984); and, Elsa M. Chaney, Mary Garcia Castro, and Margo L. Smith, eds., *Muchachas No More: Household Workers in Latin America and the Caribbean* (Philadelphia: Temple

University Press, 1989). Chaney, Garcia Castro, and Smith agreed that analyses of the role of the state are necessary for a better understanding of the changing form and content of domestic service. In the introduction to their edited volume, the authors called for studies of the state's relation to domestic service.

13. On the private-personal point, see Mary Romero's interesting discussion of her academic colleague's relation to his domestic worker in *M.A.I.D. in the USA*, chapter 1. Sedef Arat-Koc argues that overall feminist aversion to the study of domestic service in the West is due to personal discomfort, especially that of white employer-servant of color relations ("In the Privacy of Our Own Homes: Foreign Domestic Workers as a Solution to the Crisis in the Domestic Sphere in Canada," *Studies in Political Economy* 28 [1989]: 33–58).

14. Overall, theories of international migration are not able to fully account for the causes and consequences of the transnationalization of migrant female domestic labor. The dominant "push-pull" or equilibrium perspective would have us believe that peoples are "pushed" out of their home countries and "pulled" into host countries primarily because of wage differentials. At the individual or aggregate levels, this neoliberal perspective on migration fails to account for the role of states and key nonstate actors in constructing and sustaining the demand and supply of foreign female domestic workers. Historical-structural approaches, on the other hand, address some of these flaws by focusing on the constraints of social structures. At the global level, the world systems approach posits that the expansion of global capitalist markets inevitably causes migratory flows within states, and also international migration from periphery to core states. South-South migration that has no historical antecedent is explained in terms of the rise of global cities. Yet, there is no adequate explanation of the increasingly gendered nature of transnational labor migration. Even the dual labor market approach, which explains transnational labor migration as the result of specific demands emanating from the host country, cannot fully account for the transnationalization of migrant female domestic labor. Feminist scholars critique the dual labor market approach for privileging analyses of the relationship between transnational male migrant labor and the industrial sector. Primacy placed on the relationship between low wage male migrant labor, economic growth, and a particular mode of production, to a certain extent has obscured the need to conceptualize the interrelationship among gender, transnational labor migration, and the service sector. For an extensive review of migration theories, see Donald J. Massey et al., "Theories of International Migration: A Review and Appraisal," *Population and Development Review* 19, no. 3 (1993): 431–466. For a feminist critique of the dual labor market perspective, see Jane Jenson, Elisabeth Hagen, and Ceallaigh Reddy, eds., *Feminization of the Labor Force: Paradoxes and Promises* (New York: Oxford University Press, 1988). I offer a more extensive discussion of the transnationalization of migrant female domestic labor in chapter 4.

15. "Private patriarchy is characterized by the domination of patriarchal relations in the household. Public patriarchy is dominated by employment and the state. In private patri-

archy the mode of expropriation of the woman is individual, by the woman's husband or father. In public patriarchy it is collective, by many men acting in common." Sylvia Walby, "Woman and Nation," *International Journal of Contemporary Sociology* 33, nos. 1–2: 89.

16. Enloe, *Bananas, Beaches and Bases*, and J. Ann Tickner, *Gender in International Relations: Feminist Perspectives on Achieving Global Security* (New York: Columbia University Press, 1992).

17. Shellee Colen, "Housekeeping for the Green Card: West Indian Household Workers, the State and Stratified Reproduction in New York," in *At Work in Homes*, eds. Sanjek and Colen, p. 110. See also Arat-Koc, "In the Privacy of Our Homes"; Frances Henry, "The West Indian Domestic Scheme in Canada," *Social and Economic Studies* 17, no. 1 (1968): 83–91; Virginia Dominguez, *From Neighbor to Stranger: The Dilemma of Caribbean Peoples in the United States* (New Haven: Yale University, Antilles Research Program, 1975); Saskia Sassen-Koob, "Notes on the Incorporation of Third World Women into Wage Labor Through Immigration and Off-Shore Production," *International Migration Review* 18, no. 4 (1984): 1144–1167; and Abigail B. Bakan and Daiva K. Stasiulis, "Making the Match: Domestic Placement Agencies and the Racialization of Women's Household Work," *Signs: Journal of Women in Culture and Society* 20, no. 2 (1995): 303–335. A number of these studies deal with immigration rules: employing families act as sponsors for Caribbean and/or Asian women who wish to apply for permanent residency, or who are looking for temporary higher wage work in North America. Migrant women are obligated legally to work as live-in servants for the employers. In this sense, the state helps to ensure a constant supply of domestic workers who will stay with their employing families—especially throughout the duration of permanent residency applications.

18. Arat-Koc, "In the Privacy of Our Own Homes," p. 52.

19. See especially Enloe, *Bananas, Beaches and Bases*, chapter 8.

20. Joseph A. Camilleri, Anthony P. Jervis, and Albert J. Paolini, eds., *The State in Transition: Reimagining Political Space* (Boulder: Lynne Rienner, 1995); Robert W. Cox, *Production, Power, and World Order: Social Forces in the Making of History* (New York: Columbia University Press, 1987); Stephen Gill, "Theorizing the Interregnum: The Double Movement and Global Politics in the 1990s," in *International Political Economy: Understanding Global Disorder* ed. Björn Hettne (London: Zed Books, 1995); and James H. Mittelman, "Rethinking the International Division of Labour in the Context of Globalisation," *Third World Quarterly* 16, no. 2 (1995): 273–294.

21. Jeremy Bentham, *The Principles of Morals and Legislation*, edited with an Introduction by L. J. LaFleur (New York: Hafner Press, 1948), p. 19.

22. For excellent critiques of the epistemological foundations in key studies on Southeast Asian development, see P. W. Preston, *Rethinking Development: Essays on Development and Southeast Asia* (London: Routledge and Kegan Paul, 1987), and *Discourses of Development: State, Market, and Polity in the Analysis of Complex Change* (Hants, England: Avebury, 1994).

23. "By utility is meant that property in any object, whereby it tends to produce benefit, advantage, pleasure, good or happiness (all this in the present case comes to the same thing) to prevent the happening of mischief, pain, evil, or unhappiness to the party whose intent is considered: if that party be the community in general, then the happiness of the community: if a particular individual, then the happiness of that individual." Bentham, *Morals and Legislation*, p. 2.

24. The World Bank's rationale and prescription for the expansion of export-oriented development in Asia, can be found in its publication, *The East Asian Miracle: Economic Growth and Public Policy: Summary* (Washington D.C.: World Bank, 1994). For a concise description and critical analysis of structural adjustment and stabilization policies in Africa, see Ecumenical Coalition for Economic Justice, *Recolonization or Liberation: The Bonds of Structural Adjustment and Struggles for Emancipation* (Toronto: Ecumenical Coalition for Economic Justice, 1990).

25. According to Antonio Gramsci, the state's hegemonic ideology that inheres in state agencies, institutions, legislation, and policies, binds social forces into a cohesive "historic bloc." The Gramscian phrase, "counterhegemonic historic bloc" is the collective term for various forms of opposition to the theory and practice of neoliberalism within a country. The Coxian phrase "transnational counterhegemonic historic bloc" is the collective term for opposition on the transnational level (see Cox, *Production, Power and World Order*, chapter 10 "The Formation of Classes and Historic Blocs,"). For various examples of national and transnational oppositional forces, see Bice Maiguscha, "The Role of Ideas in a Changing World Order: The Case of the International Indigenous Peoples Movement, 1975–1991," Paper presented at the International Conference on Changing World Order and the United Nations System, Yokohama, Japan, March 24–27, 1992; James R. Rush, *The Last Tree: Reclaiming the Environment in Tropical Asia* (New York: Asia Society, 1991); and Dana Allston, ed., *We Speak for Ourselves: Social Justice, Race and Environmentalism* (Washington D.C.: Panos Institute, 1990).

26. Antonio Gramsci, *Selections from the Prison Notebooks of Antonio Gramsci*, trans. and ed. Quintin Hoare and Geoffrey Nowell Smith (New York: International Publishers, 1971), p. 246.

27. Barrington Moore Jr., *The Social Origins of Dictatorship and Democracy: Lord and Peasant in the Making of the Modern World* (Boston: Beacon Press, 1966); Samuel P. Huntington, *Political Order in Changing Societies* (New Haven: Yale University Press, 1968), and "Will More Countries Be Democratic?" *Political Science Quarterly* 99, no. 2 (1984): 193–218.

28. For a good detailed summary of debates between class theorists, see especially Scott McNall, Rhonda Levine, and Rick Fantasia, *Bring Class Back In: Contemporary and Historical Perspectives* (Boulder: Westview, 1991). For studies of the middle classes in the developing and/or rapidly industrializing worlds, see Dale L. Johnson, ed., *Middle Classes in Dependent Countries* (Beverly Hills: Sage Publications, 1985); Richard Tanter and Kenneth Young, eds., *The Politics of Middle Class Indonesia*, Monash Papers on Southeast

Asia no. 19 (Clayton, Australia: Centre for Southeast Asian Studies, Monash University, 1990); and Richard Robison and David S. G. Goodman, eds., *The New Rich in Asia: Mobile Phones, McDonalds and Middle Class Revolution* (London: Routledge, 1996).

29. Helen Arshat, Tan Boon Ann, Tay Nai Ping, and M. Subbiah, *Marriage and Family Formation in Peninsular Malaysia* (Kuala Lumpur: National Population and Family Development Board, 1989), p. 160.

30. Robert W. Cox, in his path-breaking volume *Production, Power and World Order* argued that the expansion of neoliberalism affects and is affected by the interplay between changing state-society relations and social relations of production. While this is a theoretically valid point that is supported by empirical evidence, in our preoccupation with social relations of production we have overlooked the other equally important side of the coin, i.e., changes in consumption patterns and the ensuing political, economic, and social consequences. In other words, people do not wake up on a given day and practice capitalist social relations and lifestyle, but that they are socialized to pursue these relations and lifestyle. Changes in consumption patterns have interesting and compelling ramifications for the politics of governance in various regions of the world (see Catherine Jones, "Hong Kong, Singapore, South Korea and Taiwan: Oikonomic Welfare States," *Government and Opposition* 25, no. 4 (1990): 446–462; Janet W. Salaff, *State and Family in Singapore: Restructuring a Developing Society* (Ithaca: Cornell University Press, 1988); and Diane Singerman, *Avenues of Participation: Family, Politics and Networks in Urban Quarters of Cairo* (Princeton: Princeton University Press, 1995).

31. Pierre Bourdieu, "The Social Space and the Genesis of Groups," *Theory and Society* 14, no. 6 (1985): 730.

32. Many scholars of the family use the sociobiological dimension to draw the distinction between the family and the household: a family is a kin-related network whose members may or may not reside in the same physical locale, whereas a household consists of kin and/or nonkin members who reside in the location. See Barrie Thorne and Marilyn Yalom, eds., *Rethinking the Family: Some Feminist Questions* (New York: Longman, 1982); William J. Goode, *The Family* (New Jersey: Prentice-Hall, 1964); and D. H. J. Morgan, *The Family, Politics and Social Theory* (London: Routledge and Kegan Paul, 1985).

33. Jacques Donzelot, *Policing of Families*, trans. Robert Hurley (New York: Pantheon Books, 1979).

34. Morgan, *The Family*, pp. 72–73. Christopher Lasch argues that no families are impervious to the welfare state penetration and control (*Haven in a Heartless World: The Family Besieged* [New York: Basic Books, 1977]), whereas Donzelot drew a distinction between the state's "policing" of working and middle class families (*Policing of Families*). See also Freidrich Engels's classic text on capitalist development and changes in household relations (*The Origin of the Family, Private Property, and the State: In the Light of the Researches of Lewis H. Morgan by Frederick Engels*, with an Introduction and Notes by Eleanor Burke Leacock [New York: International Publishers, 1972]). Engels exam-

ined the interrelationships among the development of private property, the shift in production beyond the household, and concomitant changes in gender relations.

35. Donzelot, *Policing of Families*, p. 49.

36. Christopher Blaydon and Carol Stack, "Income Support Policies and the
Family," in *The Family*, eds. Alice Rossi, Jerome Kagan, and Tamara Hareven (New
York: Norton, 1978).

37. Gramsci discussed the state's educative role in the following way: "Government
with the consent of the governed—but with this consent organized, and not generic and
vague as it is expressed in the intent of elections. The State does have and request consent, but it also 'educates' this consent, by means of the political and syndical associa-
tions" (*Prison Notebooks*, p. 259). Although Gramsci did not specifically address the
state's relation to the family, his concept of the "ethical" state which interpenetrates
political and civil society, and which uses legislation to facilitate the construction of a
higher level of civilization, creates the theoretical opening or space for scholars to further theorize the state's relation to the family (see *Prison Notebooks*, chapter 2.

38. The phrase "redraft morality" is borrowed from M. Jacqui Alexander, "Redrafting
Morality: the Postcolonial State and the Sexual Offenses Bill of Trinidad and Tobago,"
in *Third World Women and the Politics of Feminism*, eds. Chandra Talpade Mohanty,
Anne Russo, and Lourdes Torres (Bloomington: Indiana University Press, 1993).

39. Peter L. Berger and Thomas Luckmann, *The Social Construction of Reality: A
Treatise in the Sociology of Knowledge* (Garden City: Doubleday, 1966).

40. In this sense, there is similarity between postmodern and critical theorists. While
postmodern theorists frequently cite Jacques Derrida in discussions of the method of
deconstruction (especially in deconstructing dyadic relations/constructs that inherently
privilege one side over the other), critical theory (whether it is of the Coxian or
Habermasian perspective) also is premised on the processes of taking apart social institutions and structures which have been constructed in particularly skewed ways that legitimize the oppression or subjugation of certain groups of peoples (see Jacques Derrida,
Writing and Difference [London: Routledge and Kegan Paul, 1978; and Jürgen Habermas,
Knowledge and Interests, trans. Jeremy Shapiro [Boston: Beacon Press, 1971]). For a dis-
cussion of the various strands of postmodern thought, see Pauline Marie Rosenau, "Once
Again Into the Fray: International Relations Confronts the Humanities," *Millennium:
Journal of International Studies* 19, no. 1 (1990): 83–110, and *Postmodernism and the Social
Sciences: Insights, Inroads and Intrusions* (Princeton: Princeton University Press, 1992).

41. Robert W. Cox, "Social Forces, States and World Orders: Beyond International
Relations Theory," in *Neorealism and Its Critics*, ed. Robert O. Keohane (New York:
Columbia University Press, 1986), pp. 208–9.

42. James C. Scott, *Domination and the Arts of Resistance: Hidden Transcripts* (New
Haven: Yale University Press, 1990).

43. Sidney Verba, Joseph DiNunzio, and Christine Spaulding, "Unwanted Attention:
Report on a Sexual Harassment Survey," Report to the Faculty Council of the Faculty of

Arts and Sciences, Harvard University, September 1983, as quoted in Shulamith Reinharz, *Feminist Methods in Social Research* (New York: Oxford University Press, 1992), p. 90.

44. Roger Sanjek, "On Ethnographic Validity," in *Fieldnotes: The Making of Anthropology*, ed. Roger Sanjek (Ithaca: Cornell University Press, 1990). As the reader can discern readily, I have adhered to the first two guidelines in this introductory chapter. Chapters 4, 5, and 6 offer extensive fieldnote quotations.

45. Margaret R. Somers, "The Narrative Constitution of Identity: A Relational and Network Approach," *Theory and Society* 23, no. 5 (1994): 618.

46. These are open-air night markets replete with hawker stalls that are set up in various neighborhoods. The hawker stalls are the Malaysian version of fast food since those who are tired after work and/or do not feel like cooking at home can walk just a few blocks beyond their houses, sit down at one of the tables set up by the food vendors, and have dinner served within minutes.

47. Some DOMs set aside residential houses for Filipina servants to go to on their rest days—as opposed to running the risk of exposing servants to negative or criminal influences in public space. To date, I am not aware of any agency residential houses for Indonesian maids.

48. Roger Sanjek, "Fieldnotes and Others," in *Fieldnotes*, ed. Sanjek, p. 398.

49. I would converse also with taxi drivers, when they drove me to houses with Indonesian servants, and wait while I interviewed the domestic workers. One time, a taxi driver drove me to the place where his Indonesian girlfriend worked. We quickly discovered that her employers were still in the house, so we waited around the corner for what seemed an eternity, before I heard a whistle. He drove around the corner and found his girlfriend standing at the gate with a smile on her face—her employers had just left the house.

50. Bonnie Thorton Dill wrote of a similar experience: "[T]hey [domestic servants] were primarily interested in helping me; and if this would help me get my degree, whatever it was, they were glad to do it" (*Across the Boundaries*, p. 3). The qualitative difference is that middle-class respondents in my study tried to talk me out of writing about "maids." Many of them believed that it was more interesting for me to research "[high] politics." One even mentioned that a study of gender relations at the various new restaurant-bars in Kuala Lumpur would have been a more fruitful use of my time.

51. Simon Ottenberg, "Thirty Years of Fieldnotes: Changing Relationships to the Text," in *Fieldnotes*, ed. Sanjek, p. 146.

52. Dill, *Across the Boundaries*, p. 34.

53. Clifford Geertz, Foreword, to *Knowledge and Power in Morocco: The Education of a Twentieth Century Notable*, Dale F. Eickelman (Princeton: Princeton University Press, 1985), p. xi.

54. For example, the act of swimming at a country/sporting club would have been part of my everyday, or to be more precise, my every other week experience. Yet, the kind of car window sticker provided by the club became a "symbol" of my middle-class sta-

tus that effectively coopted me—in the eyes of the middle-class respondents—as a member of an "imagined community of middle classes." Thus, I was privy to selected kinds of information that a foreign or a local researcher who did not belong to that class, would have had perhaps a longer and more difficult time in eliciting from the respondents. The question then, is "How was I able to successfully interview foreign female domestic workers?" Here, I draw on Carol Smart's notion of "interviewing up" and "interviewing down" ("Researching Prostitutes: Some Problems for Feminist Researchers," in *A Feminist Ethic for Social Science Research* [Laviston: Edwin Mellen Press, 1988], pp. 37–46). In my conversations with Filipina and Indonesian servants, I addressed them as my equal, in terms of my nonverbal and verbal gestures. In other words, I did not relate to them as if they belonged to a lower social stratum. A number of foreign female domestic workers validated my attitude and behavior with statements such as "You are not like the rest," "You respect us," or "I like you because you do not think we are all prostitutes."

55. Reinharz, *Feminist Methods*, p. 46.

56. Cox, "Social Forces"; Habermas, *Knowledge and Human Interests*; Ben Agger, *Gender, Culture and Power: Toward A Feminist Postmodern Critical Theory* (Westport: Praeger, 1993); and Sandra Harding, ed., *Feminism and Methodology: Social Science Issues* (Bloomington: Indiana University Press, 1987).

57. The postmodern strand that practices and validates the method of deconstructing social institutions, dyads, and so forth, I would argue, is a version of critical theory (even though some postmodernists reject the notion of theory) since postmodern scholars are driven to "address the hierarchy of value over the allegedly valueless" (Agger, *Gender, Culture, Power*, p. 96). Taken to one of the logical conclusions, some postmodernists can and do adopt a relativist stance. Nevertheless, as Sandra Harding eloquently wrote, "The articulation of relativism as an intellectual process emerges historically only as an attempt to dissolve challenges to the legitimacy of purportedly universal beliefs and ways of life. Multirelativism is an objective problem or a solution to a problem only from the perspective of the dominating groups. For groups that are subjugated and marginalized, a relativist stance expresses a false consciousness because it accepts the dominating group's insistence on their right to hold distorted views as intellectually legitimate" ("Introduction: Is There A Feminist Method?" in *Feminism and Methodology*, ed. Harding, p. 10).

58. Harding, "Is There a Feminist Method?," p. 9.

2. Arranging and Rearranging the Interior Frontiers

1. The phrase "interior frontiers" is borrowed from Fichte. For an excellent analysis of different colonial manipulations of the interior frontiers of Southeast Asian societies, see Ann Stoler, "Sexual Affronts and Racial Frontiers: European Identities and the Cultural Politics of Exclusion in Colonial Southeast Asia," *Comparative Studies in Society and History* 34, no. 3 (1992): 514–551.

2. For at least six years after independence in 1957, the formal name of the independent geopolitical entity was the Federation of Malaya, which consisted of eleven "states" on the peninsula. In 1963 with the inclusion of the three British protectorates of Singapore, Sabah, and Sarawak (the latter two are on the island of Borneo), the official name was changed from the Federation of Malaya to the Federation of Malaysia. Until recently, it was common to use the nouns West Malaysia and East Malaysia in reference to the two geographically separate subunits of the Federation of Malaysia. Today, official discourse has replaced East Malaysia with the names of the two "states" of Sabah and Sarawak so as to avoid confusing the east coast of Peninsular Malaysia with East Malaysia. Subsequently, "West Malaysia" was replaced with "Peninsular Malaysia."

3. David Joel Steinberg, et. al., *In Search of Southeast Asia: A Modern History*, revised edition (Honolulu: University of Hawaii Press, 1987), p. 77.

4. "He, who, by clearing or cultivation, or by building a house, causes that to live with which was dead (*meng-hidup-kan bumi*), acquires a proprietary right in the land, which now becomes *tanah hidup* (live land) in contradistinction to *tanah mati* (dead land). His right to the land is absolute as long as occupation continues, or as long as the land bears signs of appropriation." W. E. Maxwell, quoted in Paul Kratoska, "The Peripatetic Peasant and Land Tenure in British Malaya," *Journal of Southeast Asian Studies* 16, no. 1 (1985): 19.

5. Judith Nagata, *Reflowering of Malaysian Islam: Modern Religious Radicals and Their Roots* (Vancouver: University of British Columbia, 1984), p. 3.

6. J. M. Gullick, *Indigenous Political Systems of Western Malaya* (London: Athlone Press, 1958); and Steinberg, et. al., *In Search of Southeast Asia*.

7. Islamic scholars were present in Malaya as early as the thirteenth century. Mary Turnbull argues that Islam did not gain a strong foothold until the fifteenth century because of fundamental differences between Muslim tenets and practices, and traditional Malay animism. According to the earliest known written record of Malay social life (*Sejarah Melayu*), the Melakan ruler dreamt of the Prophet who told him that a missionary from Jeddah would arrive on the Melakan coast (see especially Richard O. Windstedt, "The Malay Annals or *Sejarah Melayu*" *Journal of the Malayan Branch of the Royal Asiatic Society* 16, no. 3 [1938]: 1–226). The prophecy manifested the very next day, after which the Malay ruler and his subjects converted to Islam. For a concise history of precolonial Malaya, see Mary Turnbull, *A Short History of Malaya, Singapore and Brunei* (Singapore: Graham Brash, 1980), pp. 21–23.

8. "[T]he limits of Malay identity, while stretched and partly democratized by Islam, were still constrained by political loyalties and by ties to a certain kind of established authority. By the end of the nineteenth century, most Malay rulers had succeeded in formalizing this association between royal and religious authority by appointing official interpreters of the religious law (*mufti*, or in some states, *Syeikh al-Islam*) who were dependent on princely patronage and upheld the moral power, or Brahmin-like, even added to its aura. These *mufti* were empowered to issue doctrinal rulings (*fatwa*)

regarded as valid and legally binding on all Muslim residents in the sultan's domain. It follows that, in some cases, their rulings tended to support the political status quo." Nagata, *Reflowering*, pp. 11–12.

9. Wazir Jahan Karim, *Women and Culture: Between Malay Adat and Islam* (Boulder: Westview, 1992).

10. Rudyard Kipling's poem "The White Man's Burden" belonged to part of the larger Romanticist movement that was preoccupied with the construction of "otherness." During the nineteenth century, the combination of the already-proven effectiveness of typography, with that of British mercantilist expansion further stimulated the Romanticist quest for difference, arguably only to culminate in social Darwinism (e.g., the construction and ordering of sociobiological categories). See Jacques Barzun for the argument that Romanticism was not an enemy of "science" or the "scientific project." Barzun did not consider the novelist/poet and the scientist as fundamentally different in their schemata for understanding social life (*Classic, Romantic and Modern* [Chicago: University of Chicago Press, 1975]).

11. W. L. Blythe, "Historical Sketch of Chinese Labour in Malaysia," *Journal of the Malayan Branch of the Asiatic Society* 20 (1947): 64–114; R. N. Jackson, *Immigrant Labour and the Development of Malaysia, 1786–1920* (Kuala Lumpur: Government Press, 1961); and Saw Swee Hock, *The Population of Peninsular Malaysia* (Singapore: Singapore University Press, 1988).

12. C. Northcote Parkinson, *British Intervention in Malay 1876–1887* (Singapore: University of Malaya Press, 1960); and C. D. Cowan, *Nineteenth Century Malaya: The Origins of British Colonial Control* (London: Oxford University Press, 1961).

13. Gullick, *Indigenous Political System*, chapters 4 and 5, passim; and, Steinberg, ed., *In Search of Southeast Asia*, part I.

14. Donald Nonini, *British Colonial Rule and the Resistance of the Malay Peasantry, 1900–1957*, Monograph series no. 38 (New Haven: Yale University Southeast Asia Studies, Yale Center for International and Area Studies, 1992), p. 52.

15. Ibid., p. 48.

16. Members of secret societies "were bound together by the rituals of sworn brotherhood around a charismatic and semi-mystical head. Being tightly knit, and glorifying martial prowess, they were particularly suited to the task of colonization and self-protection demanded on a pioneering community." Heng Pek Koon, *Chinese Politics in Malaysia: A History of the Malaysian Chinese Association* (Singapore: Oxford University Press, 1988), p. 15. For detailed descriptions of secret society rituals, see J. D. Vaughan, *The Mannerisms and Customs of the Straits Chinese* (Kuala Lumpur: Oxford University Press, 1879); and Mak Lau Fong, *The Sociology of Secret Societies: A Study of Chinese Secret Societies in Singapore and Peninsular Malaysia* (Kuala Lumpur: Oxford University Press, 1981).

17. Blythe, "Historical Sketch," p. 104.

18. Ibid., pp. 68–97.

19. "The comparative Chinese success in the tin mines was an affront to European expertise. An effective spread of European plantations might retrieve not only profits but also face." Philip Loh, *The Malay States: 1877–1895: Political Change and Social Policy* (London: Oxford University Press, 1969), p. 155.

20. Colin E. R. Abraham, "Racial and Ethnic Manipulation in Colonial Malaya," *Ethnic and Racial Studies* 6, no. 1 (1983): 24.

21. It is known that labor contractors also lied to the migrants by promising a better life in Malaya. Upon arrival, many migrant workers refused to work in deplorable conditions found in the plantations. Kernial Singh Sandhu argues that tenuous Dutch-British relations also contributed to administrative problems in regulating Javanese migrants (*Indians in Malaya: Some Aspects of Their Immigration and Settlement (1786–1957)* [London: Cambridge University Press, 1969]). See also Saw, *Peninsular Malaysia*.

22. Abraham, "Racial and Ethnic Manipulation," p. 24.

23. Saw, *Peninsular Malaysia*, pp. 23–24.

24. Julian Lim, "Social Problems of Chinese Women Immigrants in Malaysia, 1925–1940," *Malaysian History* 23 (1989): 101–109; Sharon Lee, "Female Immigrants and Labour in Colonial Malaya 1860–1947," *International Migration Review* 23, no. 2 (1990): 309–331; and Lai Ah Eng, *Peasants, Proletarians and Prostitutes: A Preliminary Investigation Into the Work of Chinese Women in Colonial Malaya*, Research Notes and Discussion Papers no. 59 (Singapore: Institute for Southeast Asian Studies, 1986).

25. Lee, "Female Immigrants," pp. 314–316.

26. Frank A. Swettenham wrote that Indian workers were preferred over Chinese laborers because "[T]hey have this advantage over the Chinese, that while the Indian women and children emigrate with the men of the family, the Chinese do not" (*The Real Malay* [London: J. Lane, 1900], p. 40). See also, J. Parmer, *Colonial Labour Policy and Administration* (New York: J. J. Augustin, 1960).

27. See especially C. Kondapi, *Indians Overseas: 1838–1949* (New Delhi: Oxford University Press, 1951); Ravindra K. Jain, *South Indians on the Plantation Frontier in Malaya* (New Haven: Yale University Press, 1970); Sandhu, *Indians in Malaya*; and Michael Stenson, *Race and Colonialism in Western Malaysia: The Indian Case* (St. Lucia: University of Queensland Press, 1980).

28. Prakash Jain, "Exploitation and Reproduction of Migrant Indian Labour in Colonial Guyana and Malaysia," *Journal of Contemporary Asia* 18, no. 2 (1988): 189–206.

29. Julian Lim ("Social Problems of Chinese Women Immigrants") identified three categories of prostitutes: sold, pawned, and voluntary. He argued that the last category of women were not "coerced" into prostitution—i.e., the women were not financially obligated to work as prostitutes. I take issue with his category of "voluntary" prostitutes because "voluntary" implies a degree of "free" choice. It is hard to assume that women would have favored prostitution over other kinds of work. Perhaps, further historical research on this category of sex-workers will shed more light on the matter. For more discussion on the *mui tsai* system, see Bruno Lasker, *Human Bondage in Southeast Asia*

(Westport: Greenwood Press, 1972); and Janet Lim, *Sold For Silver* (Ohio: World Publishing Co., 1958).

30. Lee, "Female Immigrants"; Lim, "Social Problems of Chinese Women Immigrants"; Lai, *Peasants, Proletarians and Prostitutes;* and Kenneth Gaw, *Superior Servants: The Legendary Cantonese Amahs of the Far East* (Singapore: Oxford University Press, 1991).

31. Lim, "Social Problems of Chinese Women Immigrants," p. 106.

32. Lee, "Female Immigrants," p. 316.

33. Nonini, *British Colonial Rule*, p. 73.

34. Cited in William R. Roff, *The Origins of Malay Nationalism* (New Haven: Yale University Press, 1967), p. 125.

35. Nonini, *British Colonial Rule*, p. 74.

36. Li Dun Jen, *British Malaya: An Economic Analysis* (New York: The American Press, 1955), p. 40.

37. See especially Paul H. Kratoska, "Rice Cultivation and the Ethnic Division of Labor in British Malaya," *Comparative Studies in Society and History* 24, no. 2 (1982): 280–314, and "The Peripatetic Peasant."

38. For example, R. J. Wilkinson, the Federal Inspector of Schools said, "The best and most promising boys, who will form the nucleus of proposed Lower Division of the Civil Service, can be kept on for three years more for advanced studies in England, and for the study of law, history and literature" (quoted in Rex Stevenson, *Cultivators and Administrators: British Educational Policy Towards the Malays, 1875–1906* [Kuala Lumpur: Oxford University Press, 1975], p. 179).

39. For more in-depth discussion of the consequences of the introduction of mass literacy and the contents of textbooks in Malay schools, see Amin Sweeney, *A Full Hearing: Orality and Literacy in the Malay World* (Berkeley: University of California Press, 1987).

40. Stevenson, *Cultivators and Administrators*, p. 10.

41. "Not a single Malay can be pointed out as having raised himself by perseverance and diligence, as a merchant or otherwise, to a prominent position in the Colony. The Klings, natives of the Coromandel Coast, are an active, industrious race it is true, but neither can it be said that any of them has risen to any distinction. The Chinese are sober, industrious, crafty, proud, conceited, treacherous." J. D. Vaughan, *Mannerisms and Customs*, p. 1. See also, Syed Hussein Alatas, *The Myth of the Lazy Native: A Study of the Image of the Malays, Filipinos, and Javanese from the 16th to the 20th Century and its Function in the Ideology of Colonial Capitalism* (London: Frank Cass, 1977).

42. Leslie O'Brien critiques mainstream scholars' reliance on Furnivall's concept of the "plural" society to describe colonial and postcolonial Malaysian society. She argues that Malaysian society was not as "plural" (distinct but parallel social institutions for each group of peoples) as we have been led to believe by scholarly reconstructions of social life ("Class, Gender and Ethnicity: The Neglect of An Integrated Framework," *Southeast Asian Journal of Social Science* 10, no. 2 (1982): 1–12). I agree with her to the

extent that the plural society framework neglects the possibilities of horizontal bonds, i.e., class formation, maintenance, and contestation. However, the issue here is not whether the "races" intermingled in their everyday lives—especially during the colonial period. The point is that colonial intentions were to keep them apart. Hence, the perceived existence of a plural colonial society.

43. James Puthucheary, *Ownership and Control in the Malayan Economy: A Study of the Structure of Ownership and Control and its Effects on the Development of Secondary Industries and Economic Growth in Malaya and Singapore* (Singapore: Eastern Universities Press, 1960), p. xiv.

44. James Jedudason, *Ethnicity and the Economy: The State, Chinese Business, and Multinationals in Malaysia* Singapore: Oxford University Press, 1989), p. 32.

45. In colonial Malaya during the 1920s, Muslims educated in the Middle East (especially in Egypt), questioned the legitimacy of the religious bureaucracy that the British had constructed. The debates between Kaum Muda (foreign-educated reformists) and Kaum Tua (Malay-educated conservatives) during that decade revealed radically different interpretations of Islam's role in emancipation from colonialism. Reformists argued that the development of Malay society depended on the modernization of Islam, i.e., to eliminate the institution of Malay monarchy (since monarchies were considered by some to be anti-Islamic); and to "purify" Malay culture of *adat* (customary law). Conservatives however supported the continuation of the status quo.

A significant development during this period was the construction of different categories of Malay identity. Members of Kaum Muda either were foreign-born Muslims from the Middle East, India, and Indonesia who settled in Malaya, or Malays of mixed descent. Members of Kaum Tua, on the other hand, were Malays born in Malaya. Kaum Tua members saw themselves as *Melayu Jati* or "true Malays," whereas the following categories were constructed for members of Kaum Muda: *Darah Keturunan Kling* (lit: descended from "Klings" or South Indians) for Indian-Muslims, and *Darah Keturunan Arab* (lit: descended from Arabs) for Arab-Muslims. In the next two decades, Kaum Tua members would prevail in retaining traditional Malay institutions and restricting non-Malay Muslim entry into the community of Malays. See Roff, *Origins of Malay Nationalism*.

46. Gordon P. Means, *Malaysian Politics*, 2nd. ed. (London: Hodder & Stoughton, 1976), p. 69.

47. Albert Lau, "Malayan Union Citizenship: Constitutional Change and Controversy in Malaya 1942–48," *Journal of Southeast Asian Studies* 20, no. 2 (1989): 216–243.

48. Jedudason, *Ethnicity and the Economy*, pp. 42–43.

49. R. S. Milne and Diane K. Mauzy, *Politics and Government in Malaysia* (Singapore: Federal Publishers, 1978); Means, *Malaysian Politics*; and Cynthia Enloe, *Multi-Ethnic Politics: The Case of Malaysia* (Berkeley: Center for South and Southeast Asian Studies, University of California, 1970).

50. "Essentially the bargain provided for Malay political domination in return for a free enterprise system which would allow the continuation of Chinese economic power.

Specifically, it offered liberal citizenship requirements as a major concession by the Malays in return for non-Malay concessions on special rights, religion and community." Milne and Mauzy, *Politics and Government*, p. 130.

51. Virginia Dancz, *Women and Party Politics in Peninsular Malaysia* (Singapore: Oxford University Press, 1987).

52. Aihwa Ong, "State versus Islam: Malay Families, Women's Bodies, and the Body Politic in Malaysia," *American Ethnologist* 17, no. 2 (1990): 259.

53. Saw, *Peninsular Malaysia*, p. 65.

54. Indonesia opposed the creation of the Federation of Malaysia and accused Malaysian leaders of pandering to the British (hence, slogans of "neocolonialism"). Consequently, the Indonesian state embarked on a "*konfrontasi* [confrontation] policy" of using overt and subversive military tactics to harass the coastal areas of the peninsula. The confrontation ended when Indonesian President Sukarno fell from power in 1965–1966.

55. Joel S. Kahn, "Growth, Economic Transformation, Culture and the Middle Classes in Malaysia," in *The New Rich in Asia: Mobile Phones, McDonalds and Middle-Class Revolution*, eds. Richard Robison and David S. G. Goodman (London: Routledge, 1996).

56. A few years before independence, the World Bank published a report identifying the Malayan economy's dependence on commodity exports, the lack of human resource development, and high wages as major obstacles to sustained economic growth (see World Bank/International Bank for Reconstruction and Development, *The Economic Development of Malaya* [Baltimore: Johns Hopkins University Press, 1955]. A key solution, according to the World Bank, was to impose tariff protection to nurture and to protect infant manufacturing industries. While colonialists were reluctant to follow the World Bank's advice because of objections from entrenched European business interests, the postcolonial state elite appeared to depart from their predecessors' policy in their willingness to impose export duties and excess profit taxes on corporations; to undertake deficit spending to finance development projects as opposed to ensuring annual balanced budgets; and to implement ISI. Even though the postcolonial state elite put into practice Articles 152, 153 and 181 of the Constitution, they continued the colonial legacy of a laissez faire attitude toward non-Malay ownership of the economy, i.e., Europeans retained ownership and management of key industries. Within the context of ISI, traditional European agency houses merely "diversified" by adding palm oil to their list of commodity exports, and substituted the import of foreign goods with that of semi-assembled or semi-processed goods (cigarettes, soap, nonferrous metals and automobile parts) for final assembly/processing and sale in the protected domestic market. By the late 1960s, foreigners owned more than 60 percent of share capital in agriculture, manufacturing, and trading companies. Meanwhile, Chinese business interests began to transform from the role of middleman/broker for Malays and Europeans, to that of nascent conglomerates in property development, manufacturing, and so forth (see Jedudason, *Ethnicity and the Economy*; Jomo Kwame Sundaram, *Growth and*

Structural Change in the Malaysian Economy [New York, St. Martin's Press, 1990]; and George Cho, *The Malaysian Economy: Spatial Perspectives* [London: Routledge, 1990]).

57. Folker Fröebel, Otto Kreye, and Jürgen Heinrichs, *The New International Division of Labour: Structural Unemployment in Industrialized Countries and Industrialization in Developing Countries,* trans. Peter Burgess (Cambridge: Cambridge University Press, 1980).

58. The Investment Incentive Act 1968 charged the Federal Investment Development Authority or FIDA (formed in 1965) with the responsibility to attract foreign investments. Labor laws were amended to provide a more depoliticized work environment for foreign firms.

59. See Lim Mah Hui, "Affirmative action, ethnicity and integration: the case of Malaysia," *Ethnic and Racial Studies* 8, no. 2 (1985): 250–276, and "Contradiction in the Development of Malay Capital: State, Accumulation and Legitimation," *Journal of Contemporary Asia* 15, no. 1 (1985): 37–63; Fatimah Halim, "The Transformation of the Malaysian State," *Journal of Contemporary Asia,* 20, no. 1 (1990): 64–88; and Jomo, *Growth and Structural Change.*

60. "In 1957/8, intra-ethnic inequality was highest for the Chinese and lowest for the Malays, but by 1970 and 1973, this ranking was reversed. Anand (1973) and Ishak and Rogayah (1978) found that nearly 90 per cent of overall income inequality in Peninsular Malaysia in 1970 was due to differences within ethnic groups, rather than between them." Jomo, *Growth and Structural Change,* p. 91.

61. The noun "Bumiputera" or "sons of the soil" is synonymous with the noun Malay. "Bumiputera" was coined during the 1920s to symbolize Malay peoples' claim to their status as the original peoples in Malaya: "Non-Muslim indigenes are thus Bumiputera, whereas Muslims of 'non-indigenous' races are not. Put another way, all Malays are Bumiputera, but not all Bumiputera are Malays." Nagata, *Reflowering,* p. 194. See also Judith Nagata, "What is a Malay? Situational Selection of Ethnic Identity in a Plural Society," *American Ethnologist* 1, no. 2 (1974): 331–50. In the 1970s, the postcolonial Malaysian state replaced the noun "Malay" with "Bumiputera" in official discourse so as to include all aboriginal peoples in the NEP, while legitimizing the status of Malays as the indigenous peoples. Today, the nouns "Bumiputera" and "Malay" are used interchangeably.

62. Karl Von Vorys, *Democracy without Consensus: Communalism and Political Stability in Malaysia* (Princeton: Princeton University Press, 1975), p. 216. See also Donald R. Snodgrass, *Inequality and Economic Development in Malaysia* (Kuala Lumpur: Oxford University Press, 1980).

63. Mainstream scholars insist that physical violence between Malays and Chinese occurred because of a breakdown of consensus or democracy among elite ethnic leaders (see R. K. Vasil, *The Malaysian General Elections of 1969* (Singapore: Oxford University Press, 1972); Felix V. Gagliano, *Communal Violence in Malaysia 1969: The Political Aftermath* [Athens: Center for International Studies, Ohio University, 1970]; and Means,

Malaysian Politics). Put simply, it is argued that the Malay and Chinese elite no longer consented to abide by the unstated rules of the "Bargain" that institutionalized Malay political supremacy in return for continued Chinese domination of the economy. This argument, however, neglects the phenomenon of new social forces that, given the colonial legacy of ethnic relations and development in Malaysia, found their only viable channel of expression along the ethnic as opposed to the class dimension. This does not mean that "class" was *the* cause of the riots. Rather, development structures and processes fragmented Malaysian peoples along a specific class-ethnic nexus that led to the crisis (see Martin Brennan, "Class, Politics and Race in Modern Malaysia," *Journal of Contemporary Asia* 12, no. 2 [1982]: 188–215).

64. Means, *Malaysian Politics*, p. 403.

65. Government of Malaysia, *Second Malaysia Plan 1971–1975* (Kuala Lumpur: Government Printing Press, 1971), p. 1.

66. Ozay Mehmet, *Development in Malaysia: Poverty, Wealth and Trusteeship* (London: Croom Helm, 1986).

67. Jomo Kwame Sundaram, cited in Loong Wong and Beverly Blaslett, "Manipulating Space in a Postcolonial State," in *The State in Transition: Reimagining Political Space*, eds. Joseph A. Camilleri, Anthony D. Jervis, and Albert J. Paolini (Boulder: Lynne Rienner, 1995), p. 177.

68. "The second prong of the NEP strategy sought to restructure society by eliminating ideas of race with economic function. This objective was to be achieved through restructuring of employment patterns, ownership of share capital in the corporate sector and creation of BCIC." Government of Malaysia, *Second Outline Perspective Plan 1991–2000* (Kuala Lumpur: National Printing Department, 1991), p. 32.

69. For detailed analyses of non-Malay ownership of corporate wealth during the 1950s, see Puthucheary's *Ownership and Control*. For more recent studies, see Lim Mah Hui, *Ownership and Control of the 100 Largest Corporations in Malaysia* (Kuala Lumpur: Oxford University Press, 1981); and McVey, ed., *South East Asian Capitalists* (Ithaca: Cornell Southeast Asia Program, Cornell University, 1992).

70. "The introduction of modern industries in rural areas and the development of new growth centers in new areas to the migration of rural inhabitants to urban areas are essential to economic balance between the urban and rural areas and the elimination of race with vocation as well as location." Government of Malaysia, *Second Malaysia Plan*, p. 45. In order to ensure a continuing stream of Malay urban inmigrants together with the economic viability of migrants in the cities, state agencies offered Malays liberal credit (e.g., below market interest rates) to facilitate the purchase of low and medium cost housing and transportation required for urban living (see Cho, *Malaysian Economy*).

71. Y. M. Liang, "Malaysia's NEP and the Chinese Community," *Review of Indonesian and Malaysian Affairs* 21, no. 2 (1987): 131–142; and G. Sivalingam, "The NEP and the Differential Economic Performance of the Races in West Malaysia 1970–1985," in

Economic Performance in Malaysia: The Insider's View, ed. Manning Nash (New York: Professors World Peace Academy, 1990).

72. Pavalavalli Govindasamy and Julie Da Vanzo, "Ethnicity and Fertility Differentials in Peninsular Malaysia: Do Policies Matter?" *Population and Development Review* 18, no. 2 (1992): 249.

73. Saw, *Peninsular Malaysia,* pp. 96–101. See also, M. S. Sidhu and G. W. Jones, *Population Dynamics in a Plural Society: The Case of Peninsular Malaysia* (Kuala Lumpur: UMCB Publishers, 1981).

74. For example, the Industrial Coordination Act 1975 (ICA) empowered the Minister of Trade and Information to revoke or refuse to issue manufacturing licenses if it was determined that they were not in the "national interest." Even though the concept of national interest was never defined, it can be inferred from the context of the NEP that national interest was synonymous with the state's perception and definition of the overall interest of the Malay community. The ICA elicited negative responses, e.g., foreign investors complained about the state's direct involvement in regulating manufacturing industries. It quickly became clear that ICA was directed to control or limit Chinese participation in the manufacturing sector. Manufacturing licenses were awarded on the following conditions: (a) firms that produced for the domestic market must have a 70 percent Malaysian ownership with at least a 30 percent Malay equity; (b) 30 percent Malay ownership of all distributorships; (c) if possible, local materials were to be used in the production process; and (d) ministerial approval at all stages from conception to implementation of production plants. Since most Chinese firms were operated as family businesses, the ICA then was seen as an incursion in Chinese families' private decisionmaking structures and processes. The gradual decline of foreign and Chinese capital from the manufacturing sector prompted the state to amend the ICA several times during the 1970s and early 1980s. See Jedudason, *Ethnicity and the Economy,* pp. 135–137.

75. Jamilah Ariffin, *Women and Development in Malaysia* (Petaling Jaya: Pelanduk Publications, 1992), p. 121.

76. Cho, *Malaysian Economy,* p. 198.

77. Ibid. See also Jürgen Ruland, *Urban Development in South East Asia: Regional Cities and Local Government* (Boulder: Westview, 1992).

78. Jedudason, *Ethnicity and the Economy,* p. 38.

79. According to Jedudason, revenues from resource-based and nonresource based exports respectively in 1975 were RM9.2 billion and RM1.86 billion. By 1980, resource-based exports remained the larger source of revenue: RM28.2 billion as opposed to RM6.3 billion from non-resource based exports (*Ethnicity and Economy,* p. 121).

80. Heavy Industries Corporation of Malaysia (HICOM) was the leading publicly owned corporation to initiate heavy industrialization, e.g., cement, steel, and automobile projects. The most famous and successful HICOM project is the production of Proton, the national car. Lacking sufficient capital and technological knowhow, HICOM

solicited help from Mitsubishi Corporation to manufacture the automobile. As Jomo wrote: "[A]lthough the Mitsubishi Corporation and the Mitsubishi Motor Corporation each hold only 15 percent of stock [in the Proton project], they have already reaped handsome profit from supplying the production and assembly technology, as well as about 70 percent of Proton car components and various consultancy, training and other service, besides charging patent, design and other fees—regardless of whether Proton makes money" (*Growth and Structural Change*, pp. 131–132). For detailed critiques of the industrialization policy, see Jomo Kwame Sundaram, ed., *The Sun Also Sets: Lessons in Looking East*, 2nd. edition (Kuala Lumpur: INSAN, 1985).

81. Richard Robison, "Structures of Power and the Industrialization Process in Southeast Asia," *Journal of Contemporary Asia* 19, no. 4 (1989): 381. See also Jomo Kwame Sundaram, "Economic Crisis and Policy Response in Malaysia," in *Southeast Asia in the 1980s: The Politics of Economic Crisis*, eds. Richard Robison, Kevin Hewison, and Richard Higgott (Sydney: Allen & Unwin, 1987), pp. 113–148.

82. Garry Rodan, "The Rise and Fall of Singapore's Second Industrial Revolution," in *Southeast Asia in the 1980s*, eds. Robison, Hewison, and Higgott; and "Industrialization and the Singapore State in the Context of the New International Division of Labour," in *Southeast Asia: Essays in the Political Economy of Structural Change*, eds. Richard Higgott and Richard Robison (London: Routledge and Kegan Paul, 1985).

83. The Singapore state legislated pay raises to induce higher level skills training and application. A few years later, the pay raise was reverted as a result of declining investments by transnational corporations. See J. W. Henderson, "The New International Division of Labour and American Semiconductor Production in South East Asia," in *Multinational Corporations and the Third World*, eds. C. J. Dixon, D. Drakakis-Smith, and H. D. Watts (Boulder: Westview, 1986), and *Globalisation of High Technology Production: Society, Space and Semiconductors in the Restructuring of the Modern World* (London: Routledge, 1989).

84. The irony is that in 1979, the country's revenues from the electronics industry only registered a surplus of US$30 million (US$4020 million export revenue minus US$3990 million import cost) before discounting royalty fees for technology, the repatriation of profits, and so forth. See Jomo, *Growth and Structural Change*, p. 137; and Chris Dixon, *Southeast Asia in the World Economy* (Cambridge: Cambridge University Press, 1991), p. 187.

85. In 1986, Bumiputera corporate equity holdings increased 108-fold as a result of privatization. See Fang Chan Onn, *The Malaysian Economic Challenge: Transformation for Growth* (Singapore: Longman, 1989), pp. 75–77. Also see R. S. Milne, "Privatization in the ASEAN States: Who Gets What, Why and With What Effect?" *Pacific Affairs* 65, no. 1 (1992): 7–24. For excellent mapping of the networks of cross-ownership by UMNO, MCA and MIC, see Edmund Terence Gomez, *Politics in Business: UMNO's Corporate Investments* (Kuala Lumpur: Forum, 1990), *Money Politics in the Barisan Nasional* (Kuala Lumpur: Forum, 1991, and *Political Business: Corporate Involvement of Malaysian Political Parties* (Queensland: James Cook University of North Queensland, 1994).

86. J. Saravanamuttu cited in Kahn, "The Middle Classes," p. 50.

87. Kahn, "The Middle Classes," p. 63.

88. See especially Jamilah Ariffin, *Women and Development.*

89. Sylvia Walby, "Woman and Nation," *International Journal of Contemporary Sociology* 33, nos. 1–2 (1992): 81–100.

90. See the studies of Edmund Terence Gomez (note 85).

91. Government of Malaysia, *Second Outline Perspective Plan 1991–2000* (Kuala Lumpur: National Printing Department, 1991), p. 46.

92. Government of Malaysia, *Second Outline,* p. 15. "The National Development Policy will continue the efforts to correct economic imbalance to create a more just, united, peaceful and prosperous society."

93. Ahmad Sarji Abdul Hamid, ed., *Malaysia's Vision 2020: Understanding the Concept, Implications and Challenges* (Petaling Jaya: Pelanduk Publications, 1993), pp. 397–402.

94. Ibid.

95. Karl Polanyi argued that disruptions caused by the development of market economies give rise to society's demands for defensive/protective measures (*The Great Transformation: The Political and Economic Origins of Our Time* [Boston: Beacon Press, 1944]). A classic example of the Polanyian double movement was the emergence of the welfare state with policies and legislation that buffered the more vulnerable groups against the negative effects of a self-regulating market system. Since the 1980s, the gradual decline of the welfare state in the United States and Great Britain, signalled the reemergence of neoclassical economic orthodoxy. For the very interesting conceptualization of Asian Newly Industrializing Countries (NICs) as modified versions of the welfare state, see Catherine Jones, "Hong Kong, Singapore, South Korea and Taiwan: Oikonomic Welfare States," *Government and Opposition* 25, no. 4 (1990): 446–462.

96. A series of material and symbolic contestations occurred between the Malay-dominated state and the Chinese community. The 1982 National Cultural Policy attempted to legitimize Malay culture as the foundation of a national culture. Put simply, the symbolic dimension of the state's hegemonic historic bloc would, in part, be constructed out of Malay cultural symbols, e.g., religion and language. Non-Malay fear of cultural desecration further intensified when the Melakan state government in 1984, proposed the commercial development of the oldest Chinese cemetery in the country. Chinese mainstream (MCA) and opposition parties (DAP) joined ranks to oppose the state which in turn, relented to Chinese demands by registering the cemetery as a historic preservation site.

97. Lim, "Development of Malay Capital," p. 57.

98. Suhaini Aznam, "From the Campus Back to the Mainstream," *Far Eastern Economic Review* (January 22, 1987), p. 22.

99. See Nagata, *Reflowering;* Jomo Kwame Sundaram and Ahmad Shaberry Cheek, "The Politics of Malaysia's Islamic Resurgence," *Third World Quarterly* 19, no. 2 (1988): 843–869, and "Malaysia's Islamic Movements," in *Fragmented Visions: Culture and Politics in Malaysia,* eds. Joel S. Kahn and Francis Loh Kok Wah (Sydney: Allen & Unwin, 1992);

and Clive S. Kessler, "Malaysia: Islamic Revivalism and Political Dissatisfaction in a Divided Society," *South East Asian Chronicle* 75 (1980): 3–11.

100. Darul Arqam offered its members an alternative to capitalist modes of production by creating a consumer goods business organized along Islamic principles. Today, popular consumer support for the group's products has transformed Darul Arqam into a commercial powerhouse in the domestic and regional production and distribution of Muslim food products. According to Jonathan Karp, "[Al-Arqam] . . vilified by the Malaysian Government for its messianic teachings and deemed reactionary for its Islamic communes, cult-like devotion and distinctive attire—is a budding international business empire with estimated assets of MR400 million. The state has tried to control the group by insisting that it is a threat to national security" ("Allah's Bounty," *Far Eastern Economic Review* [September 1, 1994]: 78).

101. Nagata, *Reflowering*, p. 71.

102. PAS was coopted into the National Front (which emerged from the Alliance Party's cooptation of several opposition parties) after the 1969 riots. However, it was expelled from the National Front in 1978 for holding extremist views. PAS's explusion only increased Islamicists' fervor. In fact, conflicts between PAS and the state sometimes disintegrated into bloodshed, e.g., the 1978 Kerling Incident in which Islamicists sacked a Hindu temple, the 1980 Batu Pahat Islamicist attack on a police station, and the 1985 Memali tragedy in which PAS members clashed with police.

103. Chan Looi Tat, "A Storm in the North," *Asiaweek* (24 Aug 1984): 30.

104. Jomo, *Growth and Structural Change*, p. 156.

105. Ruland, *Urban Development Asia*, p. 259.

106. For a list of wealthy Malay politicians and businessmen, see Lim, "Development of Malay Capital."

107. Michael Kusnic and Julie Da Vanzo, *Income Inequality and the Definition of Income* (Santa Monica: The Rand Corporation for the Agency of International Development, 1980).

108. Jedudason, *Ethnicity and the Economy*, p. 115.

109. Ibid., p. 160.

110. Milne and Mauzy, *Politics and Government*, p. 345.

111. Malay bureaucrats or trustees collected "quasi-rents" and also failed to reinvest revenues to generate additional profit or productivity. See Ozay Mehmet, "The Social Costs of Trusteeship: Deficits, 'Distributional Coalitions,' and Quasi-Rents," in *Development in Malaysia*. Yoshihara Kunio argues that the Southeast Asian brand of capitalism or "ersatz capitalism," is not capitalism grounded in indigenous efforts (*The Rise of Ersatz Capitalism in South-East Asia* [Singapore: Oxford University Press, 1988]). Ruth McVey and her contributors in the edited volume, *South East Asian Capitalists*, take issue with Kunio's position in their discussions on the role of big business in Southeast Asian economic development.

112. See Lim, *Ownership and Control of 100 Largest Corporations*; Richard Robison, "Structures of Power and the Industrialisation Process in Southeast Asia," *Journal of*

Contemporary Asia 19, no. 4 (1989): 371–397; Cheong Kee Cheok, et al., *Malaysia: Some Contemporary Issues in Socio-Economic Development* (Kuala Lumpur: Malaysian Economic Association, 1979); Tan Tat Wai, *Income Distribution and Determination in West Malaysia* (Kuala Lumpur: Oxford University Press, 1982); McVey, ed., *South East Asian Capitalists*; and Edmund Terence Gomez's studies.

To be sure, the Malaysian middle classes, especially the Malay middle classes, had expanded as a result of education and employment opportunities. And Malay control of corporate wealth increased. The question was, "Who really controlled the redistributed wealth, and did the wealth trickle down to the majority of Malays?" Heng Pek Koon writes: "Government statistics . . . show that Malay ownership of corporate wealth in the country has grown from 2.4 percent in 1970 to 17.8 percent in 1985 while the foreign share has dropped from 63.3 percent to 25.5 percent. During the same period the non-Malay (largely Chinese) share grew from 34.3 percent to 56.7 percent. These figures, however, have been strongly disputed by Chinese political and business leaders. . . . There is reason to think they are right. The holdings of nominee companies and locally controlled subsidiaries of foreign-based corporations, in which Malay ownership is considerable, have been counted in their entirety as non-Malay owned" ("The Chinese Business Elite of Malaysia," in *Southeast Asian Capitalists*, ed. Ruth McVey, p. 130).

113. For example, Bank Rakyat, which was established in the 1970s to facilitate the distribution of credit to rural Malays, had lost approximately RM100 million. Investigations into the loss implicated the bank's chief executive officer and the chief minister of Selangor in the misappropriation of bank funds. In the early 1980s, Bank Bumiputera's officers used funds to speculate in the Hong Kong property market. The bank lost approximately RM2 billion, which was more than its RM1.2 billion paid-up capital. Politicians at the highest levels were accused of covering up irregular and concealed payments to a corporation in Hong Kong (Gordon P. Means, *Malaysian Politics: The Second Generation* [Singapore Oxford University Press, 1991], p. 56).

114. MCA, the largest Chinese political party (and arguably the most organized and financially well-endowed of predominantly Chinese political parties) in the National Front coalition, had been rendered relatively politically ineffective by the NEP. To compensate for its political impotence, MCA pooled the Chinese community's economic resources to establish Multi-Purpose Holdings Berhad (MPHB), the party's corporate investment arm. MPHB initially was formed as MCA's self-help answer to the NEP. MCA politicians and key supporters also controlled a number of Chinese Deposit-Taking Cooperatives. In the 1980s, over RM3.6 billion cooperative funds were lost as a result of fraud, theft, and the economic recession (which substantially devalued the cooperatives' institutional investments). See Means, *Second Generation*, pp. 120–3.

115. For arguments based on culture or ethnicity, see Nagata, *Reflowering*; and Chandra Muzaffar, *Islamic Resurgence in Malaysia* (Petaling Jaya: Penerbit Fajar Bakti, 1987). For a class analysis of Islamic revivalism, see Kessler, "Malaysia: Islamic Revivalism."

116. Nagata, *Reflowering*, p. 72.

117. Ibid, p. 71. See also Ong, "State Versus Islam."

118. Prior to Dr. Mahathir Mohamad's ascent to power, Prime Minister Hussein Onn explained the state's Islamization program in the following way in 1980: "You may wonder why we spend so much on Islam. You may think it is a waste of money. If we didn't, we would face two major problems. First, Parti Islam [PAS] will get at us. The party will and does claim that we are not religious and the people will lose faith. Second, we have to strengthen the faith of the people, which is another way to fight against communist ideology" (Ameer Ali, "Islamic Revivalism in Harmony and Conflict: The Experience in Sri Lanka and Malaysia," *Asian Survey* 24, no. 3 [1984]: 299).

119. Means, *The Second Generation*, p. 147.

120. Ibid., p. 199.

121. For example, Team B accused Team A of awarding the North-South Highway contract (the largest in Malaysian history) to the latter's supporters. Harold Crouch asserted that there were no major policy differences between Teams A and B ("Authoritarian Trends, the UMNO Split and the Limits to State Power," in *Fragmented Visions*, eds. Kahn and Loh). However, Khoo Kay Jin ("Grand Vision: Mahathir and Modernization," in the same edited volume) argued to the contrary in that the underlying cause of the challenge was fundamental policy differences between the competing teams: Team B wanted more aggressive bureaucratic efforts to shift economic resources into Malay hands, while Team A moved to relax equity rules for foreign participation in the economy.

122. Subsequently, Prime Minister Dr. Mahathir Mohamad restructured the judicial system by removing Supreme Court justices who had ruled against Team A in several key cases. The justices were accused by the state of undermining its ability to govern Malaysian society. Gordon Means posited that the ultimate blow to the independent judiciary was its acceptance of Team B's lawsuit against Team A. To cut a long story short, UMNO was deregistered as a result of the legal suit. The Prime Minister immediately reregistered UMNO as UMNO Baru (New UMNO).

123. "Many Chinese viewed this move as a violation of the 1986 election manifesto pledge and as the first move in a ploy to undermine or possibly eliminate Chinese-medium primary schools.' " Means, *The Second Generation*, p. 208.

124. Rehman Rashid, who is a Malaysian journalist, offers a humourous yet bittersweet description his experiences in a police interrogation room (*A Malaysian Journey* [Petaling Jaya: Rehman Rashid, 1993]).

125. See Means, *The Second Generation* for more detail.

126. Loong and Wong argue that, in spite of coercive-repressive legislation, the Malaysian state enjoyed much "support" from the populace primarily because of the ability to resurrect the memory of the 1969 ethnic riots as a weapon of fear that controls the nature and extent of dissent ("Manipulating Space," in *The State in Transition*, eds. Camilleri, Jervis, and Paolini). Michael Peletz makes a similar argument ("Sacred Texts and Dangerous Words: The Politics of Law and Cultural Rationalization in Malaysia," *Comparative Studies in Society and History* 35, no. 1 [1993]: 66–109). While I would readily

agree with the cogency of this argument, one still needs to explain why and how Malays and non-Malays are encouraged to support, if not strengthen, the path of export-oriented development. Reminding peoples of the possibility of another interethnic riot may very well be an effective tool in silencing or subverting dissent. Yet, the success of encouraging Malaysians to act in ways that strengthen the development and expansion of capitalist markets is a somewhat different issue.

127. Saw, *Peninsular Malaysia*, p. 225.

128. Ibid., p. 238.

129. Jamilah Arrifin, *Women and Development*, p. 34.

130. Azizah Kassim, "The Unwelcome Guests: Indonesian Immigrants and Malaysian Public Responses," *Southeast Asian Studies* 25, no. 2 (1987): 267.

131. Patrick Pillai, *People on the Move: An Overview of Recent Immigration and Emigration in Malaysia* (Kuala Lumpur: Institute for Strategic and International Studies, 1992), p. 8.

132. Ibid.

133. Richard Dorall, "Foreign Workers in Malaysia: Issues and Implications of Recent Illegal Economic Migrants from the Malay World," in *The Trade in Domestic Helpers: Causes, Mechanisms and Consequences*, Asian and Pacific Development Centre (Kuala Lumpur: Asian and Pacific Development Centre, 1989).

134. *Straits Times* February 17, 1981.

135. *Asiaweek* December 19, 1980, cited in Dorall, "Foreign Workers in Malaysia," p. 298.

136. Dorall, "Foreign Workers in Malaysia," pp. 299–300.

137. "Based on the amount and type of labor needed by Malaysia, the Indonesian Manpower Ministry would recruit workers and facilitate their entry into Malaysia by such means as providing them with travel documents and exempting them from exit taxes." Azizah Kassim, "The Unwelcome Guests," p. 268.

138. According to Patrick Guinness, only 750 migrants were processed, of which 498 ran away from their place of employment during that period ("Indonesian Migrants in Johor: An Itinerant Labour Force," *Bulletin of Indonesian Economic Studies* 26, no. 1 [1990]: 127).

139. Ministry of Human Resources, *Labour and Manpower Report 1987/88* (Kuala Lumpur: Ministry of Labour/Ministry of Human Resources 1988), p. 2.

140. *Malay Mail* May 10, 1987.

3. "Boys, *Amahs*, and Girls": Domestic Workers of the Past and Present

1. Linzi Manicom, "Ruling Relations: Rethinking State and Gender in South African History," *Journal of African History* 33, no. 3 (1992): 441–465.

2. J. D. Vaughan, *The Mannerisms and Customs of the Straits Chinese* (London: Oxford University Press, 1879).

3. J. M. Gullick wrote that the institution of debt-bondage was somewhat similar to slavery in that debt-bondspeople were not guaranteed their freedom even after a period of service to their creditors. A Malay man or woman who borrowed money from, and who could not repay the debt to a ruler or chief consequently became a debt-bondsman or woman to the creditor. Freedom from debt-bondage did not depend on calculating the value of labor performed on behalf of the creditor. Rather, freedom from debt bondage was granted at the discretion of the creditor. In traditional Malay society, debt-bondspeople were still considered members of society since most were taken to live with their creditor-masters. Slaves, however, belonged outside of society. According to Gullick, since Islamic law prohibited the enslavement of Muslims, slaves in traditional Malay society were "Africans, aborigines, and Bataks (a non-Muslim Sumatran tribe)" (*Indigenous Political System of the Malays* [London: Athlone Press, 1958], p. 104). For the discussion of the debates on distinguishing between Malay debt-slaves and debt-bondspersons, see Wazir Jahan Karim, *Women and Culture: Between Malay Adat and Islam* (Boulder: Westview, 1992), pp. 72–79.

4. Gullick, *Indigenous Political System*, pp. 103–4. "A chief thus gained two objects. He had the means of attracting to him men in search of mistresses and ultimately wives. Secondly by providing his followers with the means of satisfying their sexual needs at home the chief prevented them from making forays among his peasant subjects to seduce or abduct their women. No doubt the chief had first to abduct some of these women himself under a more or less legal procedure."

5. Ibid., 103.

6. Vaughan, *Mannerisms and Customs*, p. 21.

7. In fact, Lai Ah Eng argued that Chinese secret societies' control over the wage and working conditions of Chinese male domestic servants further reinforced the *mui-tsai* system in Malaya. Chinese employers, upset with the demands of male servants, turned to young Chinese girls who not only performed housework for free, but also eventually could become future mistresses or daughters-in-law (*Peasants, Proletarians, and Prostitutes: A Preliminary Investigation into the Work of Chinese Women in Colonial Malay*, Research Notes and Discussion Papers, no. 59 [Singapore: Institute for Southeast Asian Studies, 1986], p. 28).

8. For a discussion of successive transformations in colonial perceptions of Malays, see Charles Hirschmann, "The Meaning and Measurement of Ethnicity in Malaysia: An Analysis of Census Classification," *Journal of Asian Studies* 40, no. 3 (1987): 555–582.

9. Vaughan, *Mannerisms and Customs*, p. 20.

10. This also was the case with Chinese male servants on the west coast of the United States during the nineteenth and early twentieth century, and with African-American male slaves in the South. See Mary Romero, *M.A.I.D. in the USA* (London: Routledge, 1992); David M. Katzman, *Seven Days a Week: Women and Domestic Service in Industrializing America* (New York: Oxford University Press, 1978); and Evelyn Nakano Glenn, *Issei, Nisei, War Bride: Three Generations of Japanese-American Women in Domestic Service* (Philadelphia: Temple University Press, 1986).

11. Vaughan, *Mannerisms and Customs*, pp. 14–18.

12. *Straits Times* September 18, 1933.

13. Ibid.

14. Fatimah Halim, "The Transformation of the Malaysian State," *Journal of Contemporary Asia* 20, no. 1 (1990): 68.

15. *Straits Times* September 18, 1933.

16. Kenneth Gaw, *Superior Servants: The Legendary Cantonese Amahs of the Far East* (Singapore: Oxford University Press, 1991), p. 87. Gaw's study is based on oral histories of *amahs*. To date, it is the only comprehensive published study of *amahs* in colonial Malaya.

17. Ibid., p. 44. According to Gaw (citing T. C. Lai's edited volume *Things Chinese* [Hong Kong: Swindon Book Co., 1979]), the movement began as a distinctly female custom in the district of Shun Tak. Many young village women refused to marry men who were chosen by their parents. If women were forced to marry, then some could and did resist by committing suicide. Whenever the parents of a young servant insisted that their daughter get married, her group of young servant-friends would hold a funeral rite for her. The funeral rite was symbolic of the death of her economic and social independence.

18. Ibid., p. 41.

19. *The Star* March 6, 1994.

20. "Ah" is the prefix attached to Malaysian Chinese first names in everyday speech.

21. Gaw, *Superior Servants*, chapter eight.

22. *The Star* March 6, 1994.

23. Gaw, *Superior Servants*, p. 130. Chinese women earned between (Malayan dollars) $5–$10 per month working for Chinese employers, and between $8–$15 working for European employers. In the 1950s, Chinese employers paid female servants $90–$120 a month, while Europeans paid servants between $130–$170 a month.

24. In comparing the working conditions of Filipina and Indonesian servants with that of *amahs*, Noeleen Heyzer and Vivian Wee write that: "[The *amah*] has the protection of her guild and the unwritten understanding of the employing household in that the servant cannot be subject to instant dismissal. She must have control over her labour activities and her labour cannot be called upon after a certain hour of the night" ("Lessons from the *Kongsi Fong* System of Guangdong Province, China," *Issues in Gender and Development*, no. 5 [1993]: 16).

25. Romero, *M.A.I.D.*, p. 106.

26. During the interviews, I learned more about various aspects of her "children's" lives than I did her life. Ah Ling Cheh's "son," who recently graduated from an English university, told her that he planned to marry an Englishwoman. She was visibly upset because she wanted grandchildren of her own race.

27. "In fact, the familiar black and white dress of the amahs has been attributed to the British. They liked their servants to look neat and to have a recognizable uniform—to be identifiably 'servants.' " Gaw, *Superior Servants*, p. 105.

28. Ibid.

29. Ibid., p. 115.

30. *Straits Times* October 18, 1958. I was not able to trace the origins of the Domestic Employee's Union or its fate beyond 1958. The three *amahs* in this study were not aware of the labor union.

31. For a comparative analysis of ethnic women's participation in the three major political parties in Malaysia, UMNO, MCA, and MIC, see Virginia Dancz, *Women and Party Politics in Peninsular Malaysia* (Singapore: Oxford University Press, 1987).

32. The relative absence of studies of contemporary domestic service is made most salient in a comprehensive bibliography of Malaysian women and development entitled *Status and Role of Malaysian Women in Development: A Bibliographic Essay* that was compiled by the Bibliographic Project Team led by Khoo Siew Mun (Kuala Lumpur: Faculty of Economics, University of Malaya; National Population and Family Development Board, Ministry of National Unity and Social Development, 1992). There were no citations to paid domestic service in sections on "Women in Economic Production by Sector," "Women in Employment," "Home Economics, Household and Housekeeping," and "Maternal and Childcare."

33. As opposed to research on female factory workers, especially since the late 1960s. Examples of oft cited research are that of Aihwa Ong, *Spirits of Resistance and Capitalist Discipline: Factory Women in Malaysia* (Albany: State University of New York Press, 1987); Linda Y.C. Lim, *Women Workers in Multinational Corporations: The Case of the Electronic Industry in Malaysia and Singapore*, Occasional Papers, no. 9 (Michigan: University of Michigan, 1987); and Janet Salaff and Aline K. Wong, "Women Workers: Factory, Family and Social Class in an Industrializing Order," in *Women in the Urban and Industrial Workforce: Southeast and East Asia*, ed. Gavin W. Jones, Monograph no. 33 (Canberra: Development Studies Centre, The Australian National University, 1984).

To argue that domestic service in Malaysia is ignored as an area of intellectual inquiry because domestic servants are women, is without foundation since there continue to be studies of women in factory work, and so forth. Rather, it is to argue that the study of domestic service is ignored primarily because it is ascribed "nonwork" performed by women in the private domain that, in turn, is perceived as synonymous with women's space.

34. Sedef Arat-Koc, "In the Privacy of Our Own Homes: Foreign Domestic Workers as a Solution to the Crisis in the Domestic Sphere in Canada," *Studies in Political Economy* 28 (1989): 37–58.

35. *Straits Times* September 19, 1963.

36. Siew Ean Khoo, and Peter Pirie, "Female Rural to Urban Migration in Peninsular Malaysia," in *Women in the Cities of Asia: Migration and Urban Adaptation*, eds. James T. Fawcett, Siew Ean Khoo, and Peter C. Smith (Boulder: Westview, 1984), p. 136.

37. Fawcett, Khoo, and Smith, eds., *Women in the Cities of Asia*; Jamilah Ariffin, *Women and Development in Malaysia* (Petaling Jaya: Pelanduk Publications, 1992); and Hing Ai Yun, "Women and Work in West Malaysia," *Journal of Contemporary Asia* 14, no. 2 (1984): 204–218.

38. Azizah Kassim, "The Squatter Women and the Informal Economy: A Case Study," in *Women and Employment in Malaysia*, eds. Hing Ai Yun and Rokiah Talib (Kuala Lumpur: Department of Anthropology and Sociology, University of Malaya; Women's Association; Asia Pacific and Development Centre, 1986), p. 52. For a discussion on urban squatter settlements, see Nurizan Yahaya, "A Profile of the Urban Poor in Malaysia," *Journal of Contemporary Asia* 21, no. 2 (1991): 212–227.

39. Azizah Kassim, "Squatter Women," p. 52.

40. M. Jocelyn Armstrong, "Female Household Workers in Industrializing Malaysia," in *At Work in Homes: Household Workers in World Perspectives*, eds. Roger Sanjek and Shellee Colen (Washington D.C.: American Anthropological Association, 1990), pp. 156–157.

41. Jamilah Ariffin, *Women and Development*, pp. 46–47.

42. *Straits Times* (which later became *New Straits Times*) August 11, 1967; *New Straits Times* May 15, 1973; November 20, 1974; October 16, 1978; and June 7, 1981.

43. *New Straits Times* May 15, 1973 and June 28, 1975; and *Malay Mail* May 27, 1976.

44. *New Straits Times* June 29, 1975.

45. L. K. Yap, *Domestic Servants in Malaysia: A Sociolegal Study*, Faculty of Law, University of Malaya, 1984.

46. *New Straits Times* April 15, 1974.

47. Ibid., April 15, 1974; March 31, 1974; July 17, 1973; June 1, 1976; June 25, 1975; September 26, 1976; June 7, 1980; and July 10, 1980.

48. Ibid., February 1, 1973.

49. Chinese New Villages were established by the British during the 1950s along the peripheries of urban centers. The intent was to contain Chinese peasant support for, and communist penetration into, rural areas. Villagers were rounded up and relocated to these centers. See Judith Strauch, *Chinese Village Politics in the Malaysian State* (Cambridge: Harvard University Press, 1981).

50. *New Straits Times* June 27, 1973. During the 1920s and in another part of the world, the San Francisco Bay Area's YWCA also offered housekeeping classes to Japanese immigrant women (Nakano Glenn, *Issei, Nisei, War Bride*).

51. *New Straits Times* June 6, 1982.

52. Ibid., June 23, 1987.

53. The Ministry of Labour was renamed the Ministry of Human Resources in the late 1980s.

54. *The Star* April 27, 1994.

55. Raja Rohana Raja Mamat, *The Role and Status of Malay Women in Malaysia: Social and Legal Perspectives* (Kuala Lumpur: Dewan Bahasa dan Pustaka, 1991), p. 52.

56. Jamilah Ariffin, *Women and Development*, pp. 104–107.

57. Hing Ai Yun argued that: "[I]n Malaysia, religious inhibitions on women working outside the home have alleviated somewhat pressures to socialize childcare but to resort to other alternative sources of labor—immigrants. Politically, this could be the more accept-

able solution to the current labor shortage in selected sectors of the economy." ("Women and Work in West Malaysia," *Journal of Contemporary Asia* 14, no. 2 [1984]: 214.) In a footnote clarifying "religious inhibitions," Hing writes, "This is probably relevant more for the Muslim community than for the Chinese." See chapter 6 for further discussion.

58. "As in other countries, rural-urban migration was induced by higher expectations among educated rural youths, the decline of agricultural jobs in the occupational prestige scale, and a desire for social independence (Lim, 1988a: 124). However, in Malaysia the outflow was exacerbated by the establishment of labor-intensive factories where wage and working conditions were better than in the plantations, and by the NEP, which encouraged the participation of rural youths in urban activities." Patrick Pillai, *People on the Move: An Overview of Recent Immigration and Emigration in Malaysia* (Kuala Lumpur: Institute of Strategic and International Studies, 1992), p. 7.

59. *New Straits Times* June 25, 1986.

60. It can be argued that the MTUC's labor organizing power has been severely restrained since 1975 when the Registrar of Trade Unions prohibited MTUC from organizing workers in TNC-owned factories. See Rohana Ariffin, "Women and Trade Unions in West Malaysia," *Journal of Contemporary Asia* 19, no. 1 (1989): 78–94. In 1988, the state allowed the establishment of in-house electronics unions following the U.S. threat to drop Malaysia from the Generalized Special Preferences (GSP) list. The nature of the MTUC's response to foreign female domestic workers may also indicate that the particularities of nationality have yet to be transcended in the construction of transnational labor rights.

61. Richard Dorall, "Foreign Workers in Malaysia: Issues and Implications of Recent Illegal Economic Migrants from the Malay World," in Asian and Pacific Development Centre, *The Trade in Domestic Helpers: Causes, Mechanisms, and Consequences* (Kuala Lumpur: Asian and Pacific Development Centre, 1989), p. 299.

62. *New Straits Times* October 18, 1986.

63. Ibid., December 11, 1986.

64. *Malay Mail* January 10, 1987.

65. Ibid., May 10, 1987.

66. *New Straits Times* January 12, 1989.

67. Ibid.

68. *New Straits Times* October 26, 1991.

69. Ibid., "Datuk Megat Junid also said that Indonesian maids of the Christian faith would be deported as the regulations state that Indonesia maids must be Muslim."

70. *The Star* October 28, 1991.

71. See *New Straits Times, Malay Mail, The Star,* and *Business Times,* October 26, 1991.

72. *Business Times* October 21, 1991.

73. *Malay Mail* December 14, 1991.

74. For interviews of middle class Malaysian employers' view of the state's deportation policy, see *The Star* October 27, 1991.

75. *New Straits Times* November 4, 1991.

76. *The Star* November 9, 1991.

77. Ibid., December 18, 1991.

78. Hence, the unspoken rule of "no pork meat, no dog in the household."

79. *New Straits Times* December 18, 1991.

4. The Malaysian-Philippine-Indonesian Maid Trade

1. This is the view taken by publications such as The World Bank, *The East Asian Miracle: Economic Growth and Public Policy: A Summary* (Washington D.C.: The World Bank, 1994); Bela Balassa, *The Newly Industrializing Countries in the World Economy* (New York: Pergamon Press, 1981); Helen Hughes, ed., *Achieving Industrialization in East Asia* (Cambridge: Cambridge University Press, 1988); and Michael Michaely, et al., *Liberalizing Foreign Trade: Lessons of Experience from Developing Countries*, vols. 1–7 (Oxford: Basil Blackwell, 1991).

2. Donald J. Massey, et al., "Theories of International Migration: A Review and Appraisal," *Population and Development Review* 19, no. 3 (1993): 431. For critiques of the push-pull perspective, see also Charles Woods, "Equilibrium and Historical-Structural Perspectives on Migration," *International Migration Review* 16, no. 2 (1982): 298–319; and James H. Mittelman, "The Global Restructuring of Production and Migration," in *Global Transformation: Challenges to the State System*, ed. Yoshikazu Sakamoto (New York: United Nations University Press, 1994).

3. Larry Sjaastad, "The Costs and Returns of Human Migration," *Journal of Political Economy* 70, no. 5 (1962): 80–92; Michael P. Todaro, *Internal Migration in Developing Countries: A Review of Theory, Evidence, Methodology and Research* (Geneva: International Labour Office, 1976); and Paul R. Shaw, *Migration Theory and Fact: A Review and Bibliography of Current Literature* (Philadelphia: Regional Science Research Institute, 1975).

4. Although there is not absolute agreement on this issue, I accept the argument that from the nineteenth century to the 1960s, there have been successively two distinct world orders, Pax Britannica and Pax Americana, in which Great Britain and the United States institutionalized the expansion of international liberal economic systems (for critical analyses of hegemonic succession, see Robert W. Cox, *Production, Power and World Order: Social Forces in the Making of History* [New York: Columbia University Press, 1987]; and Robert Gilpin, *War and Change in World Politics* [New York: Cambridge University Press, 1981]). The decline of Pax Americana since the late 1960s, however, has left the world without an undisputed hegemon (for the argument that international regimes make possible cooperation in the era of declining American hegemony, see Robert O. Keohane, *After Hegemony: Cooperation and Discord in the World Political Economy* [Princeton: Princeton University Press, 1984]). In spite of and because of this, a key feature in the contemporary emerging new world order is the expansion of neolib-

eralism or the belief that the best path of development is export-led growth that is constituted by and constitutes the drive for globally integrated open markets and free trade.

5. In theory, the good life meant that noncommunist states and peoples eventually would benefit from capitalist development. In practice, not only did former colonies continue to export raw materials to, and import manufactured goods from the West and Japan under unfavorable terms, but also state and private sector elites in former colonies were better positioned than the masses to accumulate material wealth that is generated from development.

6. ISI was conceptualized and proposed by Raul Prebisch who led the United Nations Economic Commission for Latin America (ECLA). He argued that open markets and free trade served only the more developed countries since postcolonial states continued to experience declining terms of trade as a result of colonial legacies of specializing in commodity exports. The solution then was greater protectionist policies (see Celso Furtado, *Development and Underdevelopment*, trans. Ricardo W. de Aquiar and Eric Charles Drysdal [Berkeley: University of California Press, 1964]). ISI was designed to develop manufacturing industries behind trade/tariff barriers. Lacking capital and control over technology, most developing states depended on foreign knowledge and capital. ISI may have slowed the penetration of imported manufactured goods, but the policy continued to allow the free flow of capital. Transnational corporations (TNCs) flourished behind protective barriers by producing goods for domestic consumption while repatriating profits.

7. Richard Higgott and Richard Robison, eds., *Southeast Asia: Essays in the Political Economy of Structural Change* (London: Routledge and Kegan Paul, 1985); and Stephan Haggard, "The Newly Industrializing Countries in the International System: A Review Article," *World Politics* 28, no. 2 (1986): 343–370.

8. Richard Leaver, "Reformist Capitalist Development and the New International Division of Labour," in *Southeast Asia*, eds. Higgott and Robison, pp. 149–171.

9. Folker Fröebel, Otto Kreye, and Jürgen Heinrichs, *The New International Division of Labour: Structural Unemployment in Industrialized Countries and Industrialization in Developing Countries*, trans. Peter Burgess (Cambridge: Cambridge University Press, 1980).

10. For data on foreign aid and development, see the entire section of Annex C in John W. Sewell et al., *Growth, Exports and Jobs in a Changing World Economy: Agenda 1988* (New Brunswick: Transaction Books, 1988); and Stephen Hellinger, Douglas Hellinger, & Fred M. O' Regan, *Aid for Just Development: Report on the Future of Foreign Assistance* (Boulder: Lynne Rienner, 1988).

11. We also know today, that petrodollar loans "alleviated" economic problems, partly, by financing ill-conceived "white elephant" projects, and by adding to the private treasuries of state elite and supporters in Africa, Asia, and Latin America. For a concise explanation of the structural causes of, and key actors in the debt crisis, see Debt Crisis Network, *From Debt to Development: Alternatives to the International Debt Crisis* (Washington D.C.: Institute for Policy Studies, 1986), p. 25.

12. "The labor emigration policies of most of the Asian labor exporters are essentially the result of governmental reaction to the massive increase in labor demand in the Middle East. . . . The reasoning was that labor export would serve as a 'safety valve,' reducing the pressures on the domestic labor market." C. W. Stahl and Ansanul Habib, "Emigration and Development in South and Southeast Asia," in *The Unsettled Relationship: Labor Migration and Economic Development,* eds. Demetrious G. Papademitreou and Philip Martin (Connecticut: Greenwood Press, 1991), pp. 163–164. See also C. W. Stahl, "South-North Migration in the Asia-Pacific Region," *International Migration* 28 (1991): 163–193; and Ronald Skeldon, "International Migration Within and From the East and Southeast Asian Region, *Asia and Pacific Migration Journal* 1, no. 1 (1992): 19–63.

13. Christian Conference of Asia-Rural Urban Mission [CCA-URM], *Asian Labor: Migration From Poverty To Bondage,* Report of the Workshop on Asian Labor Migration, Hong Kong, August 9–15, 1990, p. 10.

14. World Bank, *World Bank Development Report 1990* (New York: Oxford University Press, 1990), pp. 93–94.

15. Stahl and Habib, "Emigration and Development," p. 164.

16. Patrick Guinness, "Indonesian Migrants in Johor: An Itinerant Labour Force," *Bulletin of Indonesian Economic Studies* 26, no. 1 (1990): 117–131; Azizah Kassim, "The Unwelcome Guests: Indonesian Immigrants and Malaysian Public Responses," *Southeast Asian Studies* 25, no. 2 (1987): 265–278; and Richard Dorall and Shanmugam R. Paramasivam, "Gender Perspectives on Indonesian Labour Migration to Peninsular Malaysia: A Case Study," Paper presented at the Population Studies Unit's International Colloquium, "Migration, Development and Gender in the ASEAN Region," Coral Beach Resort, Kuantan, Pahang, October 28–31, 1992.

17. Patrick Pillai, *People on the Move: An Overview of Recent Immigration and Emigration in Malaysia* (Kuala Lumpur: Institute for Strategic and International Studies, 1992), p. 25.

18. Reginald Appleyard, ed., *The Impact of International Migration on Developing Countries* (Paris: Development Centre of the Organisation for Economic Co-operation and Development, 1989); Fred Arnold and Nasra M. Shah, eds., *Asian Labor Migration: Pipeline to the Middle East* (Boulder: Westview, 1986); George Cremer, "Deployment of Indonesian Migrants to the Middle East: Present Situation and Prospects," *Bulletin for Indonesian Economic Studies* 24, no. 3 (1988): 73–86; Stahl, "South-North Migration"; and Shahid Javed Burki, "Migration from Pakistan to the Middle East," in *The Unsettled Relationship,* eds. Papademitreou and Martin.

19. Cremer, "Deployment," p. 74.

20. Debt Crisis Network, *From Debt to Development,* p. 33.

21. For a good and clear description of the "standard menu" in World Bank and IMF structural adjustment and stabilization policies, see Ecumenical Coalition for Economic Justice, *Recolonization or Liberation: The Bonds of Structural Adjustment and Struggles for Emancipation* (Toronto: Ecumenical Coalition for Economic Justice, 1990).

22. Philippine Senator Bobby Tanada in a speech at the International Conference on Human Rights of Migrant Workers, Manila, November 19–20, 1992, quoted in "Migrant Workers and Trade Unions," *Asian Migrant Forum* no. 6 (1993): 19.

23. Stahl, "South-North Migration," p. 184.

24. Malsiri Dias, "Mechanisms of Migration Including Support Systems With Special Reference to Female Labour," *Issues in Gender and Development* no. 5 (1993): 2.

25. "Government Performance in the Middle East Labour Market," *Philippine Migration Review*, reprinted in *Newspaper Clippings and Reprints of Periodicals* Asian Regional Programme on International Labour Migration (Bangkok: International Labour Organization, 1991), n.p.

26. Karl Polanyi, *The Great Transformation: The Political and Economic Origins of Our Time* (Boston: Beacon Press, 1944).

27. Appleyard, *Impact of International Migration*, p. 30.

28. CCA-URM, *Migration From Poverty to Bondage*, p. 13.

29. "Making the Export of Labor Really Temporary," *Asian Migrant Forum*, p. 19.

30. Cremer, "Deployment," p. 77.

31. Migrants have been known to rely more on informal (such as friends or families traveling back to their home countries) as opposed to formal channels of remittances.

32. "There are several measurement problems: worker remittances are often lumped together with migrant transfers and other private transfers (such as gifts and inheritances) as 'unrequited transfers'; reporting of worker remittances by some countries is minimal or sporadic, and remittances below some cut-off point may not be reported; and commercial banks may not report remittances to the central bank so that they can use the foreign exchange from remittances without the usual government controls (Stahl and Habib n.d.)." Fred Arnold, "The Contribution of Remittances to Economic and Social Development," in *International Migration Systems: A Global Approach*, eds. Mary Kritz, Lin Lean Lim, and Hania Zlotnik (New York: Oxford University Press, 1992), p. 205. See also Sharon Stanton Russell, "Remittances from International Migration: A Review in Perspective," *World Development* 14, no. 6 (1986): 677–696; and Sharon Stanton Russell and Michael S. Teitelbaum, *International Migration and International Trade*, World Bank Discussion Papers no. 160 (Washington D.C.: World Bank, 1992).

The difficulty in accessing economic data, together with transnational organizations' and labor sending states' different methods of categorizing remittances, contribute to the lack of accurate statistics on migrant remittances. See Russell and Teitelbaum, *International Migration* for further discussion on the issue.

33. Scholars of migration have been debating the use of migrant remittances, i.e., for consumptive or productive purposes (Kritz et. al., *International Migration Systems*; and Mary Kritz, Charles B. Keely, and Silvano M. Tomasi, eds. *Global Trends in Migration: Theory and Research on International Population Movements* [Staten Island: Center for Migration Studies, 1981]). Empirical studies on the use of Asian migrant remittances indicate that most of the income migrant families receive are used to repay debts, pur-

chase consumer goods, and renovate or buy homes, as opposed to investing in industrial activities. The argument that remittances have not and do not directly benefit development is based on the assumption that labor out-migration policies should be implemented directly and visibly to promote industrialization rather than represent labor-sending states' neo-Malthusian method of coping with the pressures of under/unemployment, overpopulation, and balance of payments deficits.

On the other hand, there are scholars who call for a reconceptualization of the relationship between remittances and development (see Stanton Russell, "Remittances"; and Stanton Russell and Teitelbaum, *International Migration and International Trade*). It is argued that remittances that are used to pay off personal debts can indirectly promote development by providing recipients with the context eventually to invest in the formal sectors of the economy. Remittances initiate a "chain reaction" that strengthens industrialization. Additional theoretical and empirical research is required further to clarify the relation between remittances and development.

If applied to the case of foreign female domestic workers, then the debate will focus on whether or not the women's remittances contribute to industrialization. I would argue that to frame discourse solely around the issue of remittances, at this point, is to sidestep the normative dimension and consequences of the transnationalization of migrant female domestic labor.

34. CCA-URM, *Migration From Poverty to Bondage*, p. 10.

35. Nasra M. Shah, Sulayman Al-Qudsi, and Makhdoom Shah, "Asian Women Workers in Kuwait," *International Migration Review* 25, no. 3 (1991): 467.

36. "Bill for Remittances of OCWs [Overseas Contract Workers] Passed," *New Chronicle* May 27, 1991, reprinted in *Newspaper Clippings*, Asian Regional Programme on International Labour Migration.

37. Cremer, "Deployment," pp. 76–82.

38. Richard Dorall, "Foreign Workers in Malaysia: Issues and Implications of Recent Illegal Economic Migration From the Malay World," in Asian and Pacific Development Centre, *The Trade in Domestic Helpers: Causes, Mechanisms and Consequences* (Kuala Lumpur: Asian and Pacific Development Centre, 1989), p. 300.

39. Pang Eng Fong, *Regionalisation and Labour Flows in Pacific Asia* (Paris: OECD, 1994).

40. Stahl, "South-North Migration," p. 186.

41. Noeleen Heyzer and Vivian Wee, "Who Benefits, Who Profits? Domestic Workers in Transient Overseas Employment," *Issues in Gender and Development* no. 5 (1993): 10.

42. Patricia Weinert, *Help Wanted!*; Asian and Pacific Development Centre, *Trade in Domestic Helpers*; Asian Migrant Forum, Special Issue: Migrant Workers and Trade Unions, no. 6 (1992): 1–37; *Issues in Gender and Development*, Special Issue: International Migration of Women, no. 5 (1993): 1–39; and *Middle East Watch: Women's Rights Project*, Special Issue: Punishing the Victim: Rape and Mistreatment of Asian Maids in Kuwait, 4, no. 8 (1992): 1–44.

43. Patricia Weinert in *Help Wanted!* identifies the list of labor-receiving countries in Asia, Western Europe, and the Middle East that do not legislate domestic service.

44. See my comments on conducting field research in chapter 1. Linda Low's study of migrant workers in Singapore also made a similar argument about the difficulty in obtaining accurate statistics ("Population Movement in the Asia Pacific Region: Singapore Perspective," *International Migration Review* 29, no. 3 [1995]: 745–764).

45. The interview with the Philippine representative took place on January 25, 1994 at the Philippine Embassy, Kuala Lumpur; and the interview with his Indonesian counterpart occurred on February 21, 1994 at the Indonesian embassy, Kuala Lumpur.

46. A cursory examination of the articles on labor migration that are cited in this chapter will reveal the frequency with which the words "deployment" and "deployed" are used uncritically.

47. Jean Bethke Elshtain, in her study *Women and War*, discusses the use of metaphors and tropes that constitute and represent women in a variety of roles and images to sustain national war efforts (New York: Basic Books, 1987). Cynthia Enloe's study offers more contemporary examples of how women assume particular roles—e.g., prostitutes for military servicemen in the Philippines, wives of diplomats, and so forth—in the service of national and international politics (*Bananas, Beaches and Bases: Making Feminist Sense of International Politics* [Berkeley: University of California Press, 1989]). See also the following for more detailed conceptualizations of the relationship between language and politics, see James Der Darian and Michael J. Shapiro, eds., *International/Intertextual Relations: Postmodern Readings in World Politics* (Lexington: Lexington Books, 1989); and Michael J. Shapiro, *Language and Politics* (New York: New York University Press, 1984). For further details on how patterned verbal and nonverbal social interactions over time construct reality, see the classic texts by Peter L. Berger and Thomas Luckmann, *The Social Construction of Reality: A Treatise in the Sociology of Knowledge* (Garden City: Doubleday, 1966); Ludwig Wittgenstein, *Philosophical Investigations*, trans. G. E. Manscombe (New York: Macmillan, 1953); Peter Winch, *The Idea of a Social Science and Its Relation to Philosophy* (London: Routledge and Kegan Paul, 1958; and J. L. Austin, *How To Do Things With Words* (Cambridge: Harvard University Press, 1962).

What is significant today is how female servants are taking center stage in the restructuring of national and regional economies. To "deploy" servants in the economic "war" effort is to expect, on some level, that some migrants will be sacrificed for the sake of the country and peoples. The frequent and uncritical use of the noun "deployment" defines or shapes the boundaries/parameters that guide labor-sending states' responses to foreign female domestic workers' complaints of abuse. In other words, the sacrifice of some for the good of many is perceived as *not* too high a price to pay for state legitimacy and social stability.

48. In 1994, the other occupations were low-wage restaurant, plantation and construction work.

49. In 1995, the state in Singapore convicted and executed a Filipina servant for (allegedly—since there was insufficient evidence, according to her defense attorney and activists) murdering her employer's child. The Philippine state did not immediately ban the out-migration of female nationals to Singapore. Instead, a flight was chartered to bring back to the Philippines any Filipina who had wanted to leave Singapore: "According to news reports, the embassy often has been accused of indifference in responding to the complaints of Filipinos who allege mistreatment" (*New York Times* March 18, 1995).

50. Personal communication with Agile and Irene Fernandez of *Tenaganita* on January 26, 1994; Caridad Tharan of International Council on Management of Population Programmes on January 17, 1994; Ivy Josiah of Women's Aid Organization on January 31, 1994.

51. *Malay Mail* January 13, 1993.

52. For more indepth discussion of Philippine state agencies involved in the out-migration of Filipinas, see Vivian Tornea and Esther Habana, "Women in International Labour Migration: The Philippine Experience," in *The Trade in Domestic Helpers*, Asian and Pacific Development Centre, pp. 63–125.

53. Interview on January 28, 1994, Kuala Lumpur.

54. The Immigration Department's ruling on male domestic servants was made public in *New Straits Times* April 30, 1993.

55. Arguably, economic cooperation between Malaysia and Indonesia has its historical origins: prior to colonialism, Malaysia and Indonesia were part of the "Malay world." Since the construction of the two separate geopolitical units, political and economic relations between the Malaysian and Indonesian states have been fair, with the clear exception of Indonesia's 1960s *konfrontasi* policy.

56. Several Filipina and Indonesian domestic workers mentioned that some women have bypassed the state's two plus one additional year work contract. They would complete their work contracts after the third and final year, travel back to the Philippines or Indonesia, and wait approximately six months to a year before applying as new applicants for work permits.

57. In 1993, the Immigration Department collected RM276 million in levies from all categories of migrant workers (*New Straits Times* February 6, 1994).

58. Prime Minister Mahathir Mohamad admitted in 1993 that Malaysia was home to approximately one million illegal Indonesian migrants (*The Sun* December 12, 1993). The 1993 *Operasi Nyah I* (Operation Go Away I) involved patrolling the coastline of Peninsular Malaysia to deter illegal migrants who arrive by boat. In 1994, *Operasi Nyah II* (Operation Go Away II) targeted public places frequented by migrants.

59. For the Immigration Department's guidelines on hiring migrants from depots, see *Business Times* April 28, 1993. In 1994, it was reported that the eight depots housed 4,886 illegal migrants (*New Straits Times* February 27, 1994).

60. *New Straits Times* November 25, 1993.

61. See for example, *New Straits Times* October 25, 1991, May 11, 1992, and September 7, 1993; and *Malay Mail* November 30, 1993.

62. The state explained the March 1994 raid on St. John's Church in Kuala Lumpur in terms of the need to stop Filipina servants from selling goods without a business license, and from prostituting themselves (*New Straits Times* March 28, 1994).

63. Foreign female domestic workers' undergo medical tests for venereal disease, Hepatitis B, tuberculosis, Acquired Immune Deficiency Syndrome, and pregnancy (*New Straits Times* January 3, 1991).

64. *The Star* April 16, 1994.

65. *The Star* November 20, 1992; *New Straits Times* September 7, 1993; *Malay Mail* May 11, 1992, November 30, 1993, and December 1, 1993.

66. He was well-prepared to engage in a shouting match with us, which would have then attracted the kind of attention that my research did not need in an environment filled with fear and suspicion.

67. Personal communication on January 17, 1994 with Caridad Tharan from the International Council on Management of Population Programmes, and on January 20, 1994 with Needra Weerakoon, a researcher of transnational migrant female domestic labor at the Asia and Pacific Development Centre, Kuala Lumpur.

68. Ernst Spaan, "Taikongs and Calos: The Role of Middlemen and Brokers in Javanese International Migration," *International Migration Review* 28, no. 1 (1994): 93–113.

69. See the interview of Benny Jacoeb Tumbo, director of ATMI (Asosiasi Tenaga Kerja Migran Indonesia) a nonprofit organization concerned with Indonesian migrant workers' rights in Malaysia, in a newspaper article titled "Sindiket Jual Gadis Indon" (*Utusan Malaysia* October 22, 1991). In my interview with Mr. Tumbo on March 29, 1994, he stated that his organization, in an attempt to undermine the *taikong* enterprise, offers to process illegal Indonesian female workers' work permits and to place the domestic servants in prescreened Malaysian families for a nominal fee.

70. During the mid 1980s, there were only a handful of legal DOMs in Malaysia. By 1994, the Immigration Department's list of legally registered DOMs included the names and addresses of well over 100 companies. Elsewhere in Bangladesh and Sri Lanka, there were respectively 55 and 4 DOMs in 1977. By 1980, the numbers had risen to 300 and 544 DOMs. In the Philippines there were 650 DOMs in 1980. Within five years, there were 964 DOMs. There is scant publicly available or accessible information on the number of Indonesian DOMs. See Manolo Abello, "Contemporary Labour Migration: Policies and Perspectives of Sending Countries," in *International Migration Systems*, eds. Kritz, Lim, and Zlotnik, p. 271.

71. *New Straits Times* August 1, 1992.

72. "One maid complained to her agency about the verbal abuse and ill treatment she received. 'They told me it was my mistake and not my employer's fault. As long as my employer has paid the fees, the agency doesn't bother what happens to us.'" *New Straits Times* September 16, 1993.

73. "*Yan lay*" is Cantonese (Wade-Giles system) for Indonesia/n, and "*bun*" is the third syllable of the Cantonese word for Philippine.

74. More than 70 percent of Filipina servants in another study were university or college graduates. See Jojie Samuel M. C. Samuel, *Pembantu-pembantu Rumah Wanita Filipina diMalaysia: Satu Kajian Kes diKawasan Kuala Lumpur dan Petaling Jaya*, Ijazah Sarjana Muda Sastera, Fakulti Literatur dan Sains Sosial, Universiti Malaya, 1987/8.

75. In Zakiyah bte Jamaluddin's study of Indonesian servants, most of the women were married or divorced (*Pembantu Rumah Wanita Indonesia diKuala Lumpur dan Petaling Jaya*, Ijazah Sarjana Muda Sastera, Fakulti Anthropologi dan Sosial, Universiti Malaya, 1991–92).

76. This occurred over the course of a dinner organized by a female employer. The dinner guests were three female employers, a Malaysian woman who was in the process of selecting a foreign servant, and myself. All of the employers agreed that the younger and less experienced the domestic worker, the better it would be for the employing families.

77. Married and single Indonesian women freely mentioned that they "sat at home and did nothing." However, when I asked them to describe a typical day in the house, most of the women talked about performing household chores. Migrant women who looked for work beyond their homes but who did not succeed in doing so (prior to migration), also did not consider household labor as "work." The Indonesian women's perception of housework as "nonwork" reflects the pervasiveness of patriarchal-capitalist definitions of what should legitimately constitute work.

78. For more description, see Caridad Tharan, "Filipina Maids," in *The Trade in Domestic Helpers*, Asian and Pacific Development Centre, p. 277.

79. Mirjana Morokvasic argues that what are generally perceived as personal reasons in fact are structurally determined ("Women in Migration: Beyond A Reductionist Outlook," in *One Way Ticket: Migration and Female Labour*, ed. Annie Phizacklea [London: Routledge and Kegan Paul, 1983]; and "Birds of Passage are also Women . . . ," *International Migration Review* 18, no. 4 [1984]: 886–907).

80. *The Star* January 25, 1994. *Sijil Perjalanan Laksana Paspot* (SPLP) is issued by the Indonesian state to its nationals for exclusive travel between Malaysia and Indonesia.

81. Her bedroom used to be the employer's storage room, thus there was no proper ventilation. And, she was not allowed to eat food from the refrigerator unless her employer gave her permission. Many times, her employer would leave the house for hours without ensuring that Ami, who was prohibited from leaving the house, had enough food to eat.

82. Tharan, "Filipina Maids," p. 276. My experience supports Caridad Tharan's observations. Field interviews in this study were greatly facilitated by the presence of hundreds of servants at shopping malls on Sundays in Kuala Lumpur. Interviews were conducted while the women tried on new clothes, ate in mall restaurants, selected cameras, and so forth.

83. According to the CCA-URM report, nearly 6 percent of Philippine households rely on remittances as the main source of income. Elsewhere, Sri Lankan maids remit as

much as 92 percent of their earnings (see J. W. Huguet, "International Labour Migration from the ESCAP Region," in *Impact of International Migration*, ed. Appleyard, p. 100).

84. CCA-URM, "From Poverty To Bondage," p. 13.

5. Infrapolitics of Domestic Service: Strategies of, and Resistances to, Control

1. James C. Scott, *Domination and the Arts of Resistance: Hidden Transcripts* (New Haven: Yale University Press, 1990), chapters 1 and 7, passim. See also James C. Scott, *Weapons of the Weak: Everyday Forms of Peasant Resistance* (New Haven: Yale University Press, 1985).

2. Scott, *Domination*, p. 18. In this chapter, I take the position that story-telling by employers and domestic workers involves the verbal and nonverbal dimensions, e.g., how both parties negotiate or fail to negotiate the use of physical space, demeanor, and so forth.

3. Ibid., pp. 198–200.

4. Martha Lee Osbourne, ed., *Women in Western Thought* (New York: Random House, 1979); Alison Jaggar, *Feminist Politics and Human Nature* (New Jersey: Rowman and Allanheld, 1983); Anne W. Saxonhouse, *Women in the History of Political Thought: Ancient Greece to Machiavelli* (New York: Praeger, 1985); and Jean Bethke Elshtain, *Public Man, Private Woman: Women in Social and Political Thought* (Princeton: Princeton University Press, 1981).

5. In France and England, domestic workers were not given citizenship until the late nineteenth and early twentieth centuries. Prior to that, they were considered too dependent on their master-employers to be given such responsibilities. See Teresa McBride, *Domestic Revolution: The Modernization of Household Service in England and France 1820–1920* (New York: Holmes and Meier, 1976).

6. *New Straits Times* December 11, 1993.

7. Scott, *Domination*, p. 199.

8. Naomi Abrahams, "Toward Reconceptualizing Political Action," *Sociological Inquiry* 62, no. 3 (1992): 327–347.

9. Since the 1960s, two key tenets of feminist scholarship that are encapsulated in the slogans "the political is personal, the personal is political" and "housework is work" have challenged directly intellectual and conventional acceptance of the domestic domain and reproductive labor respectively as nonpublic-nonpolitical space and activities. For representative literature on the gender division of labor in housework, see Ann Oakley, *Woman's Work: The Housewife, Past and Present* (New York: Pantheon, 1974/5); Susan Gardiner, "Women's Domestic Labour," *New Left Review* 89 (1975): 47–59; Margaret Benston, "The Political Economy of Women's Liberation," *Monthly Review* 21, no. 4 (1969): 13–27; Mariarosa Dalla Costa and Selma James, *The Power of Women and the Subversion of Community* (Bristol: Falling Wall Press, 1975). For representative literature

on the politics of female sexuality, see Catherine MacKinnon, *Toward A Feminist Theory of the State* (Cambridge: Harvard University Press, 1989); Andrea Dworkin, *Our Blood: Prophecies and Discourses on Sexual Politics* (New York: Harper and Row, 1976); Kate Millett, *Sexual Politics* (Garden City: Doubleday, 1970); and Mary Daly, *Beyond God the Father: Toward A Philosophy of Women's Liberation* (Boston: Beacon Press, 1973).

10. Tan Poo Chang, *Status and Role of Malaysian Women in Development and Family Welfare: Policy Implications and Recommendations* (Kuala Lumpur: National Population and Family Development Board and Ministry of National Unity and Social Development), 1992; and Husna Sulaiman and Christina Lam, "Family Care and Interactive Time of Professional Mothers," *Malaysian Journal of Family Studies* 1, no. 1 (1989): 14–24.

11. See especially Ester Boserup, *Woman's Role in Economic Development* (New York: St. Martin's Press, 1970); Julie Matthaei, *An Economic History of Women in America: Women's Work, the Sexual Division of Labor and the Development of Capitalism* (New York: Schocken Books, 1982); Irene Tinker, ed., *Persistent Inequalities: Women and World Development* (New York: Oxford University Press, 1990); Gavin W. Jones, ed., *Women in the Urban and Industrial Workforce: Southeast and East Asia*, Monograph no. 33 (Canberra: Development Studies Centre, The Australian National University, 1984); and Cynthia Enloe, *Bananas, Beaches and Bases: Making Feminist Sense of International Politics* (Berkeley: University of California Press, 1989).

12. See especially Phyllis Palmer, *Domesticity and Dirt: Housewives and Domestic Servants in the United States 1920–1945* (Philadelphia: Temple University Press, 1989); Mary Romero, *M.A.I.D. in the U.S.A.* (New York: Routledge, 1992); and Judith Rollins, *Between Women: Domestics and Their Employers* (Philadelphia: Temple University Press, 1985).

13. Anna Rubbo and Michael Taussig, "Up Off Their Knees: Servanthood in Southwest Colombia," *Latin American Perspectives* 10, no. 4 (1983): 14–15. Rollins emphasizes that, "[Deference-giving] remains one of the functions of the domestic servant—the validation of the employer's class status (and thus the hierarchical class system" (*Between Women*, p. 180).

14. "Material and objective conditions that allow domestic tasks to be redistributed within the household, regardless of age and gender, will not develop as long as middle class women can transfer most of the household tasks to domestic servants. In effect, the very presence of the domestic workers discourages the collaboration of male household members, children and teenagers. The fact that domestic service is available, therefore reaffirms mechanisms of patriarchy in the heart of the family." Isis Duarte, "Household Workers in the Dominican Republic: A Question for the Feminist Movement," *Muchachas No More: Household Workers in Latin America and the Caribbean*, eds. Elsa M. Chaney, Mary Garcia Castro, and Margo L. Smith (Philadelphia: Temple University Press, 1989), p. 179.

15. Pamela Horn, *Rise and Fall of the Victorian Servant* (New York: St. Martin's Press, 1975), pp. 126–130.

16. This is according to several Filipina servants whose friends worked for wealthy employers.

17. Several interviews of female employers were conducted in country clubs. The employers insisted that the clubs offered a more private, exclusive environment in which to converse.

18. Scott, *Weapons of the Weak*, pp. 306–312.

19. This is similar to the case in which a corporate employer/manager gives bonuses and/or presents to employees at the end of a profitable fiscal year, or on special occasions in celebration of employees' service to the corporation. The act of gift-giving, then, serves as an expression of the employer/manager's gratitude, and at the very same time, allows for the purchase of obligation and loyalty from employees. A key difference between the corporate and household environment is that the latter is unlegislated. Regardless of the intended and unintended consequences of giving gifts to corporate employees, most of the employees are protected by labor legislation in the event of disputes with employers over working relations and conditions. In the household context, gift-giving further complicates an already tenuous relationship that is not recognized by law, and that, in certain cases, can take the form of pseudo-familial relations. This is not to say that employers who give gifts to their servants are not genuinely expressing their gratitude. Rather, it is to point out that gift-giving is another method of purchasing obligation and reaffirming social status. After all, why would an employer of a domestic worker give gifts that are for immediate consumption as opposed to raising the woman's monthly salary, which then may allow her to better plan for the future?

20. Rollins, *Between Women*; Donald M. Katzman, *Seven Days a Week: Women and Domestic Service in Industrializing America* (New York: Oxford University Press, 1978); Evelyn Nakano Glenn, *Issei, Nisei, and War Bride: Three Generations of Japanese American Women in Domestic Service* (Philadelphia: Temple University Press, 1986); and Romero, *M.A.I.D.*

21. See especially Palmer, *Domesticity and Dirt*.

22. See especially David Joel Steinberg, et. al., *In Search of Southeast Asia: A Modern History* (Honolulu: University of Hawaii, 1987).

23. In 1987, the Immigration Department's bond requirements were RM100,000 from DOMs, and RM1000 from employers. During my field research in 1994, I saw a poster on a wall in the Immigration Department that listed the bond monies for all categories of migrant workers. If employers choose personally to apply for foreign domestic workers' entry permits as opposed to contracting with DOMs, then employers of Filipina servants must give the Department a RM5000 bond, while those who wish to employ Indonesian servants are required to provide a RM500 bond. See *The Star* October 3, 1993, in which the state prosecuted several DOMs for runaway servants and other matters. While it can be said that most employers choose to contract with DOMs to handle their applications, the lower bond deposits required of those who do so then encourage a greater level of employer dependence on DOMs. Taken to its logical conclusion, the greater the number of employers who contract with DOMs, the greater the profit for DOMs, and revenue for the state.

24. *New Straits Times* January 6, 1993.

25. Azizah Kassim, "The Unwelcome Guests: Indonesian Immigrants and Malaysian Public Responses," *Southeast Asian Studies* 25, no. 2 (1987): 271.

26. "And, while other women fantasized about the perfect male (if articles in magazines are anything to go by), I fantasized about the perfect maid. Faced with a mountain of ironing in the evening after a full day at the office, I would cry hot salty tears onto the ironing board and wonder sadly whether I was indeed destined for a lifetime of drudgery. . . . As usual, I took solace in looking forward to calling my dear friend Premita, at the earliest opportunity I had and pouring all my grievances to her about maids and their sexploits down the telephone line." Elina Abdul Majid, "The Maid in Malaysia," *Her World* (February 1994), pp. 152–153. *Her World* is one of the most popular Malaysian magazines for modern urban middle-class and aspiring middle-class women.

27. Similarly, Judith Rollins experienced invisibility during her fieldwork as a domestic servant in Boston. She wrote that, "Unlike a third person who chose not to take part in the conversation [between members of the employing family] I knew I was not expected to take part . . . I wouldn't speak and was related to as if I wouldn't hear" (*Between Women*, p. 208).

28. See especially Katzman, *Seven Days A Week;* and McBride, *Domestic Revolution.*

29. Scott, *Domination,* p. 193.

30. Ibid., p. 4.

31. Ibid., p. 200. Servants who were not given rest days by employers, but who ran errands outside of employers' houses, were interviewed in farmers' markets and neighborhood grocery and/or hardware stores.

32. "The information grapevine is the informal network of domestic workers who know each other through kinship and friendship. These tend to be built on domestic workers living in the same sending country. . . . one constraint on this network is the mobility of the worker outside her employer's home. If she has no days off, it is highly unlikely she would be able to meet any of her compatriots. Indeed, some employers deliberately choose not to give their maids any day off, for fear that their employees will meet other maids to compare their relative working conditions. The maid's ignorance is then construed as an employer's bliss." Noleen Heyzer and Vivien Wee, "Who Benefits, Who Profits? Domestic Workers in Transient Overseas Employment," *Issues in Gender and Development* no. 5 (1993): 11.

33. Rollins, *Between Women,* p. 231.

34. Kathy Robinson, in her discussion of public discourse on the exploitation of Indonesian servants overseas, writes that: "[D]omestic service in Indonesia, in particular, is the invocation of familial relations as the appropriate model. Their [servants'] exploitation were seen as more heinous than the exploitation of workers in an industrial workforce" ("Housemaids: The Effects of Gender and Culture in the Internal and International Migration of Indonesian Women," in *Intersexions: Gender, Class, Culture and Ethnicity* eds. Gill Bottomley, Marie de Lepervanche, and Jeannie Martin [Sydney:

Allen & Unwin, 1991], p. 49). See also Jean Taylor, *The Social World of Batavia: European and Eurasian Dutch Asia* (Madison: University of Wisconsin Press, 1983).

35. Scott, *Domination*, pp. 32–33.

36. Ami went on to work for another family. I do not know if she worked legally or illegally for the family. I asked her if she had official permission to change employers. She was quiet and then answered yes. Sensing Ami's reluctance, I chose not to pursue the matter further.

37. *Malay Mail* December 1, 1990.

38. Personal communication with Caridad Tharan, March 21, 1994.

39. *The Star* October 29, 1991.

6. Modernity Via Consumption: Domestic Service and the Making of the Modern Malaysian Middle Class

1. For example, *Malay Mail* published an article on December 9, 1993, that graphically described how an unidentified female employer abused her domestic worker: "Among the allegations against the woman employer were pouring hot water on the maid's private parts, smashing her head against the wall, pulling her hair, and poking her stomach with a fork." Between 1990 and 1994, a cursory examination of the *New Straits Times, Malay Mail,* and *The Star* will show that relatively less abusive actions are discussed only in a few "special" articles.

2. "The growth rate dropped from 2.8 in 1960–70 to 2.5 in 1970–1982; the projected growth rate for 1980–2000 is 2.0. Based on this, the population is expected to grow to 17 million in 1990, 21 million in 2000 and to stabilize at 33 million in 2005." Chee Heng Leng, "Babies to Order: Official Population Policies in Malaysia and Singapore," in *Structures of Patriarchy: The State, The Community and The Household in Modernising Asia,* ed. Bina Agarwal (London: Zed Books, 1988), p. 164.

3. Singapore is another exception. In this case, Prime Minister Lee Kuan Yew explicitly introduced his eugenic policy by encouraging Singaporean female university graduates to have more babies in order to replenish a shrinking *skilled* workforce. See Chee Heng Leng, "Babies to Order."

4. Essentially, Malaysian law derives from civil/secular law and Islamic law. In the early 1990s Islamic law remained decentralized: each of the eleven "states" has independent jurisdiction over the interpretation and application of family law that specifically applies to Muslims. Michael Peletz explains: "The state, for example, not only confines the jurisdiction of the Islamic legal system to Malaysia's Muslim population, which includes all Malays but is nonetheless only about half of the country's total population; the state also limits the jurisdiction of Islamic law to a rather narrow range of Muslims' affairs. In terms of civil matters, Islamic law is largely restricted to what is sometimes referred to as 'family law,' such as the registration of marriage and divorce and the issues of conjugal maintenance and child support. In criminal matters, Islamic law is confined

in practice to various types of sexual offenses, failure to fast during the fasting month and non-payment of religious tithes and taxes." ("Sacred Texts and Dangerous Words: The Politics of Law and Cultural Rationalization in Malaysia," *Comparative Studies in Society and History* 35, no. 1 [1993]: pp. 78–79).

I discuss aspects of only Malaysian civil/secular law at the federal level because it is the Malaysian state's juridical-legislative dimension that constructs and legitimizes all Malaysian women's civil-political rights. For discussions on Malay women and Muslim family law, please consult Betty Jaime Chung and Ng Shui Meng, *The Status of Women in Law: A Comparison of Four Asian Countries*, Occasional Papers no. 49 (Singapore: Institute of Southeast Asian Studies, 1977); Jamilah Ariffin, *Women and Development in Malaysia* (Petaling Jaya: Pelanduk Publications, 1992); and Raja Rohana Raja Mamat, *The Role and Status of Malay Women in Malaysia: Social and Legal Perspectives* (Kuala Lumpur: Dewan Bahasa dan Pustaka, 1991).

5. "The construction by the state of relations in the private domain, i.e., marriage and the family, is what has determined women's status as citizens within the public domain." Nira Yuval-Davis, "The Citizenship Debate: Women, Ethnic Processes and the State," *Feminist Review* no. 39 (1991): 64. Of interest is that as late as the 1960s in Britain, the former colonial ruler of Malaya, immigration law reinforced men as heads of family and defined women "only (a) in relation to men; and (b) through the heterosexual nuclear family model" (Chandra Talpade Mohanty, "Introduction: Cartographies of Struggle: Third World Women and the Politics of Feminism," in *Third World Women and The Politics of Feminism*, eds. Chandra Talpade Mohanty, Ann Russo, and Lourdes Torres [Bloomington: Indiana University Press, 1991], p. 26).

6. Jamilah Ariffin, *Women and Development in Malaysia*, pp. 128–131.

7. *Federal Constitution* (Kuala Lumpur: International Law Books Service, 1993).

8. "According to the origin myths of liberalism, men come out of the 'state of nature' to procure rights for themselves in society; they do not establish the state to protect or empower individuals inside families." Wendy Brown, "Finding the Man in the State," *Feminist Studies* 18, no. 1 (1992): 18. For classical liberal constructions of the state, see Thomas Hobbes, *Leviathan*, ed. with an Introduction by C. B. MacPherson (London: Penguin Books, 1968), and John Locke, *Two Treatises of Government*, ed. Peter Laslett (Cambridge: Cambridge University Press, 1960).

9. As is known today, the classical liberal construction and location of the family in the nonpolitical and emotive realm obscures the fact that as late as the seventeenth century in Europe, there was no distinction between economic and domestic life (see Louis Tilly and Joan W. Scott, *Women, Work and Family* [New York: Holt, Reinhart and Winston, 1978]). The shift from a family-based economy to a family-wage economy (or, production shifted outside the household) occurred during industrialization. For more details, see Friedrich Engels, *The Origin of the Family, Private Property and the State: In the Light of the Researches of Lewis H. Morgan, by Frederick Engels* with an Introduction and Notes by Eleanor Burke Leacock [New York: International Publishers, 1972]).

10. This is most evident from the writings of Aristotle and St. Augustine, to that of Immanuel Kant and Georg Hegel. Wendy Brown argues that: "Moreover, because the liberal state does not recognize the family as a political entity or reproduction as a social relation, women's situation as unpaid workers within the family is depoliticized" ("Finding the Man," p. 19).

11. Carol Pateman, "The Fraternal Social Contract," in *Civil Society and the State: New European Perspectives*, ed. John Keane (London: Verso, 1988); Wendy Brown, "Finding the Man"; and Susan Tiano, "Public-Private Dichotomy: Theoretical Perspectives on Women in Development," *The Social Science Journal* 21, no. 4 (1984): 11–28.

12. Mohanty., "Introduction," p. 23.

13. Zainab Wahidin, "Engendering the NDP—An Afterthought," Paper presented at the First ISIS Conference on Women, "Towards and Engendered Millennium," Kuala Lumpur, Malaysia, May 7–8, 1993, p. 5.

14. Linda Y. C. Lim, *Women Workers in Multinational Corporations: The Case of the Electronics Industry in Malaysia and Singapore*, Occasional Papers no. 9 (Michigan: University of Michigan, 1978); Mary Hancock, "Transnational Production and Women Workers," in *One Way Ticket: Migration and Female Labour*, ed. Annie Phizacklea (London: Routledge and Kegan Paul, 1983); and Aihwa Ong, *Spirits of Resistance and Capitalist Discipline: Factory Women in Malaysia* (New York: State University of New York Press, 1987).

15. Cited in Ong, *Spirits of Resistance*, p. 152. Rosalind Tong writes that, "The fact that nearly half of the work force is female indicates that capital wants and indeed needs women in the work force. What this bald statistic does not show, however, is that capital wants/needs women in the work force largely because women's work does not command as much compensation as men's work" (*Feminist Thought: A Comprehensive Introduction* [Boulder: Westview, 1989], pp. 57–8).

16. Jamilah Ariffin cited in Ong, "State versus Islam: Malay Families, Women's Bodies and the Body Politics in Malaysia," *American Ethnologist* 17, no. 2 (1990): 171. Ong's article is reprinted in Aihwa Ong and Michael Peletz, eds., *Bewitching Women and Pious Men: Gender and Body Politics in Southeast Asia* (Berkeley: University of California Press, 1995).

17. "Since many of the women workers live an 'unchaperoned' life without male relations to supervise them or to provide an anchor to the rest of Malay society, some inevitably relieve their daily drudgery with films or discos. Whatever the circumstances however, all workers tend to be tarred with the same slanderous brush, and they have been accorded the popular epithet, *minah karan*, which carries the sense of girls who seek thrills, like an electric current, or hot stuff." Judith Nagata, *The Reflowering of Malaysian Islam: Modern Religious Radicals and Their Roots* (Vancouver: University of British Columbia Press, 1984), p. 73. See also Margaret Scott, "Brave New World," *Far Eastern Economic Review* (December 21, 1989): 32–34.

18. According to the *Malaysian Family Life Survey*, 36 percent of all women between the ages of 18 and 29 were married in 1970. By 1988, only 12 percent were married. The

fertility rate declined from 6.8 percent in 1957 to 3.3 percent in 1990. See Saw Swee Hock's *Population of Peninsular Malaysia* for additional data on Malaysian demographics (Singapore: Singapore University Press, 1988).

19. For a discussion of Malay male villagers' rejection of contraceptives, see Ong, "State Versus Islam."

20. Ibid., p. 268.

21. See Nagata, *Reflowering*, and Ong, "State Versus Islam" for detailed discussions Malay women's adoption of the veil.

22. Ong, "State Versus Islam," p. 269.

23. Helen Arshat, et al., *Marriage and Family Formation in Peninsular Malaysia* (Kuala Lumpur: National Population and Family Development Board, 1989), p. 160.

24. Pavalavalli Govindasamy and Julie Da Vanzo, "Ethnicity and Fertility Differentials in Peninsular Malaysia. Do Policies Matter?" *Population and Development Review* 18, no. 2 (1992): 243–267.

25. R. Leete, "Dual Fertility Trends in Malaysia's Multiethnic Society," *International Family Planning Perspectives* 15, no. 2 (1989): 58–65.

26. Chee, "Babies to Order," p. 167.

27. Ibid., p. 166.

28. The unemployment rate in 1994 was 3 percent. In the proposed 1995 Malaysian budget, the state projected that the unemployment rate would decline to approximately 2.8 percent. See YB Dato' Seri Anwar Ibrahim, "The 1995 Malaysian Budget Proposals," Speech to Dewan Rakyat, Kuala Lumpur, Malaysia, October 28, 1994. The entire text is available on the Malaysia website of the World Wide Web at the time of this writing.

29. Datuk Paduka Napsiah Omar, Minister of National Unity and Social Development, "Keynote Address," Presented at the First ISIS National Conference on Women, "Towards an Engendered Millennium," Kuala Lumpur, Malaysia, May 7–8, 1993.

30. "Thus, at the moment, the increased participation of women in the labor force does not really represent an emancipation but is mainly a reconstruction of women's role within the sexual division of labor." Mei Ling Yong and Kamal Salih, "The Malay Family, Structural Change and Transformation—A Research Proposal," in *Geography and Gender in the Third World*, eds. Janet Momsen and Juliet Townsend (New York: State University of New York, 1987), p. 351.

31. Kumari Jayawardena, *Feminism and Nationalism in the Third World* (London: Zed Books, 1986); Wazir Jahan Karim, "Malay Women's Movements: Leadership and Processes of Change," *International Social Science Journal* 35, no. 4 (1983): 719–731; Lenore Manderson, *Women, Politics and Change: The Kaum Ibu Malaysia, 1945–1972* (Kuala Lumpur: Oxford University Press, 1980); and Virginia Dancz, *Women and Party Politics in Peninsular Malaysia* (Singapore: Oxford University Press, 1987).

32. M. Jacqui Alexander, "Redrafting Morality: The Postcolonial State and the Sexual Offenses Bill of Trinidad and Tobago," in *Third World Women*, eds. Mohanty, Russo and Torres.

33. Some might argue that the failure to qualify for state approval is a blessing in disguise that socializes able-bodied Malaysians to serve themselves, as opposed to being served by others. If the patriarchal conceptualization of the relationship between gender and housework is unchallenged, then women still will remain the gender responsible for the performance of unpaid reproductive labor.

34. It is in this sense that marxist and socialist feminists agree that the "family" is more than an institution primarily characterized by love. It also can be a site of women's subjugation. This is not to say that both schools of thought are able to agree on the root cause of female subjugation. The more orthodox marxist feminists such as Margaret Benston, Selma James, and Mariarosa Dalla Costa identify capitalism rather than patriarchy as the defining ideology of women's oppression within the family. Socialist feminists such as Alison Jaggar assert otherwise. The "compromise" (for lack of a more appropriate word) is found in Heidi Hartmann's work on dual systems or the way capitalism and patriarchy interact to doubly oppress women in the domestic domain. See Hartmann, "The Family as the Locus of Gender, Class and Political Struggle: The Example of Housework," *Signs: Journal of Women in Culture and Society* 6, no. 3 (1981): 366–394.

I believe that Jean Bethke Elshtain has a point when she criticizes marxist feminists for reducing the family to a set of economistic relations (*Public Man, Private Women: Women in Social and Political Thought* [Princeton: Princeton University Press, 1981]). Elshtain's call for the return of the family as a last sanctuary (characterized by love) that protects members against the social ravages of capitalism is commendable and affirms the experiences of immigrant ethnic women and families in the advanced industrialized countries. Still, her solution is problematic in other contexts because it obscures the kinds of unequal distribution of social and economic power in household relations that may and do negatively affect some, but not all women's everyday lives.

35. See, especially Heidi Hartmann, "Capitalism, Patriarchy and Job Segregation by Sex," *Signs* 1, no. 3 (1976): 137–169; Michele Barrett and Mary McIntosh, *The Anti-Social Family* (London: NLB, 1982); Kate Young, Carol Wolkowitz, and Roslyn McCullagh, *Of Marriage and the Market: Women's Subordination Internationally and Its Lessons* (London: Routledge and Kegan Paul, 1984); D. H. J. Morgan, *The Family, Politics and Social Theory* (London: Routledge and Kegan Paul, 1985); and Tilly and Scott, *Women, Work and Family*.

36. See, especially, Jane Ursel, *Private Lives, Public Policy: One Hundred Years of State Intervention in the Family* (Toronto: Women's Press, 1994); Jacques Donzelot, *The Policing of Families*, trans. Robert Hurley (New York: Pantheon Books, 1979; and Catherine MacKinnon, *Toward A Feminist Theory of the State* (Cambridge: Harvard University Press, 1989).

37. R. W. Connell, *Gender and Power: Society, the Person and Sexual Politics* (Stanford: Stanford University Press, 1987). For direct and indirect criticisms for Connell, see especially, Mohanty, Russo, and Lourdes, *Third World Women*; bell hooks, *Feminist Theory: From Margin to Center* (Boston: South End Press, 1984); Jacqueline Bhabha, Francesca Klug, and Sue Shutter, eds., *Worlds Apart: Women Under Immigration and Nationality*

Law (London: Pluto Press, 1985); and Nira Yuval-Davis, "The Citizenship Debate: Women, Ethnic Processes and the State," *Feminist Review*, no. 39 (1991): 56–68.

38. "In recent years, the nuclear family has been seen as one of the roots of the development of capitalism in North America, Europe, and even Japan. The Singapore government is not the first to embark on family reform to encourage the capitalist political economy." Janet W. Salaff, *State and Family in Singapore: Restructuring a Developing Society* (Ithaca: Cornell University Press, 1988), p. 266. See also Engels, *Origin of the Family*.

39. Salaff, *State and Family*, pp. 266–268.

40. Ibid., p. 268.

41. "Few government departments and agencies offered childcare support services." Tan Poo Chang, *Status and Role of Malaysian Women in Development and Family Welfare: Policy Implications and Recommendations* (Kuala Lumpur: National Population and Family Development Board and Ministry of National Unity and Social Development, 1992), p. 14.

42. Child Protection Act 1984 and 1991, and Care Centers Act 1993. See Kamariah Ismail's work for a discussion on the absence of state regulation of creches ("Childcare Services for Working Women in Malaysia," in *Women and Work in Malaysia*, eds. Hing Ai Yun and Rokiah Talib [Kuala Lumpur: Department of Anthropology and Sociology, University of Malaya, National Population and Family Development Board, Ministry of National Unity and Social Development, 1986]).

43. Tan, *Status and Role of Malaysian Women*, p. 12.

44. Rohani A. Razak, "Women's Labour Participation in Peninsular Malaysia," in *Report of the Malaysian Family Life Survey II 1988* (Kuala Lumpur: National Population and Family Development Board, 1992); Tan, *Status and Role of Malaysian Women*; and Nor Alemawati Mohamad Zain, "Childcare Providers in Peninsular Malaysia," in *Report of the Malaysian Family Life Survey II 1988*.

45. Husna Sulaiman and Christina Lam, "Family Care and Interactive Time of Professional Mothers," *Malaysian Journal of Family Studies* 1, no. 1 (1989): 14–24.

46. The Malay phrase is used to connote laziness. Its literal meaning is to sit down, cross one leg over the other, and then sway the top leg to symbolize a level of comfortability with one's surrounding environment.

47. And, there are Malaysian women who religiously practice patriarchal definitions of women's primary role and status as wives and mothers. During the first two weeks in February 1994 *The Star* published a series of responses to a letter written by a Malaysian man on the virtues of beating his wife. Most of the responses vehemently chastised the man. Yet, one Malaysian woman insisted that: "Regarding domestic irritations, I dare say some women can really irritate their husbands to the point of misery. The common ways are constant nagging, constant demand for money, disrespect for in-laws, neglect of children's welfare, gossip with neighbours, comparing husbands with other men, sulking, denial of sex, refusal to cook, refusal to wash, and long absence from home to mention only a few" (*The Star* February 13, 1994).

48. *New Straits Times* July 8, 1993.

49. *New Straits Times* November 12, 1991.

50. Interview on March 29, 1994 with the Deputy Counsel General of the Ministry of National Unity and Social Development, Kuala Lumpur.

51. Telephone interviews of representatives from four formal/regulated creches on 8 and March 9, 1994, and in-person interviews with three informal creches respectively on March 17 and 25, 1994, and April 18, 1994.

52. For summaries of the history of intellectual debates between Marxian and Weberian class theorists, see Stephen Edgell, *Class* (London: Routledge, 1993); Reinhard Bendix and Seymour Martin Lipset, *Class, Status and Power: A Reader in Social Stratification* (New York: Free Press, 1966); Reinhard Bendix, "Inequality and Social Structure: A Comparison of Marx and Weber," *American Sociological Review* 44 (1974): 149–191; Anthony Giddens, *Capitalism and Modern Social Theory: An Analysis of the Writings of Marx, Durkheim, and Max Weber* (Cambridge: Cambridge University Press, 1971); and Anthony Giddens and David Held, eds., *Classes, Power and Conflict* (Berkeley: University of California Press, 1982).

53. Weberians would conceptualize the middle class as permanently located in the center of the divide although each class contains status groups that have higher or lower status than each other, while orthodox Marxists would insist that the middle class, by nature, is "pseudo-proletarian." Take for instance, the development of Marxist class theory. Marx, in *Das Kapital* volume I, argued that capitalist development would eventually eliminate the distinction between land and capital, and in the process lead to the emergence of two classes—capitalists and proletarians—with distinctly opposing interests. Marx predicted that the "*dritte personen*" of shopkeepers, lawyers, intellectuals, priests, and so forth, would disappear with the expansion of capitalist development because they were "unproductive workers." However, by volume III, in which Marx had to confront the emergence of the corporation, he then revised his argument to allow for the growth of a managerial class (*Contribution to the Critique of the Political Economy* trans. and ed. by N. I. Stone [London: Paul, Trench, and Trubner, 1904]). Even since then, latter-day Marxists have had to grapple theoretically with what is commonly referred to as the middle class. Some have remained true to the Marx of volume I by insisting that the middle class ("pseudo-proletarians") is an aberration that, sooner or later, would be subsumed into the proletarian class (e.g., Harry Braverman, *Labor and Monopoly Capital: The Degradation of Work in the Twentieth Century* [New York: Monthly Review Press, 1974]; and Guglielmo Carchedi, *On the Economic Identification of Social Classes* [London: Routledge and Kegan Paul, 1977]). Others argue that the middle class has become a legitimate class in and of itself (e.g., Barbara Ehrenreich and John Ehrenreich, "The Professional-Managerial Class," in *Between Labour and Capital*, ed. P. Walker [Brighton: Harvester Press, 1979]).

54. Eric Olin Wright, "Reconstructing Class Analysis," Paper presented at Work, Class and Culture Symposium, University of Witwatersrand, South Africa, June 28–30, 1993; Scott McNall, Rhonda Levine, and Rick Fantasia, eds., *Bringing Class Back In: Con-*

temporary and Historical Perspectives (Boulder: Westview, 1991); Edgell, *Class*; and Malcolm Waters, "Collapse and Convergence in Class Theory: The Return of the Social in the Analysis of Stratification Arrangements," *Theory and Society* 20, no. 2 (1991): 141–172.

55. "Class lies neither in structure nor agency alone but in their relations as it is historically produced, reproduced and transformed. That is, political and symbolic factors necessarily play a crucial role in the constitution of the middle class (and of any class, for that matter): class identifications, practices, and 'lived experience' are not 'afterthoughts' tacked on preexisting classes; they enter into the very making of these classes." Löic J. D. Wacquant, "Making Class: The Middle Class(es) in Social Theory and Social Structure," in *Bringing Class Back In*, eds. McNall, Levine, and Fantasia, p. 52.

56. Pierre Bourdieu, "The Social Space and the Genesis of Groups," *Theory and Society* 14, no. 6 (1985): 730. For an analysis of the Marxian and Weberian origins of Bourdieu's writings, see Rogers Brubaker, "Rethinking Classical Theory: The Sociological Vision of Pierre Bourdieu," *Theory and Society* 14, no. 6 (1985): 745–775.

57. Benedict Anderson's concept, "imagined community," encapsulates the relationship between capitalist development, print technology, and the construction of national identity (*Imagined Communities: Reflections on the Origin and Spread of Nationalism*, 2nd. ed. [London: Verso, 1991]).

58. "Membership of the middle class is not, however, just a matter of levels of income and expenditure. It is sharply defined by social behaviour, reflecting what may be described as the privatization of the means of consumption, this is readily apparent from the contrast between middle-class and kampung [village] society." H. W. Dick, "The Rise of a Middle Class and the Changing Concept of Equity in Indonesia: An Interpretation," *Indonesia* no. 39 (1985): 75.

59. Mahathir Mohamad, "The Second Outline Perspective Plan 1991–2000," in *Malaysia's Vision 2020: Understanding the Concept, Implications and Challenges*, ed. Ahmad Sarji Abdul Hamid (Petaling Jaya: Pelanduk Publications, 1993), pp. 435–437.

60. For discussions of the media's role in constructing a consumer-oriented version of modernity, see Anthony David Smith, *Age of Behemoths: The Globalization of Mass Media Firms* (London: Priority Press, 1991); and Herbert Schiller, *Culture Inc.: The Corporate Takeover of Public Expression* (London: Oxford University Press, 1989).

61. Ulf Hannerz, "Cosmopolitans and Locals in World Culture," in *Global Culture: Nationalism, Globalization and Modernity*, ed. Mike Featherstone (London: Sage Publications, 1990).

62. Arjun Appadurai, "Disjuncture and Difference in the Global Political Economy," in *Global Culture*, ed. Featherstone, p. 299.

63. The other two television stations, RTM1 and RTM2 are owned and controlled by the state. See Gordon P. Means, *Malaysian Politics: The Second Generation* (Singapore: Oxford University Press, 1991). For discussions of intricate cross-ownership of media and other corporations by UMNO, MCA and MIC, see the works of Edmund Terence Gomez.

64. Zaharom Nain, "The State, the Malaysian Press, and the War," in *Triumph and Image: The Media's War in the Persian Gulf,* eds. Hamid Mowlana, George Gerbner, and Herbert Schiller (Boulder: Westview, 1992).

65. Means, *The Second Generation,* p. 140.

66. *New Straits Times* January 19, 1994.

67. "With the booming economy, Malaysians have more disposable income and many more middle class families can now indulge in recreational activities including water sports." *Business Times* December 27, 1993.

68. The phrase "cultural industry" was coined by the Frankfurt School of Critical Theory. See, for example, Theodore Adorno, "Television and Patterns of Mass Culture," in *Mass Culture: The Popular Arts in America,* eds. Bernard Rosenberg and David Manning White (New York: Free Press, 1957); and Herbert Marcuse, *One Dimensional Man: Studies in the Ideology of Advanced Industrial Society* (Boston: Beacon Press, 1964). Culture industries encompass the structures and processes involved in the objectivation and mass commodification of cultural symbols (e.g., particular kinds of clothing, sports and art).

69. Since Lazarsfeld's "limited effects paradigm," communication scholars continue to debate the effects of advertising messages. Lazarsfeld argued in the 1940s, that audiences actively selected information for processing. By the 1960s and 1970s, however, critical scholars asserted to the contrary, thus strengthened developing states' demand for a New World Information and Communication Order (NWICO) that, in part, was designed to protect nonwestern cultures from the massive influx of western cultural industries. The failure of NWICO and the reemergence of the limited effects paradigm in the form of the "active audience" theory (e.g., one hundred or more cable channels to select from) appear to resurrect the argument that media audiences are active rather than passive in processing of information. Hamid Mowlana and Laurie Wilson argue that proponents and opponents of the "limited effects paradigm" miss the entire point that the structures and processes of owning, producing, and distributing information, are beyond the control of audiences in developing countries. Thus, "the software aspect of communication technology, for example, in the forms of programs, shows and film, enters into a national system seeking to reflect some popular cultural tastes; the product in turn feeds back into the system and reinforces that which has already been found popular" (*The Passing of Modernity: Communication and the Transformation of Society* [New York: Longman, 1990], pp. 96–97).

70. According to an official from the Ministry of Human Resources, the average income of a middle class person in 1994 was RM1000 per month. The average income of middle class families of civil servants was RM2000 per month, approximately RM500–800 less than their private sector counterparts.

71. In the last decade or so, privately owned Malaysian colleges offering twinning programs were established, especially in Kuala Lumpur. Twinning programs allow Malaysians to study at a private Malaysian college for the first two years, after which they

are sent to universities/colleges abroad for the final year or two years of tertiary education. In this way, the cost of sending Malaysians overseas for the entire period of tertiary
education is substantially reduced.

72. See the following for advertising strategies to promote Malaysian consumption
of high-end consumer products: Deng Shengliang, Smita Jivan, and Mary-Louise
Hassan, "Advertising in Malaysia: A Cultural Perspective," *International Journal of
Advertising* 13, no. 2 (1994): 153–166; Jonathan Karp, "Paper Chase," *Far Eastern
Economic Review* (October 6, 1994): 70–71; and Jo Anne Parke, "The Case for Going
Global," *Target Marketing* 17, no. 11 (1994): 8–13.

73. "Class situation thus intersects with the individual at the point of the market to
provide for the emergence of social classes. . . . [T]he particular characteristic of these
social classes is not simply that some have reward and opportunity advantages over others, but that they are able to maintain and even enhance those advantages by excluding
the members of inferior groups." Waters, "Collapse and Convergence," p. 149–150.

74. For discussions on the meanings that inhere in visual texts, see Roland Barthes,
S/Z, trans. Richard Miller (New York: Hill and Wang, 1974).

75. Jomo Kwame Sundaram, *Growth and Structural Change in the Malaysian
Economy* (New York: St. Martin's Press, 1990), p. 230.

7. Conclusion

1. Jeremy Bentham, *The Principles of Morals and Legislation*, edited with an introduction by L. J. LaFleur (New York: Hafner Press, 1948), p. 2.

2. For a discussion on the felicific calculus in the global expansion of financial credit
services, see Stephen Gill, "The Global Panopticon: The Neoliberal State, Economic
Life, and Democratic Surveillance," *Alternatives* 2 (1995): 1–44.

3. As stated by Prime Minister Dr. Mahathir Mohamad in response to questions
from participants at the seminar entitled "Towards a Developed and Industrialized
Society: Understanding the Concept, Implications and Challenges" (see Ahmad Sarji
Abdul Hamid, ed., *Malaysia's Vision 2020: Understanding the Concept, Implications and
Challenges* [Petaling Jaya: Pelanduk Publications, 1993], p. 26).

4. Mahathir Mohamad, "The Second Outline Perspective Plan 1991–2000," in
Malaysia's Vision 2020, p. 445.

5. As Anne Archer writes in the context of the globalization of information technology: "To begin with, "desires" are postulated without any general theory of humanity
(which has the job inter alia of distinguishing between propensities and conduct in such
terms of good/evil, virtue/vice, grace/sin, rational/irrational, free/determined, etc.).
Since our theorists turn their back on this job, yet want to make other peoples' desires
carry the moral burden, then the simple act of wanting something has to be seen as
rationally desirable on this view, otherwise the blank ethical check cannot be issued. In
other words, good reason is presumed to be forthcoming from anyone who desires any-

thing: the only way of making ethical check-outs redundant. Then, such actors harness their wants to *Zwenkrätionalitat*, they survey the technological means available, and the end result is dubbed "progressive" for mankind as a whole" ("Theory, Culture and Post-Industrial Society," in *Global Culture: Nationalism, Globalization and Modernity*, ed. Mike Featherstone [London: Sage Publications, 1990], p. 8).

6. Mahathir Mohamad, "Malaysia: The Way Forward, "in *Malaysia's Vision 2020*, p. 403.

7. Michael Vatikiotis, "Making of a Maverick," *Far Eastern Economic Review* (August 20, 1992): 18.

Bibliography

Abello, Manolo. "Contemporary Labour Migration: Policies and Perspectives of Sending Countries." In *International Migration Systems: A Global Approach*, eds. Mary Kritz, Lin Lean Lim, and Hania Zlotnik. New York: Oxford University Press, 1992.

Abraham, Colin E. R. "Racial and Ethnic Manipulation in Colonial Malaya." *Ethnic and Racial Studies* 6, no. 1 (1983): 18–32.

Abrahams, Naomi. "Towards Reconceptualizing Political Action." *Sociological Inquiry* 62, no. 3 (1992): 327–347.

Adorno, Theodore. "Television and Patterns of Mass Culture." In *Mass Culture: The Popular Arts in America*, eds. Bernard Rosenberg and David Manning White. New York: Free Press, 1957.

Agarwal, Bina, ed. *Structures of Patriarchy: The State, The Community and The Household in Modernising Asia.* London: Zed Books, 1988.

Agger, Ben. *Gender, Culture, and Power: Toward A Feminist Postmodern Critical Theory.* Westport: Praeger, 1993.

Ahmad Sarji Abdul Hamid, ed. *Malaysia's Vision 2020: Understanding the Concept, Implications and Challenges.* Petaling Jaya: Pelanduk Publications, 1993.

Alexander, M. Jacqui. "Redrafting Morality: The Postcolonial State and the Sexual Offenses Bill of Trinidad and Tobago." In *Third World Women and the Politics of Feminism*, eds. Chandra Talpade Mohanty, Ann Russo, and Lourdes Torres. Bloomington: Indiana University Press, 1993.

Ali, Ameer. "Islamic Revivalism in Harmony and Conflict: The Experience in Sri Lanka and Malaysia." *Asian Survey* 24, no. 3 (1984): 296–313.

Allston, Dana, ed. *We Speak for Ourselves: Social Justice, Race and Environment.* Washington D.C.: Panos Institute, 1990.

Amsden, Alice. *Asia's Next Giant: South Korea and Late Industrialization.* New York: Oxford University Press, 1989.

Andersen, Margaret L. *Thinking About Women: Sociological Perspectives on Sex and Gender.* New York: Macmillan, 1988.

Anderson, Benedict. *Imagined Communities: Reflections on the Origin and Spread of Nationalism.* 2nd ed. London: Verso, 1991.

Appadurai, Arjun. "Disjuncture and Difference in the Global Political Economy." In *Global Culture: Nationalism, Globalization and Modernity*, ed. Mike Featherstone. London: Sage Publications, 1990.

Appleyard, Reginald, ed. *The Impact of International Migration on Developing Countries*. Paris: Development Centre of the Organisation for Economic Co-operation and Development, 1989.

Arat-Koc, Sedef. "In the Privacy of Our Own Homes: Foreign Domestic Workers as a Solution to the Crisis in the Domestic Sphere in Canada." *Studies in Political Economy* 28 (1989): 33–58.

Archer, Anne. "Theory, Culture and Post-Industrial Society." In *Global Culture: Nationalism, Globalization and Modernity*, ed. Mike Featherstone. London: Sage Publications, 1990.

Armstrong, M. Jocelyn. "Female Household Workers in Industrializing Malaysia." In *At Work in Homes: Household Workers in World Perspectives*, eds. Roger Sanjek and Shellee Colen. Washington D.C.: The American Anthropological Association, 1990.

Arnold, Fred, and Nasra M. Shah, eds. *Asian Labor Migration: Pipeline to the Middle East*. Boulder: Westview, 1986.

Arnold, Fred. "The Contribution of Remittances to Economic and Social Development." In *International Migration Systems: A Global Approach*, eds. Mary Kritz, Lin Lean Lim, and Hania Zlotnik. New York: Oxford University Press, 1992.

Arshat, Helen, Tan Boon Ann, Tay Nai Ping and M. Subbiah. *Marriage and Family Formation in Peninsular Malaysia*. Kuala Lumpur: National Population and Family Development Board, 1989.

Asian and Pacific Development Centre. *The Trade in Domestic Helpers: Causes, Mechanisms and Consequences*. Kuala Lumpur: Asian and Pacific Development Centre, 1989.

Asian Development Bank. *Key Indicators of Developing Asian and Pacific Countries*. Manila: Asian Development Bank, 1994.

Asian Migrant Forum. Special Issue: Migrant Workers and Trade Unions. no. 6 (1992): 1–37.

Asian Regional Programme on International Labour Migration. *Newspaper Clippings and Reprints of Periodicals*. Bangkok: International Labour Organisation, 1991.

Austin, J. L. *How To Do Things With Words*. Cambridge: Harvard University Press, 1962.

Azizah Kassim. "The Unwelcome Guests: Indonesian Immigrants and Malaysian Public Responses." *Southeast Asian Studies* 25, no. 2 (1987): 265–278.

——. "The Squatter Women and the Informal Economy: A Case Study." In *Women and Work in Malaysia*, eds. Hing Ai Yun and Rokiah Talib. Kuala Lumpur: Department of Anthropology and Sociology, University of Malaya; University of Malaya's Women's Association; Asian and Pacific Development Centre, 1986.

Bakan, Abigail, and Daiva K. Stasiulis. "Making the Match: Domestic Placement Agencies and the Racialization of Women's Household Work." *Signs: Journal of Women in Culture and Society* 20, no. 2 (1995): 303–335.

Balassa, Bela. *The Newly Industrializing Countries in the World Economy.* New York: Pergamon Press, 1981.

Barrett, Michele, and Mary McIntosh. *The Anti-Social Family.* London: NLB, 1982.

Barthes, Roland. *S/Z.* Trans. Richard Miller. New York: Hill and Wang, 1974.

———. *The Semiotic Challenge.* Trans. Richard Howard. London: Hill & Wang, 1988.

Barzun, Jacques. *Classic, Romantic and Modern.* Chicago: University of Chicago Press, 1975.

Bello, Walden, and Stephanie Rosenfeld. "Dragons in Distress: The Crisis of NICs." *World Policy Journal* 7, 3 (1990): 431–468.

Bendix, Reinhard, and Seymour Martin Lipset. *Class, Status and Power: A Reader in Social Stratification.* New York: Free Press, 1966.

Bendix, Reinhard. "Inequality and Social Structure: A Comparison of Marx and Weber." *American Sociological Review* 44 (1974): 149–191.

Benston, Margaret. "The Political Economy of Women's Liberation." *Monthly Review* 21, no. 4 (1969): 13–27.

Bentham, Jeremy. *The Principles of Morals and Legislation.* Ed. with an Introduction by L. J. LaFleur. New York: Hafner Press, 1948.

Berger, Peter L., and Thomas Luckmann. *The Social Construction of Reality: A Treatise in the Sociology of Knowledge.* Garden City: Doubleday, 1966.

Bhabha, Jacqueline, Francesca Klug, and Sue Shutter, eds. *Worlds Apart: Women Under Immigration and Nationality Law.* London: Pluto Press, 1985.

Blaydon, Christopher, and Carol Stack. "Income Support Policies and the Family." In *The Family*, eds. Alice Rossi, Jerome Kagan, and Tamara Hareven. New York: W. W. Norton and Co., 1978.

Blythe, W. L. "Historical Sketch of Chinese Labour in Malaysia." *Journal of the Malayan Branch of the Asiatic Society* 20 (1947): 64–114.

Boserup, Ester. *Woman's Role in Economic Development.* New York: St. Martin's Press, 1970.

Bottomley, Gill, Marie de Lepervanche, and Jeannie Martin, eds. *Intersexions: Gender, Class, Culture and Ethnicity.* Sydney: Allen & Unwin, 1991.

Bourdieu, Pierre. "The Social Space and the Genesis of Groups." *Theory and Society* 14, no. 6 (1985): 723–744.

Braudel, Fernand. *Afterthoughts on Material Civilization and Capitalism.* Trans. Patricia M. Ranum. Baltimore: Johns Hopkins University Press, 1977.

Braverman, Harry. *Labor and Monopoly Capital: The Degradation of Work in the Twentieth Century.* New York: Monthly Review Press, 1974.

Brennan, Martin. "Class, Politics and Race in Modern Malaysia." *Journal of Contemporary Asia* 12, no. 2 (1982): 188–215.

Brown, Wendy. "Finding the Man in the State." *Feminist Studies* 18, no. 1 (1992): 7–34.

Brubaker, Rogers. "Rethinking Classical Theory: The Sociological Vision of Pierre Bourdieu." *Theory and Society* 14, no. 6 (1985): 745–776.

Bunster, Ximena and Elsa M. Chaney. *Sellers and Servants: Working Women in Lima, Peru*. New York: Praeger, 1985.

Burki, Shahid Javed. "Migration from Pakistan to the Middle East." In *The Unsettled Relationship: Labor Migration and Economic Development*, eds. Demetrious G. Papademitreou and Philip Martin. Connecticut: Greenwood, 1991.

Butler, Judith, and Joan Scott, eds. *Feminists Theorize The Political*. New York: Routledge, 1992.

Camilleri, Joseph A., Anthony P. Jervis, and Albert J. Paolini, eds. *The State in Transition: Reimagining Political Space*. Boulder: Lynne Rienner, 1995.

Carchedi, Guglielmo. *On the Economic Identification of Social Classes*. London: Routledge and Kegan Paul, 1977.

Chan Looi Tat. "A Storm in the North." *Asiaweek* (24 Aug 1984): 30–33.

Chandra Muzaffar. *Islamic Revivalism and the Political Process in Malaysia*. Petaling Jaya: Penerbit Fajar Bakti, 1987.

———. *Islamic Resurgence in Malaysia*. Petaling Jaya: Penerbit Fajar Bakti, 1987.

Chaney, Elsa M., Mary Garcia Castro, and Margo L. Smith, eds. *Muchachas No More: Household Workers in Latin America and the Caribbean*. Philadelphia: Temple University Press, 1989.

Chaplin, David. "Domestic Service and Industrialization." *Comparative Studies in Sociology* 1 (1978): 97–127.

Chee Heng Leng. "Babies to Order: Official Population Policies in Malaysia and Singapore." In *Structures of Patriarchy: The State, The Community and The Household in Modernising Asia*, ed. Bina Agarwal. London: Zed Books, 1988.

Cheong Kee Cheok, et. al. *Malaysia: Some Contemporary Issues in Socio-Economic Development*. Kuala Lumpur: Malaysian Economic Association, 1979.

Cho, George. *The Malaysian Economy: Spatial Perspectives*. London: Routledge, 1990.

Christian Conference of Asia-Urban Rural Mission. *Asian Labor: Migration from Poverty to Bondage*. Report of the Workshop on Labor Migration, Hong Kong, 9–15 August, 1990.

Chuang Tzu. *Wandering on the Way: Early Taoist Tales and Parables of Chuang Tzu*. Trans. Victor H. Mair. New York: Bantam Books, 1994.

Chung, Betty Jaime, and Ng Shui Meng. *The Status of Women in Law: A Comparison of Four Asian Countries*. Occasional Papers no. 49. Singapore: Institute of Southeast Asian Studies, 1977.

Cock, Jacklyn. *Maids and Madams: A Study in the Politics of Exploitation*. Johannesburg: Ravan Press, 1980.

Colen, Shellee. "Housekeeping for the Green Card: West Indian Household Workers, the State and Stratified Reproduction in New York City." In *At Work in Homes:*

Household Workers in World Perspective, eds. Roger Sanjek and Shellee Colen. Washington D.C.: American Anthropological Association, 1990.

——. "Just a Little Respect: West Indian Domestic Workers in New York City." In *Muchachas No More: Household Workers in Latin America and the Caribbean*, eds. Elsa M. Chaney, Mary Garcia Castro, and Margo L. Smith. Philadelphia: Temple University Press, 1989.

Connell, R. W. *Gender and Power: Society, the Person, and Sexual Politics.* Stanford: Stanford University Press, 1987.

Costa, Mariarosa Dalla, and Selma James. *The Power of Women and the Subversion of Community.* Bristol: Falling Wall Press, 1975.

Cowan, C. D. *Nineteenth Century Malaya: The Origins of British Colonial Control.* London: Oxford University Press, 1961.

Cox, Robert W. "Social Forces, States and World Orders: Beyond International Relations Theory." In *NeoRealism and Its Critics*, ed. Robert Keohane. Princeton: Princeton University Press, 1986.

——. *Production, Power and World Order: Social Forces in the Making of History.* New York: Columbia University Press, 1987.

Cremer, George. "Deployment of Indonesian Migrants to the Middle East: Present Situation and Prospects." *Bulletin for Indonesian Economic Studies* 24, no. 3 (1988): 73–86.

Crouch, Harold. "Authoritarian Trends, the UMNO Split and the Limits to State Power." In *Fragmented Visions: Culture and Politics in Contemporary Malaysia*, eds. Joel S. Kahn and Francis Loh Kok Wah. Sydney: Allen & Unwin, 1992.

Daly, Mary. *Beyond God the Father: Toward A Philosophy of Women's Liberation.* Boston: Beacon Press, 1973.

Dancz, Virginia. *Women and Party Politics in Peninsular Malaysia.* Singapore: Oxford University Press, 1987.

Debt Crises Network. *From Debt to Development: Alternatives to the International Debt Crises.* Washington D.C.: Institute for Policy Studies, 1986.

Deng Shengliang, Smita Jivan, and Mary-Louise Hassan. "Advertising in Malaysia: A Cultural Perspective." *International Journal of Advertising* 13, no. 2 (1994): 153–166.

Der Darian, James, and Michael J. Shapiro, eds. *International/Intertextual Relations: Postmodern Readings of World Politics.* Lexington: Lexington Books, 1989.

Derrida, Jacques. *Writing and Difference.* London: Routledge and Kegan Paul, 1978.

Deyo, Frederic C, ed. *The Political Economy of the New Asian Industrialism.* Ithaca: Cornell University Press, 1987.

Dias, Malsiri. "Mechanisms of Migration Including Support Systems with Special Reference to Female Labour." *Issues in Gender and Development* no. 5 (1993): 2–3.

Dick, H. W. "The Rise of a Middle Class and the Changing Concept of Equity in Indonesia: An Interpretation." *Indonesia* no. 39 (1985): 71–85.

Dill, Bonnie Thornton. *Across the Boundaries of Race and Class: An Exploration of Work and Family Among Black Female Domestic Servants*. New York: Garland, 1994.

Dixon, C. J., D. Drakakis-Smith, and H. D. Watts. *Multinational Corporations and the Third World* London: Croom Helm, 1986.

Dixon, Chris. *Southeast Asia in the World Economy*. Cambridge: Cambridge University Press, 1991.

Dominguez, Virginia. *From Neighbor to Stranger: The Dilemma of Caribbean Peoples in the United States*. New Haven: Antilles Research Program, Yale University, 1975.

Donzelot, Jacques. *The Policing of Families*. Trans. Robert Hurley. New York: Pantheon Books, 1979.

Dorall, Richard, and Shanmugam R. Paramasivam. "Gender Perspectives on Indonesian Labour Migration to Peninsular Malaysia: A Case Study." Paper presented at the Population Studies Unit's International Colloquium, Migration, Development and Gender in the ASEAN Region, Coral Beach Resort, Kuantan, Pahang, Oct 28–31, 1992.

Dorall, Richard. "Foreign Workers in Malaysia: Issues and Implications of Recent Illegal Economic Migrants from the Malay World." In *The Trade in Domestic Helpers: Causes, Mechanisms and Consequences*. Asian Pacific and Development Center. Kuala Lumpur: Asian and Pacific Development Centre, 1989.

Duarte, Isis. "Household Workers in the Dominican Republic: A Question for the Feminist Movement." In *Muchachas No More: Household Workers in Latin America and the Caribbean*, eds. Elsa M. Chaney, Mary Garcia Castro, and Margo L. Smith. Philadelphia: Temple University Press, 1989.

Dudden, Faye. *Serving Women: Household Service in Nineteenth Century America*. Connecticut: Wesleyan University Press, 1983.

Dworkin, Andrea. *Our Blood: Prophecies and Discourses on Sexual Politics*. New York: Harper and Row, 1976.

Ecumenical Coalition for Economic Justice. *Recolonization or Liberation: The Bonds of Structural Adjustment and Struggles for Emancipation*. Toronto: Ecumenical Coalition for Economic Justice, 1990.

Edgell, Stephen. *Class*. London: Routledge, 1993.

Ehrenreich, Barbara, and John Ehrenreich. "The Professional-Managerial Class." In *Between Capital and Labour*, ed. P. Walker. Brighton: Harvester Press, 1979.

Eisenstein, Zillah, ed. *Capitalism, Patriarchy and the Case for Socialist Feminism*. New York: Monthly Review Press, 1978.

Elina Abdul Majid. "The Maid in Malaysia." *Her World* (February 1994): 152–154.

Ellul, Jacques. *The Technological Bluff*. Trans. Geoffrey W. Bromiley. Michigan: William Eerdmans, 1990.

Elshtain, Jean Bethke. *Public Man, Private Woman: Women in Social and Political Thought*. Princeton: Princeton University Press, 1981.

——. *Women and War*. New York: Basic Books, 1987.

Engels, Friedrich. *The Origin of Family, Private Property and the State, In the Light of the Researches of Lewis H. Morgan by Frederick Engels*. With an Introduction and Notes by Eleanor Burke Leacock. New York: International Publishers, 1972.

Enloe, Cynthia. *Multi-Ethnic Politics: The Case of Malaysia*. Berkeley: Center for South and Southeast Asian Studies, University of California, 1970.

——. *Bananas, Beaches and Bases: Making Feminist Sense of International Politics*. Berkeley: University of California Press, 1989.

Faaland, Justin, Rais Saniman, and J. R. Parkinson. *Growth and Ethnic Inequality: Malaysia's New Economic Policy*. London: Hurst and Co., 1990.

Fan Kok Sim. *Women in Southeast Asia: A Bibliography*. Boston: G. K. Hall, 1982.

Fang Chan Onn. *The Malaysian Economic Challenge: Transformation for Growth*. Singapore: Longman, 1989.

Fatima Daud. "Women's Economic Role in Malaysia." In *Economic Performance in Malaysia: The Insider's View*, ed. Manning Nash. New York: Professors World Peace Academy, 1990.

Fatimah Halim. "The Transformation of the Malaysian State." *Journal of Contemporary Asia*, 20, no. 1 (1990): 64–88.

Fawcett, James T., Siew Ean Khoo, and Peter C. Smith, eds. *Women in the Cities of Asia: Migration and Urban Adaptation*. Boulder: Westview, 1984.

Featherstone, Mike, ed. *Global Culture: Nationalism, Globalization, and Modernity*. London: Sage Publications, 1990.

Federal Constitution. Kuala Lumpur: International Law Books Series, 1993.

Froebel, Fölker, Otto Kreye and Jürgen Heinrichs. *The New International Division of Labour: Structural Unemployment in Industrialized Countries and Industrialization in Developing Countries*. Trans. Peter Burgess. Cambridge: Cambridge University Press, 1980.

Furtado, Celso. *Development and Underdevelopment*. Trans. Ricardo W. de Aquiar and Eric Charles Drysdal. Berkeley: University of California Press, 1964.

Gagliano, Felix V. *Communal Violence in Malaysia 1969: The Political Aftermath*. Athens: Center for International Studies, Ohio University, 1970.

Gardiner, Susan. "Women's Domestic Labour." *New Left Review* 89 (1975): 47–59.

Gaw, Kenneth. *Superior Servants: The Legendary Cantonese Amahs of the Far East*. Singapore: Oxford University Press, 1991.

Geertz, Clifford. "Foreword." In *Knowledge and Power in Morocco: The Education of a Twentieth Century Notable*, Dale F. Eickelman. Princeton: Princeton University Press, 1985.

Gereffi, Gary, and Stephanie Fonda. "Regional Paths of Development." *Annual Review of Sociology* 18 (1992): 419–448.

Giddens, Anthony, and David Held, eds. *Classes, Power and Conflict*. Berkeley: University of California Press, 1982.

Giddens, Anthony. *Capitalism and Modern Social Theory: An Analysis of the Writings of Marx, Durkheim, and Max Weber*. Cambridge: Cambridge University Press, 1971.

Gill, Stephen, and James H. Mittelman. "Innovation in International Relations Theory: Coxian Historicism as an Alternative Paradigm." Paper presented to the Eminent Scholar Panel, 1993 Annual Meeting of the International Studies Association, Acapulco, Mexico, March 1993.

Gill, Stephen. "The Global Panopticon: The Neoliberal State, Economic Life and Democratic Surveillance." *Alternatives* 2 (1995): 1–44.

———. "Theorizing the Interregnum: The Double Movement and Global Politics in the 1990s." In *International Political Economy: Understanding Global Disorder*, ed. Björn Hettne. London: Zed Books, 1995.

Gilpin, Robert. *War and Change in World Politics*. New York: Cambridge University Press, 1981.

Glenn, Evelyn Nakano. "From Servitude to Service Work: Historical Continuities in the Racial Division of Paid Reproductive Labor." *Signs: Journal of Women in Culture and Society* 18, no. 1 (1992): 1–43.

———. *Issei, Nisei, War Bride: Three Generations of Japanese American Women in Domestic Service*. Philadelphia: Temple University Press, 1986.

Gomez, Edmund Terence. *Politics in Business: UMNO's Corporate Investments*. Kuala Lumpur: Forum, 1990.

———. *Money Politics in the Barisan Nasional*. Kuala Lumpur: Forum, 1991.

———. *Political Business: Corporate Involvement of Malaysian Political Parties*. Queensland: James Cook University of North Queensland, 1994.

Goode, William J. *The Family*. New York: Prentice-Hall, 1964.

Govindasamy, Pavalavalli, and Julie Da Vanzo. "Ethnicity and Fertility Differentials in Peninsular Malaysia: Do Policies Matter?" *Population and Development Review* 18, no. 2 (1992): 243–267.

Gramsci, Antonio. *Selections from the Prison Notebooks of Antonio Gramsci*. Trans. and edited by Quintin Hoare and Geoffrey Nowell Smith. New York: International Publishers, 1971.

Guinness, Patrick. "Indonesian Migrants in Johor: An Itinerant Labour Force." *Bulletin of Indonesian Economic Studies* 26, no. 1 (1990): 117–131.

Gullick, J. M. *Indigenous Political Systems of the Malays*. London: Athlone Press, 1958.

Gunatilleke, Godfrey, ed. *Migration of Asian Workers to the Arab World*. Tokyo: The United Nations University, 1986.

Habermas, Jürgen. *Knowledge and Human Interests*. Trans. Jeremy Shapiro. Boston: Beacon Press, 1971.

Haggard, Stephan. "The Newly Industrializing Countries in the International System. Review Article." *World Politics* 28, no. 2 (1986): 343–370.

Halim Salleh. "Peasants, Proletarianisation and the State: FELDA Settlers in Pahang." In *Fragmented Visions: Culture and Politics in Contemporary Malaysia*, eds. Joel S. Kahn and Francis Loh Kok Wah. Sydney: Allen & Unwin, 1992.

Hancock, Mary. "Transnational Production and Women Workers." In *One Way Ticket: Migration and Female Labour*, ed. Annie Phizacklea. London: Routledge and Kegan Paul, 1983.

Hannerz, Ulf. "Cosmopolitans and Locals in World Culture." In *Global Culture: Nationalism, Globalization and Modernity*, ed. Mike Featherstone. London: Sage Publications, 1990.

Hansen, Karen Tranberg. "Sex and Gender Among Domestic Servants in Zambia." *Anthropology Today* 2, no. 3 (1986): 18–23.

Harding, Sandra. "Introduction: Is There a Feminist Method?" In *Feminism and Methodology: Social Science Issues*, ed. Sandra Harding. Bloomington: University of Indiana Press, 1987.

Hartmann, Heidi. "The Family as the Locus of Gender, Class and Political Struggle: The Examples of Housework." *Signs: Journal of Women in Culture and Society* 6, no. 3 (1981): 316–394.

———. "Capitalism, Patriarchy and Job Segregation by Sex." *Signs: Journal of Women in Culture and Society* 1, no. 3 (1976): 137–169.

Hawes, Gary, and Hong Liu. "Explaining the Dynamics of the Southeast Asian Political Economy." *World Politics* 45, no. 4 (1993): 629–660.

Hellinger, Steven, Douglas Hellinger, and Fred M. O'Regan. *Aid for Just Development: Report on the Future of Foreign Assistance.* Boulder: Lynne Rienner, 1988.

Henderson, J. W. "The New International Division of Labour and American Semiconductor Production in South East Asia." In *Multinational Corporations and the Third World*, eds. C. J. Dixon, D. Drakakis-Smith and H. D. Watts. Boulder: Westview, 1986.

———. *Globalisation of High Technology Production: Society, Space and Semiconductors in the Restructuring of the Modern World.* London: Routledge, 1989.

Heng Pek Koon. *Chinese Politics in Malaysia: A History of the Malaysian Chinese Association.* Singapore: Oxford University Press, 1988.

———. "The Chinese Business Elite of Malaysia." In *Southeast Asian Capitalists*, ed. Ruth McVey. Ithaca: Cornell Southeast Asia Program, Cornell University, 1992.

Henry, Frances. "The West Indian Domestic Scheme in Canada." *Social and Economic Studies* 17, no. 1 (1968): 83–91.

Hewison, Kevin, Richard Robison, and Garry Rodan, eds. *Southeast Asia in the 1990s: Authoritarianism, Democracy and Capitalism.* Sydney: Allen & Unwin, 1993.

Hewison, Kevin, Richard Robison, and Garry Rodan. "Introduction: Changing Forms of State Power in Southeast Asia." In *Southeast Asia in the 1990s: Authoritarianism, Democracy, and Capitalism*, eds. Hewison, Robison, and Rodan. Sydney: Allen & Unwin, 1993.

Heyzer, Noeleen, and Vivian Lee. "Lessons from the *Kongsi Fong* System in Guangdong Province, China." *Issues in Gender and Development* no. 5 (1993): 16–17.

———. "Who Benefits, Who Profits? Domestic Workers in Transient Overseas Employment." *Issues in Gender and Development*, no. 5 (1993): 10–14.

Higgott, Richard, and Richard Robison, eds. *Southeast Asia: Essays in the Political Economy of Structural Change.* London: Routledge and Kegan Paul, 1985.

Hing Ai Yun, and Rokiah Talib, eds. *Women and Work in Malaysia.* Kuala Lumpur: Department of Anthropology and Sociology, University of Malaya; National Population and Family Development Board, Ministry of National Unity and Social Development, 1986.

Hing Ai Yun. "Women and Work in West Malaysia." *Journal of Contemporary Asia* 14, no. 2 (1984): 204–218.

Hirschmann, Charles. "The Meaning and Measurement of Ethnicity in Malaysia: An Analysis of Census Clarification." *Journal of Asian Studies* 40, no. 3 (1987): 555–582.

Hobbes, Thomas. *Leviathan.* Ed. with an Introduction by C. B. MacPherson. London: Penguin Books, 1968.

Hofheinz, Roy, and Kent E. Calder. *The East Asia Edge.* New York: Basic Books, 1982.

hooks, bell. *Feminist Theory: From Margin to Center.* Boston: South End Press, 1984.

Horn, Pamela. *Rise and Fall of the Victorian Servant.* New York: St. Martin's Press, 1975.

Hughes, Helen, ed. *Achieving Industrialization in East Asia.* Cambridge: Cambridge University Press, 1988.

Huguet, J. W. "International Labour Migration from the ESCAP Region." In *The Impact of International Migration on Developing Countries,* ed. Reginald Appleyard. Paris: Development Centre of the Organisation for Economic Co-operation and Development, 1989.

Huntington, Samuel. "Will More Countries Be Democratic?" *Political Science Quarterly* 99, no. 2 (1984): 193–218.

——. *Political Order in Changing Societies.* New Haven: Yale University Press, 1968.

Husna Sulaiman, and Christina Lam. "Family Care and Interactive Time of Professional Mothers." *Malaysian Journal of Family Studies* 1, no. 1 (1989): 14–24.

International Labour Organisation. *Yearbook of Labour Statistics.* Geneva: International Labour Organisation, 1994 (and past series).

Issues in Gender and Development. Special Issue: International Migration of Women. no. 5 (1993): 1–39.

Jackson, R. N. *Immigrant Labour and the Development of Malaysia, 1786–1920.* Kuala Lumpur: Government Press, 1961.

Jaggar, Alison. *Feminist Politics and Human Nature.* New Jersey: Rowman & Allanheld, 1983.

Jain, Prakash. "Exploitation and Reproduction of Migrant Indian Labour in Colonial Guyana and Malaysia." *Journal of Contemporary Asia* 18, no. 2 (1988): 189–206.

Jain, Ravindra K. *South Indians on the Plantation Frontier in Malaya.* New Haven: Yale University Press, 1970.

Jamilah Ariffin. *Women and Development in Malaysia.* Petaling Jaya: Pelanduk Publications, 1992.

Jayawardena, Kumari. *Feminism and Nationalism in the Third World.* London: Zed Books, 1986.

Jedudason, James. *Ethnicity and the Economy: The State, Chinese Business, and Multinationals in Malaysia.* Singapore: Oxford University Press, 1989.

Jelin, Elizabeth. "Migration and Labor Force Participation of Latin American Women: Domestic Service in the Cities." *Signs: Journal of Women in Culture and Society* 3, no. 1 (1977): 129–141.

——. "Migration and Labor Force Participation of Latin American Women: The Domestic Servants in the Cities." In *Muchachas No More: Household Workers in Latin America and the Caribbean.* eds. Elsa Chaney, Mary Garcia Castro, and Margo L. Smith. Philadelphia: Temple University Press, 1989.

Jenson, Jane, Elisabeth Hagen, and Ceallaigh Reddy, eds. *Feminization of the Labor Force: Paradoxes and Promises.* New York: Oxford University Press, 1988.

Johnson, Dale L., ed. *Middle Classes in Dependent Countries.* Beverly Hills: Sage Publications, 1985.

Jomo Kwame Sundaram, and Ahmad Shaberry Cheek. "The Politics of Malaysia's Islamic Resurgence." *Third World Quarterly* 19, no. 2 (1988): 843–869.

——. "Malaysia's Islamic Movements." In *Fragmented Visions: Culture and Politics in Contemporary Malaysia,* eds. Joel S. Kahn and Francis Loh Kok Wah. Sydney: Allen & Unwin, 1992.

Jomo Kwame Sundaram. "Economic Crisis and Policy Response in Malaysia." In *Southeast Asia in the 1980s: The Politics of Economic Crisis,* eds. Richard Robison, Kevin Hewison, and Richard Higgott. Sydney: Allen & Unwin, 1987.

——. .*Growth and Structural Change in the Malaysian Economy.* London: St. Martin's Press, 1990.

——. "Whither Malaysia's New Economic Policy?" *Pacific Affairs* 63, no. 4 (1990–1): 469–500.

——, ed. *The Sun Also Sets: Lessons in Looking East.* 2nd. edition, Kuala Lumpur: INSAN, 1985.

Jones, Catherine. "Hong Kong, Singapore, South Korea and Taiwan: Oikonomic Welfare States." *Government and Opposition* 25, no. 4 (1990): 446–462.

Jones, Gavin W, ed. *Women in the Urban and Industrial Workforce: Southeast and East Asia.* Monograph no. 33. Canberra: Development Studies Centre, The Australian National University, 1984.

Kahn, Joel S. "Class, Ethnicity and Diversity: Some Remarks on Malay Culture in Malaysia." In *Fragmented Visions: Culture and Politics in Malaysia,* eds. Joel S. Kahn and Francis Loh Kok Wah. Sydney: Allen & Unwin, 1992.

——. "Growth, Economic Transformation, Culture and the Middle Classes in Malaysia." In *The New Rich in Asia: Mobile Phones, McDonalds and Middle Class Revolution,* eds. Richard Robison and David S. G. Goodman. London: Routledge, 1996.

Kahn, Joel, and Francis Loh Kok Wah, eds. *Fragmented Visions: Culture and Politics in Malaysia.* Sydney: Allen & Unwin, 1992.

Kamariah Ismail. "Childcare Services for Working Women in Malaysia." In *Women and Work in Malaysia*, eds. Hing Ai Yun and Rokiah Talib. Kuala Lumpur: Department of Anthropology and Sociology, University of Malaya; National Population and Family Development Board, Ministry of National Unity and Social Development, 1986.

Karim, Wazir Jahan. *Women and Culture: Between Malay Adat and Islam.* Boulder: Westview, 1992.

——. "Malay Women's Movements: Leadership and Processes of Change." *International Social Science Journal* 35, no. 4 (1983): 719–731.

Karp, Jonathan. "Allah's Bounty." *Far Eastern Economic Review* (1 September 1994): 78.

——. "Paper Chase." *Far Eastern Economic Review* (6 October 1994): 70–71.

Katzman, Donald M. *Seven Days A Week: Women and Domestic Service in Industrializing America.* New York: Oxford University Press, 1978.

Keohane, Robert O. *After Hegemony: Cooperation and Discord in the World Political Economy.* Princeton: Princeton University Press, 1984.

Kessler, Clive S. "Malaysia: Islamic Revivalism and Political Dissatisfaction in a Divided Society." *Southeast Asian Chronicle* 75 (1980): 3–11

Khoo Kay Jin. "Grand Vision: Mahathir and Modernization." In *Fragmented Visions: Culture and Politics in Contemporary Malaysia*, eds. Joel S. Kahn and Francis Loh Kok Wah. Sydney: Allen & Unwin, 1992.

Khoo Siew Ean, and Peter Pirie. "Female Rural to Urban Migration in Peninsular Malaysia." In *Women in the Cities of Asia: Migration and Urban Adaptation*, eds. James T. Fawcett, Siew Ean Khoo, and Peter C. Smith. Boulder: Westview, 1984.

Khoo Siew Mun, et. al. *Status and Role of Malaysian Women in Development: A Bibliographic Essay.* Kuala Lumpur: Faculty of Economics, University of Malaya; National Population and Family Development Board, Ministry of National Unity and Social Development, 1992.

Kingston, Maxine Hong. *China Men.* New York: Ballantine Books, 1981.

Kondapi, C. *Indian Overseas: 1838–1949.* New Delhi: Oxford University Press, 1951.

Kratoska, Paul H. "The Peripatetic Peasant and Land Tenure in British Malaya." *Journal of Southeast Asian Studies* 16, no. 1 (1985): 16–45.

——. "Rice Cultivation and the Ethnic Division of Labor in British Malaysia." *Comparative Studies in Society and History* 24, no. 2 (1982): 280–314.

Kritz, Mary, Charles B. Keely, and Silvano M. Tomasi, eds. *Global Trends in Migration: Theory and Research on International Population Movements.* Staten Island: Center for Migration Studies, 1981.

Kritz, Mary, Lin Lean Lim, and Hania Zlotnik, eds. *International Migration Systems: A Global Approach.* New York: Oxford University Press, 1992.

Kunio, Yoshihara. *The Rise of Ersatz Capitalism in South-East Asia.* Singapore: Oxford University Press, 1988.

Kusnic, Michael, and Julie Da Vanzo. *Income Inequality and the Definition of Income.* Santa Monica: The Rand Corporation for the Agency of International Development, 1980.

Lai Ah Eng. *Peasants, Proletarians and Prostitutes: A Preliminary Investigation into the Work of Chinese Women in Colonial Malaya.* Research Notes and Discussion Papers no. 59. Singapore: Institute for Southeast Asian Studies, 1986.

Lasch, Christopher. *Haven in a Heartless World: The Family Besieged.* New York: Basic Books, 1977.

Lasker, Bruno. *Human Bondage in Southeast Asia.* Westport: Greenwood Press, 1972.

Lau, Albert. "Malayan Union Citizenship: Constitutional Change and Controversy in Malaya 1942–48." *Journal of Southeast Asian Studies* 20, no. 2 (1989): 216–243.

Leaver, Richard. "Reformist Capitalist Development and the New International Division of Labour." In *Southeast Asia: Essays in the Political Economy of Structural Change,* eds. Richard Higgott and Richard Robison. London: Routledge and Kegan Paul, 1985.

Lee, Raymond. "The State, Religious Nationalism, and Ethnic Rationalization in Malaysia." *Racial and Ethnic Studies* 13, no. 4 (1990):482–502.

Lee, Sharon. "Female Immigrants and Labour in Colonial Malaya 1980–1947." *International Migration Review* 23, no. 2 (1990): 309–331.

Leete, R. "Dual Fertility Trends in Malaysia's Multiethnic Society." *International Family Planning Perspectives* 15, no. 2 (1989): 58–65.

Leung, Y. S. "The Uncertain Phoenix: Confucianism and its Modern Fate." *Asian Culture* 10 (1987): 85–94.

Li, Dun Jen. *British Malaya: An Economic Analysis.* New York: The American Press, 1955.

Liang, Y. M. "Malaysia's NEP and the Chinese Community." *Review of Indonesian and Malaysian Affairs* 21, no. 2 (1987): 131–142

Lim Mah Hui. *Ownership and Control of the 100 Largest Corporations in Malaysia.* Kuala Lumpur: Oxford University Press, 1981.

——. "Affirmative action, ethnicity and integration: the case of Malaysia." *Ethnic and Racial Studies* 8, no. 2 (1985): 250–276.

——. "Contradiction in the Development of Malay Capital: State, Accumulation and Legitimation." *Journal of Contemporary Asia* 15, no. 1 (1985): 37–63.

Lim, Janet. *Sold For Silver.* Ohio: World Publishing Co., 1958.

Lim, Julian. "Social Problems of Chinese Female Immigrants in Malaysia 1925–1940." *Malaysian History* 23 (1989): 101–109.

Lim, Linda Y. C. *Women Workers in Multinational Corporations: The Case of the Electronics Industry in Malaysia and Singapore.* Occasional Papers no. 9. Michigan: University of Michigan, 1978.

Locke, John. *Two Treatises of Government.* Ed. Peter Laslett. Cambridge: Cambridge University Press, 1960.

Loh, Philip. *The Malay States: 1877–1895: Political Change and Social Policy.* London: Oxford University Press, 1969.

Low, Linda. "Population Movement in the Asia Pacific Region: Singapore Perspective."
    International Migration Review 29, no. 3 (1995): 745–764.
MacKinnon, Catherine. *Toward A Feminist Theory of the State.* Cambridge: Harvard
    University Press, 1989.
Mahathir Mohamad. "The Second Outline Perspective Plan, 1991–2000." In *Malaysia's
    Vision 2020: Understanding the Concept, Implications and Challenges,* ed. Ahmad Sarji
    Abdul Hamid. Petaling Jaya: Pelanduk Publications, 1993.
——. "Inauguration Speech to the Malaysian Business Council." In *Malaysia's Vision
    2020: Understanding the Concept, Implications and Challenges,* ed. Ahmad Sarji Abdul
    Hamid. Petaling Jaya: Pelanduk Publications, 1993.
——. "Malaysia: The Way Forward." In *Malaysia's Vision 2020: Understanding the
    Concept, Implications and Challenges,* ed. Ahmad Sarji Abdul Hamid. Petaling Jaya:
    Pelanduk Publications, 1993.
Maiguischa, Bice. "The Role of Ideas in a Changing World Order: The Case of the
    International Indigenous Movement." Paper presented at the International Con-
    ference on the Changing World Order and the United Nations System. Yokohama,
    Japan, 24–27 March 1992.
Mak Lau Fong. *The Sociology of Secret Societies: A Study of Chinese Secret Societies in
    Singapore and Peninsular Malaysia.* Kuala Lumpur: Oxford University Press, 1981.
Malaysia, Government of. *Second Outline Perspective Plan 1991–2000.* Kuala Lumpur:
    National Printing Department, 1991.
——. *Second Malaysia Plan 1971–1975.* Kuala Lumpur: Government Printing Press, 1971.
——./Ministry of Human Resources. *Tinjauan Upah Pekerjaan Sektor Pembuatan.*
    Kuala Lumpur: Ministry of Human Resources, 1992.
——. *Labour and Manpower Report 1987/88.* Kuala Lumpur: Ministry of Labour/
    Ministry of Human Resources, 1988.
Manderson, Lenore. *Women, Politics and Change: The Kaum Ibu Malaysia, 1945–1972.*
    Kuala Lumpur: Oxford University Press, 1980.
Manicom, Linzi. "Ruling Relations: Rethinking State and Gender in South African
    History." *Journal of African History* 33 no. 3 (1992): 441–465.
Marcuse, Herbert. *One Dimensional Man: Studies in the Ideology of Advanced Industrial
    Society.* Boston: Beacon Press, 1964.
Marx, Karl. *Contribution to the Critique of Political Economy.* Trans. and Ed. N. I. Stone.
    London: Paul, Trench, and Trubner, 1904.
Massey, Donald, J. Arango, A. Kouaouci, A. Pelligrino, and J. Taylor. "Theories of
    International Migration: A Review and Appraisal." *Population and Development
    Review* 19, no. 3 (1993): 431–466.
Matthaei, Julie. *An Economic History of Women in America: Women's Work, the Sexual
    Division of Labor and the Development of Capitalism.* New York: Schocken Books, 1982.
McBride, Teresa. *Domestic Revolution: The Modernization of Household Service in
    England and France 1820–1920.* New York: Holmes and Meier, 1976.

McNall, Scott, Rhonda Levine, and Rick Fantasia, eds. *Bringing Class Back In: Contemporary and Historical Perspectives.* Boulder: Westview, 1991.

McVey, Ruth, ed. *South East Asian Capitalists.* Ithaca: Cornell Southeast Asia Program, Cornell University, 1992.

Means, Gordon P. *Malaysian Politics.* 2nd. ed. London: Hodder & Stoughton, 1976.

——. *Malaysian Politics: The Second Generation.* Singapore: Oxford University Press, 1991.

Mehmet, Ozay. *Development in Malaysia: Poverty, Wealth and Trusteeship.* London: Croom Helm, 1986.

Michaely, Michael, et. al. *Liberalizing Foreign Trade: Lessons of Experience from Developing Countries.* vols. 1–7. Oxford: Basil Blackwell, 1991.

Middle East Watch: Women's Rights Project. Special Issue: Punishing the Victim: Rape and Mistreatment of Asian Maids in Kuwait. 4, no. 8 (1992): 1–44.

Millett, Kate. *Sexual Politics.* Garden City: Doubleday, 1970.

Milne, R. S. "Privatization in the Asean States: Who Gets What, Why and With What Effect?" *Pacific Affairs* 65, no. 1 (1992): 7–24.

——. 'Malaysia—Beyond the New Economy Policy." *Asian Survey* 25 (1986): 1364–1382.

Milne, R. S., and Diane K. Mauzy. *Politics and Government in Malaysia.* Singapore: Federal Publishers, 1978.

Mitchell, Juliet. *Woman's Estate.* New York: Pantheon Books, 1971.

Mittelman, James H. "Rethinking the international division of labour in the context of globalisation." *Third World Quarterly* 16, no. 2 (1995): 273–294.

——. "The Global Restructuring of Production and Migration." In *Global Transformation: Challenges to the State System,* ed. Yoshikazu Sakamoto. New York: United Nations University Press, 1994.

Mohanty, Chandra Talpade. "Introduction: Cartographies of Struggle: Third World Women and the Politics of Feminism." In *Third World Women and the Politics of Feminism,* eds. Chandra Talpade Mohanty, Ann Russo, and Lourdes Torres. Bloomington: Indiana University Press, 1991.

Moore Jr., Barrington. *The Social Origins of Dictatorship and Democracy: Lord and Peasant in the Making of the Modern World.* Boston: Beacon Press, 1966.

Morgan, D. H. J. *The Family, Politics and Social Theory.* London: Routledge and Kegan Paul, 1985.

Morishima, Michio. *Why Has Japan Succeeded?: Western Technology and the Japanese Ethos.* New York: Cambridge University Press, 1982.

Morokvasic, Mirjana. "Women in Migration: Beyond the Reductionist Outlook." In *One Way Ticket, Migration and Female Labour,* ed. Annie Phizacklea. London: Routledge and Kegan Paul, 1983.

——. "Birds of Passage Are Also Women . . . " *International Migration Review* 18, no. 4 (1984): 886–907.

Mowlana, Hamid, and Laurie Wilson. *The Passing of Modernity: Communication and the Transformation of Society.* New York: Longman, 1990.

Nagata, Judith. "What is a Malay? Situational Selection of Ethnic Identity in a Plural Society." *American Ethnologist* 1, no. 2 (1974): 331–50.

——. *The Reflowering of Malaysian Islam: Modern Religious Radicals and Their Roots.* Vancouver: University of British Columbia Press, 1984.

Napsiah Omar. "Keynote Address." Presented at the First ISIS Conference on Women, Towards An Engendered Millennium. Kuala Lumpur, Malaysia, 7–8 May 1993.

Nonini, Donald. *British Colonial Rule and the Resistance of the Malay Peasantry, 1900–1957.* Monograph Series no. 38. New Haven: Yale University Southeast Asia Studies, Yale Center for International and Area Studies, 1992.

Nor Alemawati Mohamad Zain. "Childcare Providers in Peninsular Malaysia." *Report of the Malaysian Family Life Survey II 1988.* Kuala Lumpur: National Population and Family Development Board, 1992.

Nurizan Yahaya. "A Profile of the Urban Poor in Malaysia." *Journal of Contemporary Asia* 21, no. 2 (1991): 212–227.

O'Brien, Leslie. "Class, Gender and Ethnicity: The Neglect of an Integrated Framework." *Southeast Asian Journal of Social Science* 10, no. 2 (1982): 1–12.

Oakley, Ann. *Woman's Work: The Housewife, Past and Present.* New York: Pantheon, 1974/5.

Ong, Aihwa, and Michael Peletz, eds. *Bewitching Women and Pious Men: Gender and Body Politics in Southeast Asia.* Berkeley: University of California Press, 1995.

Ong, Aihwa. "State versus Islam: Malay Families, Women's Bodies, and the Body Politic in Malaysia." *American Ethnologist* 17, no. 2 (1990): 258–276.

——. *Spirits of Resistance: and Capitalist Discipline: Factory Women in Malaysia.* Albany: State University of New York Press, 1987.

Osbourne, Martha Lee, ed. *Women in Western Thought.* New York: Random House, 1979.

Ottenberg, Simon. "Thirty Years of Fieldnotes: Changing Relationships to the Text." In *Fieldnotes: The Making of Anthropology,* ed. Roger Sanjek. Ithaca: Cornell University Press, 1990.

Palabrico-Costello, M. "Female Domestic Servants in Cagayan de Oro, Philippines: Social and Economic Implications of Employment in a Pre-Modern Occupation." In *Women in the Urban and Industrial Workforce: Southeast and East Asia,* ed. Gavin W. Jones. Monograph no. 33. Canberra: Development Studies Centre, The Australian National University, 1984.

Palmer, Phyllis. *Domesticity and Dirt: Housewives and Domestic Servants in the United States 1920–1945.* Philadelphia: Temple University Press, 1989.

Pang Eng Fong. *Regionalisation and Labour Flows in Pacific Asia.* Paris: OECD, 1994.

Parke, Jo Anne. "The Case for Going Global." *Target Marketing* 17, no. 11 (1994): 8–13.

Parkinson, C. Northcote. *British Intervention in Malay 1876–1887.* Singapore: University of Malaya Press, 1960.

Parmer, J. *Colonial Labour Policy and Administration.* New York: J. J. Augustin, 1960.

Pateman, Carol. "The Fraternal Social Contract." In *Civil Society and the State: New European Perspectives,* ed. John Keane. London: Verso, 1988.

Peletz, Michael. "Sacred Texts and Dangerous Words: The Politics of Law and Cultural Rationalization in Malaysia." *Comparative Studies in Societies and History* 35, no. 1 (1993): 66–109.

Phizacklea, Annie, ed. *One Way Ticket: Migration and Female Labour.* London: Routledge and Kegan Paul, 1983.

Pillai, Patrick. *People on the Move: An Overview of Recent Immigration and Emigration in Malaysia.* Kuala Lumpur: Institute for Strategic and International Studies, 1992.

Piore, Michael. *Birds of Passage: Migrant Labour in Industrial Societies.* Cambridge: Cambridge University Press, 1979.

Polanyi, Karl. *The Great Transformation: The Political and Economic Origins of Our Time.* Boston: Beacon Press, 1944.

Preston, P. W. *Discourses of Development: State, Market and Polity in the Analysis of Complex Change.* Hants, England: Avebury, 1994.

——. *Rethinking Development: Essays on Development and Southeast Asia.* London: Routledge and Kegan Paul, 1987.

Puthucheary, James. *Ownership and Control in the Malayan Economy: A Study of the Structure of Ownership and Control and its Effects on the Development of Secondary Industries and Economic Growth in Malaya and Singapore.* Singapore: Eastern Universities Press, 1960.

Pye, Lucian W. *Asian Power and Politics: The Cultural Dimensions of Authority.* Cambridge: Belknap Press, 1985.

Raja Rohana Raja Mamat. *The Role and Status of Malay Women in Malaysia: Social and Legal Perspectives.* Kuala Lumpur: Dewan Bahasa dan Pustaka, 1991.

Rehman Rashid. *A Malaysian Journey.* Petaling Jaya: Rehman Rashid, 1993.

Reinharz, Shulamith. *Feminist Methods in Social Research.* New York: Oxford University Press, 1992.

Robinson, Kathy. "Housemaids: The Effects of Gender and Culture on the Internal and International Migration of Indonesian Women." In *Intersexions: Gender, Class, Culture and Ethnicity*, eds. Gill Bottomley, Marie de Lepervanche, and Jeannie Martin. Sydney: Allen & Unwin, 1991.

Robison, Richard, Kevin Hewison, and Richard Higgott, eds. *Southeast Asia in the 1980s: The Politics of Economic Crisis.* Sydney: Allen & Unwin, 1987.

Robison, Richard. "Structures of Power and the Industrialisation Process in Southeast Asia." *Journal of Contemporary Asia* 19, no. 4 (1989): 371–397.

Robison, Richard, and David S. G. Goodman, eds. *The New Rich in Aisa: Mobile Phones, McDonalds and Middle Class Revolution.* London: Routledge, 1996.

Rodan, Garry. "The Rise and Fall of Singapore's Second Industrial Revolution." In *Southeast Asia in the 1980s: The Politics of Economic Crisis*, eds. Richard Robison, Kevin Hewison, and Richard Higgott. Sydney: Allen & Unwin, 1987.

——. "Industrialization and the Singapore State in the Context of the New International Division of Labour." In *South East Asia: Essays in the Political Economy of*

Structural Change, eds. Richard Higgott and Richard Robison. London: Routledge and Kegan Paul, 1985.

Roff, William R. *The Origins of Malay Nationalism.* New Haven: Yale University Press, 1967.

Rogers, Everett. *Communication and Development: Critical Perspectives.* Beverly Hills: Sage Publications, 1976.

Rohana Ariffin. "Women and Trade Unions in West Malaysia." *Journal of Contemporary Asia* 19, no. 1 (1989): 78–94.

Rohani A. Razak. "Women's Labour Participation in Peninsular Malaysia." In *Report of the Malaysian Family Life Survey II 1988.* Kuala Lumpur: National Population and Family Development Board, 1992.

Rollins, Judith. *Between Women: Domestics and Their Employers.* Philadelphia: Temple University Press, 1985.

Romero, Mary. *M.A.I.D. in the USA.* New York: Routledge, 1992.

Rosenau, Pauline Marie. *Postmodernism and the Social Science: Insights, Inroads and Intrusions.* Princeton: Princeton University Press, 1992.

———. "Once Again into the Fray: International Relations Confronts the Humanities." *Millennium: Journal of International Studies* 19, no. 1 (1990): 83–110.

Rossi, Alice, Jerome Kagan, and Tamara Harevan, eds. *The Family.* New York: W. W. Norton and Co., 1978.

Rubbo, Ann and Michael Taussig. "Up Off Their Knees: Servanthood in Southwest Colombia." *Latin American Perspectives* 10, no. 4 (1983): 5–23.

Ruland, Jürgen. *Urban Development in South East Asia: Regional Cities and Local Government.* Boulder: Westview, 1992.

Rush, James R. *The Last Tree: Reclaiming the Environment in Tropical Asia.* New York: Asia Society, 1991.

Russell, Sharon Stanton, and Michael S. Teitelbaum. *International Migration and International Trade.* World Bank Discussion Papers no. 160. Washington D.C.: World Bank, 1992.

Russell, Sharon Stanton. "Remittances from International Migration: A Review in Perspective." *World Development* 14, no. 6 (1986): 677–696.

Salaff, Janet W. *State and Family in Singapore: Restructuring a Developing Society.* Ithaca: Cornell University Press, 1988.

Salaff, Janet, and Aline K. Wong. "Women Workers: Factory, Family and Social Class in an Industrializing Order." In *Women in the Urban and Industrial Workforce: Southeast and East Asia*, ed. Gavin W. Jones. Monograph no. 33. Canberra: Development Studies Centre, The Australian National University, 1984.

Samuel, M. C. Jojie Samuel. *Pembantu-pembantu Rumah Wanita Filipina diMalaysia: Satu Kajian Kes diKawasan Kuala Lumpur dan Petaling Jaya.* Ijazah Sarjana Muda Sastera, Fakulti Literatur dan Sains Sosial, Universiti Malaya, 1987/8.

Sandhu, Kernial Singh. *Indians in Malaya: Some Aspects of Their Immigration and Settlement (1786–1957).* London: Cambridge University Press, 1969.

Sanjek, Roger, and Shellee Colen, eds. *At Work in Homes: Household Workers in World Perspective.* Washington D.C.: American Anthropological Association, 1990.

Sanjek, Roger. "Fieldnotes and Others." In *Fieldnotes: The Making of Anthropology,* ed. Roger Sanjek. Ithaca: Cornell University Press, 1990.

Sanjek, Roger. "On Ethnographic Validity." In *Fieldnotes: The Making of Anthropology,* ed. Roger Sanjek. Ithaca: Cornell University Press, 1990.

Sassen-Koob, Saskia. "Notes on the Incorporation of Third World Women into Wage - labor Through Immigration and Off-Shore Production." *International Migration Review* 18, no. 4 (1984): 1144–1167.

Saw Swee Hock. *The Population of Peninsular Malaysia.* Singapore: Singapore University Press, 1988.

Saxonhouse, Arlene W. *Women in the History of Political Thought: Ancient Greece to Machiavelli.* New York: Praeger, 1985.

Schiller, Herbert. *Culture Inc.: The Corporate Takeover of Public Expression.* London: Oxford University Press, 1989.

Scott, James C. *Domination and the Arts of Resistance: Hidden Transcripts.* New Haven: Yale University Press, 1990.

——. *Weapons of the Weak: Everyday Forms of Peasant Resistance.* New Haven: Yale University Press, 1985.

Scott, Margaret. "Brave New World." *Far Eastern Economic Review* (21 December 1989): 32–34.

Sewell, John, et. al. *Growth, Exports and Jobs in a Changing World Economy: Agenda 1988.* New Brunswick: Transaction Books, 1988.

Shah, Nasra, M. Sulayman Al-Qudsi, and Makhdoom Shah. "Asian Women Workers in Kuwait." *International Migration Review* 25, no. 3 (1991): 464–486.

Shapiro, Michael J. *Language and Politics.* New York: New York University Press, 1984.

Shaw, Paul R. *Migration Theory and Fact: A Review and Bibliography of Current Literature.* Philadelphia: Regional Science Research Institute, 1975.

Shawcross, John. *Shelley's Literary and Philosophical Criticism.* London: H. Milford, 1909.

Sidhu, M. S. , and G. W. Jones. *Population Dynamics in a Plural Society: The Case of Peninsular Malaysia.* Kuala Lumpur: UMCB Publishers, 1981.

Singerman, Diane. *Avenues of Participation: Family, Politics and Networks in Urban Quarters of Cairo.* Princeton: Princeton University Press, 1995.

Sivalingam, G. "The NEP and the Differential Economic Performance of the Races in West Malaysia 1970–1985." In *Economic Performance in Malaysia: The Insider's View,* ed. Manning Nash. New York: Professors World Peace Academy, 1990.

Sjaastad, Larry. "The Costs and Returns of Human Migration." *Journal of Political Economy* 70, no. 5 (1962): 80–92.

Skeldon, Ronald. "International Migration Within and From the East and Southeast Asian Region." *Asia and Pacific Migration Journal* 1, no. 1 (1992): 19–63.

Smart, Carol. "Researching Prostitutes: Some Problems for Feminist Researchers." *A Feminist Ethic for Social Science Research.* Laviston: Edwin Mellen Press, 1988.

Smith, Anthony David. *Age of Behemoths: The Globalization of Mass Media Firms*. London: Priority Press Publications, 1991.

Snodgrass, Donald R. *Inequality and Economic Development in Malaysia*. Kuala Lumpur: Oxford University Press, 1980.

Somers, Margaret R. "The Narrative Constitution of Identity: A Relational and Network Approach." *Theory and Society* 23, no. 5 (1994): 605–649.

Spaan, Ernst. "Taikongs and Calos: The Role of Middlemen and Brokers in Javanese International Migration." *International Migration Review* 28, no. 1 (1994): 93–113.

Stahl, C. W. and Ansanul Habib. "Emigration and Development in South and Southeast Asia." In *The Unsettled Relationship: Labor Migration and Economic Development*, eds. Demetrious G. Papademitreou and Philip Martin. Connecticut: Greenwood Press, 1991.

Stahl, C. W. "South-North Migration in the Asia-Pacific Region." *International Migration* 29 (1991): 163–193.

Steinberg, David Joel, et. al. *In Search of Southeast Asia: A Modern History*. Honolulu: University of Hawaii Press, 1987.

Stenson, Michael. *Class, Race and Colonialism in Western Malaysia: The Indian Case*. St. Lucia: University of Queensland Press, 1980.

Stevenson, Rex. *Cultivators and Administrators: British Educational Policy Towards the Malays, 1875–1906*. Kuala Lumpur: Oxford University Press, 1975.

Stoler, Ann. "Sexual Affronts and Racial Frontiers: European Identities and the Cultural Politics of Exclusion in Colonial Southeast Asia." *Comparative Studies in Societies and History* 34, no. 3 (1992): 514–551.

Strauch, Judith. *Chinese Village Politics in the Malaysian State*. Cambridge: Harvard University Press, 1981.

Suhaini Aznam. "From the Campus Back to the Mainstream." *Far Eastern Economic Review* (22 January 1987): 56.

Sweeney, Amin P. L. *A Full Hearing: Orality and Literacy in the Malay World*. Berkeley: University of California Press, 1987.

Swettenham, Frank A. *The Real Malay*. London: J. Lane, 1900.

Syed Hussein Alatas. *The Myth of the Lazy Native: A Study of the Image of the Malays, Filipinos and Javanese from the 16th to the 20th Century and its Function in the Ideology of Colonial Capitalism*. London: Frank Cass, 1977.

Tan Poo Chang. *Status and Role of Malaysian Women in Development and Family Welfare: Policy Implications and Recommendations*. Kuala Lumpur: National Population and Family Development Board and Ministry of National Unity and Social Development, 1992.

Tan Tat Wai. *Income Distribution and Determination in West Malaysia*. Kuala Lumpur: Oxford University Press, 1982.

Tanter, Richard, and Kenneth Young, eds. *The Politics of Middle Class Indonesia*. Monash Papers on Southeast Asia, no. 19. Clayton: Centre for Southeast Asian Studies, Monash University, 1990.

Taylor, Jean. *The Social World of Batavia: European and Eurasian Dutch Asia*. Madison: University of Wisconsin Press, 1983.

Tharan, Caridad. "Filipina Maids." In *The Trade in Domestic Helpers: Causes, Mechanisms and Consequences*. Asian and Pacific Development Centre. Kuala Lumpur: Asian and Pacific Development Centre, 1989.

Thorne, Barrie and Marilyn Yalom, eds. *Rethinking the Family: Some Feminist Questions*. New York: Longman, 1982.

Tiano, Susan. "Public-Private Dichotomy: Theoretical Perspectives on Women in Development." *The Social Science Journal* 21, no. 4 (1984): 11–28.

Tickner, J. Ann. *Gender in International Relations: Feminist Perspectives on Achieving Global Security*. New York: Columbia University Press, 1992.

Tilly, Louise, and Joan W. Scott. *Women, Work and Family*. New York: Holt, Reinhart and Winston, 1978.

Tinker, Irene, ed. *Persistent Inequalities: Women and World Development*. New York: Oxford University Press, 1990.

Todaro, Michael P. *Internal Migration in Developing Countries: A Review of Theory, Evidence, Methodology and Research Priorities*. Geneva: International Labour Office, 1976.

Toer, Pramoedya Ananta. *This Earth of Mankind*. Trans. Max Lane. New York: Avon Books, 1993.

Tong, Rosalind. *Feminist Thought: A Comprehensive Introduction*. Boulder: Westview, 1989.

Tornea, Vivian and Esther Habana. "Women in International Labour Migration: The Philippine Experience." In *The Trade in Domestic Helpers: Causes, Mechanisms, and Consequences*. Asian and Pacific Development Centre. Kuala Lumpur: Asian and Pacific Development Centre, 1989.

Tucker, Susan. *Telling Memories Among Southern Women: Domestic Workers and Their Employers in the Segregated South*. Baton Rouge: Louisiana State University Press, 1988.

Turnbull, Mary. *A Short History of Malaya, Singapore and Brunei*. Singapore: Graham Brash, 1980.

United Nations Conference on Trade and Development. *Handbook of International Trade and Development Statistics*. New York: United Nations Conference on Trade and Development, 1993.

Ursel, Jane. *Private Lives, Public Policy: One Hundred Years of State Intervention in the Family*. Toronto: Women's Press, 1994.

Vasil, R. K. *The Malaysian General Elections of 1969*. Singapore: Oxford University Press, 1972.

Vatikiotis, Michael. "Making of a Maverick." *Far Eastern Economic Review* (20 August 1992): 18.

Vaughan, J. D. *The Mannerisms and Customs of the Straits Chinese*. London: Oxford University Press, 1879.

Von Vorys, Karl. *Democracy without Consensus: Communalism and Political Stability in Malaysia*. Princeton: Princeton University Press, 1975.

Wacquant, Löic J. D. "Making Class: The Middle Class(es) in Social Theory and Social Structure." In *Bringing Class Back In: Contemporary and Historical Perspectives*, eds. Scott McNall, Rhonda Levine, and Rick Fantasia. Boulder: Westview, 1991.

Wade, Robert. "East Asia's Economic Success: Conflicting Perspectives, Partial Insights, Shaky Evidence." *World Politics* 44, no. 2 (1992): 270–320.

——. *Governing the Market: The Role of Government in East Asian Industrialization*. Princeton: Princeton University Press, 1990.

Walby, Sylvia. "Woman and Nation." *International Journal of Contemporary Sociology* 33, nos. 1–2 (1992): 81–100.

Waley, Arthur, ed. *Three Ways of Thought in Ancient China*. Garden City: Doubleday Anchor Books, 1939.

Waters, Malcolm. "Collapse and Convergence in Class Theory: The Return of the Social in the Analysis of Stratification Arrangements." *Theory and Society* 20, no. 2 (1991): 141–172.

Weinert, Patricia. *Foreign Female Domestic Workers: Help Wanted!* Working Paper on International Migration for Employment. Geneva: International Labour Organization, 1991.

Winch, Peter. *The Idea of a Social Science and Its Relation to Philosophy*. London: Routledge and Kegan Paul, 1958.

Winstedt, Richard O. "The Malay Annals or *Sejarah Melayu*." *Journal of the Malayan Branch of the Royal Asiatic Society* 16, no. 3 (1938): 1–226.

Wittgenstein, Ludwig. *Philosophical Investigations*. Trans. G. E. Manscombe. New York: Macmillan, 1953.

Wong, Loong, and Beverly Blaslett. "Manipulating Space in a Postcolonial State," in *The State in Transition: Reimagining Political Space*, eds. Joseph A. Camilleri, Anthony D. Jervis, and Albert J. Paolini. Boulder: Lynne Rienner, 1995.

Woods, Charles. "Equilibrium and Historical-Structural Perspectives on Migration." *International Migration Review* 16, no. 2 (1982): 298–319.

World Bank/International Bank for Reconstruction and Development. *World Tables*. Baltimore: Johns Hopkins University Press, 1995.

——. *The East Asian Miracle: Economic Growth and Public Policy: Summary*. Washington D.C.: The World Bank, 1994.

——. *World Bank Development Report 1990*. New York: Oxford University Press, 1990.

——. *World Bank Development Report 1980*. New York: Oxford University Press, 1984.

——. *The Economic Development of Malaya*. Baltimore: Johns Hopkins University Press, 1955.

Wright, Eric Olin. "Reconstructing Class Analysis." Paper presented at the Work, Class and Culture Symposium. University of Witwatersrand, South Africa, June 28–30, 1993.

Yap, L. K. *Domestic Servants in Malaysia: A Sociolegal Study.* Faculty of Law, Universiti Malaya, 1984.

Yong, Mei Ling, and Kamal Salih. "The Malay Family, Structural Change and Trans-formation—A Research Proposal." In *Geography and Gender in the Third World,* eds. Janet Momsen and Juliet Townsend. New York: State University of New York, 1987.

Young, Kate, Carol Wolkowitz, and Roslyn McCullagh. *Of Marriage and the Market: Women's Subordination Internationally and Its Lessons.* London: Routledge and Kegan Paul, 1984.

Yuval-Davis, Nira. "The Citizenship Debate: Women, Ethnic Processes and the State." *Feminist Review* no. 39 (1991): 58–68.

Zaharom Nain. "The State, the Malaysian Press and the War." In *Triumph and Image: The Media's War in the Persian Gulf,* eds. Hamid Mowlana, George Gerbner, and Herbert Schiller. Boulder: Westview, 1992.

Zainab Wahidin. "Engendering the NDP—An Afterthought." Paper presented at the First ISIS Conference on Women, Towards an Engendered Millennium. Kuala Lumpur, Malaysia, May 7–8, 1993.

Zakiyah bte Jamaluddin. *Pembantu Rumah Wanita Indonesia diKuala Lumpur dan Petaling Jaya.* Ijazah Sarjana Muda Sastera, Fakulti Anthropologi dan Sosial, Universiti Malaya, 1991–92.

Newspapers:
Business Times
Malay Mail
New Straits Times (including *New Sunday Times*)
Straits Times
The Star (including *Sunday Star*)
The Sun
Utusan Malaysia

Weekly Magazines
Asiaweek
Far Eastern Economic Review

Index